T0301537

Derivatives
Analytics
with Python

For other titles in the Wiley Finance series
please see www.wiley.com/finance

Derivatives Analytics with Python

Data Analysis, Models, Simulation, Calibration and Hedging

YVES HILPISCH

WILEY

This edition first published 2015
© 2015 John Wiley & Sons Ltd

Registered office
John Wiley & Sons Ltd, The Atrium, Southern Gate, Chichester, West Sussex, PO19 8SQ, United
Kingdom

For details of our global editorial offices, for customer services and for information about how to apply
for permission to reuse the copyright material in this book please see our website at www.wiley.com.

Wiley publishes in a variety of print and electronic formats and by print-on-demand. Some material
included with standard print versions of this book may not be included in e-books or in
print-on-demand. If this book refers to media such as a CD or DVD that is not included in the version
you purchased, you may download this material at http://booksupport.wiley.com. For more information
about Wiley products, visit www.wiley.com.

Designations used by companies to distinguish their products are often claimed as trademarks. All
brand names and product names used in this book are trade names, service marks, trademarks or
registered trademarks of their respective owners. The publisher is not associated with any product or
vendor mentioned in this book.

Limit of Liability/Disclaimer of Warranty: While the publisher and author have used their best efforts
in preparing this book, they make no representations or warranties with respect to the accuracy or
completeness of the contents of this book and specifically disclaim any implied warranties of
merchantability or fitness for a particular purpose. It is sold on the understanding that the publisher is
not engaged in rendering professional services and neither the publisher nor the author shall be liable
for damages arising herefrom. If professional advice or other expert assistance is required, the services
of a competent professional should be sought.

Library of Congress Cataloging-in-Publication Data

Hilpisch, Yves J.
  Derivatives analytics with Python : data analysis, models, simulation, calibration and hedging /
Yves Hilpisch.—1
      pages cm.—(The Wiley finance series)
  Includes bibliographical references and index.
  ISBN 978-1-119-03799-6 (hardback)
  1. Derivative securities.   2. Hedging (Finance)   3. Python (Computer program language)
I. Title.
  HG6024.A3H56 2015
  332.64'5702855133—dc23   2015010191

A catalogue record for this book is available from the British Library.

ISBN 978-1-119-03799-6 (hardback)   ISBN 978-1-119-03793-4 (ebk)
ISBN 978-1-119-03800-9 (ebk)   ISBN 978-1-119-03801-6 (obk)

Cover Design: Wiley
Cover Images: Top image (c)iStock.com/agsandrew; Bottom image (c)iStock.com/stocksnapper

Set in 10/12pt Times by Aptara Inc., New Delhi, India
Printed in Great Britain by TJ International Ltd, Padstow, Cornwall, UK

Contents

PART THREE

Market-Based Valuation

List of Tables

List of Figures

Preface

This book is an outgrowth of diverse activities of myself and colleagues of mine in the fields of financial engineering, computational finance and Python programming at our company The Python Quants GmbH on the one hand and of teaching mathematical finance at Saarland University on the other hand.

The book is targeted at practitioners, researchers and students interested in the market-based valuation of options from a practical perspective, i.e. the single numerical and technical implementation steps that make up such an effort. It is also for those who want to learn how Python can be used for derivatives analytics and financial engineering. However, apart from being primarily practical and implementation-oriented, the book also provides the necessary theoretical foundations and numerical tools.

My hope is that the book will contribute to the increasing acceptance of Python in the financial community, and in particular in the analytics space. If you are interested in getting the Python scripts and IPython Notebooks accompanying the book, you should visit http://wiley.quant-platform.com where you can register for the Quant Platform which allows browser-based, interactive and collaborative financial analytics. Further resources are found on the website http://derivatives-analytics-with-python.com. You should also check out the open source library DX Analytics under http://dx-analytics.com which implements the concepts and methods presented in the book in standardized, reusable fashion.

I thank my family—and in particular my wife Sandra—for their support and understanding that such a project requires many hours of solitude. I also want to thank my colleague Michael Schwed for his continuous help and support. In addition, I thank Alain Ledon and Riaz Ahmad for their comments and feedback. Discussions with participants of seminars and my lectures at Saarland University also helped the project significantly. Parts of this book have benefited from talks I have given at diverse Python and finance conferences over the years.

I dedicate this book to my lovely son Henry Nikolaus whose direct approach to living and clear view of the world I admire.

YVES HILPISCH
Saarland, February 2015

## CHAPTER 1

A Quick Tour

1.1 MARKET-BASED VALUATION

This book is about the market-based valuation of (stock) index options. In the domain of derivatives analytics this is an important task which every major investment bank and buy-side decision maker in the financial market is concerned with on a daily basis. While theoretical valuation approaches develop a model, parametrize it and then derive values for options, the market-based approach works the other way round. Prices from liquidly traded options are taken as given (i.e. they are inputs instead of outputs) and one tries to parametrize a market model in a way that replicates the observed option prices as well as possible. This activity is generally referred to as *model calibration*. Being equipped with a calibrated model, one then proceeds with the task at hand, be it valuation, trading, investing, hedging or risk management. A bit more specifically, one might be interested in pricing and hedging an exotic derivative instrument with such a model—hoping that the results are in line with the overall market (i.e. arbitrage-free and even "fair") due to the previous calibration to more simple, vanilla instruments.

To accomplish a market-based valuation, four areas have to be covered:

1. **market**: knowledge about market realities is a conditio sine qua non for any sincere attempt to develop market-consistent models and to accomplish market-based valuation
2. **theory**: every valuation must be grounded on a sound market model, ensuring, for example, the absence of arbitrage opportunities and providing means to derive option values from observed quantities
3. **numerics**: one cannot hope to work with analytical results only; numerical techniques, like Monte Carlo simulation, are generally required in different steps of a market-based valuation process
4. **technology**: to implement numerical techniques efficiently, one is dependent on appropriate technology (hard- and software)

This book covers all of these areas in an integrated manner. It uses equity index options as the prime example for derivative instruments throughout. This, among others, allows to abstract from dividend related issues.

1.2 STRUCTURE OF THE BOOK

The book is divided into three parts. The first part is concerned with market-based valuation as a process and empirical findings about market realities. The second part covers a number of topics for the theoretical valuation of options and derivatives. It also develops tools much needed during a market-based valuation. The third part finally covers the major aspects related to a market-based valuation and also hedging strategies in such a context.

Part I "The Market" comprises two chapters:

- **Chapter 2**: this chapter contains a discussion of topics related to market-based valuation, like risks affecting the value of equity index options
- **Chapter 3**: this chapter documents empirical and anecdotal facts about stocks, stock indices and in particular volatility (e.g. stochasticity, clustering, smiles) as well as about interest rates

Part II "Theoretical Valuation" comprises four chapters:

- **Chapter 4**: this chapter covers arbitrage pricing theory and risk-neutral valuation in discrete time (in some detail) and continuous time (on a higher level) according to the Harrison-Kreps-Pliska paradigm (cf. Harrison and Kreps (1979) and Harrison and Pliska (1981))
- **Chapter 5**: the topic of this chapter is the complete market models of Black-Scholes-Merton (BSM, cf. Black and Scholes (1973), Merton (1973)) and Cox-Ross-Rubinstein (CRR, cf. Cox et al. (1979)) that are generally considered benchmarks for option valuation
- **Chapter 6**: Fourier-based approaches allow us to derive semi-analytical valuation formulas for European options in market models more complex and realistic than the BSM/CRR models; this chapter introduces the two popular methods of Carr-Madan (cf. Carr and Madan (1999)) and Lewis (cf. Lewis (2001))
- **Chapter 7**: the valuation of American options is more involved than with European options; this chapter analyzes the respective problem and introduces algorithms for American option valution via binomial trees and Monte Carlo simulation; at the center stands the Least-Squares Monte Carlo algorithm of Longstaff-Schwartz (cf. Longstaff and Schwartz (2001))

Finally, **Part III "Market-Based Valuation"** has seven chapters:

- **Chapter 8**: before going into details, this chapter illustrates the whole process of a market-based valuation effort in the simple, but nevertheless still useful, setting of Merton's jump-diffusion model (cf. Merton (1976))
- **Chapter 9**: this chapter introduces the general market model used henceforth, which is from Bakshi-Cao-Chen (cf. Bakshi et al. (1997)) and which accounts for stochastic volatility, jumps and stochastic short rates
- **Chapter 10**: Monte Carlo simulation is generally the method of choice for the valuation of exotic/complex index options and derivatives; this chapter therefore discusses in some detail the discretization and simulation of the stochastic volatility model by Heston

(cf. Heston (1993)) with constant as well as stochastic short rates according to Cox-Ingersoll-Ross (cf. Cox et al. (1985))

- **Chapter 11**: model calibration stays at the center of market-based valuation; the chapter considers several general aspects associated with this topic and then proceeds with the numerical calibration of the general market model to real market data
- **Chapter 12**: this chapter combines the results from the previous two to value European and American index options via Monte Carlo simulation in the calibrated general market model
- **Chapter 13**: this chapter analyzes dynamic delta hedging strategies for American options by Monte Carlo simulation in different settings, from a simple one to the calibrated market model
- **Chapter 14**: this brief chapter provides a concise summary of central aspects related to the market-based valuation of index options

In addition, the book has an **Appendix** with one chapter:

- **Appendix A**: the appendix introduces some of the most important Python concepts and libraries in a nutshell; the selection of topics is clearly influenced by the requirements of the rest of the book; those not familiar with Python or looking for details should consult the more comprehensive treatment of all relevant topics by the same author (cf. Hilpisch (2014))

1.3 WHY PYTHON?

Although Python has established itself in the financial industry as a powerful programming language with an elaborate ecosystem of tools and libraries, it is still not often used for financial, derivatives or risk analytics purposes. Languages like C++, C, C#, VBA or Java and toolboxes like Matlab or domain-specific languages like R often dominate this area. However, we see a number of good reasons to choose Python even for computationally demanding analytics tasks; the following are the most important ones we want to mention, in no particular order, (see also chapter 1 in Hilpisch (2014)):

- **open source**: Python and the majority of available libraries are completely open source; this allows an entry to this technology at no cost, something particularly important for students, academics or other individuals
- **syntax**: Python programming is easy to learn, the code is quite compact and in general highly readable; at universities it is increasingly used as an introduction to programming in general; when it comes to numerical or financial algorithm implementation, the syntax is pretty close to the mathematics in general (e.g. due to code vectorization approaches)
- **multi-paradigm**: Python is as good for procedural programming (which suffices for the purposes of this book) as well as at object-oriented programming (which is necessary in more complex/professional contexts); it also has some functional programming features to offer
- **interpreted**: Python is an interpreted language which makes rapid prototyping and development in general a bit more convenient, especially for beginners; tools like IPython

Notebook and libraries like pandas for time series analysis allow for efficient and productive interactive analytics workflows

■ **libraries**: nowadays, there is a wealth of powerful libraries available and the supply grows steadily; there is hardly a problem that cannot be easily tackled with an existing library, be it a numerical problem, a graphical one or a data-related problem

■ **speed**: a common prejudice with regard to interpreted languages—compared to compiled ones like C++ or C—is the slow speed of code execution; however, financial applications are more or less all about matrix and array manipulations and operations which can be done at the speed of C code with the essential Python library NumPy for array-based computing; other performance libraries, like Numba for dynamic code compiling, can also be used to improve performance

■ **market**: in the London area (mainly financial services) the number of Python developer contract offerings was 485 in the third quarter of 2012; the comparable figure in the same period 2013 was already 864;[1] large financial institutions like Bank of America, Merrill Lynch and J.P. Morgan have millions of lines of Python code in production, mainly in risk management; Python is also really popular in the hedge fund industry

All in all, Python seems to be a good choice for our purposes. The cover story "Python Takes a Bite" in the March 2010 issue of *Wilmott* magazine (cf. Lee (2010)) also illustrates that Python is gaining ground in the financial world. A modern introduction into Python for finance is given by Hilpisch (2014).

One of the easiest ways to get started with Python is to register on the *Quant Platform* which allows for browser-based, interactive and collaborative financial analytics and development (cf. http://quant-platform.com). This platform offers all you need to do efficient and productive financial analytics as well as financial application building with Python. It also provides, for instance, integration with R, the free software environment for statistical computing and graphics.

1.4 FURTHER READING

The book covers a great variety of aspects which comes at the cost of depth of exposition and analysis in some places. Our aim is to emphasize the red line and to guide the reader easily through the different topics. However, this inevitably leads to uncovered aspects, omitted proofs and unanswered questions. Fortunately, a number of good sources in book form are available which may be consulted on the different topics:

■ **market**: cf. Bittmann (2009) to learn about options fundamentals, the main microstructure elements of their markets and the specific lingo; Gatheral (2006) is a concise reference about option and volatility modeling in practice; Rebonato (2004) is a book that comprehensively covers option markets, their empirical specialities and the models used in theory and practice

---

[1] Source: www.itjobswatch.co.uk/contracts/london/python.do on 07. October 2014.

- **theory**: Pliska (1997) is a comprehensive source for discrete market models; the book by Delbaen and Schachermayer (2004) covers the general arbitrage theory in continuous time and is quite advanced; less advanced, but still comprehensive, treatments of arbitrage pricing are Björk (2004) for continuous processes based on Brownian motion and Cont and Tankov (2004a) for continuous processes with jumps; Wilmott et al. (1995) offers a detailed discussion of the seminal Black-Scholes-Merton model
- **numerics**: Cherubini et al. (2009) is a book-length treatment of the Fourier-based option pricing approach; Glasserman (2004) is *the* standard textbook on Monte Carlo simulation in financial applications; Brandimarte (2006) covers a wide range of numerical techniques regularly applied in mathematical finance and offers implementation examples in Matlab[2]
- **implementation**: probably the best introduction to Python for the purposes of this book is another book by same author (cf. Hilpisch (2014)) which is called *Python for Finance*; that book covers the main tools and libraries needed for this book, like IPython, NumPy, matplotlib, PyTables and pandas, in a detailed fashion and with a wealth of concrete financial examples; the excellent book by McKinney (2012) about data analysis with Python should also be consulted; good general introductions to Python from a scientific perspective are Haenel et al. (2013) and Langtangen (2009); Fletcher and Gardener (2009) provides an introduction to the language also from a financial perspective, but mainly from the angle of modeling, capturing and processing financial trades; London (2005) is a larger book that covers a great variety of financial models and topics and shows how to implement them in C++; in addition, there is a wealth of Python documentation available for free on the Internet.

This concludes the Quick Tour.

---

[2]Python in combination with NumPy comes quite close to the syntax of Matlab such that translations are generally straightforward.

The Market

## CHAPTER 2

What is Market-Based Valuation?

2.1 OPTIONS AND THEIR VALUE

An equity option represents the right to buy (*call*) or sell (*put*) a unit of the underlying stock at a prespecified price (*strike*) at a predetermined date (*European option*) or over a determined period of time (*American option*). Some options are settled in actual stocks; most options, like those on an index, are settled in cash. People or institutions selling options are called *option writers*. Those buying options are called *option holders*.

For a European call option on an index with strike 8,000 and index level of 8,200 at maturity, the option holder receives the difference $8,200 - 8,000 = 200$ (e.g. in EUR or USD) from the option writer. If the index level is below the strike, say at 7,800, the option expires worthless and the writer does not have to pay anything. We can formalize this via the so-called *inner value* (or *intrinsic value* or *payoff*)—from the holder's viewpoint—of the option

$$h_T(S, K) = \max[S_T - K, 0]$$

where T is the maturity date of the option, S_T the index level at this date and K represents the strike price. We can now use Python for the first time and plot this inner value function.

A script could look like:

```
#
# European Call Option Inner Value Plot
# 02_MBV/inner_value_plot.py
#
# (c) Dr. Yves J. Hilpisch
# Derivatives Analytics with Python
#
import numpy as np
import matplotlib as mpl
import matplotlib.pyplot as plt
mpl.rcParams['font.family'] = 'serif'
```

```
# Option Strike
K = 8000

# Graphical Output
S = np.linspace(7000, 9000, 100)  # index level values
h = np.maximum(S - K, 0)  # inner values of call option

plt.figure()
plt.plot(S, h, lw=2.5)  # plot inner values at maturity
plt.xlabel('index level $S_t$ at maturity')
plt.ylabel('inner value of European call option')
plt.grid(True)
```

The output of this script is shown in Figure 2.1.

Three scenarios have to be distinguished with regard to the so-called *moneyness* of an option:

- **in-the-money (ITM)**: a call (put) is in-the-money if $S > K$ ($S < K$)
- **at-the-money (ATM)**: an option, call or put, is at-the-money if $S \approx K$
- **out-of-the-money (OTM)**: a call (put) is out-of-the-money if $S < K$ ($S > K$)

However, what influences the *present value* of such a call option today? Here are some factors:

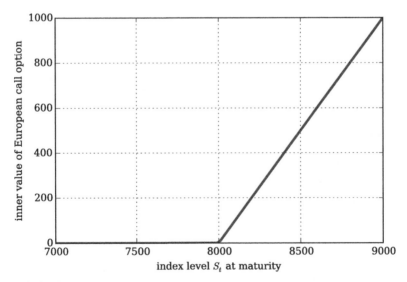

FIGURE 2.1   Inner value of a European call option on a stock index with strike of 8,000 dependent on the index level at maturity

■ **initial index level**: of course, it is important what the current index level is since this influences how probable it is that the index level exceeds the strike at maturity; if the index level is 7,900 it should be much more probable that the call option expires with positive value than if the level was at 7,500

■ **volatility of the index**: put simply, (annualized) volatility is a measure for the randomness of the index's returns over a year; suppose the extreme case that the index is at 7,900 and there is no risk/no movement at all—then the index would not surpass the strike at maturity; however, if the index is at 7,900 and fluctuating strongly then there is a chance that the option will expire with positive value—and the bigger the fluctuations (the higher the volatility) the better from the option holder's viewpoint

■ **time-to-maturity**: again suppose the index is at 7,900; if time-to-maturity is only one day then the probability of the option being valuable at maturity is much lower than if time-to-maturity was 1 month or even 1 year

■ **interest rate**: cash flows from a European option occur at maturity only which represents a future date; these cash flows have to be discounted to today to derive a present value

These heuristic insights are formalized in the seminal work of Black-Scholes-Merton (cf. Black and Scholes (1973) and Merton (1973)) who for the first time derived a closed option pricing formula for a parsimonious set of input parameters. Their formula says mainly the following

$$C_0^* = C^{BSM}(S_0, K, T, r, \sigma)$$

In words, the fair present value of a European call option C_0^* is given by their formula $C^{BSM}(\cdot)$ which takes as input parameters:

1. S_0 the current index level
2. K the strike price of the option
3. T the maturity date (equals time-to-maturity viewed from the present date)
4. r the constant risk-less short rate
5. σ the volatility of the index, i.e. the standard deviation of the index level returns

The Black-Scholes-Merton formula can also be plotted and the result is shown in Figure 2.2.[1] The present value of the option is always above the (undiscounted) inner value. The difference between the two is generally referred to as the *time value* of the option. In this sense, the option's present value is composed of the inner value plus the time value. Time value is suggestive of the fact that the option still has time to get in-the-money or to get even more in-the-money.

Here is the Python script that generates Figure 2.2.

---

[1]Cf. Chapter 5 for a treatment of the Black-Scholes-Merton model and their pricing formula, reproduced there as equation (5.7). The Python script in sub-section 5.6.2, which we have used to generate Figure 2.2, implements the formula for calls and puts.

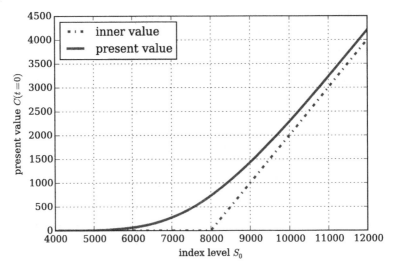

FIGURE 2.2   Black-Scholes-Merton value of a European call option on a
stock index with $K = 9000, T = 1.0, r = 0.025$ and $\sigma = 0.2$ dependent on the
initial index level S_0; for comparison, the undiscounted inner value is also shown

```
#
# European Call Option Value Plot
# 02_mbv/BSM_value_plot.py
#
# (c) Dr. Yves J. Hilpisch
# Derivatives Analytics with Python
#
import numpy as np
import matplotlib as mpl
import matplotlib.pyplot as plt
mpl.rcParams['font.family'] = 'serif'

# Import Valuation Function from Chapter 5
import sys
sys.path.append('05_com')
from BSM_option_valuation import BSM_call_value

# Model and Option Parameters
K = 8000   # strike price
T = 1.0   # time-to-maturity
r = 0.025   # constant, risk-less short rate
vol = 0.2   # constant volatility

# Sample Data Generation
S = np.linspace(4000, 12000, 150)   # vector of index level values
```

```
h = np.maximum(S - K, 0)   # inner value of option
C = [BSM_call_value(S0, K, 0, T, r, vol) for S0 in S]
   # calculate call option values

# Graphical Output
plt.figure()
plt.plot(S, h, 'b-.', lw=2.5, label='inner value')
   # plot inner value at maturity
plt.plot(S, C, 'r', lw=2.5, label='present value')
   # plot option present value
plt.grid(True)
plt.legend(loc=0)
plt.xlabel('index level $S_0$')
plt.ylabel('present value $C(t=0)$')
```

2.2 VANILLA VS. EXOTIC INSTRUMENTS

Financial markets distinguish between *plain vanilla* or *flow* equity derivatives, like European call options written on an equity index, and *exotic* equity derivatives, like options on an equity index with Asian features, barriers and/or American exercise.[2] In general, there exist liquid markets for plain vanilla products but not for exotic ones. In contrast, exotic derivatives are often tailored by financial institutions to specific client needs and are not traded at all (or "only once" if you like).[3]

Nevertheless, financial institutions writing exotic equity options (so-called *sell side*) or clients buying these options (i.e. the *buy side*) must have a mechanism to derive fair values regularly and transparently. In addition, option writers must be able to hedge their exposure. In relation to exotic equity derivatives, sellers and buyers must often resort to numerical methods, like Monte Carlo simulation, to come up with fair values and appropriate hedging strategies.

Here we face for the first time what is meant by *market* in market-based valuation. The market is represented by liquidly traded vanilla instruments (for example, European or American call options) on the underlying in question. If I want to value a non-traded equity derivative in a market-based manner then I should include in this process the information available from the relevant vanilla options market. This requirement is based on a belief in efficient markets and the claim that *the market is always right*.

More formally, whatever model I use for the valuation and hedging of exotic equity derivatives, a minimum requirement is that the model reproduce the values of liquidly traded instruments sufficiently well. Two areas have to be considered carefully:

■ **qualitative features**: given the underlying of the derivative to be valued and the options on this underlying liquidly traded, what qualitative features should the model exhibit? for

---

[2]Cf. de Weert (2008) for an overview and explanation of exotic options and their features.
[3]As a proxy of market liquidity you can think of the frequency with which option quotes are updated. For plain vanilla instruments this might be in the range of seconds during trading hours; for exotic derivatives this might be once a day or even once a week.

example, it would make sense to assume that an equity index will (positively) trend in the long term; however, this assumption is not appropriate if the underlying is an interest rate or volatility measure which tend to fluctuate around long-term equilibrium values

- **quantitative features**: given the basic qualitative features of the model, there are in general infinitely many possibilities to parametrize it; while in physics there are often universal constants to rely on, this is hardly ever the case in finance; on the positive side, this allows parameters to be set in a way that best fits model prices to market-observed prices from vanilla instruments (a task called *calibration* and central in what follows)

In Chapter 3, we discuss a number of issues related to the question of what qualitative features an appropriate model should exhibit. Part II of the book then explains how to build such models theoretically. Part III of the book is mainly concerned with simulation, model calibration (i.e. parameter specification), valuation and hedging.

2.3 RISKS AFFECTING EQUITY DERIVATIVES

This section focuses on market risks affecting the price of derivative instruments as well as other risks that play a role in this context.

2.3.1 Market Risks

To come up with fair values for equity derivatives and sound hedging strategies, one has to consider first which market risks influence their values. Among the market risks that influence equity derivatives are:

- **price risk**: this relates to uncertain changes in the underlying's price, like index or stock price movements
- **volatility risk**: volatility refers to the standard deviation of the underlying's returns; however, volatility itself fluctuates over time, i.e. volatility is not constant but rather stochastic
- **jump or crash risk**: the stock market crashes of 1987, 1998, 2001 and 2008 as well as implied volatilities of stock index options (see the next chapter) indicate that there is a significantly positive probability for large market drops; such discontinuities may break down, for example, otherwise sound dynamic hedging strategies
- **interest rate risk**: although equity derivatives generally do not rely on interest rates or bonds directly[4] their value is indirectly influenced by interest rates via risk-neutral discounting with the short rate
- **correlation risk**: simply spoken, correlation measures the co-movement of two or more assets/quantities; correlation may change over time and become close to 1, i.e. perfect, among asset classes during times of stress
- **liquidity risk**: dynamic and static hedging strategies depend on market liquidity; for example, if certain options are not liquidly traded a desired hedge may not be executable

---

[4]Otherwise they would be classified as *hybrids*.

■ **default risk**: in case of the default of a company represented in the underlying assets, stocks and/or bonds of this company depreciate in value (often to zero)

In what follows, the discussion addresses all market risks mentioned above, apart from default and liquidity risk. *Default risk* does not play a significant role since the discussion mainly focuses on benchmark indices where the possibility of default of a single company is generally negligible.[5]

Liquidity risk is more oriented towards the implementation of hedging programs and in that sense "only" an important operational aspect depending on the specific market environment an option seller or buyer operates in. In addition, the focus of this book is mainly on stock index derivatives where liquidity risk seldom is a problem—index futures, for example, are among the most liquid instruments. Although an active area of research,[6] a broadly accepted theoretical approach to incorporate liquidity in financial models is still missing. Cetin et al. (2004) point out:

"From a financial engineering perspective, the need is paramount for a simple yet robust method that incorporates liquidity risk into arbitrage pricing theory."

They propose what they call the "liquidity risk arbitrage pricing theory" with a stochastic supply curve for a security's price as a function of trade size.[7] As long as there is no solution to this, one has to keep in mind what *The New York Times* summarizes as follows:

"That failure [of risk models] suggests new frontiers for financial engineering and risk management, including trying to model the mechanics of panic and the patterns of human behavior.

'What wasn't recognized was the importance of a different species of risk—liquidity risk,' said Stephen Figlewski, a professor of finance at the Leonard N. Stern School of Business at New York University....."[8]

2.3.2 Other Risks

In addition to market risks, there are other sources of risk like, for instance, models and operations. *Model risk* refers to the risk that valuation and risk management finally rely on the specific model used. Even if your model addresses, say, volatility risk you may nevertheless address it in a harmful way—i.e. via the wrong model generating inappropriate hedging strategies. *Operational risk* refers to all aspects of implementing valuation and risk management processes as well as risks related to IT systems used. For example, knowledge of the right

---

[5]Gatheral (2006), ch. 6, analyzes default risk in the context of options on single stocks. Duffie and Singleton (2003) analyze default risk in a broader context and more comprehensively.

[6]Frey (2000) analyzes market illiquidity as a source of model risk in the context of dynamic hedging. Hilpisch (2001) provides a survey of research addressing valuation and dynamic hedging in imperfectly liquid markets.

[7]Cf. Jarrow (2005) for a discussion of this theory's implications in terms of valuation, hedging and risk measurement.

[8]*The New York Times* (13. September 2009): "Wall Street's Math Wizards Forgot a Few Variables."

hedging program is surely of great importance—but the timely and correct execution of the program is at least equally important.

2.4 HEDGING

Hedging describes the activity of minimizing or even *eliminating risks* resulting from option positions. Getting back to our previous example, an option writer who faces the risk of paying out 200 EUR to an option holder might want to set up a hedge program that pays her the exact amount in the exact case—leaving her with net debt of zero. The program should also pay 300 EUR or 100 EUR or whatever might be the amount due to writing the index option. In such a way, the writer would completely eliminate the risks attached to the short position in the option. In general, option writers do exactly this since as market participants they are not speculators but rather want to earn a steady income from their activities.

A hedge program can be either *dynamic* or *static* or a combination of both. Assume the equity index option of the example has time-to-maturity of 1 year. In order to hedge the option dynamically—in general with positions in the underlying—the writer sets up a hedge portfolio at the date of writing the option and then adjusts the portfolio frequently. A static hedge program—in general with positions in other options—would be set up at issuance and hold constant until maturity. More sophisticated hedge strategies generally combine both elements.

In general, there is neither a unique objective nor a unique set of principles for setting up hedge programs. For example, Gilbert et al. (2007) report three main objectives of variable annuities providers, i.e. life insurers, when implementing hedging programs:

1. accounting level
2. accounting volatility and
3. economic risks

This book focuses on economic risks only since accounting issues are highly dependent on the concrete reporting standards and may therefore vary from country to country. In that sense, the perspective of this book is cash flow driven and intentionally neglects accounting issues. The approach is that of *arbitrage* or *risk-neutral* pricing/hedging as comprehensively explained in Björk (2004) for models with continuous price processes and in Cont and Tankov (2004a) for models where price processes may jump.

Generally speaking, the main goal of a hedging program in economic or cash terms is to perfectly replicate the hedged derivative's payoff and thus eliminate all risk. However, in practice this is seldom realized due to two main issues. The first is the *frequency of hedge rebalancings*. In theory, dynamic hedging requires continuous rebalancings but practice only allows discrete rebalancings due to transaction costs and other market microstructure elements. This leads to a sequence of hedge errors which might add up over time or which may cancel each other out to some extent. The second is *market incompleteness*. If jumps of the underlying are possible, for example, markets become incomplete in the sense that risks cannot be hedged away since an infinite number of hedge instruments would be necessary to do so. One must rather resort to a risk minimization program where an (expected) hedge error, for example, is minimized. Another possibility would be to super-replicate the derivative—a strategy that can be rather costly.

In summary, if markets are sufficiently complete, hedgers generally strive to completely eliminate all cash flow risks resulting from options. If they are incomplete, hedgers can often only try to minimize the (expected) hedge error.

2.5 MARKET-BASED VALUATION AS A PROCESS

This book mainly takes the perspective of a corporate or financial institution investing or trading in—possibly exotic—equity derivatives. A canonical example might be a quantitative hedge fund. In order to make profound decisions and to build a sustainable business around equity derivatives, the institution must consider the following fundamental aspects:

1. **market realities**: what characterizes the market of the underlying and of the liquidly traded options on the underlying?
2. **market model**: the institution should apply a theoretical market model which is capable of providing a realistic framework for valuation and hedging purposes in the specific underlying and option market
3. **vanilla instrument valuation**: there should be available efficient methods to price vanilla instruments on a large scale
4. **model calibration**: a minimum requirement the market model must fulfill is that it reproduce prices of actively traded vanilla instruments reasonably well; to this end, the model parameters have to be calibrated to market data
5. **exotic instrument valuation**: there must be available flexible numerical methods to value exotic derivatives based on the calibrated market model; the most flexible method in this regard is Monte Carlo simulation (MCS)
6. **hedging**: as a general rule, if you can value a derivative instrument you can derive information needed to hedge this instrument; regarding exotic equity derivatives, numerical methods also have to be applied more often than not to come up with hedge parameters, like the delta of an option

This book addresses all six aspects. However, it abstracts in general from market microstructure aspects like bid/ask spreads, market liquidity, transaction costs, trade execution, etc. and also from dividends (which may be justified by the focus on index options).

Being equipped with an understanding of what characterizes the market-based valuation process, the next chapter reproduces some of the most important stylized facts with regard to stock indices and index options.

## CHAPTER 3

Market Stylized Facts

3.1 INTRODUCTION

In science one often takes the route from the specific to the general—from a number of real world observations to a theory or model describing the phenomenon in general fashion. This chapter therefore mainly conducts an analysis of real world data as a basis for the further modeling and implementation efforts. Our main objects of analysis are the DAX stock index—composed of stocks of large German companies—and European call options on the EURO STOXX 50 stock index—composed of stocks of large European companies.

The chapter first introduces some notions central to equity markets and equity derivatives, like volatility and correlation. It then conducts a simulation study in a laboratory fashion based on the benchmark geometric Brownian motion model of Black-Scholes-Merton (BSM). However, the main part of the chapter is concerned with the analysis of a financial time series of daily DAX index level movements. This is done in a tutorial style where the simplicity and replicability of results (with the provided Python scripts) are the main objectives. The chapter then turns to equity options markets in section 3.5. Here, pricing conventions and practices, the volatility smile/skew and its term structure are the main topics. Section 3.6 then rather briefly takes a look at market realities with regard to short rates.

3.2 VOLATILITY, CORRELATION AND CO.

Volatility may be the most central notion in option and derivatives analytics. There is not a single volatility concept but rather a family of concepts related to the notion of an "undirected dispersion/risk measure". For our purposes, we need to distinguish between the following different—but somehow related—volatility concepts (always in relation to a stochastic process or a financial time series):

- **historical volatility**: this refers to the standard deviation of log returns of a financial time series; suppose we observe N (past) log returns[1] $r_n, n \in \{1, \dots, N\}$, with mean return

$$\hat{\mu} = \frac{1}{N} \sum_{n=1}^{N} r_n$$

---

[1]Assume a time series with quotes $S_n, n \in \{0, \dots, N\}$. The log return for $n > 0$ is defined by $r_n \equiv \log S_n - \log S_{n-1} = \log(S_n / S_{n-1})$.

the historical volatility $\hat{\sigma}$ is then given by[2]

$$\hat{\sigma} = \sqrt{\frac{1}{N-1} \sum_{n=1}^{N} (r_n - \hat{\mu})^2}$$

- **instantaneous volatility**: this refers to the volatility factor of a diffusion process; for example, in the Black-Scholes-Merton model the instantaneous volatility σ is found in the respective (risk-neutral) stochastic differential equation (SDE)

$$dS_t = rS_t dt + \sigma S_t dZ_t$$

- **implied volatility**: this is the volatility that, if put into the Black-Scholes-Merton option pricing formula, gives the market-observed price of an option; suppose we observe today a price of C_0^* for a European call option; the implied volatility σ^{imp} is the quantity that solves ceteris paribus the implicit equation[3]

$$C_0^* = C^{BSM}(S_0, K, T, r, \sigma^{imp})$$

These volatilities all have squared counterparts which are then named *variance*. For example, in some financial models where volatility is stochastic—in contrast to the BSM assumption—the variance is modeled instead of the volatility.

Two other (sample) moments of distribution are of importance:

- **skewness**: this is a measure of the location of sample values relative to the mean ("more to the left or more to the right")[4]; again suppose we observe N (past) log returns $r_n, n \in \{1, \ldots, N\}$, with mean return $\hat{\mu}$; the (sample) skewness $\hat{s}$ is

$$\hat{s} = \frac{\frac{1}{N} \sum_{n=1}^{N} (r_n - \hat{\mu})^3}{\left(\frac{1}{N} \sum_{n=1}^{N} (r_n - \hat{\mu})^2 \right)^{3/2}}$$

- **kurtosis**: this is a measure for the peakedness of a distribution and/or the size of the tails of the distribution ("fat tails" are implied by a high kurtosis); again suppose we observe N (past) log returns $r_n, n \in \{1, \ldots, N\}$, with mean return $\hat{\mu}$; the (sample) kurtosis $\hat{k}$ is

$$\hat{k} = \frac{\frac{1}{N} \sum_{n=1}^{N} (r_n - \hat{\mu})^4}{\left(\frac{1}{N} \sum_{n=1}^{N} (r_n - \hat{\mu})^2 \right)^2} - 3$$

here 3 is subtracted such that the (standard) normal distribution has a kurtosis of 0

---

[2]This formula is often called the *corrected* (or unbiased) sample standard deviation in contrast to the case of the *uncorrected* (or biased) sample standard deviation where the multiplier is $1/N$ instead of $1/(N-1)$. Note that in Python and in particular NumPy, the uncorrected sample standard deviation is generally implemented.

[3]Implied volatility could in principle also be defined with respect to a different model. However, throughout this book *implied* always means "implied by the Black-Scholes-Merton formula".

[4]For the normal distribution the skewness is 0, implying a symmetric distribution around the mean.

Another important statistical notion is correlation. We mainly need to distinguish two types[5]:

- **historical correlation**: this refers to a measure for the co-movement of two financial time series; suppose we observe from two series a and b a total of N (past) pairs of log returns $(r_n^a, r_n^b), n \in \{1, \dots, N\}$, with mean returns $\hat{\mu}^a$ and $\hat{\mu}^b$; the historical (or sample) correlation $\hat{\rho}$ is then defined as

$$\hat{\rho} = \frac{\sum_{n=1}^{N} \left(r_n^a - \hat{\mu}^a \right) \left(r_n^b - \hat{\mu}^b \right)}{\sqrt{\sum_{n=1}^{N} \left(r_n^a - \hat{\mu}^a \right)^2 \sum_{n=1}^{N} \left(r_n^b - \hat{\mu}^b \right)^2}}$$

- **instantaneous correlation**: suppose we are given two standard Brownian motions Z^a, Z^b; the instantaneous correlation ρ between both is then given by $\langle Z^a, Z^b \rangle_t = \rho t$ where $\langle \cdot \rangle_t$ denotes the quadratic variation process (cf. Protter (2005), pp. 66–77); one can also write $dZ^a dZ^b = \rho dt$ where the meaning of "instantaneous" becomes more evident

Equipped with this set of definitions we can now proceed and apply (some of) them to both artificial data and real data.

3.3 NORMAL RETURNS AS THE BENCHMARK CASE

As the benchmark case, we consider the geometric Brownian motion model of BSM given by the SDE

$$dS_t = rS_t dt + \sigma S_t dZ_t$$

A discrete version, which can easily be simulated, is given by the difference equation

$$S_t = S_{t-\Delta t} e^{\left(r - \frac{1}{2}\sigma^2 \right) \Delta t + \sigma \sqrt{\Delta t} z_t}$$

for times $t \in \{\Delta t, 2\Delta t, \dots, T\}$ and the z_t being standard normally distributed random variables.

We parametrize the model with $S_0 = 100, T = 10.0, r = 0.05, \sigma = 0.2$. The Python script in sub-section 3.8.1 contains these parameters and a simulation algorithm as well as implementing a number of test routines. In addition, it generates a variety of graphical plots.[6]

Figure 3.1 presents a simulated path for the index level in combination with the daily log returns. From first inspection, the index development seems realistic and indistinguishable from typical charts seen in the financial press. Figure 3.2 shows the frequency of daily log returns and compares these to a normal distribution. The fit seems quite good—a fact to be expected since the characteristic feature of geometric Brownian motion is normally distributed returns.

Similarly, Figure 3.3 illustrates the normality of the returns by a so-called quantile-quantile plot or Q-Q plot. All return realizations lie on the straight line in such a case.

---

[5]Cf. Rebonato (2004) for an in-depth discussion of correlation in the context of option pricing.
[6]The script assumes 252 business days per year for the artificial data.

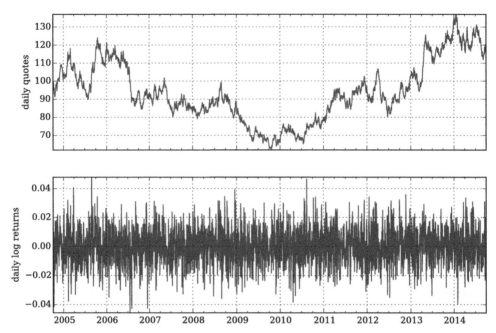

FIGURE 3.1   A single simulated path for the geometric Brownian motion over a 10-year period with daily log returns

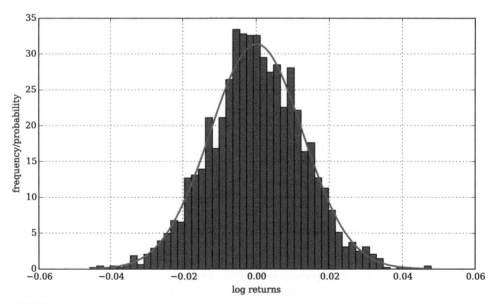

FIGURE 3.2   Histogram of the daily log returns (bars) and for comparison the probability density function of the normal distribution with the sample mean and volatility (line)

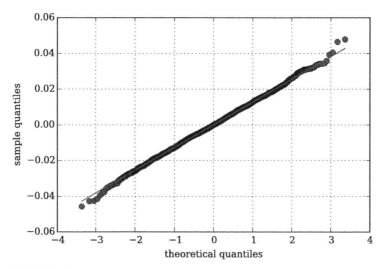

FIGURE 3.3 Quantile-quantile plot of the daily log returns of the geometric Brownian motion

However, statistical tests may help in gaining further confirmation of the graphical evidence. To this end, the Python script calculates several sample statistics and conducts a total of three tests. For the particular process shown in Figure 3.1, the statistics are:

```
 1   RETURN SAMPLE STATISTICS
 2   -----------------------------------------------
 3   Mean of Daily  Log Returns  0.000078
 4   Std  of Daily  Log Returns  0.012746
 5   Mean of Annua. Log Returns  0.019689
 6   Std  of Annua. Log Returns  0.202336
 7   -----------------------------------------------
 8   Skew of Sample Log Returns  -0.024305
 9   Skew Normal Test p-value     0.617420
10   -----------------------------------------------
11   Kurt of Sample Log Returns  0.127744
12   Kurt Normal Test p-value    0.190342
13   -----------------------------------------------
14   Normal Test p-value          0.374472
15   -----------------------------------------------
16   Realized Volatility          0.202340
17   Realized Variance            0.040941
```

Some comments on the results:

1. **volatility**: the annualized standard deviation of the log returns equals almost exactly the instantaneous volatility $\sigma = 0.2$ of the geometric Brownian motion

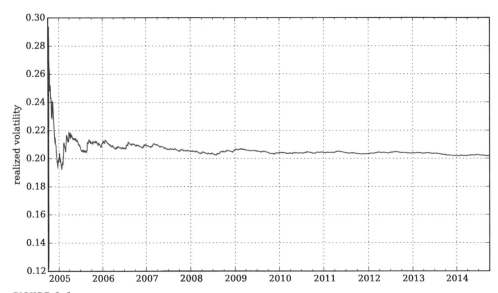

FIGURE 3.4   Realized volatility for the simulated path of the geometric Brownian motion

2. **skewness**: the skewness is almost zero and the high p-value of the normal skewness test indicates that the distribution of the log returns is normal
3. **kurtosis**: although the kurtosis is slightly positive, the p-value of the normal kurtosis test nevertheless also indicates normal distribution
4. **normality**: finally, the joint test for normality indicates a normal distribution with a p-value of 0.426

All in all, we can conclude that the simulated index level path exhibits, as desired, normally distributed log returns. The sample annualized volatility also coincides with the instantaneous volatility of the BSM model.

What about realized volatility and variance? To begin with, realized volatility is a special form of historical volatility and can be seen as a process. While historical volatility is computed for a fixed time window or a fixed number of observations, realized volatility evolves over time. Assume we started in January 2004 with say five observations and compute the sample volatility for the first time. Now, one day later when the 6th observation is available we update the volatility value to include the 6th observation as well. In this fashion, realized volatility is constantly updated.[7]

Figure 3.4 illustrates the evolution of realized volatility over time. It obviously converges to the above reported value of 0.202 which is almost the same as the instantaneous volatility.

Finally, Figure 3.5 shows the rolling mean return and the rolling (realized) volatility for time windows of 252 days, i.e. 1 year. In addition, the figure also displays the rolling correlation between the two over a time window of same length. Even though the realized volatility and the sample volatility for all returns coincide with the constant instantaneous volatility, the rolling

---

[7]Cf. Andersen and Benzoni (2009) for a survey of realized volatility and related research.

FIGURE 3.5   Rolling mean log return (252 days), rolling volatility (252 days) and rolling correlation between both (252 days) for geometric Brownian motion; dashed lines are averages over the whole period shown

volatility varies strongly around the level of 20%. The volatility and return measures are sometimes positively correlated (move in the same direction) and sometimes negatively—on average the correlation is $\hat{\rho} = -0.0529$.

3.4 INDICES AND STOCKS

Before turning to options, this section reproduces stylized facts of stock indices and stocks.

3.4.1 Stylized Facts

In this sub-section, we briefly list and describe some stylized facts about stock index returns. Stylized facts can be described as follows (cf. Cont (2001), p. 223):

> "A set of [statistical] properties, common across many instruments, markets and time periods, has been observed by independent studies and classified as 'stylized facts'."

Below we list a selection of stylized facts. The emphasis is on comparing these facts with the benchmark case of BSM where volatility is constant and returns are normally distributed. Among those stylized facts about index returns that are important for our purposes are[8]:

- **stochastic volatility**: volatility is neither constant nor deterministic; there is no mechanism to forecast volatility at a high confidence level
- **volatility clustering**: empirical data suggests that high volatility events seem to cluster in time; there is often a positive autocorrelation of volatility measures
- **volatility mean reversion**: volatility is a mean-reverting quantity—it never reaches zero nor does it go to infinity; however, the mean can change over time
- **leverage effect**: studies suggest that volatility is negatively correlated with asset returns; if return measures increase, volatility measures often decrease and vice versa
- **fat tails**: compared to a normal distribution large positive and negative index returns are more frequent
- **jumps**: index levels may move by magnitudes that cannot be explained within a Gaussian, i.e. normal, diffusion setting; some jump component may be necessary to explain certain large moves

3.4.2 DAX Index Returns

We will now test whether we can identify evidence for the stylized facts of the previous subsection in the log returns of the DAX index. We analyze the period from 01. October 2004 to 30. September 2014.[9] The following is a small selection of the raw data used. All results and graphics reported hereafter are based on the adjusted close numbers from Yahoo! Finance.

		index	returns	rea_var	rea_vol
2	Date				
3	2014-09-24	9661.97	0.006952	0.047792	0.218614
4	2014-09-25	9510.01	-0.015853	0.047798	0.218628
5	2014-09-26	9490.55	-0.002048	0.047780	0.218586
6	2014-09-29	9422.91	-0.007153	0.047766	0.218555
7	2014-09-30	9474.30	0.005439	0.047751	0.218519

Figure 3.6 shows the index levels and the daily log returns graphically. On first inspection, the development of the index is not too different from the picture for the geometric Brownian motion. However, the daily log returns speak quite a different language: the (average) amplitudes change over time indicating at least *time-varying volatility* and there also seems to be *volatility clustering.*

Figure 3.7 compares the sample frequency of log returns with a normal distribution that has the same mean and standard deviation. The sample distribution has both a *higher peak*

---

[8]Cf. Cont (2001) for a concise survey. Cf. Rebonato (2004), in particular chapter 7, for a wealth of information regarding empirical findings about equity markets and equity options.

[9]Source of DAX index quotes http://finance.yahoo.com. We use the data as delivered by the site, no adjustments have been made.

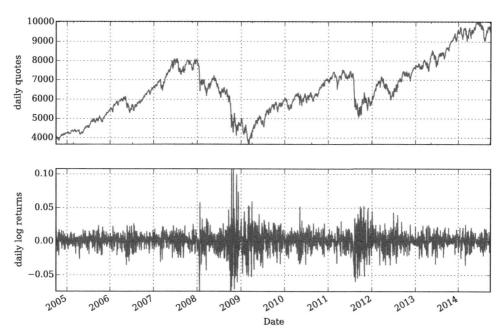

FIGURE 3.6 DAX index level quotes and daily log returns over the period from 01. October 2004 to 30. September 2014

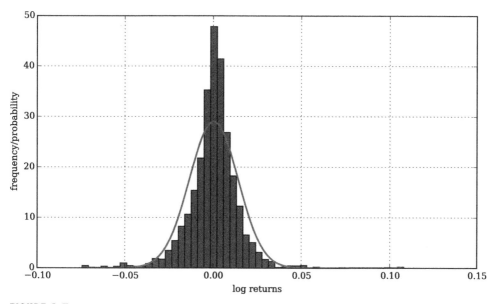

FIGURE 3.7 Histogram of the daily log returns of the DAX over the period from 01. October 2004 to 30. September 2014 (bars) and for comparison the probability density function of the normal distribution with the sample mean and volatility (line)

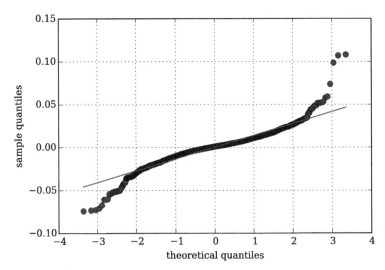

FIGURE 3.8 Quantile-quantile plot of the daily log returns of the DAX over the period from 01. October 2004 to 30. September 2014

and *heavier tails*. However, skewness seems comparable—there is neither "left-leaning" nor "right-leaning" of the sample distribution.

Finally, Figure 3.8 shows the Q-Q plot for the DAX log returns. This also illustrates well the deviation from the normal distribution.

We can also test our findings more rigorously, at least with respect to the obviously non-normal distribution. Here is the output of the Python script of sub-section 3.8.2:

```
1   RETURN SAMPLE STATISTICS
2   ---------------------------------------------
3   Mean of Daily  Log Returns  0.000348
4   Std  of Daily  Log Returns  0.013761
5   Mean of Annua. Log Returns  0.087656
6   Std  of Annua. Log Returns  0.218449
7   ---------------------------------------------
8   Skew of Sample Log Returns  0.025083
9   Skew Normal Test p-value    0.603591
10  ---------------------------------------------
11  Kurt of Sample Log Returns  7.205877
12  Kurt Normal Test p-value    0.000000
13  ---------------------------------------------
14  Normal Test p-value         0.000000
15  ---------------------------------------------
16  Realized Volatility         0.218519
17  Realized Variance           0.047751
18
```

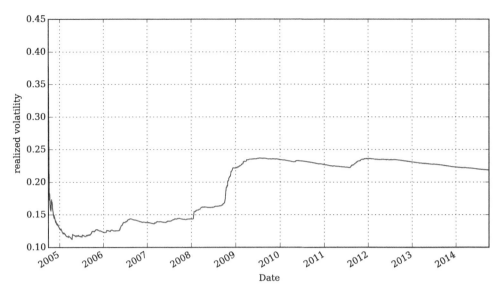

FIGURE 3.9 Realized volatility for the DAX over the period from 01. October 2004 to 30. September 2014

Over the sample period, the DAX index generates an annualized return of about 8.7%. The historical/realized volatility is about 21.9%. All test results say that the null hypothesis that "the sample distribution is normal" can be rejected with high significance. The impression about the kurtosis is also supported by the high value of 7.2—we have fat tails.

What about realized volatility over time? Figure 3.9 illustrates that the realized volatility varies over time and that it does not seem to converge (at least not strongly). In the beginning, it goes down to below 15%, rises again to about 24% to drop and rise again for a bit. This provides further evidence that volatility is time varying.

The last point is even better illustrated in Figure 3.10 which shows a rolling yearly volatility measure. This measure varies between 11% and about 40%. These large deviations are much stronger than the deviations observed in Figure 3.5 for the geometric Brownian motion. This holds true for both *deviations from the average* and with respect to the *difference between maxima and minima*. Nevertheless, volatility obviously is *mean reverting*.

What about the leverage effect? Comparison of the upper and middle sub-plots of Figure 3.10 indeed indicates a negative correlation. This is supported by the negative average (line) in the lower sub-plot. However, the yearly rolling correlation measure in the lower sub-plot varies strongly taking almost extreme values in regular cycles. Regularly, correlation even comes quite close to $+1.0$ or -1.0.

So far, we have found evidence for time-varying/stochastic volatility, clustering, mean reversion, leverage effect and fat tails. What about jumps? If we say, somehow arbitrarily, that a jump is a daily log return of more than $\pm5\%$, we have a total of 31 jumps in the historical DAX data. Assuming a normal distribution with the DAX log returns' sample mean and standard deviation, the probabilities are $P(r_n < -0.05) = 0.0002911$ and $P(r_n > -0.05) = 0.0003402$ for observing such extraordinary returns given a specific return observation r_n. Multiplying these probabilities with the sample size of 2,557 we could expect 0.74 returns lower than -5%

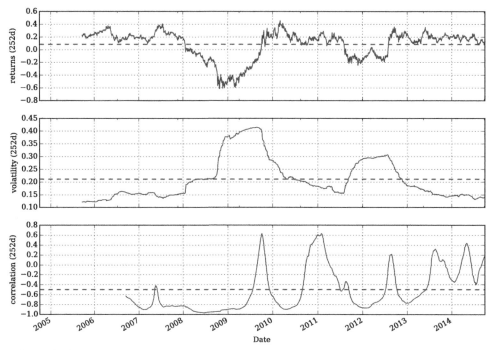

FIGURE 3.10   Rolling mean log return (252 days), rolling volatility (252 days) and rolling correlation between both (252 days); dashed lines are averages over the whole period shown

and 0.87 returns higher than +5%. Again, we see evidence for fat tails and can interpret these figures also as hints towards the existence of jumps.[10]

All in all, if we want to model an index like the DAX realistically, the model should take account of:

1. autocorrelated stochastic volatility
2. mean reversion of volatility
3. leverage effect, i.e. negative correlation between returns and volatility
4. fat tails of and jumps in the index returns

3.5   OPTION MARKETS

This section now turns to options markets, in particular to bid/ask spreads in these markets and implied volatilities.

---

[10]These considerations are quite heuristic in nature and are lacking a sound conceptual grounding. For example, a central question is how to assess the distinct contributions of the jump and diffusion component, respectively, to observed index movements in a jump-diffusion model. Cf. Klössner (2010) for a survey of econometric tests for jumps in financial time series.

3.5.1 Bid/Ask Spreads

A market-based valuation of equity derivatives, both vanilla and exotic, should yield sufficiently accurate values. However, markets are far from being perfect and a number of so-called market microstructure elements influences prices directly or indirectly. With regard to valuation accuracy it is important that there is in general not a single quote for an option but at least two: a *bid* quote at which market makers would buy the option and an *ask* quote at which they would sell the option.

Table 3.1 reports average option quote spreads for call options on stocks in the Dow Jones Industrial Average (DJIA) index for the period from 1996 to 2010. For the total sample of about 1.1 mn options, the average spread is 0.227 USD or 7.92% relative to the average mid-price. These values vary with maturity of the call options and moneyness levels. The *smallest absolute spread* with 0.136 USD is observed for out-of-the-money options with short maturity. The *smallest relative spread* emerges with 3.7% for in-the-money options with long maturity. Table 3.2 paints a consistent picture for put option quotes and spreads.

To put these observations differently, one cannot in general expect to reach a market-based valuation accuracy of say "1 cent or better" or "1% or better". The market itself does not quote options in such a manner and exchanges generally have tick sizes—i.e. minimum allowed changes of the price of an option—much higher than 1 cent. For example, in Tables 3.1 and 3.2 the tick size for options with bid quotes below 3 USD is 5 cents. For options with bid quotes above 3 USD the tick size is 10 cents.

3.5.2 Implied Volatility Surface

Recall that the implied volatility of a European call option with market quote C_0^* is the value σ^{imp} that solves the implicit equation

$$C_0^* = C^{BSM}(S_0, K, T, r, \sigma^{imp}) \tag{3.1}$$

given the BSM call option formula. Chapter 5 discusses the model, the formula and the sensitivity of the formula with respect to the input volatility (the so-called vega) in detail. At

TABLE 3.1 Option bid/ask spreads for call options on stocks of the DJIA index[a]

Category	Type	Number	Maturity	Mid-Price	Spread	Rel. Spread
All	All	1,095,327	96.60	5.185	0.227	7.92%
Short	OTM	125,575	44.26	1.069	0.136	18.72%
Short	ATM	118,027	44.74	2.956	0.184	7.44%
Short	ITM	173,607	44.30	6.561	0.265	4.74%
Long	OTM	191,127	127.57	1.593	0.147	12.63%
Long	ATM	203,790	129.63	4.563	0.226	5.72%
Long	ITM	283,201	128.81	9.967	0.318	3.70%

[a]Data for the period 1996–2010; OTM, ATM, ITM = out-of-the, at-the, in-the-money options; number = number of call options included in the sample; maturity = average option maturity in days; mid-price = middle of bid and ask quotes in USD; spread = USD difference of bid and ask quote; relative spread = spread relative to mid-price.
Source: Chaudhury (2014).

TABLE 3.2   Option bid/ask spreads for put options on stocks of the DJIA index[a]

Category	Type	Number	Maturity	Mid-Price	Spread	Rel. Spread
All	All	1,105,028	96.07	5.093	0.229	7.80%
Short	OTM	158,486	44.55	1.339	0.148	15.98%
Short	ATM	120,257	44.63	3.443	0.204	7.12%
Short	ITM	146,979	43.86	6.858	0.279	4.91%
Long	OTM	267,847	128.80	2.238	0.172	10.26%
Long	ATM	201,100	129.33	5.769	0.255	5.18%
Long	ITM	210,359	127.34	10.621	0.317	3.50%

[a]Data for the period 1996–2010; OTM, ATM, ITM = out-of-the, at-the, in-the-money options; number = number of put options included in the sample; maturity = average option maturity in days; mid-price = middle of bid and ask quotes in USD; spread = USD difference of bid and ask quote; relative spread = spread relative to mid-price.
Source: Chaudhury (2014).

this stage, it is only important to know, that the vega, i.e. the first derivative of the formula with respect to volatility, is strictly positive implying a bijective relationship between call values and volatilities and therewith a unique solution to equation (3.1). Sub-section 3.8.3 provides a Python script implementing the BSM formula for calls and a numerical routine to solve the implicit equation (3.1).

Equipped with this knowledge, we now want to briefly analyze a real volatility surface. Volatility surface means the volatilities implied for different option strikes and different option maturities on the same underlying. Our objects of study will be implied volatilities from European call options on the EURO STOXX 50 stock index.

As with index returns, there are some stylized facts about the volatility surface for stock indices (cf. Rebonato (2004), chapter 7):

- **smiles**: option implied volatilities exhibit a smile form, i.e. for calls the OTM implied volatilities are higher than the ATM ones; sometimes they rise again for ITM options; this is a phenomenon present in the financial markets mainly since the market crash of 1987
- **term structure**: smiles are more pronounced for short-term options than for longer-term options; a phenomenon sometimes called volatility term structure

The script in sub-section 3.8.4 uses a set of option quotes for different strikes and different option maturities. Options are European call options on the EURO STOXX 50 index and the quotes are from 30. September 2014. The following is a small excerpt from the data used.

```
1          Date      Strike  Call    Maturity    Put
2    498   2014-09-30  3750    27.4    2015-09-18  635.9
3    499   2014-09-30  3800    21.8    2015-09-18  680.3
4    500   2014-09-30  3850    17.2    2015-09-18  725.7
5    501   2014-09-30  3900    13.4    2015-09-18  772.0
6    502   2014-09-30  3950    10.4    2015-09-18  818.9
```

The script calculates the implied volatilities of the different options and generates a graphical output as shown in Figure 3.11. The results reflect the stylized facts rather well.

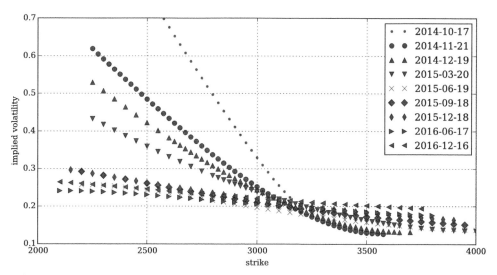

FIGURE 3.11   Implied volatilities from European call options on the EURO STOXX 50 on 30. September 2014

3.6   SHORT RATES

Short rates and associated discount factors are not only important for the valuation of options. Short rates are, in a sense, the least common denominator of all asset pricing models—be it for primary asset classes (e.g. stocks, bonds, commodities) or derivative assets, be it in complete or incomplete market models (cf. Hansen and Renault (2009)). As intensively discussed in Chapter 4, short rates and their corresponding discount factors are a basic building block for the risk-neutral valuation approach and the Fundamental Theorem of Asset Pricing.

However, empirical evidence about the dynamics of short rates is not as clear as one would wish. A recent empirical study by Bali-Wu opens with the words (cf. Bali and Wu (2006), pp. 1269–1270):

> "The short-term interest rate is a fundamental variable in both theoretical and empirical finance because of its central role in asset pricing. An enormous amount of work has been directed towards the understanding of the stochastic behavior of short-term interest rates. Nevertheless, based on different data sets and/or different parametric or non-parametric specifications, these studies have generated confusing and sometimes conflicting conclusions."

Nevertheless, some stylized facts are also worth reporting with respect to short rates.[11] Those that are most important in terms of financial modeling requirements are:

- **positivity**: (nominal) interest rates are positive in general; a formal model should take this into account

---

[11]Cf. Björk (2009) for a concise survey of interest rate types and modeling. Cf. Brigo and Mercurio (2006) for a comprehensive treatment of current interest rate modeling.

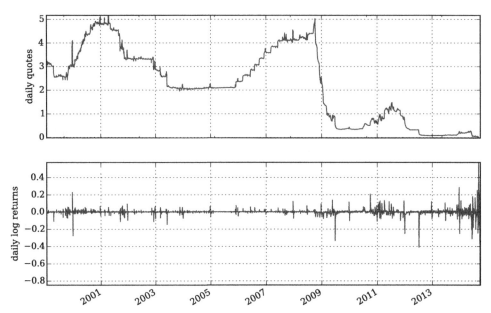

FIGURE 3.12   Daily quotes of 1 week Euribor and daily log changes over the period from 01. January 1999 to 30. September 2014

- **stochasticity**: interest rates in general and short rates in particular move in random fashion; there are no means to forecast interest rates movements with high confidence
- **mean reversion**: interest rates can neither trend to zero nor infinity in the long term such that there must always be the phenomenon of mean reversion
- **term structure**: yields of benchmark bonds—like German bunds—as well as rates in interbank lending vary with time to maturity implying different (instantaneous) forward rates, i.e. different future short rate levels

The Euribor, which stands for "Euro InterBank Offered Rate", is a benchmark rate for interbank lending. There are Euribor rates for different maturities, starting with 1 week and ranging to 1 year. Figure 3.12 shows the daily quotes of the 1 week Euribor from January 1999 to the end of September 2014 as well as the daily log changes. With regard to the daily changes there are a number of outliers and we can also observe something like volatility clustering. The figure also provides support for the first three stylized facts. This figure has been produced with the Python script found in sub-section 3.8.5. This script uses an Excel workbook which contains the whole Euribor dataset from 1999 to September 2014.[12] Figure 3.13 shows the histogram of the daily log changes in comparison to a normal distribution with same mean and standard deviation. The histogram has a relatively high peak.

Figure 3.14 illustrates the deviation of the daily log change distribution from normality by a Q-Q plot.

Figure 3.15 shows the daily quotes of the Euribor for 1 week, 1 month, 6 months and 1 year in comparison. The general picture is one with a normal term structure (longer horizons show

---

[12]Source: http://www.euribor-ebf.eu/euribor-org/euribor-rates.html.

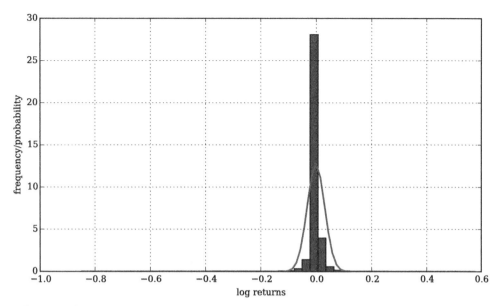

FIGURE 3.13 Histogram of daily log changes in 1 week Euribor in comparison to a normal distribution with same mean and standard deviation (line)

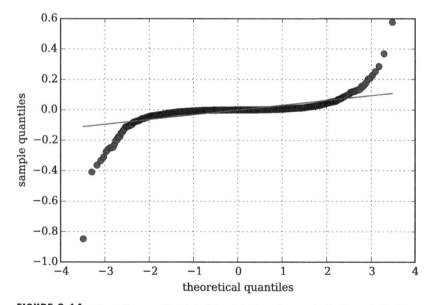

FIGURE 3.14 Quantile-quantile plot of the daily log changes in the 1 week Euribor

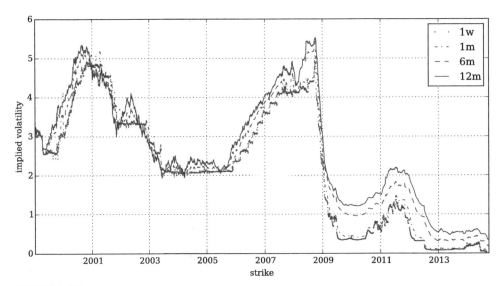

FIGURE 3.15 Daily quotes of 1 week (dotted), 1 month (dot-dashed), 6 months (dashed) and 1 year Euribor (solid line) over the period from 01. January 1999 to 30. September 2014

higher rates) but there are also periods with inverted term structure where short-term borrowing becomes more expensive than long-term borrowing. The financial crisis of 2008/2009 caused a large drop in the overall level of Euribor rates accompanied by a widening of the spreads (steeper term structure).

3.7 CONCLUSIONS

A realistic market model …

- … has to take into account that index volatility
  - varies over time (stochasticity, mean reversion, clustering)
  - is negatively correlated with returns (leverage effect)
  - varies for different option strikes (volatility smile)
  - varies for different option maturities (volatility term structure)
- … has to account for jumps in the index development
- … has to take into account that interest rates
  - vary over time (positivity, stochasticity, mean reversion)
  - vary for different time horizons (term structure)

Such a model therefore comprises (at least)

- a stochastic volatility component
- a jump component and
- a stochastic short rate component

3.8 PYTHON SCRIPTS

3.8.1 GBM Analysis

```python
#
# Analyzing Returns from Geometric Brownian Motion
# 03_stf/GBM_returns.py
#
# (c) Dr. Yves J. Hilpisch
# Derivatives Analytics with Python
#
import math
import numpy as np
import pandas as pd
import scipy.stats as scs
import statsmodels.api as sm
import matplotlib as mpl
import matplotlib.pyplot as plt
mpl.rcParams['font.family'] = 'serif'


#
# Helper Function
#


def dN(x, mu, sigma):
    ''' Probability density function of a normal random variable x.

    Parameters
    ==========
    mu: float
        expected value
    sigma: float
        standard deviation

    Returns
    =======
    pdf: float
        value of probability density function
    '''
    z = (x - mu) / sigma
    pdf = np.exp(-0.5 * z ** 2) / math.sqrt(2 * math.pi * sigma ** 2)
    return pdf


#
# Simulate a Number of Years of Daily Stock Quotes
#
```

```python
def simulate_gbm():
    # model parameters
    S0 = 100.0  # initial index level
    T = 10.0  # time horizon
    r = 0.05  # risk-less short rate
    vol = 0.2  # instantaneous volatility

    # simulation parameters
    np.random.seed(250000)
    gbm_dates = pd.DatetimeIndex(start='30-09-2004',
                                 end='30-09 2014',
                                 freq='B')
    M = len(gbm_dates)  # time steps
    I = 1  # index level paths
    dt = 1 / 252.  # fixed for simplicity
    df = math.exp(-r * dt)  # discount factor

    # stock price paths
    rand = np.random.standard_normal((M, I))  # random numbers
    S = np.zeros_like(rand)  # stock matrix
    S[0] = S0  # initial values
    for t in range(1, M):  # stock price paths
        S[t] = S[t - 1] * np.exp((r - vol ** 2 / 2) * dt
                        + vol * rand[t] * math.sqrt(dt))

    gbm = pd.DataFrame(S[:, 0], index=gbm_dates, columns=['index'])
    gbm['returns'] = np.log(gbm['index'] / gbm['index'].shift(1))


    # Realized Volatility (eg. as defined for variance swaps)
    gbm['rea_var'] = 252 * np.cumsum(gbm['returns'] ** 2) / np.arange(len(gbm))
    gbm['rea_vol'] = np.sqrt(gbm['rea_var'])
    gbm = gbm.dropna()
    return gbm

# Return Sample Statistics and Normality Tests

def print_statistics(data):
    print "RETURN SAMPLE STATISTICS"
    print "---------------------------------------------"
    print "Mean of Daily  Log Returns %9.6f" % np.mean(data['returns'])
    print "Std  of Daily  Log Returns %9.6f" % np.std(data['returns'])
    print "Mean of Annua. Log Returns %9.6f" % (np.mean(data['returns']) * 252)
    print "Std  of Annua. Log Returns %9.6f" % \
                (np.std(data['returns']) * math.sqrt(252))
    print "---------------------------------------------"
    print "Skew of Sample Log Returns %9.6f" % scs.skew(data['returns'])
    print "Skew Normal Test p-value   %9.6f" % scs.skewtest(data['returns'])[1]
    print "---------------------------------------------"
```

```
    print "Kurt of Sample Log Returns %9.6f" % scs.kurtosis(data['returns'])
    print "Kurt Normal Test p-value    %9.6f" % \
            scs.kurtosistest(data['returns'])[1]
    print "----------------------------------------------"
    print "Normal Test p-value         %9.6f" % \
            scs.normaltest(data['returns'])[1]
    print "----------------------------------------------"
    print "Realized Volatility         %9.6f" % data['rea_vol'].iloc[-1]
    print "Realized Variance           %9.6f" % data['rea_var'].iloc[-1]

#
# Graphical Output
#

# daily quotes and log returns
def quotes_returns(data):
    ''' Plots quotes and returns. '''
    plt.figure(figsize=(9, 6))
    plt.subplot(211)
    data['index'].plot()
    plt.ylabel('daily quotes')
    plt.grid(True)
    plt.axis('tight')

    plt.subplot(212)
    data['returns'].plot()
    plt.ylabel('daily log returns')
    plt.grid(True)
    plt.axis('tight')

# histogram of annualized daily log returns
def return_histogram(data):
    ''' Plots a histogram of the returns. '''
    plt.figure(figsize=(9, 5))
    x = np.linspace(min(data['returns']), max(data['returns']), 100)
    plt.hist(np.array(data['returns']), bins=50, normed=True)
    y = dN(x, np.mean(data['returns']), np.std(data['returns']))
    plt.plot(x, y, linewidth=2)
    plt.xlabel('log returns')
    plt.ylabel('frequency/probability')
    plt.grid(True)

# Q-Q plot of annualized daily log returns
def return_qqplot(data):
    ''' Generates a Q-Q plot of the returns.'''
    plt.figure(figsize=(9, 5))
    sm.qqplot(data['returns'], line='s')
    plt.grid(True)
    plt.xlabel('theoretical quantiles')
    plt.ylabel('sample quantiles')
```

```python
# realized volatility
def realized_volatility(data):
    ''' Plots the realized volatility. '''
    plt.figure(figsize=(9, 5))
    data['rea_vol'].plot()
    plt.ylabel('realized volatility')
    plt.grid(True)


# mean return, volatility and correlation (252 days moving = 1 year)
def rolling_statistics(data):
    ''' Calculates and plots rolling statistics (mean, std, correlation). '''
    plt.figure(figsize=(11, 8))

    plt.subplot(311)
    mr = pd.rolling_mean(data['returns'], 252) * 252
    mr.plot()
    plt.grid(True)
    plt.ylabel('returns (252d)')
    plt.axhline(mr.mean(), color='r', ls='dashed', lw=1.5)

    plt.subplot(312)
    vo = pd.rolling_std(data['returns'], 252) * math.sqrt(252)
    vo.plot()
    plt.grid(True)
    plt.ylabel('volatility (252d)')
    plt.axhline(vo.mean(), color='r', ls='dashed', lw=1.5)
    vx = plt.axis()

    plt.subplot(313)
    co = pd.rolling_corr(mr, vo, 252)
    co.plot()
    plt.grid(True)
    plt.ylabel('correlation (252d)')
    cx = plt.axis()
    plt.axis([vx[0], vx[1], cx[2], cx[3]])
    plt.axhline(co.mean(), color='r', ls='dashed', lw=1.5)
```

3.8.2 DAX Analysis

```python
#
# Analyzing DAX Index Quotes and Returns
# Source: http://finance.yahoo.com
# 03_stf/DAX_returns.py
#
# (c) Dr. Yves J. Hilpisch
# Derivatives Analytics with Python
#
```

```python
import pandas.io.data as web
from GBM_returns import *


# Read Data for DAX from the Web
def read_dax_data():
    ''' Reads historical DAX data from Yahoo! Finance, calculates log returns,
    realized variance and volatility.'''
    DAX = web.DataReader('^GDAXI', data_source='yahoo',
                   start='30-09-2004', end='30-09-2014')
    DAX.rename(columns={'Adj Close' : 'index'}, inplace=True)
    DAX['returns'] = np.log(DAX['index'] / DAX['index'].shift(1))
    DAX['rea_var'] = 252 * np.cumsum(DAX['returns'] ** 2) / np.arange(len(DAX))
    DAX['rea_vol'] = np.sqrt(DAX['rea_var'])
    DAX = DAX.dropna()
    return DAX


def count_jumps(data, value):
    ''' Counts the number of return jumps as defined in size by value. '''
    jumps = np.sum(np.abs(data['returns']) > value)
    return jumps
```

3.8.3   BSM Implied Volatilities

```python
#
# Valuation of European Call Options in BSM Model
# and Numerical Derivation of Implied Volatility
# 03_stf/BSM_imp_vol.py
#
# (c) Dr. Yves J. Hilpisch
# from Hilpisch, Yves (2014): Python for Finance, O'Reilly.
#
from math import log, sqrt, exp
from scipy import stats
from scipy.optimize import fsolve


class call_option(object):
    ''' Class for European call options in BSM Model.

    Attributes
    ==========
    S0: float
        initial stock/index level
    K: float
        strike price
    t: datetime/Timestamp object
        pricing date
```

```
M:  datetime/Timestamp object
    maturity date
r:  float
    constant risk-free short rate
sigma:  float
    volatility factor in diffusion term

Methods
=======
value:  float
    return present value of call option
vega:  float
    return vega of call option
imp_vol:  float
    return implied volatility given option quote
'''

def __init__(self, S0, K, t, M, r, sigma):
    self.S0 = float(S0)
    self.K = K
    self.t = t
    self.M = M
    self.r = r
    self.sigma = sigma

def update_ttm(self):
    ''' Updates time-to-maturity self.T. '''
    if self.t > self.M:
        raise ValueError("Pricing date later than maturity.")
    self.T = (self.M - self.t).days / 365.

def d1(self):
    ''' Helper function. '''
    d1 = ((log(self.S0 / self.K)
        + (self.r + 0.5 * self.sigma ** 2) * self.T)
        / (self.sigma * sqrt(self.T)))
    return d1

def value(self):
    ''' Return option value. '''
    self.update_ttm()
    d1 = self.d1()
    d2 = ((log(self.S0 / self.K)
        + (self.r - 0.5 * self.sigma ** 2) * self.T)
        / (self.sigma * sqrt(self.T)))
    value = (self.S0 * stats.norm.cdf(d1, 0.0, 1.0)
        - self.K * exp(-self.r * self.T) * stats.norm.cdf(d2, 0.0, 1.0))
    return value
```

```
def vega(self):
    ''' Return Vega of option. '''
    self.update_ttm()
    d1 = self.d1()
    vega = self.S0 * stats.norm.pdf(d1, 0.0, 1.0) * sqrt(self.T)
    return vega

def imp_vol(self, C0, sigma_est=0.2):
    ''' Return implied volatility given option price. '''
    option = call_option(self.S0, self.K, self.t, self.M,
                         self.r, sigma_est)
    option.update_ttm()
    def difference(sigma):
        option.sigma = sigma
        return option.value() - C0
    iv = fsolve(difference, sigma_est)[0]
    return iv
```

3.8.4 EURO STOXX 50 Implied Volatilities

```
#
# Black-Scholes-Merton Implied Volatilities of
# Call Options on the EURO STOXX 50
# Option Quotes from 30. September 2014
# Source: www.eurexchange.com, www.stoxx.com
# 03_stf/ES50_imp_vol.py
#
# (c) Dr. Yves J. Hilpisch
# Derivatives Analytics with Python
#
import numpy as np
import pandas as pd
from BSM_imp_vol import call_option
import matplotlib as mpl
import matplotlib.pyplot as plt
mpl.rcParams['font.family'] = 'serif'

# Pricing Data
pdate = pd.Timestamp('30-09-2014')

#
# EURO STOXX 50 index data
#

# URL of data file
es_url = 'http://www.stoxx.com/download/historical_values/hbrbcpe.txt'
# column names to be used
```

```python
cols = ['Date', 'SX5P', 'SX5E', 'SXXP', 'SXXE',
        'SXXF', 'SXXA', 'DK5F', 'DKXF', 'DEL']
# reading the data with pandas
es = pd.read_csv(es_url,  # filename
                 header=None,  # ignore column names
                 index_col=0,  # index column (dates)
                 parse_dates=True,  # parse these dates
                 dayfirst=True,  # format of dates
                 skiprows=4,  # ignore these rows
                 sep=';',  # data separator
                 names=cols)  # use these column names
# deleting the helper column
del es['DEL']
S0 = es['SX5E']['30-09-2014']
r = -0.05


#
# Option Data
#
data = pd.HDFStore('./03_stf/es50_option_data.h5', 'r')['data']


#
# BSM Implied Volatilities
#

def calculate_imp_vols(data):
    ''' Calculate all implied volatilities for the European call options
    given the tolerance level for moneyness of the option.'''
    data['Imp_Vol'] = 0.0
    tol = 0.30  # tolerance for moneyness
    for row in data.index:
        t = data['Date'][row]
        T = data['Maturity'][row]
        ttm = (T - t).days / 365.
        forward = np.exp(r * ttm) * S0
        if (abs(data['Strike'][row] - forward) / forward) < tol:
            call = call_option(S0, data['Strike'][row], t, T, r, 0.2)
            data['Imp_Vol'][row] = call.imp_vol(data['Call'][row])
    return data


#
# Graphical Output
#
markers = ['.', 'o', '^', 'v', 'x', 'D', 'd', '>', '<']
def plot_imp_vols(data):
    ''' Plot the implied volatilites. '''
    maturities = sorted(set(data['Maturity']))
    plt.figure(figsize=(10, 5))
```

```
    for i, mat in enumerate(maturities):
        dat = data[(data['Maturity'] == mat) & (data['Imp_Vol'] > 0)]
        plt.plot(dat['Strike'].values, dat['Imp_Vol'].values,
                'b%s' % markers[i], label=str(mat)[:10])
    plt.grid()
    plt.legend()
    plt.xlabel('strike')
    plt.ylabel('implied volatility')
```

3.8.5 Euribor Analysis

```
#
# Analyzing Euribor Interest Rate Data
# Source: http://www.emmi-benchmarks.eu/euribor-org/euribor-rates.html
# 03_stf/EURIBOR_analysis.py
#
# (c) Dr. Yves J. Hilpisch
# Derivatives Analytics with Python
#
import pandas as pd
from GBM_returns import *

# Read Data for Euribor from Excel file
def read_euribor_data():
    ''' Reads historical Euribor data from Excel file, calculates log returns,
    realized variance and volatility.'''
    EBO = pd.read_excel('./03_stf/EURIBOR_current.xlsx',
                    index_col=0, parse_dates=True)
    EBO['returns'] = np.log(EBO['1w'] / EBO['1w'].shift(1))
    EBO = EBO.dropna()
    return EBO

# Plot the Term Structure
markers = [',', '-.', '-', '-']
def plot_term_structure(data):
    ''' Plot the term structure of Euribor rates. '''
    plt.figure(figsize=(10, 5))
    for i, mat in enumerate(['1w', '1m', '6m', '12m']):
        plt.plot(data[mat].index, data[mat].values,
                'b%s' % markers[i], label=mat)
    plt.grid()
    plt.legend()
    plt.xlabel('strike')
    plt.ylabel('implied volatility')
    plt.ylim(0.0, plt.ylim()[1])
```

Theoretical Valuation

## CHAPTER 4

Risk-Neutral Valuation

4.1 INTRODUCTION

Every sincere attempt to value financial derivatives needs to be grounded on a sound theory, formally represented in general by some kind of market model. A market model embodies a simplifying mathematical description of a real financial market. A priori, it is not clear what features a market model should have. These are mainly dictated by the market under observation and the tasks to be accomplished (e.g. pricing, trading, hedging, risk management). However, there is a minimum set of requirements a market model should obey. The most important are the *absence of arbitrage opportunities* (NA) and *no free lunches with vanishing risk* (NFLVR).

A central result in mathematical finance is the *Fundamental Theorem of Asset Pricing* which relates, for a given market model, the conditions of NA or NFLVR to the existence of an equivalent martingale measure (EMM) making all discounted stochastic processes of the market model martingales. A martingale is a stochastic process that does not change its value on average (under some suitable conditions). An important corollary of this result is that the (discounted) price processes of attainable, i.e. redundant, options are also martingales giving rise to a pure probabilistic approach to option pricing. Namely, the value of a European option maturing at some date in the future is simply its expected payoff at that date under the EMM discounted back to today by the risk-free short rate.

The market-based valuation of options is a mainly numerical discipline and therefore works generally in discrete time and with discrete state spaces. This is due to computers being able only to store discrete sets of quantities. However, in the valuation process analytical results from continuous time, continuous state space models are used whenever appropriate. Unfortunately, the mathematical machinery needed to establish the Fundamental Theorem for such types of models is well beyond the scope of this book.

We therefore take a typical—and for our purposes appropriate—route by introducing the main building blocks of the theory in discrete time and with discrete state space. The mathematics needed remains on an undergraduate level. Nevertheless, all the fundamental notions and results of arbitrage pricing and risk-neutral valuation can be presented in an almost self-contained fashion. The intuitive grasp gained in this discrete model world should then carry over to the continuous world with its numerous complications. In this setting, the central results are only stated and references are given for the respective proofs.

There is a large literature on the concepts and results presented in this chapter. Cf. Bhattacharya and Waymire (2007) or Williams (1991) for the fundamental probabilistic concepts. Cf. Protter (2005) for a comprehensive treatment of stochastic processes and stochastic integration needed for the continuous time, continuous state space context. The seminal paper by Harrison and Pliska (1981) is still a highly readable source, in particular for the discrete case. The book by Pliska (1997) coveres comprehensively arbitrage theory in discrete models while the book by Delbaen and Schachermayer (2004) should be consulted on the general theory. The article by Protter (2001) provides a concise survey of the general theory.

Sections 4.2 through 4.4 cover the discrete time case. Section 4.5 considers continuous time models. A number of proofs are provided in section 4.7.

4.2   DISCRETE-TIME UNCERTAINTY

In this section, we develop a mathematical model that can capture the notions of risk and uncertainty in financial markets.[1] We consider an economy over a fixed time interval $[0, T] \subset \mathbb{R}_+$. T is called the terminal date where we assume $T \in \mathbb{N}$, the set of natural numbers. At date 0 there is uncertainty about the true state of the economy at the terminal date T. The set of possible states, however, is known. The set of all possible states ω is denoted Ω and called the state space. Subsets of Ω are called events. The family of sets that forms the set of observable events is an algebra in Ω.

Definition 1 (Algebra).   *A family $\mathcal{F}$ of sets is an* algebra *in Ω if:*

1. $\Omega \in \mathcal{F}$
2. $\mathbb{E} \in \mathcal{F} \Rightarrow \mathbb{E}^c \in \mathcal{F}$
3. $\mathbb{E}_1, \mathbb{E}_2, \ldots, \mathbb{E}_I \in \mathcal{F} \Rightarrow \bigcup_{i=1}^{I} \mathbb{E}_i \in \mathcal{F}$

$\mathbb{E}^c$ denotes the complement of the set $\mathbb{E}$. It is easy to see that the power set $\wp(\Omega)$ of Ω, i.e. the set of all subsets of Ω, is the largest algebra in Ω and that the family $\{\emptyset, \Omega\}$ is the smallest one. On the set of observable events $\mathcal{F}$, we can define a probability measure. The probability measure carries information about the probability of observable events to occur.

Definition 2 (Probability Measure).   *Let $\mathcal{F}$ be an algebra in Ω. A function $P : \mathcal{F} \to [0, 1]$ is a* probability measure *if:*

1. $\forall \mathbb{E} \in \mathcal{F} : P(\mathbb{E}) \geq 0$
2. $P\left(\bigcup_{i=1}^{I} \mathbb{E}_i\right) = \sum_{i=1}^{I} P(\mathbb{E}_i)$ *for disjoint sets* $\mathbb{E}_1, \mathbb{E}_2, \ldots, \mathbb{E}_I \in \mathcal{F}$
3. $P(\Omega) = 1$

Two probability measures P and Q, defined on an algebra $\mathcal{F}$, are equivalent if they agree on the same null-sets, $P(\mathbb{E}) = 0 \Leftrightarrow Q(\mathbb{E}) = 0$, where $\mathbb{E} \in \mathcal{F}$. A collection $(\Omega, \mathcal{F}, P)$ of a state space Ω, a set of observable events $\mathcal{F}$, where $\mathcal{F}$ is an algebra, and a probability measure P defined on $\mathcal{F}$ is called a probability space.

---

[1]The material of this section is standard, cf. Williams (1991).

In general, securities traded in financial markets are risky bets since their future prices are uncertain. In our simple setup, a natural way to model securities with uncertain future prices is via functions of the economy's state at the terminal date. This motivates the introduction of random variables and random vectors into the model.

Definition 3 (Random Variable). *Given a probability space* $(\Omega, \mathcal{F}, P)$, *a random variable S is a function*

$$S : \Omega \to \mathbb{R}_+, \omega \mapsto S(\omega)$$

that is $\mathcal{F}$-*measurable, i.e., for each* $\mathbb{E} \in \{[a, b[: a, b \in \mathbb{R}, \ a < b\}$ *one has*

$$S^{-1}(\mathbb{E}) \equiv \{\omega \in \Omega : S(\omega) \in \mathbb{E}\} \in \mathcal{F}$$

A function

$$S : \Omega \to \mathbb{R}_+^K, \omega \mapsto S(\omega)$$

is a random vector *if its component functions*

$$S^k : \Omega \to \mathbb{R}_+, \omega \mapsto S^k(\omega), k \in \{1, \dots, K\}$$

are $\mathcal{F}$-*measurable. A random vector S is* $\mathcal{F}$-*measurable if all component functions* S^k *are* $\mathcal{F}$-*measurable.*

It is sometimes convenient to write $S \in \mathcal{F}$ for "S is $\mathcal{F}$-measurable' where S can be either a random variable or a random vector.

Definition 4 (Expectation). *Let a probability space* $(\Omega, \mathcal{F}, P)$ *be given where* Ω *is finite. The expectation* $\mathbf{E}^P[S]$ *of a random variable (or vector) S under a probability measure P is defined as*

$$\mathbf{E}^P[S] \equiv \sum_{\omega \in \Omega} P(\omega) \cdot S(\omega)$$

The expectation of a random variable is real-valued whereas the expectation of a random vector is again a vector.

With respect to this definition, it is important to recall that we have defined random variables as taking only positive values on the real line. Otherwise we ought to be more careful.

So far we have assumed that at date 0 there is uncertainty with regard to the state of the economy at the terminal date T. It seems more realistic, however, to assume that uncertainty resolves gradually over time. As before, let Ω be the set of all possible states of the economy at date T. Assume now that new information about the true state of the economy at date T arrives at dates $t \in \{0, 1, \dots, T\}$. This concept is general enough for us to interpret the time interval $[t, t + 1[, 0 \leq t < T$, between two consecutive dates as a week, a day, an hour or any other unit of "real" time.[2] We have:

Definition 5 (Filtration). *A filtration $\mathbb{F}$ is a non-decreasing family of algebras in Ω, i.e.* $\mathbb{F} \equiv (\mathcal{F}_t)_{t \in \{0, \dots, T\}}$ *where* $\mathcal{F}_0 \subseteq \mathcal{F}_1 \subseteq \dots \subseteq \mathcal{F}_{T-1} \subseteq \mathcal{F}_T$.

We call the collection $(\Omega, \mathcal{F}, \mathbb{F}, P)$ a filtered probability space. In the present context, the filtration is a model for the resolution of uncertainty over time. If an event $\mathbb{E} \subseteq \Omega$ is in $\mathcal{F}_t$, then it is known at date t whether the event may happen or not. In other words, if $\mathbb{E}$ is in $\mathcal{F}_t$, one can decide whether the true state ω is in $\mathbb{E}$ or not. Hence, $\mathcal{F}_t$ can be interpreted as the information set at date t. In general, we assume that $\mathcal{F}_0 = \{\emptyset, \Omega\}$ and $\mathcal{F}_T = \wp(\Omega)$, the power set of Ω. Economically, this translates into "nothing is known at the beginning of the economy" and "everything is known at the end of the economy", respectively. The requirement that the $\mathcal{F}_t$ be non-decreasing means that information cannot be lost.

In such a dynamic context, one can generalize the idea of a random variable (vector) straightforwardly to obtain a stochastic (vector) process. This enables one eventually to model price dynamics of securities.

Definition 6 (Stochastic Process). *A stochastic (vector) process $(S_t)_{t \in \{0, \dots, T\}}$ is a date-ordered sequence of random variables (random vectors) $S_t, t \in \{0, \dots, T\}$.*

Suppose that $(S_t)_{t \in \{0, \dots, T\}}$ represents the price process of a security. Since the price of a security at the terminal date depends on the state of the economy at this date, it is reasonable to assume that its price at date t depends on the information $\mathcal{F}_t$ available at date t. This gives rise to the following concept.

Definition 7 (Adaptation). *A stochastic (vector) process $(S_t)_{t \in \{0, \dots, T\}}$ is said to be adapted to a filtration $\mathbb{F} = (\mathcal{F}_t)_{t \in \{0, \dots, T\}}$ if $\forall t : S_t$ is $\mathcal{F}_t$-measurable.*

If security price processes are adapted to the filtration then the economy is informationally efficient. The mathematical formulation here corresponds to weak form efficiency. In financial models, one can sometimes find the opposite situation as well: information is generated by security price processes. To handle such situations one needs yet another concept:

Definition 8 (Algebra Generation). *The algebra generated by a random variable (or vector) S is denoted $\mathcal{F}(S)$ and is the smallest algebra with respect to which S is measurable. The algebra generated by a stochastic (vector) process $(S_t)_{t \in \{0, \dots, T\}}$ up to date t is denoted $\mathcal{F}(S_i : i \in \{0, \dots, t\})$ and is the smallest algebra with respect to which all random variables (vectors) $S_i, i \in \{0, \dots, t\}$ are measurable.*

In light of this definition, a stochastic process $(S_t)_{t \in \{0, \dots, T\}}$ generates the filtration $\mathbb{F} = (\mathcal{F}_t)_{t \in \{0, \dots, T\}}$ where $\mathcal{F}_t \equiv \mathcal{F}(S_i : i \in \{0, \dots, t\})$. Of course, the stochastic process is adapted to the filtration it generates. We also need the following definition:

---

[2]Cases with varying length of the interval $[t, t + 1[$ can also be included.

Definition 9 (Stopping Time). *Let* $(\Omega, \mathcal{F}, \mathbb{F}, P)$ *be fixed. A random variable* $\tau : \Omega \to [0, T] \subset \mathbb{R}_+$ *is a* $\mathcal{F}_t$-*stopping time if* $\{\omega : \tau(\omega) \leq t\} \in \mathcal{F}_t$ *for all* $0 \leq t \leq T$.

We now turn to martingales. Heuristically, a martingale embodies the notion of a fair investment. Consider a risk-neutral investor who plans to invest in a stock.[3] This investor would call the investment fair if the expected discounted price of the stock at some future date equals its present price. The investor would deny buying the stock if the actual price is higher. He would, however, always agree to buy if the price of the stock is below the expected discounted price. A stock price process satisfying the condition that the expected discounted price at any future date equals its price today is a so-called martingale.

To formally define a martingale, the concept of conditional expectation is needed. Taking expectations as proposed in the respective definition presumes that nothing is known about the future state of the economy at the terminal date. In other words, the minimal algebra $\{\emptyset, \Omega\}$ forms the information set. If uncertainty is gradually resolved, the information set enlarges over time and allows better expectations to be taken. Here, *better* means that expectations are taken conditional on a relatively enlarged information set. Formally, one has the following.

Definition 10 (Conditional Expectation). *Let* $(\Omega, \mathcal{F}, \mathbb{F}, P)$ *be given. The conditional expectation* $\mathbf{E}_t^P[S]$ *of a random variable (vector) S given information* $\mathcal{F}_t$ *is the unique random variable (vector) that satisfies:*

1. $\mathbf{E}_t^P[S]$ *is* $\mathcal{F}_t$-*measurable*
2. $\forall \mathbb{E} \in \mathcal{F}_t : \mathbf{E}^P[\mathbf{E}_t^P[S] \cdot \mathbf{1}_{\mathbb{E}}] = \mathbf{E}^P[S \cdot \mathbf{1}_{\mathbb{E}}]$

For notational simplicity, we denote the conditional expectation by $\mathbf{E}_t^P[\cdot]$ instead of $\mathbf{E}^P[\cdot|\mathcal{F}_t]$ as often found in the literature. This eventually enables the definition of a martingale.

Definition 11 (Martingale). *Let* $(\Omega, \mathcal{F}, \mathbb{F}, Q)$ *be given. A* $\mathbb{F}$-*adapted stochastic process* $(S_t)_{t \in \{0, \dots, T\}}$ *is a (vector) martingale under the probability measure Q if*

$$\forall t, s \geq 0, t + s \leq T : \mathbf{E}_t^Q[S_{t+s}] = S_t$$

A probability measure Q that makes a stochastic process—defined on some filtered probability space $(\Omega, \mathcal{F}, \mathbb{F}, P)$—a martingale is called a martingale measure. Whenever Q is P-equivalent, it is called a P-equivalent martingale measure.

It may become necessary to change from one probability measure to an equivalent probability measure, say from P to Q. This is where the Radon-Nikodym derivative comes into play.

---

[3] An investor is risk neutral if he/she is indifferent between a sure amount of money and a risky investment with an expected (discounted) payoff equally as high.

Definition 12 *Let $(\Omega, \mathcal{F}, P)$ be given where Ω is finite. For a P-equivalent probability measure Q, the Radon-Nikodym derivative **L**, which is actually a random variable, is defined by*

$$\forall \omega \in \Omega : \mathbf{L}(\omega) \equiv \begin{cases} \frac{Q(\omega)}{P(\omega)} & \text{for } P(\omega) \neq 0 \\ 0 & \text{for } P(\omega) = 0 \end{cases}$$

We conclude this section with a demonstration of how the Radon-Nikodym derivative may be applied in computing expectations. Let two equivalent probability measures P and Q, defined on an algebra $\mathcal{F}$ in a finite state space Ω, be given. It holds that $\mathbf{E}^Q[S] = \mathbf{E}^P[LS]$ for a random variable (vector) S defined on $(\Omega, \mathcal{F}, P)$. Easy manipulations of $\mathbf{E}^Q[S]$ verify this claim:

$$\mathbf{E}^Q[S] = \sum_{\omega \in \Omega} Q(\omega) \cdot S(\omega)$$

$$= \sum_{\omega \in \Omega} P(\omega) \cdot \frac{Q(\omega)}{P(\omega)} \cdot S(\omega)$$

$$= \sum_{\omega \in \Omega} P(\omega) \cdot \mathbf{L}(\omega) \cdot S(\omega)$$

$$= \mathbf{E}^P[LS]$$

4.3 DISCRETE MARKET MODEL

4.3.1 Primitives

We consider a model of uncertainty as examined in the previous section. The model economy lasts for a fixed period $[0, T]$, where $T \in \mathbb{N}$ and $T < \infty$. A filtered probability space $(\Omega, \wp(\Omega), \mathbb{F}, P)$ is fixed where Ω is the finite state space of which each element $\omega \in \Omega$ represents one possible state of the economy at the terminal date T. New information about the true state of the economy at date T only arrives at dates $t \in \{0, 1, \ldots, T\}$.[4] Economic activity is also observed at these dates only. At date T all economic activity ends. A time interval $]t, t+1[$ belongs to each date $t \leq T - 1$ where there is no economic activity. The filtration $\mathbb{F} = (\mathcal{F}_t)_{t \in \{0, \ldots, T\}}$ satisfies $\mathcal{F}_0 \equiv \{\emptyset, \Omega\}$ and $\mathcal{F}_T \equiv \wp(\Omega)$. The probability measure P is strictly positive for all $\omega \in \Omega$, i.e. $\forall \omega \in \Omega : P(\omega) > 0$. As a consequence, the probability measure P is uniquely defined up to equivalence.

There is a set $\mathbb{S}$ of $K + 1$ securities available in the marketplace whose price processes are modeled by the vector process

$$(S_t)_{t \in \{0, \ldots, T\}}, \forall t : S_t \in \mathbb{R}^{K+1}_{++}$$

---

[4]Typically, models in which information only arrives at certain points in time are referred to as *discrete time models*.

The first security, $k = 0$, is called *bond* and its price process is denoted $(S_t^0)_{t \in \{0,...,T\}}$. The bond plays a special role since it is assumed to be risk-less and serves as numeraire, so we set $S_0^0 \equiv 1$.[5] Formally, risk-less means that the random variable

$$S_t^0 : \Omega \to \mathbb{R}_{++}, \omega \mapsto S_t^0(\omega)$$

is $\mathcal{F}_{t-1}$-measurable, i.e. $\forall t \geq 1 : S_t^0 \in \mathcal{F}_{t-1}$. In other words, the actual value of S_t^0 is already known at date $t - 1$. The remaining K *securities* are risky and modeled by a stochastic process each. The price process of the k-th security, $k \geq 1$, is denoted $(S_t^k)_{t \in \{0,...,T\}}$ and is adapted to the filtration $\mathbb{F}$. Recall that adapted means that the random variables $S_t^k : \Omega \to \mathbb{R}_{++}, \omega \mapsto S_t^k(\omega)$ are measurable with respect to $\mathcal{F}_t$, i.e. $\forall k, t : S_t^k(\omega) \in \mathcal{F}_t$. In other words, the actual value of S_t^k is not known until date t. Finally, we denote the *discount* process by $(\beta_t)_{t \in \{0,...,T\}}$ and define $\forall t : \beta_t \equiv (S_t^0)^{-1}$.

4.3.2 Basic Definitions

We will now introduce several central expressions that are closely related to securities trading.

Definition 13 (Portfolio).   *A **portfolio** ϕ_t is a $K + 1$-dimensional vector $\phi_t \in \mathbb{R}^{K+1}$.*

A portfolio $\phi_t = (\phi_t^0, \ldots, \phi_t^K)$ gives the number ϕ_t^k of every security $k \in \{0, \ldots, K\}$ held by an agent at date t. For example, ϕ_t^0 represents the number of bonds in the portfolio ϕ_t at date t. The portfolio ϕ_0 has the natural interpretation of being the initial endowment of an agent since agents will be allowed to form a new portfolio for the first time when prices S_0 are announced. This portfolio is then labeled ϕ_1, and has to be held during the time interval $[0, 1[$.

Definition 14 (Value of Portfolio).   *The **market value** V_t of a portfolio ϕ_t in S at date t is given by a function $V_t : \mathbb{R}^{K+1} \times \mathbb{R}_{++}^{K+1} \to \mathbb{R}$ where*

$$V_t(\phi, S) \equiv \begin{cases} \phi_1 \cdot S_0 & \text{for } t = 0 \\ \phi_t \cdot S_t & \text{for } t \in \{1, \ldots, T\} \end{cases}$$

Definition 15 (Predictability).   *ϕ_t is **predictable** if it is $\mathcal{F}_{t-1}$-measurable, i.e. if $\forall t \geq 1 : \phi_t \in \mathcal{F}_{t-1}$.*

Predictability implies that the portfolio ϕ_t be formed at $t - 1$ and kept constant during the interval $[t - 1, t]$. At date t, when prices S_t are announced, the portfolio has a market value of $V_t(\phi, S) = \phi_t \cdot S_t$. This amount can then be used, for instance, to form a new portfolio ϕ_{t+1}, which is to be held constant over the interval $[t, t + 1]$, and so forth.

---

[5]This assumption comes along with virtually no real loss of generality but it facilitates intuition considerably.

Definition 16 (Trading Strategy). *A **trading strategy** is a predictable vector process*

$$(\phi_t)_{t \in \{0,\dots,T\}}$$

with component processes $(\phi_t^k)_{t \in \{0,\dots,T\}}, k \in \{0, \dots, K\}$. $(\phi_t)_{t \in \{0,\dots,T\}}$ *is predictable if* $\forall t \geq 1 : \phi_t$ *is predictable.*

Two other processes are directly associated with each trading strategy.

Definition 17 (Value Process, Gains Process). *We have the following two important processes:*

1. *The **value process** $(V_t(\phi, S))_{t \in \{0,\dots,T\}}$ of a trading strategy in S is a real-valued, $\mathbb{F}$-adapted process where $V_t(\phi, S)$ is given by definition 14.*
2. *The **gains process** $(G_t(\phi, S))_{t \in \{0,\dots,T\}}$ of a trading strategy in S is a real-valued, $\mathbb{F}$-adapted process where we set $G_0 \equiv 0$ and where $G_t : \mathbb{R}^{K+1} \times \mathbb{R}_{++}^{K+1} \to \mathbb{R}$ with $G_t(\phi, S) \equiv \sum_{i=1}^{t} \phi_i \cdot (S_i - S_{i-1})$ for $t \geq 1$.*

In the analysis to follow, two classes of trading strategies are of particular interest: *self-financing* and *admissible* trading strategies.

Definition 18 (Self-Financing Strategy). *A trading strategy is **self-financing** if and only if $\forall t : 1 \leq t \leq T - 1 : \phi_t \cdot S_t = \phi_{t+1} \cdot S_t$ or equivalently if and only if $\forall t : 1 \leq t \leq T - 1 : V_t(\phi, S) = V_0(\phi, S) + G_t(\phi, S)$. Neither are funds withdrawn nor additional funds invested at dates between $t = 1$ and $t = T - 1$.*

Definition 19 (Admissible Strategy). *A trading strategy ϕ in S is **admissible** if $\phi_0 = 0$ (no initial endowment/value), if it is self-financing and if its value process $(V_t(\phi, S))_{t \in \{0,\dots,T\}}$ is bounded from below, i.e. if it satisfies $\forall t : V_t(\phi, S) \geq -\alpha, \alpha > 0$. $\mathbb{T}$ denotes the set of all admissible trading strategies.*

Agents who can only implement admissible trading strategies are not allowed to produce a position of too much debt. In other words, agents cannot implement trading strategies that possibly lead to infinite debt (bankruptcy).

To conclude this sub-section, assume that markets are *perfect* (i.e. no transaction costs, complete and symmetric information, etc.) and *perfectly liquid*. In summary, one ends up with:

Definition 20 (Discrete Market Model). *A **discrete market model** $\mathcal{M}$ is a collection of:*

- *a finite state space Ω*
- *a filtration $\mathbb{F}$*
- *a strictly positive probability measure P defined on $\wp(\Omega)$*
- *a terminal date $T \in \mathbb{N}, T < \infty$ and*
- *a set $\mathbb{S} \equiv \{(S_t^k)_{t \in \{0,\dots,T\}} : k \in \{0, \dots, K\}\}$ of $K + 1$ strictly positive security price processes*

We write $\mathcal{M} = \{(\Omega, \wp(\Omega), \mathbb{F}, P), T, \mathbb{S}\}$.

4.4 CENTRAL RESULTS IN DISCRETE TIME

This section's main objective is to state the Fundamental Theorem of Asset Pricing in a discrete market model. In economic terms, central topics of this section are *arbitrage-freeness*, *arbitrage-free contingent claim prices* and *market completeness*.

A central problem in financial economics is the determination of fair contingent claim prices. One can think of contingent claims as being derivative securities, consumption payoffs or arbitrary claims payable at T. In order to proceed, however, a formal definition of a contingent claim is needed.

Definition 21 (Contingent Claim). *A **contingent claim** $A_T \in \mathbb{R}_+^{|\Omega|}$ is a non-negative random variable*

$$A_T : \Omega \to \mathbb{R}_+, \omega \mapsto A_T(\omega)$$

$A_T(\omega)$ is the amount payable if state $\omega \in \Omega$ unfolds.

A natural question that arises is that of the attainability of contingent claims.

Definition 22 (Attainability). *A contingent claim A_T is **attainable** if there exists an admissible trading strategy $\phi \in \mathbb{T}$ that generates its payoff at maturity[6], $V_T(\phi) = A_T$, and if $A_0 \equiv V_0(\phi)$ is the price or value of the contingent claim at $t = 0$. $\mathbb{A} \subseteq \mathbb{R}_+^{|\Omega|}$ denotes the set of attainable contingent claims.*

Another question is which contingent claims are super-replicable.

Definition 23 (Super-Replication). *A contingent claim A_T is **super-replicable** if there exists an admissible trading strategy $\phi \in \mathbb{T}$ that generates a payoff dominating the contingent claim's payoff, $V_T(\phi) \geq A_T$, and if $A_0 \equiv V_0(\phi)$ are the associated **super-replication costs** at $t = 0$.[7] Such a trading strategy is said to super-replicate the contingent claim. $\mathbb{A}^* \subseteq \mathbb{R}_+^{|\Omega|}$ denotes the set of super-replicable contingent claims.*

Obviously, the set of attainable contingent claims $\mathbb{A}$ is in general a sub-set of the set of super-replicable contingent claims $\mathbb{A}^*$.

Definition 24 (Linear Price System). *A **linear price system** is a positive linear function $\zeta : \mathbb{A} \to \mathbb{R}_+$ with*

$$\begin{matrix} \forall a, b \in \mathbb{R}_+, \\ \forall A_T, A_T' \in \mathbb{A} \end{matrix} : \begin{cases} \zeta(A_T) = 0 \Leftrightarrow A_T = 0 \\ \zeta(a \cdot A_T + b \cdot A_T') = a \cdot \zeta(A_T) + b \cdot \zeta(A_T') \end{cases}$$

---

[6]Here and in the following, we drop dependence on S in the notations $V_t(\phi, S)$ and $G_t(\phi, S)$.
[7]Sometimes the definition includes the requirement that the trading strategy be chosen such that it minimizes the super-replication costs A_0.

$\mathbb{P}$ *denotes the set of all price systems that are consistent with the market model* $\mathcal{M}$, *i.e. where*

$$\forall \zeta \in \mathbb{P}, \forall \phi \in \mathbb{T} : \zeta(V_T(\phi)) = V_0(\phi)$$

To further analyze pricing issues, the formal concept of an arbitrage opportunity proves useful.

Definition 25 (Arbitrage Opportunity). *An **arbitrage opportunity** is a self-financing, admissible trading strategy* $\phi \in \mathbb{T}$ *whose value process satisfies* $V_0(\phi) = 0$ *and* $E_0^P[V_T(\phi)] > 0$.

Definition 26 (Weak Arbitrage Opportunity). *A weak **arbitrage opportunity** is a self-financing strategy* ϕ *(not necessarily admissible) whose value process satisfies* $V_0(\phi) = 0$ *and* $V_T(\phi) \geq 0$ *with* $E_0^P[V_T(\phi)] > 0$.

It should be clear that a security market where arbitrage opportunities exist cannot be in equilibrium. An arbitrage opportunity arises, for example, if there are two or more different prices for the same contingent claim. A simple arbitrage strategy would then be to sell the contingent claim at a high price and to buy it at a lower price, thereby locking in the difference as a risk-less profit. The profit is risk-less because the payoffs at date T of one contingent claim long and one contingent claim short perfectly compensate each other. Of course, every agent would try to achieve such a risk-less profit. Local non-satiation of agents is a sufficient condition. Since agents' budget sets are unbounded in the presence of arbitrage opportunities, markets would inevitably be in disequilibrium. That is why the absence of arbitrage opportunities is a crucial property of equilibrium models. However, from an economic point of view, the assumption of arbitrage-freeness is rather mild.[8]

In light of the above considerations, establishing conditions that guarantee the absence of arbitrage opportunities in the market model $\mathcal{M}$ is obviously of great importance, which is what we will do next. To begin with, denote $\mathbb{Q}$ to be the set of all probability measures Q that are equivalent to P and that make the discounted security (vector) price process $(\beta_t S_t)_{t \in \{0,...,T\}}$ a martingale. At this point, the main concepts for reproducing some of the central results of the risk-neutral valuation approach—as originally formalized through the works of Harrison and Kreps (1979) and of Harrison and Pliska (1981) (afterwards HK79 and HP81, respectively)—are complete.

Lemma 1 (Weak Arbitrage implies Arbitrage) *The existence of a weak arbitrage opportunity* ϕ *implies the existence of an arbitrage opportunity.*

Refer to section 4.7 for a proof of this result and the following ones. The next proposition is important from an economical point of view.

---

[8]For a discussion on this and other possible model assumptions (e.g. the law of one price) refer to section 1.2 of Pliska (1997).

Proposition 1 (HP81, prop. 2.6). *There is a one-to-one correspondence in the market model* $\mathcal{M} = \{(\Omega, \wp(\Omega), \mathbb{F}, P), T, \mathbb{S}\}$ *between price systems* $\zeta \in \mathbb{P}$ *and P-equivalent martingale measures* $Q \in \mathbb{Q}$ *via:*

a. $\zeta(A_T) = \mathbf{E}_0^Q[\beta_T \cdot A_T]$ *and*
b. $Q(\mathbb{E}) = \zeta\left(S_T^0 \mathbf{1}_\mathbb{E}\right), \mathbb{E} \in \wp(\Omega)$

Proposition 1 states that there is a one-to-one correspondence between a completely economic concept, a price system, and a completely probabilistic concept, a martingale measure. It should not come as a surprise that this has important implications for the market model. The importance is impressively illustrated by the following theorem:

Theorem 1 (Fundamental Theorem). *Consider the market model*

$$\mathcal{M} = \{(\Omega, \wp(\Omega), \mathbb{F}, P), T, \mathbb{S}\}$$

The following three statements are equivalent:

1. There are no arbitrage opportunities in the market model $\mathcal{M}$.
2. The set $\mathbb{Q}$ of P-equivalent martingale measures is non-empty.
3. The set $\mathbb{P}$ of consistent linear price systems is non-empty.

This theorem can be generalized to allow for settings where time, processes and trading are *continuous* and the time horizon is *infinite*. While the objects studied remain essentially the same, the mathematical machinery needed in such cases goes well beyond the basic concepts presented in this chapter. The subsequent section considers the continuous case.

Starting with the economically plausible assumption that a market model is free of arbitrage opportunities, Theorem 1 implies that there exists an equivalent martingale measure. Why this last implication is so important should become clear in light of the following two results:

Corollary 1 (HP81, p. 228). *If the market model $\mathcal{M}$ is arbitrage-free, then there exists a unique price A_0 associated with any contingent claim $A_T \in \mathbb{A}$. It satisfies $\forall Q \in \mathbb{Q} : A_0 = \mathbf{E}_0^Q[\beta_T A_T]$.*

For arbitrary dates $t \in \{0, \ldots, T\}$, the following result emerges.

Proposition 2 (HP81, prop. 2.9). *For every $A_T \in \mathbb{A}$*

$$\beta_t V_t(\phi) = \mathbf{E}_t^Q[\beta_T \cdot A_T]$$

for all dates $t \in \{0, \ldots, T\}$, for all trading strategies $(\phi_t)_{t\in\{0,\ldots,T\}} \in \mathbb{T}$ that generate A_T and for all P-equivalent martingale measures $Q \in \mathbb{Q}$.

Proof. HP81, Harrison and Pliska (1981), p. 230. □

Suppose Theorem 1 applies to the market model $\mathcal{M}$. From corollary 1 and proposition 2 one obtains as the date t price A_t of an attainable contingent claim A_T

$$A_t = \beta_t^{-1} \cdot \mathbf{E}_t^Q[\beta_T \cdot A_T]$$

with everything defined as before and particularly $Q \in \mathbb{Q}$. This equation states that the date t price of an attainable contingent claim is simply the conditional expectation of its discounted payoff under an appropriate probability measure multiplied by the price of the bond.[9] This seems remarkably simple. Yet considerable effort has to be put in when one wishes to apply this method to the real marketplace, i.e. when a specific price has to be computed.[10]

A brief discussion of market completeness should conclude this section.

Definition 27 (Market Completeness).   *The market model $\mathcal{M}$ is* **complete** *if it is arbitrage-free and if every contingent claim is attainable or equivalently if* $\mathbb{A} = \mathbb{R}_+^{|\Omega|}$.

In discrete time, a convenient characterization of complete markets is possible.

Proposition 3 (HK79).   *Suppose that the market model $\mathcal{M}$ is arbitrage-free. The market model $\mathcal{M}$ is complete if and only if $\mathbb{Q}$ is a singleton.*

HK79 do not give a formal proof but the argument is straightforward. In discrete time, the resolution of uncertainty can generally be represented by so-called event trees.[11] If one calculates martingale branch probabilities, one observes that these are unique if markets are complete. The corresponding equivalent martingale measure is then unique as well. Hence, $\mathbb{Q}$ is a singleton if markets are complete.

The converse statement follows from the observation that if markets are incomplete then there are always many probability measures contained in $\mathbb{Q}$. In fact, there are an infinite number of such probability measures in general. So $\mathbb{Q}$ has to be a singleton for markets to be complete. For a formal proof refer to Lamberton and Lapeyre (1996), pp. 9–10.

As an aside, we want to demonstrate that, under certain circumstances, one can interpret discounted martingale probabilities as Arrow-Debreu security prices.[12] The defining property of an Arrow-Debreu security is that it pays off one unit in a predetermined state and nothing in other states. Consider an arbitrary Arrow-Debreu security, say, for example, the one that pays in state $\widetilde{\omega} \in \Omega$. Given the unique P-equivalent martingale measure Q of a complete market model $\mathcal{M}$ its price $A_0^{\widetilde{\omega}}$ at date 0 must be according to proposition 1—with the 1 at the $\widetilde{\omega}$-th position in the payoff vector

$$A_0^{\widetilde{\omega}} = \beta_T \mathbf{E}_0^Q[(0, \dots, 1, \dots, 0)]$$
$$= \beta_T Q(\widetilde{\omega}) \cdot 1$$

---

[9]Note that $\beta_t^{-1} \equiv S_t^0$.

[10]One can, for example, rely on statistical estimation methods or on calibration approaches to come up with a market-consistent martingale measure Q for a given market model.

[11]Event trees are one possible way to graphically represent filtrations. The main feature of these trees is that every node has a unique predecessor. They should be carefully distinguished from recombining trees that are sometimes used to illustrate the evolution of the stock price process in the binomial option pricing model. In recombining trees, nodes may have more than one predecessor.

[12]Yet another expression for Arrow-Debreu security price is *state price*.

Consequently, for there to be no arbitrage the price of the chosen Arrow-Debreu security must equal the discounted probability under the unique P-equivalent martingale measure for state $\widetilde{\omega}$ to pertain. This insight is central to options pricing and is also applied in the continuous case.

4.5 CONTINUOUS-TIME CASE

In the continuous-time case, both the time interval and the state space are subsets of the real line, $t \in [0, T] \subseteq \mathbb{R}_+, \Omega \subseteq \mathbb{R}$. Again, uncertainty is represented as a filtered probability space $(\Omega, \mathcal{F}, \mathbb{F}, P)$ where $\mathbb{F} \equiv \{\mathcal{F}_{t \in [0,T]}\}$ is now an increasing family of sigma algebras[13] with $\mathcal{F}_0 \equiv \{\emptyset, \Omega\}$ and $\mathcal{F}_T \equiv \mathcal{F}$.

The set of tradable assets is denoted $\mathbb{S}$ and consists of $K + 1$ stochastic processes, each one modeling the evolution of an asset's price over time, $S^k : [0, T] \times \Omega \to \mathbb{R}$. We normalize the price of the risk-less bond by assuming that $S_t^0 \equiv 1 \Leftrightarrow \beta_t \equiv 1, t \in [0, T]$, making it the numeraire of the economy and setting the risk-less rate equal to zero. For the moment, we set $K = 1$ such that there is only one risky asset in the economy (e.g. stock, stock index, short rate). We simply write S for S^1.

We now proceed, following formally Protter (2005), ch. 2, by defining "good" trading strategies for which stochastic integrals—i.e. the analogon of the gains process in definition 17—are defined.

Definition 28 (Simple Predictable Trading Strategy). *A trading strategy $(\phi_t)_{t \in [0,T]}$ is said to be simple predictable if ϕ_t can be represented by*

$$\phi_t = \phi_0 \mathbf{1}_0(t) + \sum_{i=1}^{n} \phi_i \mathbf{1}_{(\tau_i, \tau_{i+1}]}(t)$$

for a finite sequence of stopping times $0 = \tau_1 \leq \ldots \leq \tau_n \leq T < \infty$. Also, $\phi_i \in \mathcal{F}_{\tau_i}$ and $|\phi_i| < \infty$ almost surely. The set of such trading strategies is denoted $\mathbb{H}$.

Strategies of type $\mathbb{H}$ are the fundamental building block for stochastic integration in continuous time. For a given stochastic process S, we define a linear mapping $I_t : \mathbb{H} \to \mathbb{L}^0$ where $\mathbb{L}^0$ is the space of finite valued random variables with appropriate topology. To this end, let

$$I_t(\phi, S) \equiv \phi_0 S_0 + \sum_{i=1}^{n} \phi_{t_i}(S_{t_{i+1}} - S_{t_i})$$

for $\phi \in \mathbb{H}$ and times $0 = t_1 \leq \ldots \leq t_n \leq t \leq T < \infty$. We write $I_t(\phi, S) = \int_0^t \phi_s dS_s$ for the case where $n \to \infty$. The value process of a trading stragy ϕ in S is denoted $(V_t(\phi, S))_{t \in [0,T]}$.

---

[13]A *sigma algebra* is closed under countably infinite unions of sets contained in the algebra such that condition 3. in definition 3 is to be replaced by 3.' $\mathbb{E}_1, \mathbb{E}_2, \ldots, \mathbb{E}_\infty \in \mathcal{F} \Rightarrow \bigcup_{i=1}^{\infty} \mathbb{E}_i \in \mathcal{F}$. Cf. Bhattacharya and Waymire (2007), ch. 2.

Definition 29 (Gains Process).   *The gains process* $(G_t(\phi, S))_{t \in [0,T]}$ *of a trading strategy* $\phi \in \mathbb{H}$ *in S is given by*

$$G_t(\phi, S) = \int_{0+}^{t} \phi_s dS_s = \lim_{n \to \infty} \sum_{i=1}^{n} \phi_{t_i}(S_{t_{i+1}} - S_{t_i})$$

with $0 = t_1 \leq ... \leq t_n \leq t \leq T < \infty$.

We then get the following central definitions.

Definition 30 (Total Semimartingale).   *A process S is a total semimartingale if S is right continuous with left limits (càdlàg) and* $\mathbb{F}$*-adapted and if* $I_t : \mathbb{H} \to \mathbb{L}^0$ *is continuous.*

The continuity requirement in the definition ensures that small changes in the trading strategy (or a portfolio at a specific time) cannot lead to big perturbations in the value of the gains process or the value of a portfolio.

Definition 31 (Semimartingale).   *A process S is a semimartingale if, for each stopping time* $\tau \in [0, T]$, *the stopped process* $(S_{t \wedge \tau})_{t \in [0,T]}$ *is a total semimartingale.*

These concepts might seem rather abstract. However, for a continuous market model they define on the one hand the set of acceptable trading strategies and on the other hand the set of stochastic processes appropriate to model a financial market in general and the price process of a traded asset in particular, respectively. If either the trading strategy is not simple predictable or the stochastic processes, i.e. the assets' price processes, are not semimartingales then the gains process of definition 29 is not defined. Fortunately, both concepts are quite general and in particular the class of semimartingales encompasses as special cases almost any, if not every, stochastic process used in mathematical finance for asset pricing.

For financial applications, a further characterization of semimartingales is helpful (cf. for details Protter (2005), p. 55).

Definition 32 (Decomposable Process).   *An* $\mathbb{F}$*-adapted process S is decomposable if it can be decomposed as* $S_t = S_0 + M_t + A_t$ *where* $M_0 = A_0 = 0$ *and M is a locally square integrable martingale, and A is a càdlàg,* $\mathbb{F}$*-adapted process with paths of finite variations on compacts.*[14]

Two processes are worth mentioning as special cases of semimartingales (cf. Protter (2005), p. 17 and p. 20).

Definition 33 (Brownian Motion).   *Let* $(Z_t)_{t \in [0,T]}$ *be an* $\mathbb{F}$*-adapted process taking values in* $\mathbb{R}$ $(\mathbb{R}^k, 1 < k < \infty)$. *Then Z is a (k-dimensional) standard Brownian motion if:*

1. $Z_0 = 0$ *almost surely*
2. $Z_t - Z_s$ *is independent of* F_s *for* $0 \leq s < t \leq T$
3. $Z_t - Z_s$ *is a Gaussian random variable (vector) with mean zero and variance of* $t - s$
    (variance matrix $(t - s)B$ *for a given non-random matrix B and* $k > 1$)

---

[14] For example, if *A* is deterministic it has finite variations on compacts.

According to Theorem 26 in Protter (2005) there always exists a modification of a standard Brownian motion that has continuous paths almost surely.

Example 1 (Bachelier Model). *In the Bachelier model, the index process $(S_t)_{t\in[0,T]}$ is given as an arithmetic Brownian motion with $S_t = S_0 + \int_0^t \mu dt + \int_0^t \sigma dZ_s$ where Z is a standard Brownian motion and $\mu, \sigma > 0$ are fixed. Obviously, S is decomposable and therewith a semimartingale.*

Definition 34 (Lévy Process). *Let $(N_t)_{t\in[0,T]}$ be an $\mathbb{F}$-adapted process taking values in $\mathbb{R}$ and $N_0 = 0$ almost surely. Then N is a Lévy process if:*

1. *$N_t - N_s$ is independent of $\mathcal{F}_s$ for $0 \leq s < t \leq T$*
2. *$N_t - N_s$ has the same distribution as N_{t-s} for $0 \leq s < t \leq T$, i.e. it has stationary increments*
3. *$\lim_{s \to t} N_s = N_t$ almost surely, i.e. it is continuous in probability*

By Theorem 30 of Protter (2005) there always exists a unique modification of a Lévy process that is càdlàg and also a Lévy process.

Brownian motion and Lévy processes are central in modeling financial markets. In fact, all models presented in this book are either built on Brownian motion (e.g. the Black-Scholes-Merton model, cf. Black and Scholes (1973) and Merton (1973)) or on a Lévy process (e.g. the jump-diffusion model of Merton, cf. Merton (1976)) or on both (e.g. the stochastic volatility jump model of Bates, cf. Bates (1996)).

We need as before a further qualification of trading strategies.

Definition 35 (Admissible Strategy). *A trading strategy $(\phi_t)_{t\in[0,T]} \in \mathbb{H}$ in S is admissible if $\phi_0 = 0$ and if $\int_0^t \phi_s dS_s \geq -\alpha$ with $\alpha \geq 0$ and S a semimartingale. We denote this set by $\mathbb{T}$.*

Admissibility in continuous market models ensures, apart from the avoidance of bankruptcy of agents, that certain trading strategies known to generate arbitrage opportunities (e.g. the so-called doubling strategy) are excluded. This is because such strategies rely on the possibility of producing a position of infinite debt (in the limit).

Definition 36 (Self-Financing Strategy). *A trading strategy $(\phi_t)_{t\in[0,T]} \in \mathbb{H}$ is self-financing if*

$$\phi_t S_t = \phi_0 S_0 + \int_0^t \phi_s dS_s$$

Gains from trade are only induced by random changes in S. $\phi_t S_t$ is càdlàg.

The concept of an arbitrage opportunity carries over from the discrete time case.

Definition 37 (Arbitrage Opportunity). *An arbitrage opportunity in S is a self-financing, admissible trading strategy $\phi \in \mathbb{T}$ whose value process satisfies $V_0(\phi, S) = 0, V_T(\phi, S) \geq 0$ and $P\left(V_T(\phi, S) > 0\right) > 0$.*

We now follow the tradition initiated in the seminal paper by Delbaen and Schachermayer (1994) and define a number of sets central to arbitrage pricing. We have:

- $\mathbb{A} = \{\int_0^T \phi_s dS_s, \phi \in \mathbb{T}\}$: all terminal wealths (i.e. contingent claims) that can be generated by admissible trading strategies in the semimartingale S
- $\mathbb{B} = \mathbb{A} - \mathcal{L}_+^0$: all functions dominated by elements of $\mathbb{A}$ with $\mathcal{L}_+^0$ being positive finite random variables
- $\mathbb{A}^\infty = \mathbb{A} \cap \mathcal{L}^\infty$: the intersection of $\mathbb{A}$ with $\mathcal{L}^\infty$, the space of bounded functions
- $\mathbb{B}^\infty = \mathbb{B} \cap \mathcal{L}^\infty$: the intersection of $\mathbb{B}$ with $\mathcal{L}^\infty$; $\bar{\mathbb{B}}^\infty$ denotes the closure of $\mathbb{B}^\infty$

We then have the following conditions.

Definition 38 (NA—NFLVR). *A semimartingale S satisfies the no arbitrage condition (NA) if $\mathbb{B}^\infty \cap \mathcal{L}_+^\infty = \{0\}$. It satisfies the no free lunches with vanishing risk condition (NFLVR) if $\bar{\mathbb{B}}^\infty \cap \mathcal{L}_+^\infty = \{0\}$.*

Finally, we can state the Fundamental Theorem of Asset Pricing for the continuous setup.

Theorem 2 (Fundamental Theorem of Asset Pricing—One Dimensional). *Let S be a bounded real-valued semimartingale. There exists a P-equivalent martingale measure Q for S if and only if S satisfies NFLVR.*

Proof. Cf. Delbaen and Schachermayer (1994). For a comprehensive exposition of the whole theory refer to Delbaen and Schachermayer (2004). □

This version is the original one which, however, holds for the general case of a multi-dimensional semimartingale S as well.[15] With respect to the above set definitions, we have mainly to make, for $K > 1$, the change

$$\mathbb{A} = \left\{ \sum_{k=1}^K \int_0^T \phi_s^k dS_s^k, \phi^k \in \mathbb{T} \right\}$$

Here, each S^k is a semimartingale. We now have everything together to define the general continuous market model.

---

[15]"The process S, sometimes denoted $(S_t)_{t \in \mathbb{R}_+}$ is supposed to be $\mathbb{R}_+$-valued, although all proofs work with a d-dimensional process as well", cf. Delbaen and Schachermayer (1994), p. 464.

Definition 39 (Continuous Market Model). *A **continuous market model** $\mathcal{M}$ is a collection of:*

- *a continuous state space $\Omega \subseteq \mathbb{R}$*
- *a filtration $\mathbb{F}$ of non-decreasing sigma algebras*
- *a probability measure P defined on the sigma algebra $\mathcal{F}$*
- *a terminal date $T, 0 < T < \infty$*
- *a set of simple predictable trading strategies $\mathbb{H}$ for which gains processes are defined and*
- *a set of $K + 1$ tradable assets $\mathbb{S} \equiv \{(S_t^k)_{t\in[0,T]} : k \in \{0, \dots, K\}\}$ where each S^k is a semi-martingale and S^0 is (locally) risk-less and strictly positive*

We write $\mathcal{M} = \{(\Omega, \mathcal{F}, \mathbb{F}, P), T, \mathbb{H}, \mathbb{S}\}$.

We then have:

Theorem 3 (Fundamental Theorem of Asset Pricing—Multi-Dimensional). *Let a continuous market model $\mathcal{M}$ be given. There exists a P-equivalent martingale measure Q (EMM) for $\mathbb{S}$, the set of semimartingales representing tradable assets, if and only if this set satisfies NFLVR.*

In practical applications there are basically two routes to apply this theorem:

- **model without EMM**: one has a model with real-world dynamics and is able to derive an EMM thereby ensuring NFLVR
- **model with EMM**: one starts with a model with risk-neutral dynamics under an EMM and uses it—knowing that NFLVR applies—to value contingent claims (e.g. options and other financial derivatives)

Let us switch back to the case $K = 1$, i.e. with one risky asset only (the general case is easily accounted for by a change of notation). A contingent claim is a $\mathcal{F}_T$-measurable, integrable payoff A_T at time T. A contingent claim is attainable (or redundant) in the market model $\mathcal{M}$ if there exists an admissible trading strategy $\phi \in \mathbb{T}$ that is self-financing and has $V_T(\phi, S) = A_T$. In other words, the payoff can be perfectly replicated by a strategy in the tradable assets.

For an attainable contingent claim $A \in \mathbb{A}$ with replicating strategy $\phi \in \mathbb{T}$ we have

$$A_T = V_T(\phi, S) = V_0(\phi, S) + \int_{0+}^{T} \phi_s dS_s$$

Taking expectations under the EMM yields

$$\mathbf{E}_0^Q(V_T(\phi, S)) = V_0(\phi, S) + \mathbf{E}_0^Q \left(\int_{0+}^{T} \phi_s dS_s \right)$$

Since the last term equals zero due to the martingale property of S we deduce the risk-neutral pricing formula (cf. Harrison and Pliska (1981), p. 240)

$$V_0(\phi, S) = \mathbf{E}_0^Q(V_T(\phi, S)) \tag{4.1}$$

The present value of a contingent claim equals its *expected payoff under the EMM*. It is easily verified that arbitrage opportunities arise if equation (4.1) does not hold. With $\beta_t \neq 1$ we get

$$V_0(\phi, S) = \mathbf{E}_0^Q(\beta_T V_T(\phi, S)) \tag{4.2}$$

which means that the present value equals the *expectation of the discounted payoff under the EMM*. Similarly, for $0 < t < T$ we finally have

$$V_t(\phi, S) = \beta_t^{-1} \mathbf{E}_0^Q(\beta_T V_T(\phi, S)) \tag{4.3}$$

To define the value process $(A_t)_{t \in [0,T]}$ of an attainable contingent claim $A \in \mathbb{A}$ identify $A_t = V_t(\phi, S)$ for $\phi \in \mathbb{T}$, self-financing and $A_T = V_T(\phi, S)$. We then see that the discounted value process is a martingale under the EMM

$$\mathbf{E}_0^Q(\beta_t A_t) = \mathbf{E}_0^Q(\beta_T V_T(\phi, S)) = A_0$$

which follows immediately from (4.2) and (4.3).

Finally, let us consider completeness of the continuous model $\mathcal{M}$. Define the set of all $\mathcal{F}_T$-measurable, integrable payoffs A_T by $\mathbb{C}$. The market model is then complete if $\mathbb{C} = \mathbb{A}$, i.e. the set of all contingent claims coincides with the set of attainable contingent claims.

Proposition 4 (Market Completeness).   *The continuous market model $\mathcal{M}$ is complete if the set of P-equivalent martingales measures $\mathbb{Q}$ is a singleton.*

This result also holds for the multi-dimensional case. It is sometimes called the *Second Fundamental Theorem of Asset Pricing*. Cf. Björk (2004), Theorems 10.17 and 14.18, for versions of this result for the one- and multi-dimensional case, respectively, when Brownian motion drives uncertainty.

4.6 CONCLUSIONS

This chapter looks at the Fundamental Theorem of Asset Pricing and related concepts and results. It is not possible to cover all relevant aspects of this cornerstone of modern financial theory in a single chapter. However, it provides at least an overview of the fundamental framework on which all subsequent theoretical and numerical analyses are based.

In particular, all subsequent chapters will make heavy use of the risk-neutral discounting approach to value European and American options. Especially when working in higher dimensional settings (with multiple risk factors) and using Monte Carlo simulation as valuation method, the power of the risk-neutral valuation paradigm will be impressively illustrated.

4.7 PROOFS

4.7.1 Proof of Lemma 1

Proof.   If for ϕ we have $V_t(\phi) \geq 0$ then it already satisfies definition 25. So assume the contrary. Then there exist $t < T, \mathbb{E} \in \mathcal{F}_t, a < 0$ with $\phi_t \cdot S_t = a$ on $\mathbb{E}$ and $\phi_u \cdot S_u \leq 0$ for

$t < u \leq T$. Now define another trading strategy ψ through $\psi_u \equiv 0$ for $u \leq t$ and $\psi_u(\omega) \equiv 0$ if $u < t$ as well as $\omega \notin \mathbb{E}$. If $u > t$ but $\omega \in \mathbb{E}$ set

$$\psi_u^k(\omega) \equiv \begin{cases} \phi_u^0(\omega) - a/S_t^0(\omega) & \text{for } k = 0 \\ \phi_u^k(\omega) & \text{for } k = 1, 2, \ldots, K \end{cases}$$

It remains to show that this predictable trading strategy is self-financing and admissible. For $\omega \in \mathbb{E}$

$$\psi_{t+1} \cdot S_t = \left(\phi_{t+1}^0 - a/S_t^0\right)S_t^0 + \sum_{k=1}^{K} \phi_{t+1}^k S_t^k = \phi_t \cdot S_t - a = 0$$

by the definition of a such that ψ is self-financing. For $u > t$ and $\omega \in \mathbb{E}$ one has similarly

$$\psi_u \cdot S_u = \left(\phi_u^0 - a/S_t^0\right)S_u^0 + \sum_{k=1}^{K} \phi_u^k S_u^k = \phi_u \cdot S_u - \frac{aS_u^0}{S_t^0} \geq 0$$

implying $V_t(\psi) \geq 0$ and so ψ is admissible. Realizing that $S_T^0 > 0$ implies $V_T(\psi) > 0$ on $\mathbb{E}$ with $\mathbf{E}_0^P[V_T(\psi)] > 0$ yields the assertion of the lemma (cf. Harrison and Pliska (1981), p. 228). $\qquad\square$

4.7.2 Proof of Proposition 1

Proof. First, let $Q \in \mathbb{Q}$ and define ζ by (a). Take an arbitrary $\phi \in \mathbb{T}$ and write

$$\beta_T V_T(\phi) = \beta_T(\phi_T \cdot S_T) + \sum_{t=1}^{T-1} \beta_t(\phi_t - \phi_{t+1}) \cdot S_t$$

$$= \beta_1(\phi_1 \cdot S_1) + \sum_{t=2}^{T} \phi_t \cdot (\beta_t S_t - \beta_{t+1} S_{t+1})$$

after several regroupings of terms in the first sum. Now use the definition of ζ

$$\zeta(V_T(\phi)) = \mathbf{E}_0^Q \left[\beta_T V_T(\phi)\right]$$

$$= \mathbf{E}_0^Q \left[\beta_1(\phi_1 \cdot S_1)\right] + \mathbf{E}_0^Q \left[\sum_{t=2}^{T} \phi_t \cdot (\beta_t S_t - \beta_{t+1} S_{t+1})\right]$$

$$= \mathbf{E}_0^Q \left[\beta_1(\phi_1 \cdot S_1)\right]$$

since, by assumption, $(\beta_t S_t)_{t \in \{0, \ldots, T\}}$ is a martingale under Q and ϕ is predictable. The last term gives $\mathbf{E}_0^Q[\beta_1(\phi_1 \cdot S_1)] = \phi_1 \cdot \beta_0 S_0 \equiv V_0(\phi)$ showing consistency of ζ.

Second, assume $\zeta \in \mathbb{P}$ and define Q by (b). For $\omega \in \Omega$ one clearly has $Q(\omega) = \zeta(S_T^0 \mathbf{1}_\omega) > 0$ since ζ is consistent with $\mathcal{M}$. This establishes the first characteristic of a P-equivalent martingale measure. The second follows from observing that the trading strategy $\phi \in \mathbb{T}$ with $\phi^0 \equiv 1$ and $\phi^k \equiv 0$ for $k \neq 0$ yields

$$V_0(\phi) = \zeta(V_T(\phi))$$
$$= \zeta(S_T^0 \mathbf{1}_\Omega)$$
$$= 1$$

such that $Q(\Omega) = 1$. As a consequence, $\zeta(A_T) = \beta_T \mathbf{E}_0^Q[A_T]$ for $A_T \in \mathbb{A}$.

It remains to establish that Q is a martingale measure for $(\beta_t S_t)_{t \in \{0,...,T\}}$. The case $k = 0$ is trivial—this is the risk-less numeraire. Take $k \neq 0$ arbitrary and consider the trading strategy $\zeta \in \mathbb{T}$ with $\phi_t^k \equiv \mathbf{1}_{t \leq \tau}$ and $\phi_t^0 \equiv (S_\tau^k / S_\tau^0) \mathbf{1}_{t > \tau}$ for $0 < \tau < T$ being a stopping time. Furthermore, $\phi_t^i \equiv 0$ for all other securities i and all dates t. Obviously, $V_0(\phi) = S_0^k$ and $V_T(\phi) = (S_\tau^k / S_\tau^0) S_T^0 = S_T^0 \beta_\tau S_\tau^k$. We get

$$\zeta(V_T(\phi)) = \zeta\left(S_T^0 \beta_\tau S_\tau^k\right)$$
$$= \mathbf{E}_0^Q\left(\beta_T S_T^0 \beta_\tau S_\tau^k\right)$$
$$= \mathbf{E}_0^Q\left(\beta_\tau S_\tau^k\right)$$
$$= S_0^k$$

where the last equality follows from consistency of ζ. Realizing that k is arbitrary, this yields the last characteristic Q has to fulfill to make the discounted securities process $(\beta_t S_t)_{t \in \{0,...,T\}}$ a vector martingale. So $Q \in \mathbb{Q}$ completing the proof (cf. Harrison and Pliska (1981), p. 227). □

4.7.3 Proof of Theorem 1

Proof. Suppose $\mathbb{Q}$ is non-empty. Proposition 1 then implies that $\mathbb{P}$ is non-empty as well. Consider a trading strategy $\phi \in \mathbb{T}$ with $V_0(\phi) = 0$. Then there is a $\zeta \in \mathbb{P}$ such that $\zeta(V_T(\phi)) = V_0(\phi) = 0$ and so by the definition of a linear price system $V_T(\phi) = 0$. It remains to show that the first statement implies the second and third.

Start by defining two sets:

$$\mathbb{A}^+ \equiv \{A_T \in \mathbb{A} : \mathbf{E}_0^P(A_T) \geq 1\}$$
$$\mathbb{A}^0 \equiv \{A_T : A_T = V_T(\phi), V_0(\phi) = 0, \phi \text{ self-financing}\}$$

Obviously, if there are no arbitrage opportunities then $\mathbb{A}^+ \cap \mathbb{A}^0 = \emptyset$. The next step is to show that there exists a consistent linear price system $\zeta \in \mathbb{P}$. Since $\mathbb{A}^+$ is a closed and convex subset of $\mathbb{R}^{|\Omega|}$ and $\mathbb{A}^0$ is a linear subspace, the Separating Hyperplane Theorem can be applied to establish the existence of a linear functional L on $\mathbb{R}^{|\Omega|}$ such that:

1. $L(A_T) = 0$ for $A_T \in \mathbb{A}^0$ and
2. $L(A_T) > 0$ for $A_T \in \mathbb{A}^+$

Now define $\zeta(A_T) \equiv L(A_T)/L(S_T^0)$ which satisfies definition 24. One needs to show that indeed $\zeta \in \mathbb{P}$, i.e. that it is consistent with $\mathcal{M}$. Take an admissible trading strategy $\phi \in \mathbb{T}$ and define a new self-financing trading strategy by

$$\psi_t^k \equiv \begin{cases} \phi_t^0 - V_0(\phi) & \text{for } k = 0 \\ \phi_t^k & \text{for } k = 1, 2, \ldots, K \end{cases}$$

It holds $V_0(\psi) = 0$ and $V_T(\psi) = V_T(\phi) - V_0(\phi)S_T^0$ with $V_T(\psi) \in \mathbb{A}^0$ so that $\zeta(V_T(\psi)) = 0$. We get

$$\begin{aligned} \zeta(V_T(\psi)) &= \zeta\left(V_T(\phi) - V_0(\phi)S_T^0\right) \\ &= \zeta(V_T(\phi)) - V_0(\phi)\zeta\left(S_T^0\right) \\ &= \zeta(V_T(\phi)) - V_0(\phi) \\ &= 0 \end{aligned}$$

using linearity and normalization of ζ relative to S_T^0, i.e. $\zeta(S_T^0) = 1$. From this, $\zeta(V_T(\phi)) = V_0(\phi)$ for $\phi \in \mathbb{T}$ arbitrary and $\zeta \in \mathbb{P}$. Hence, $\mathbb{P}$ is non-empty and so is $\mathbb{Q}$ due to proposition 1— completing the proof (cf. Harrison and Pliska (1981), pp. 228–229). □

## CHAPTER 5

Complete Market Models

5.1 INTRODUCTION

Ever since the publication of the seminal works by Black, Scholes and Merton (BSM) in 1973 (cf. Black and Scholes (1973) and Merton (1973)), the BSM model—which is a continuous market model—and associated option pricing formulas have been considered a benchmark for option pricing. Benchmark in the sense that they provide closed-form solutions in a simple but still somehow realistic setting. The original and famous formula is derived in the papers on the basis of two different arguments. The first one in Black and Scholes (1973) is an equilibrium argument saying that a risk-less portfolio should yield the risk-less interest rate in equilibrium. The second, and rather widely applicable, one from Merton (1973) is that the value of a (European) option should equal the value of a portfolio that, in combination with an appropriate trading strategy, perfectly replicates the payoff at maturity. It is essentially the key argument of the general arbitrage pricing theory presented in Chapter 4.

Several years later, in 1979, Cox, Ross and Rubinstein presented (cf. Cox et al. (1979)) their binomial option pricing model. This model assumes in principle a BSM economy but in discrete time with discrete state space. Whereas the BSM model necessitates advanced mathematics and the handling of partial differential equations (PDE), the CRR analysis relies on fundamental probabilistic concepts only. Their representation of uncertainty by binomial (recombining) trees is still today the tool of choice when one wishes to illustrate option topics in a simple, intuitive way. Furthermore, their numerical approach allows not only European options but also American options to be valued quite as easily.

The main characterizing feature of both market models is that they are complete: every contingent claim maturing at some future date can be replicated by a trading strategy in the two tradable assets available—a risky asset (e.g. an index or stock) and a risk-less bond. The two models are also consistent in the sense that the CRR model converges to the BSM setup when the time interval between two consecutive dates tends to zero.

This chapter presents in the next section the BSM model and some associated aspects of the pricing theory. Section 5.3 analyzes how option prices and other quantities of interest react to changes in the model parameters. The major topic is the so-called Greeks, i.e. the delta and theta of an option, for example. Section 5.4 introduces the CRR model.

5.2   BLACK-SCHOLES-MERTON MODEL

5.2.1   Market Model

We consider an economy $\mathcal{M}^{BSM}$ with final date $T, 0 < T < \infty$. Uncertainty in the economy is represented by a filtered probability space $\{\Omega, \mathcal{F}, \mathbb{F}, P\}$. Ω denotes the continuous state space, $\mathcal{F}$ an σ-algebra, $\mathbb{F}$ a filtration—i.e. a family of non-decreasing σ-algebras $\mathbb{F} \equiv \{\mathcal{F}_{t \in [0,T]}\}$ with $\mathcal{F}_0 \equiv \{\emptyset, \Omega\}$ and $\mathcal{F}_T \equiv \mathcal{F}$—and P the real or objective probability measure.

Against this background, we model for $0 \leq t \leq T$ the risk-neutral evolution of the relevant *stock index* according to the stochastic differential equation (SDE)

$$\frac{dS_t}{S_t} = rdt + \sigma dZ_t \tag{5.1}$$

S_t denotes the index level at date t, r the constant risk-less short rate, σ the constant volatility of the index and Z_t a standard Brownian motion. Since we model an index instead of a single stock, we abstract from dividend related modeling issues.[1] The stochastic process S generates the filtration $\mathbb{F}$, i.e. $\mathcal{F}_t \equiv \mathcal{F}(S_{0 \leq s \leq t})$.

The differential equation that a *risk-less zero-coupon bond* satisfies is

$$\frac{dB_t}{B_t} = rdt \tag{5.2}$$

The time t value of a zero-coupon bond paying one unit of currency at T with $0 \leq t < T$ is $B_t(T) = e^{-r(T-t)}$ with $B_T \equiv 1$.

It is well-known that the BSM model

$$\mathcal{M}^{BSM} = \{\{\Omega, \mathcal{F}, \mathbb{F}, P\}, T, \{S, B\}\}$$

is complete and that the P-equivalent martingale measure Q is unique. Cf. Björk (2004), Theorems 8.3 and 10.17, for completeness and uniqueness of the risk-neutral measure Q, respectively.

5.2.2   The Fundamental PDE

We are now interested in the value V of a contingent claim, say a European call option on the index. We follow the analysis in Wilmott et al. (1995), sec. 3.5. Assume that the value depends on the index level S and time t only, i.e. $V(S, t)$. Itô's lemma, stated as proposition 5 in sub-section 5.6.1, gives the incremental change of the value V over time. Omitting time subscripts, we get

$$dV = \frac{\partial V}{\partial S} dS + \frac{1}{2} \frac{\partial^2 V}{\partial S^2} v^2 dt + \frac{\partial V}{\partial t} dt$$

---

[1]However, if the index would pay a continuous dividend yield of dy one would replace the risk-neutral drift r by $\bar{r} = r - dy$.

From equation (5.1) we know dS and $v = \sigma S$. Then

$$
\begin{aligned}
dV &= \frac{\partial V}{\partial S}(rS\,dt + \sigma S\,dZ_t) + \frac{1}{2}\frac{\partial^2 V}{\partial S^2}\sigma^2 S^2\,dt + \frac{\partial V}{\partial t}\,dt \\
&= \sigma S\frac{\partial V}{\partial S}\,dZ_t + \left(rS\frac{\partial V}{\partial S} + \frac{1}{2}\sigma^2 S^2\frac{\partial^2 V}{\partial S^2} + \frac{\partial V}{\partial t}\right)dt
\end{aligned}
\tag{5.3}
$$

Define now the delta of the contingent claim (think again of a European call option) by

$$
\Delta_t \equiv \frac{\partial V_t}{\partial S_t}
$$

and set up a portfolio $\Pi_0 = V_0 - \Delta_0 S_0$. In other words, a portfolio consisting of one option long and Δ units of the index short. How does this portfolio evolve over time? Building on equations (5.1) and (5.3)

$$
d\Pi = \sigma S\left(\frac{\partial V}{\partial S} - \Delta\right)dZ_t + \left(rS\frac{\partial V}{\partial S} + \frac{1}{2}\sigma^2 S^2\frac{\partial^2 V}{\partial S^2} + \frac{\partial V}{\partial t} - r\Delta S\right)dt
\tag{5.4}
$$

Recognizing the definition of Δ, (5.4) simplifies to

$$
d\Pi = \left(\frac{1}{2}\sigma^2 S^2\frac{\partial^2 V}{\partial S^2} + \frac{\partial V}{\partial t}\right)dt
\tag{5.5}
$$

As a consequence of adding a delta short position, the portfolio becomes (locally) risk-less. To avoid arbitrage, a risk-less portfolio must yield the risk-less short rate according to equation (5.2). We must therefore have $d\Pi = r\Pi\,dt$ as well. Equating this with (5.5)

$$
r\left(V - \frac{\partial V}{\partial S}\right)dt = \left(\frac{1}{2}\sigma^2 S^2\frac{\partial^2 V}{\partial S^2} + \frac{\partial V}{\partial t}\right)dt
$$

and rearranging, we finally arrive at the famous and central BSM partial differential equation (PDE)

$$
\frac{\partial V}{\partial S} + \frac{1}{2}\sigma^2 S^2\frac{\partial^2 V}{\partial S^2} + \frac{\partial V}{\partial t} - rV = 0
\tag{5.6}
$$

This equation holds for every contingent claim whose value V depends on S and t only. This is what makes it so important. It cannot be overemphasized that the whole argument hinges on the assumption that the portfolio made up of the contingent claim and the short delta position becomes risk-less. However, we are on quite safe ground due to the completeness of the market model.

5.2.3 European Options

Although fundamentally of high importance, the BSM equation (5.6) is not the only reason for the popularity of the BSM model.[2] It is also the fact that this PDE allows for an explicit, i.e. analytical, solution in the case of European call and put options.

To this end, denote by $C(S, t)$ the value at time t of a European call option on the index S with payoff $h_T^C = \max[S_T - K, 0]$ where $K > 0$ is the fixed strike price. Obviously, by arbitrage we have $C(S, T) = h_T^C$ such that we get a boundary condition, i.e. a final condition, for the PDE (5.6). We also know that $C(S = 0, t) = 0$ since in this case the option will never show a positive value at maturity.[3] Finally, when $S_t \to \infty$ then $C(S, t) \approx S_t$ since K becomes negligible.

Taking one of a number of different routes,[4] one can show that the time t value of the European call option is

$$C(S, K, t, T, r, \sigma) = S_t \cdot \mathbf{N}(d_1) - e^{-r(T-t)} \cdot K \cdot \mathbf{N}(d_2) \tag{5.7}$$

where

$$\mathbf{N}(d) = \frac{1}{\sqrt{2\pi}} \int_{-\infty}^{d} e^{-\frac{1}{2}x^2} dx$$

$$d_1 = \frac{\log \frac{S_t}{K} + \left(r + \frac{\sigma^2}{2}\right)(T - t)}{\sigma \sqrt{T - t}}$$

$$d_2 = \frac{\log \frac{S_t}{K} + \left(r - \frac{\sigma^2}{2}\right)(T - t)}{\sigma \sqrt{T - t}}$$

To derive the corresponding formula for a European put option, one can apply put-call parity. To this end, consider a portfolio of one unit of the index S long, one European put option with strike K long and one European call option with the same strike short. The portfolio pays at maturity T

$$S + P - C = S + \max[K - S, 0] - \max[S - K, 0]$$

You now have to distinguish two cases. First, $S < K$. Then the payoff is $S + K - S = K$. Second, $S \geq K$. In this case, the payoff is $S - S + K = K$. Alas, the portfolio $S + P - C$ pays K for sure. To avoid arbitrage, the time t value of the portfolio therefore must be

$$S_t + P_t - C_t = e^{-r(T-t)}K$$

---

[2]Robert Merton and Myron Scholes received the Nobel Prize for economics in 1997 mainly for this general approach to option pricing and its widespread applicability in mathematical finance. Cf. the article by Robert Jarrow (Jarrow, 1999)—honoring the Nobel Prize winners and their theory—whose title says "A Partial Differential Equation That Changed the World".
[3]Once $S_t = 0$, it will stay there according to equation (5.1).
[4]Cf. Wilmott et al. (1995), ch. 5, for a similarity solution approach to equation (5.6) or Björk (2004), ch. 7, for a risk-neutral/probabilistic approach.

From this, the European put option value is given by

$$P_t = C_t - S_t + e^{-r(T-t)} K \tag{5.8}$$

We therefore have for a European put option with payoff $h_T^P = \max[K - S_T, 0]$ at maturity the following BSM formula

$$P(S, t) = e^{-r(T-t)} \cdot K \cdot \mathbf{N}(-d_2) - S_t \cdot \mathbf{N}(-d_1) \tag{5.9}$$

In what follows we are mainly interested in European options. So speaking of an "option" means a European option if not otherwise indicated. To get a better feeling of how the value of an option depends on the model and option parameters, we analyze an example option with the following parameters:

- $S_0 = 100$: initial index level
- $K = 100$: strike price
- $T = 1.0$: maturity in years
- $r = 0.05$: risk-less short rate
- $\sigma = 0.2$: volatility of the index level
- $t = 0$: valuation date, i.e. present date

The Python script in sub-section 5.6.2 implements the valuation formulas for the European call option and put option, contains the above parameters and generates the graphical output for the call version of the option as shown in Figure 5.1. Figure 5.2 shows the respective output for the put option. Every sub-plot shows variations of the base case parameters with respect to a single parameter only.

We can see the following in Figures 5.1 and 5.2:

1. **moneyness**: the at-the-money call ($K = S_0 = 100$, ATM) is worth about 10.4, much more than the put which is worth about 5.6 only; the more the options become in-the-money ($K < 100$ for the call, $K > 100$ for the put, ITM) the more they become worth; the opposite is true the more the options come out-of-the-money ($K > 100$ for the call, $K > 100$ for the put, OTM)
2. **time-to-maturity**: the higher the time-to-maturity the more the options are worth; there are European options, however, for which this relationship does not necessarily hold (e.g. deep ITM European put options)
3. **short rate**: an increase in the short rate increases the value of the call option and decreases the value of the put option; under risk-neutrality the index drifts with the short rate and the higher the drift the better for the call option (probability increases for ITM expiration) and the worse for the put option (probability increases for OTM expiration)
4. **volatility**: a higher volatility increases both the value of the call and the value of the put option since the probability for ITM expiration increases in both cases

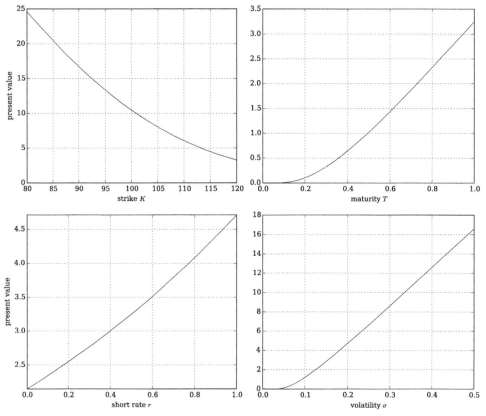

FIGURE 5.1 Value of the example European call option for varying strike K, maturity date T, short rate r and volatility σ

5.3 GREEKS IN THE BSM MODEL

In particular for hedging and risk management purposes, it is of importance to know how option values change with marginal changes in a model parameter. To derive the BSM equation (5.6), a portfolio is set up that adds a short delta position to a long position in the option. The delta $\Delta = \frac{\partial V}{\partial S}$, i.e. the first partial derivative of the option's value with respect to the index level, is one of the so-called Greeks (which refers to the Greek origin of the letter's name).

The analytical valuation formula (5.7) allows closed-form expressions to be derived for the most important Greeks as well. In what follows, we provide expressions for the Greeks of a European call option. For the **delta**, we simply get (omitting time subscripts)

$$\Delta = \frac{\partial C}{\partial S} = \mathbf{N}(d_1) \tag{5.10}$$

The **gamma** is the second partial derivative with respect to the index level

$$\Gamma = \frac{\partial^2 C}{\partial S^2} = \frac{\mathbf{N}'(d_1)}{S\sigma\sqrt{T-t}} \tag{5.11}$$

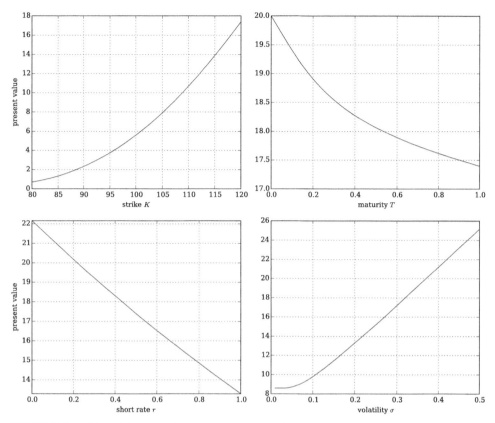

FIGURE 5.2 Value of the example European put option for varying strike K, maturity date T, short rate r and volatility σ

The **theta** of an option is, by convention, the negative first partial derivative with respect to time-to-maturity $t^* = T - t$

$$\Theta = -\frac{\partial C}{\partial t^*} = -\frac{S\mathbf{N}'(d_1)\sigma}{2\sqrt{T-t}} - re^{-r(T-t)}K\mathbf{N}(d_2) \tag{5.12}$$

The **rho** of an option is the first partial derivative with respect to the short rate r

$$\rho = \frac{\partial C}{\partial r} = K(T-t)e^{-r(T-t)}\mathbf{N}(d_2) \tag{5.13}$$

The **vega**—which is obviously not a Greek letter—is the first partial derivative with respect to the volatility σ

$$\mathbf{V} = \frac{\partial C}{\partial \sigma} = S\mathbf{N}'(d_1)\sqrt{T-t} \tag{5.14}$$

Referring to Figure 5.1 and arguing graphically, the theta, rho and vega provide closed-form expressions for the slope, given a certain parameter set, for three of the four sub-plots.

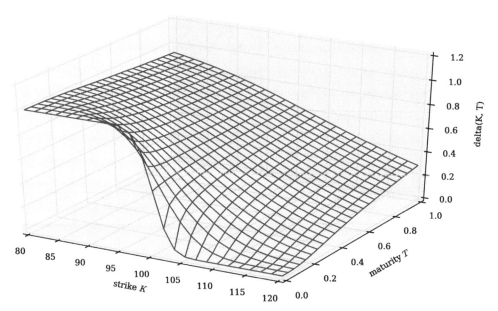

FIGURE 5.3   The delta of the European call option with respect to maturity date T and strike K

In the following, we provide plots of all the Greeks for the example call with different time-to-maturities T and different strikes K. The Python script of sub-section 5.6.3 implements the Greek formulas and generates the 3d plots.

Some observations are worth pointing out:

- **delta**: Figure 5.3 shows that the delta of the call option varies both with moneyness and maturity date T; it is between 1 and 0 for far ITM options and far OTM options, respectively, with short maturity; delta changes most around the ATM level for short maturities
- **gamma**: Figure 5.4 shows that the gamma has the highest values around the ATM level for short maturities; this is in line with the observation that delta changes most around the ATM level
- **theta**: Figure 5.5 paints a similar picture to gamma but with changed sign; theta is most important around the ATM level and for short maturities
- **rho**: Figure 5.6 illustrates that rho increases in importance with higher T (longer time-to-maturity) and with moneyness from OTM to ATM to ITM
- **vega**: Figure 5.7 shows vega increasing with T and decreasing from the ATM level in both directions, i.e. OTM and ITM

It is worth pointing out that the shapes of the Greeks in the different figures partly depend on the specific model parameters chosen and in particular on the option being a call. However, gamma and vega are the same for the put option counterpart of the call. Furthermore, some general remarks can be made:

1. **short-term**: most Greeks (delta, gamma, theta, vega) reach their highest/lowest values around the ATM level, generally at short maturities (apart from vega)

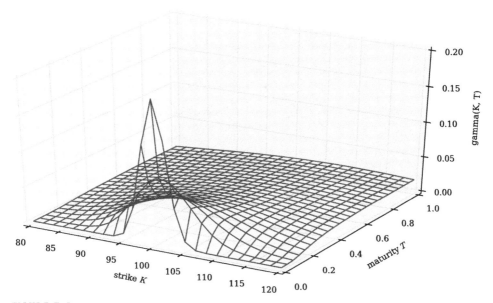

FIGURE 5.4   The gamma of the European call option with respect to maturity date *T* and strike *K*

2. **long-term**: for options with longer maturities only rho and vega have significant value impact; this is due to their role in determining how probable it is that the option expires ITM

In practice, option traders try to hedge one or several of the risks represented by the Greeks. For example, traders speak of "delta neutral" or "vega hedged" positions which means

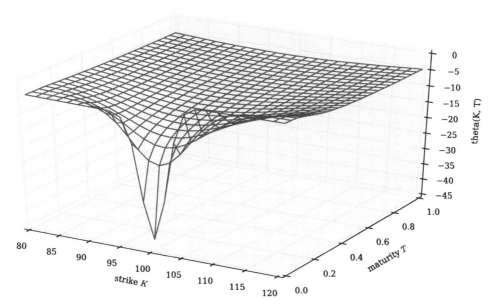

FIGURE 5.5   The theta of the European call option with respect to maturity date *T* and strike *K*

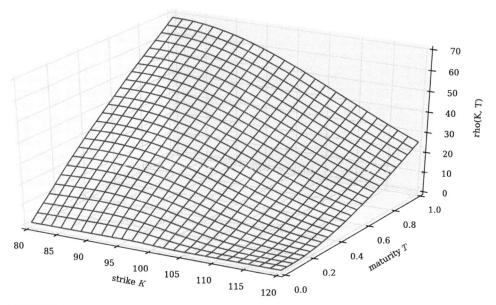

FIGURE 5.6   The rho of the European call option with respect to maturity date T and strike K

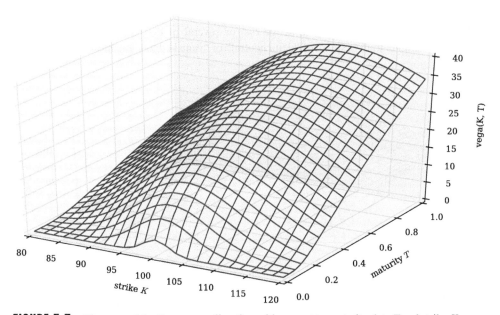

FIGURE 5.7   The vega of the European call option with respect to maturity date T and strike K

that (small) moves in the underlying or the volatility are offset by certain hedge positions in the underlying or other options.[5] Hedge activity generally does not include theta since the constant passage of time is something one has to accept and since it is what option premiums are paid for to a great extent.

5.4 COX-ROSS-RUBINSTEIN MODEL

This section presents some fundamental aspects of the binomial option pricing approach pioneered by CRR in Cox et al. (1979). We focus on those aspects that allow an implementation in Python. A detailed treatment of the model is found, for example, in Pliska (1997).

We are given a discrete market model with fixed filtered probability space $\{\Omega, \mathcal{F}, \mathbb{F}, P\}$ where Ω is finite. As in the BSM model, there are two securities traded: a risky stock index S and a risk-less zero-coupon bond B. The time horizon $[0, T]$ is divided into equidistant time intervals Δt so that one gets $T/\Delta t + 1$ points in time $t \in \{0, \Delta t, 2 \cdot \Delta t, \ldots, T\}$. The zero-coupon bond grows annually in value by the risk-less short rate r, $B_t = B_0 e^{rt}$ where we set for convenience $B_T \equiv 1$, i.e. we also have $B_t = B_T e^{-r(T-t)} = B_t = e^{-r(T-t)}$. Together

$$\mathcal{M}^{CRR} = \{\{\Omega, \mathcal{F}, \mathbb{F}, P\}, T, \{S, B\}\}$$

Starting from a strictly positive, fixed stock index level of S_0 at $t = 0$, the stock index evolves according to the law

$$S_{t+\Delta t} \equiv S_t \cdot m$$

where m is selected randomly from $\{u, d\}$. Here, $0 < d < e^{r\Delta t} < u \equiv e^{\sigma \sqrt{\Delta t}}$ as well as $u \equiv \frac{1}{d}$ as an important simplification. σ is a volatility parameter comparable to the respective BSM quantity. These assumptions lead to a recombining tree which has after n time steps $n + 1$ nodes only—instead of 2^n nodes if the tree would not recombine. This allows for a high number of time steps in the numerical implementation.

Assuming risk-neutral valuation holds, the following relationship can be derived:

$$S_t = e^{-r\Delta t} \mathbf{E}_t^Q[S_{t+\Delta t}]$$
$$= e^{-r\Delta t}(q \cdot u \cdot S_t + (1-q) \cdot d \cdot S_t)$$

Against this background, the risk-neutral (or martingale) branch probability is

$$q = \frac{e^{r\Delta t} - d}{u - d}$$

This quantity is uniquely determined by the structure of the index level tree which implies completeness of the CRR model. The value of a European call option C_0 is then obtained by

---

[5]In a BSM model, positions in the underlying can only immunize against small movements in the underlying. To hedge against volatility changes one needs a further financial instrument sensitive to such changes, in general an option. Cf. Nandi and Waggoner (2000) for an intuitive introduction to delta-vega hedging.

TABLE 5.1 Valuation results from the CRR binomial algorithm for the European call option; upper panel index level process, lower panel option value process[a]

Time	$t = 0$	Δt	$2\Delta t$	$3\Delta t$	T
S_t	100.00	110.52	122.14	134.99	149.18
		90.48	100.00	110.52	122.14
			81.87	90.48	100.00
				74.08	81.87
					67.03
C_t	9.97	15.92	24.61	36.23	49.18
		3.32	6.25	11.76	22.14
			0.00	0.00	0.00
				0.00	0.00
					0.00

[a]The true value of the European put option from the BSM formula is 10.45.

discounting the final payoffs $C(S, T) \equiv \max[S_T - K, 0]$ at $t = T$ to $t = 0$:

$$C_0 = e^{-rT} \mathbf{E}_0^Q[C_T]$$

The discounting can be done step-by-step and node-by-node backwards starting at $t = T - \Delta t$.

From an algorithmical point of view, one has to first generate the index level values, then determine the final payoffs of the call option and finally discount them back. This is what we will do in the following assuming the same model parameters as in the previous BSM example. A quite dense Python implementation of the binomial valuation approach is found in sub-section 5.6.4. Appendix A about Python discusses in sub-section A.2.2 several implementation approaches to the CRR model to illustrate different algorithmic strategies.

Table 5.1 presents results for the binomial model with four time steps, i.e. five points in time in total. From each node, the index can move upwards or downwards.[6] For example, starting at $t = 0$ with $S_0 = 100$ the index can rise to 110.52 or can drop to 90.48. Arriving with the evolution of S at T we can calculate the inner value of the option at this date by $C(S, T) \equiv \max[S_T - K, 0]$. The algorithm proceeds by taking expectations under Q and discounting backwards. For example, considering the highest node at time $t = 3\Delta t$ the option value is derived by

$$V_{3\Delta t} = e^{-r\Delta t}(q \cdot 49.18 + (1 - q) \cdot 22.14) = 36.23$$

where $r = 0.05$, $\Delta t = 0.25$ and $q = 0.5378$.

To illustrate the convergence of the CRR model value, consider Figure 5.8. In this figure, an increasing number of time intervals obviously increases valuation accuracy. The figure suggests that the CRR option value represents a lower bound to the BSM option value (i.e. that it converges to the BSM value from below). However, as Figure 5.9 illustrates, the CRR

---

[6]To save space and computer memory, "upwards" actually means sidewards in the table as well as in the arrays generated by the Python script.

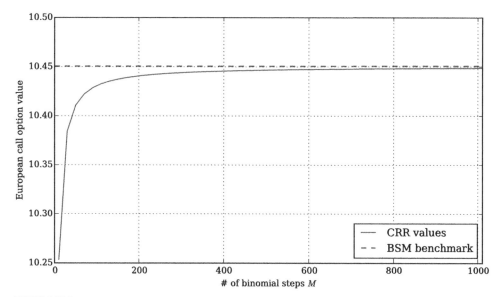

FIGURE 5.8   European call option values from the CRR model for increasing number of time intervals *M*—step size of 20 intervals

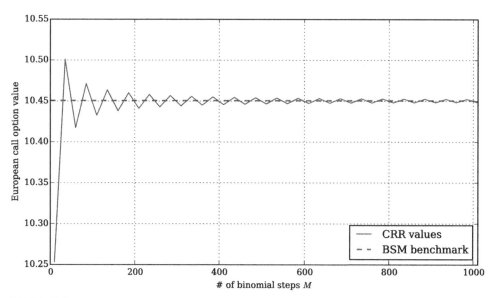

FIGURE 5.9   European call option values from the CRR model for increasing number of time intervals *M*—step size of 25 intervals

option value might also oscillate around the BSM benchmark value given a different numerical parametrization of the binomial model.

Obviously, the CRR model values converge quite well to the BSM value of 10.45. One might wonder where the advantage of the CRR model lies compared to the BSM model. With regard to standard European options there is hardly an advantage. If any, it is the simplicity of the model and the ability to analyze the workings of the algorithm step by step and node by node in a tree. In that sense, it is a good teaching tool, for instance. However, advantages arise beyond standard European options: the CRR model can also handle options with early exercise features, i.e. American or Bermudan options, as well as options with arbitrary payoffs at time T. This is illustrated in Chapter 7 which analyzes American options.

5.5 CONCLUSIONS

This chapter deals with two of the benchmark models for options pricing, the Black-Scholes-Merton (1973) continuous time model and the Cox-Ross-Rubinstein (1979) discrete time binomial model.

All of the theory and the majority of the other models covered in this book will be about some kind of enhancement relative to these benchmark models. For example, the Merton (1976) model adds a jump component to the geometric Brownian motion of BSM while the Heston (1993) model introduces a stochastic variance/volatility process.

In addition, when speaking of *implied* volatilities of option prices it is in general the BSM model that *implies* the volatility given the quoted option prices and the other market parameters.

5.6 PROOFS AND PYTHON SCRIPTS

5.6.1 Itô's Lemma

Proposition 5 (Itô's Lemma). *Let $f : \mathbb{R}^2 \to \mathbb{R}$ be a twice continuously differentiable function and S be a diffusion*

$$dS_t = m_t dt + v_t dZ_t \tag{5.15}$$

with Z a standard Brownian motion. Then for $f(S, t)$ the marginal change in time is (omitting time subscripts)

$$df(S, t) = \frac{\partial f}{\partial S} dS + \frac{1}{2} \frac{\partial^2 f}{\partial S^2} v^2 dt + \frac{\partial f}{\partial t} dt \tag{5.16}$$

Proof. First, a Taylor series expansion up to second order yields (suppressing dt^2 terms and other terms of equal or smaller order)

$$df(S, t) = \frac{\partial f}{\partial S} dS + \frac{1}{2} \frac{\partial^2 f}{\partial S^2} dS^2 + \frac{\partial f}{\partial t} dt$$

Second, note that $dS^2 = v^2 dt$. Cf. Wilmott et al. (1995), pp. 25–31, for a discussion of this simplified derivation and on the order of differential terms in the Taylor expansion. $\square$

5.6.2   Script for BSM Option Valuation

```
#
# Black-Scholes-Merton (1973) European Call & Put Valuation
# 05_com/BSM_option_valuation.py
#
# (c) Dr. Yves J. Hilpisch
# Derivatives Analytics with Python
#
import math
import numpy as np
import matplotlib as mpl
import matplotlib.pyplot as plt
mpl.rcParams['font.family'] = 'serif'
from scipy.integrate import quad


#
# Helper Functions
#


def dN(x):
    ''' Probability density function of standard normal random variable x.'''
    return math.exp(-0.5 * x ** 2) / math.sqrt(2 * math.pi)


def N(d):
    ''' Cumulative density function of standard normal random variable x. '''
    return quad(lambda x: dN(x), -20, d, limit=50)[0]


def d1f(St, K, t, T, r, sigma):
    ''' Black-Scholes-Merton d1 function.
        Parameters see e.g. BSM_call_value function. '''
    d1 = (math.log(St / K) + (r + 0.5 * sigma ** 2)
            * (T - t)) / (sigma * math.sqrt(T - t))
    return d1

#
# Valuation Functions
#


def BSM_call_value(St, K, t, T, r, sigma):
    ''' Calculates Black-Scholes-Merton European call option value.
```

```
    Parameters
    ==========
    St: float
        stock/index level at time t
    K:  float
        strike price
    t:  float
        valuation date
    T:  float
        date of maturity/time-to-maturity if t = 0; T > t
    r:  float
        constant, risk-less short rate
    sigma:  float
        volatility

    Returns
    =======
    call_value:  float
        European call present value at t
    '''
    d1 = d1f(St, K, t, T, r, sigma)
    d2 = d1 - sigma * math.sqrt(T - t)
    call_value = St * N(d1) - math.exp(-r * (T - t)) * K * N(d2)
    return call_value


def BSM_put_value(St, K, t, T, r, sigma):
    ''' Calculates Black-Scholes-Merton European put option value.

    Parameters
    ==========
    St: float
        stock/index level at time t
    K:  float
        strike price
    t:  float
        valuation date
    T:  float
        date of maturity/time-to-maturity if t = 0; T > t
    r:  float
        constant, risk-less short rate
    sigma: float
        volatility

    Returns
    =======
    put_value: float
```

```
            European put present value at t
    '''
    put_value = BSM_call_value(St, K, t, T, r, sigma) \
            - St + math.exp(-r * (T - t)) * K
    return put_value




#
# Plotting European Option Values
#


def plot_values(function):
    ''' Plots European option values for different parameters c.p. '''
    plt.figure(figsize=(10, 8.3))
    points = 100
    #
    # Model Parameters
    #
    St = 100.0  # index level
    K = 100.0  # option strike
    t = 0.0  # valuation date
    T = 1.0  # maturity date
    r = 0.05  # risk-less short rate
    sigma = 0.2  # volatility

    # C(K) plot
    plt.subplot(221)
    klist = np.linspace(80, 120, points)
    vlist = [function(St, K, t, T, r, sigma) for K in klist]
    plt.plot(klist, vlist)
    plt.grid()
    plt.xlabel('strike $K$')
    plt.ylabel('present value')

    # C(T) plot
    plt.subplot(222)
    tlist = np.linspace(0.0001, 1, points)
    vlist = [function(St, K, t, T, r, sigma) for T in tlist]
    plt.plot(tlist, vlist)
    plt.grid(True)
    plt.xlabel('maturity $T$')

    # C(r) plot
    plt.subplot(223)
    rlist = np.linspace(0, 0.1, points)
```

```
    vlist = [function(St, K, t, T, r, sigma) for r in rlist]
    plt.plot(tlist, vlist)
    plt.grid(True)
    plt.xlabel('short rate $r$')
    plt.ylabel('present value')
    plt.axis('tight')

    # C(sigma) plot
    plt.subplot(224)
    slist = np.linspace(0.01, 0.5, points)
    vlist = [function(St, K, t, T, r, sigma) for sigma in slist]
    plt.plot(slist, vlist)
    plt.grid(True)
    plt.xlabel('volatility $\sigma$')
    plt.tight_layout()
```

5.6.3 Script for BSM Call Greeks

```
#
# Black-Scholes-Merton (1973) European Call Option Greeks
# 05_com/BSM_call_greeks.py
#
# (c) Dr. Yves J. Hilpisch
# Derivatives Analytics with Python
#
import math
import numpy as np
import matplotlib as mpl
import matplotlib.pyplot as plt
mpl.rcParams['font.family'] = 'serif'
import mpl_toolkits.mplot3d.axes3d as p3
from BSM_option_valuation import d1f, N, dN


#
# Functions for Greeks
#


def BSM_delta(St, K, t, T, r, sigma):
    ''' Black-Scholes-Merton DELTA of European call option.

    Parameters
    ==========
    St: float
        stock/index level at time t
```

```
    K:   float
         strike price
    t:   float
         valuation date
    T:   float
         date of maturity/time-to-maturity if t = 0; T > t
    r:   float
         constant, risk-less short rate
    sigma:  float
         volatility

    Returns
    =======
    delta:  float
         European call option DELTA
    '''
    d1 = d1f(St, K, t, T, r, sigma)
    delta = N(d1)
    return delta


def BSM_gamma(St, K, t, T, r, sigma):
    ''' Black-Scholes-Merton GAMMA of European call option.

    Parameters
    ==========
    St: float
         stock/index level at time t
    K:   float
         strike price
    t:   float
         valuation date
    T:   float
         date of maturity/time-to-maturity if t = 0; T > t
    r:   float
         constant, risk-less short rate
    sigma:  float
         volatility

    Returns
    =======
    gamma:  float
         European call option GAMMA
    '''
    d1 = d1f(St, K, t, T, r, sigma)
    gamma = dN(d1) / (St * sigma * math.sqrt(T - t))
    return gamma
```

```
def BSM_theta(St, K, t, T, r, sigma):
    ''' Black-Scholes-Merton THETA of European call option.

    Parameters
    ==========
    St: float
        stock/index level at time t
    K:  float
        strike price
    t:  float
        valuation date
    T:  float
        date of maturity/time-to-maturity if t = 0; T > t
    r:  float
        constant, risk-less short rate
    sigma:  float
        volatility

    Returns
    =======
    theta:  float
        European call option THETA
    '''
    d1 = d1f(St, K, t, T, r, sigma)
    d2 = d1 - sigma * math.sqrt(T - t)
    theta = -(St * dN(d1) * sigma / (2 * math.sqrt(T - t))
             + r * K * math.exp(-r * (T - t)) * N(d2))
    return theta


def BSM_rho(St, K, t, T, r, sigma):
    ''' Black-Scholes-Merton RHO of European call option.

    Parameters
    ==========
    St: float
        stock/index level at time t
    K:  float
        strike price
    t:  float
        valuation date
    T:  float
        date of maturity/time-to-maturity if t = 0; T > t
    r:  float
        constant, risk-less short rate
    sigma:  float
        volatility
```

```
    Returns
    =======
    rho:  float
        European call option RHO
    '''
    d1 = d1f(St, K, t, T, r, sigma)
    d2 = d1 - sigma * math.sqrt(T - t)
    rho = K * (T - t) * math.exp(-r * (T - t)) * N(d2)
    return rho


def BSM_vega(St, K, t, T, r, sigma):
    ''' Black-Scholes-Merton VEGA of European call option.

    Parameters
    ==========
    St: float
        stock/index level at time t
    K:  float
        strike price
    t:  float
        valuation date
    T:  float
        date of maturity/time-to-maturity if t = 0; T > t
    r:  float
        constant, risk-less short rate
    sigma:  float
        volatility

    Returns
    =======
    vega:  float
        European call option VEGA
    '''
    d1 = d1f(St, K, t, T, r, sigma)
    vega = St * dN(d1) * math.sqrt(T - t)
    return vega

#
# Plotting the Greeks
#
def plot_greeks(function, greek):
    # Model Parameters
    St = 100.0  # index level
    K = 100.0  # option strike
    t = 0.0  # valuation date
    T = 1.0  # maturity date
```

```
r = 0.05  # risk-less short rate
sigma = 0.2  # volatility

# Greek Calculations
tlist = np.linspace(0.01, 1, 25)
klist = np.linspace(80, 120, 25)
V = np.zeros((len(tlist), len(klist)), dtype=np.float)
for j in range(len(klist)):
    for i in range(len(tlist)):
        V[i, j] = function(St, klist[j], t, tlist[i], r, sigma)

# 3D Plotting
x, y = np.meshgrid(klist, tlist)
fig = plt.figure(figsize=(9, 5))
plot = p3.Axes3D(fig)
plot.plot_wireframe(x, y, V)
plot.set_xlabel('strike $K$')
plot.set_ylabel('maturity $T$')
plot.set_zlabel('%s(K, T)' % greek)
```

5.6.4   Script for CRR Option Valuation

```
#
# Cox-Ross-Rubinstein Binomial Model
# European Option Valuation
# 05_com/CRR_option_calcuation.py
#
# (c) Dr. Yves J. Hilpisch
# Derivatives Analytics with Python
#
import math
import numpy as np
import matplotlib as mpl
import matplotlib.pyplot as plt
mpl.rcParams['font.family'] = 'serif'
from BSM_option_valuation import BSM_call_value

#
# Model Parameters
#
S0 = 100.0  # index level
K = 100.0  # option strike
T = 1.0  # maturity date
r = 0.05  # risk-less short rate
sigma = 0.2  # volatility
```

```
# Valuation Function
def CRR_option_value(S0, K, T, r, sigma, otype, M=4):
    ''' Cox-Ross-Rubinstein European option valuation.

    Parameters
    ==========
    S0: float
        stock/index level at time 0
    K:  float
        strike price
    T:  float
        date of maturity
    r:  float
        constant, risk-less short rate
    sigma:  float
        volatility
    otype:  string
        either 'call' or 'put'
    M:  int
        number of time intervals
    '''
    # Time Parameters
    dt = T / M  # length of time interval
    df = math.exp(-r * dt)  # discount per interval

    # Binomial Parameters
    u = math.exp(sigma * math.sqrt(dt))  # up movement
    d = 1 / u  # down movement
    q = (math.exp(r * dt) - d) / (u - d)  # martingale branch probability

    # Array Initialization for Index Levels
    mu = np.arange(M + 1)
    mu = np.resize(mu, (M + 1, M + 1))
    md = np.transpose(mu)
    mu = u ** (mu - md)
    md = d ** md
    S = S0 * mu * md

    # Inner Values
    if otype == 'call':
        V = np.maximum(S - K, 0)  # inner values for European call option
    else:
        V = np.maximum(K - S, 0)  # inner values for European put option

    z = 0
    for t in range(M - 1, -1, -1):  # backwards iteration
        V[0:M - z, t] = (q * V[0:M - z, t + 1]
```

```
                        + (1 - q) * V[1:M - z + 1, t + 1]) * df
        z += 1
    return V[0, 0]

def plot_convergence(mmin, mmax, step_size):
    ''' Plots the CRR option values for increasing number of time
    intervals M against the Black-Scholes-Merton benchmark value.'''
    BSM_benchmark = BSM_call_value(S0, K, 0, T, r, sigma)
    m = xrange(mmin, mmax, step_size)
    CRR_values = [CRR_option_value(S0, K, T, r, sigma, 'call', M) for M in m]
    plt.figure(figsize=(9, 5))
    plt.plot(m, CRR_values, label='CRR values')
    plt.axhline(BSM_benchmark, color='r', ls='dashed', lw=1.5,
                label='BSM benchmark')
    plt.grid()
    plt.xlabel('# of binomial steps $M$')
    plt.ylabel('European call option value')
    plt.legend(loc=4)
    plt.xlim(0, mmax)
```

## CHAPTER 6

Fourier-Based Option Pricing

6.1 INTRODUCTION

Chapter 4 introduces the elegant and general theory of arbitrage pricing by risk-neutral discounting. Chapter 5 discusses the rather special setting of Black-Scholes-Merton and presents the famous analytical valuation formula for European options. In the first case, the generality of the approach is what is appealing. In the second case, the highly specific but very useful valuation formula is the advantage.

The question is whether there is an approach to derive formulas as useful as the BSM one in more general settings, thereby bridging the gap between generality of risk-neutral pricing and the specificity of the BSM formula. Fortunately, there is an approach: Fourier-based option pricing. This approach allows the use of semi-analytic valuation formulas for European options whenever the characteristic function of the stochastic process representing the underlying is known.

The Fourier approach, presented in this chapter, has three main advantages:

1. **generality**: as pointed out, the approach is applicable whenever the characteristic function of the process driving uncertainty is known; and this is the case for the majority of processes/models applied in practice
2. **accuracy**: the semi-analytic formulas can be evaluated numerically in such a way that a high degree of accuracy is reached at little computational cost (e.g. compared to simulation techniques)
3. **speed**: the formulas can in general be evaluated very fast such that 10s, 100s or even 1,000s of options can be valued per second

These three advantages make Fourier-based option pricing an indispensible tool in practice. In particular, when calibrating a model to option quotes or implied volatilities, there is often no real alternative. In this chapter, the discussion focuses on European call options since these are in general the instruments of choice for the calibration of financial models. However, using put-call parity, put prices are only one step away.

There is a large body of literature dealing with Fourier-based pricing methods. For practical purposes, the valuation formulas of Lewis (2001) and Carr and Madan (1999) are of high importance. Duffie et al. (2000) provides an in-depth analysis of this method in the context of affine jump-diffusion models. Cheng and Scaillet (2007) generalizes the results of Duffie et al. (2000) to the class of linear quadratic jump-diffusion models. Cherubini et al. (2009) is a focused monograph on derivatives valuation via Fourier transforms. Schmelzele (2010) is a recent survey article comparing a number of approaches in Fourier-based option pricing. Černý (2004) discusses several fundamental aspects and shows how to apply this approach to the binomial model. Generally, the introduction of this method to mathematical finance is attributed to Heston (1993).

Section 6.2 reformulates the risk-neutral pricing problem and shows how Fourier-based option pricing can help in solving it. Section 6.3 introduces the fundamental concepts of Fourier transforms of functions and of characteristic functions. Section 6.4 presents the two popular pricing approaches as developed by Lewis (cf. Lewis (2001)) and Carr-Madan (cf. Carr and Madan (1999)). Full proofs are given due to the importance for later chapters. Section 6.5 treats Fourier series and the Fast Fourier Transform algorithm as numerical methods for function approximation and option valuation. Section 6.6 then applies the approaches presented in a continuous and a discrete market model. The continuous theory is extensively used and illustrated in later chapters. Therefore the focus lies on the application to the binomial model of Cox-Ross-Rubinstein which allows a closer look into the inner workings of Fourier pricing and allows a first assessment of the accuracy and speed of the approach.

6.2   THE PRICING PROBLEM

We consider a continuous market model

$$\mathcal{M} = \{(\Omega, \mathcal{F}, \mathbb{F}, P), T, (S, B)\}$$

with the fixed filtered probability space $(\Omega, \mathcal{F}, \mathbb{F}, P)$ and a final date $0 < T < \infty$. Two assets are traded in the economy, a (positive) stock index $S_{t \in [0,T]}$ which is a semimartingale and a risk-less bond B paying one unit of currency at T with time t value $B_t \equiv e^{-r(T-t)}$ where $r \geq 0$ represents the constant short rate. We assume *no free lunches with vanishing risk* such that there is a P-equivalent martingale measure Q making the discounted index process a martingale.

We then know that the arbitrage value of an attainable call option is

$$C_t = e^{-r(T-t)} \mathbf{E}_t^Q(C_T)$$

where $C_T \equiv \max[S_T - K, 0]$ for a strike $K > 0$. In integral from, setting $t = 0$, the call option pricing reads

$$
\begin{aligned}
C_0 &= e^{-rT} \int_0^\infty C_T(s) Q(ds) \\
&= e^{-rT} \int_0^\infty C_T(s) q(s) ds
\end{aligned}
\tag{6.1}
$$

where $q(s)$ is the risk-neutral probability density function (pdf) of S_T. Unfortunately, the pdf is quite often not known in closed form—whereas the characteristic function (CF) of S_T is.

The fundamental insight of Fourier-based option pricing is to replace both the pdf by the CF and the call option payoff C_T by its Fourier transform.

Therefore we will first define these fundamental terms and will then present two different versions of the Fourier-based pricing approach.

6.3 FOURIER TRANSFORMS

In a continuous setting, we have the following definition:

Definition 40 (Fourier Transform). *The Fourier transform of the integrable function $f(x)$ is*

$$\hat{f}(u) \equiv \int_{-\infty}^{\infty} e^{iux} f(x) dx$$

with u either real or complex. e^{iux} is called the phase factor.

By Fourier inversion

$$f(x) = \frac{1}{2\pi} \int_{-\infty}^{\infty} e^{-iux} \hat{f}(u) du$$

for u real and

$$f(x) = \frac{1}{2\pi} \int_{-\infty+iu_i}^{\infty+iu_i} e^{-iux} \hat{f}(u) du$$

for u complex with $u = u_r + iu_i$ where u_r and u_i denote the real and imaginary part of u, respectively.

Denote the inner product of two complex-valued, square-integrable functions f, g by

$$\langle f, g \rangle \equiv \int_{-\infty}^{\infty} f(x)\overline{g(x)} dx$$

with $\bar{u}$ denoting the complex conjugate of u, i.e. for $u = u_r + iu_i$ it holds $\bar{u} = u_r - iu_i$.

Theorem 4 (Parseval's Relation). *f, g as before, then*

$$\langle f, g \rangle = \frac{1}{2\pi} \int_{-\infty}^{\infty} \hat{f}(k)\overline{\hat{g}(k)} dk$$

$$= \frac{1}{2\pi} \langle \hat{f}, \hat{g} \rangle \tag{6.2}$$

Proof. By the inner product definition $\langle f, g \rangle \equiv \int_{-\infty}^{\infty} f(x)\overline{g(x)}dx$. By Fourier inversion $f(x) = \frac{1}{2\pi}\int_{-\infty}^{\infty} e^{-iux}\hat{f}(k)dk$. Inserting the latter in the former gives (cf. Schmelzele (2010))

$$
\begin{aligned}
\langle f, g \rangle &= \int_{-\infty}^{\infty} \frac{1}{2\pi}\int_{-\infty}^{\infty} e^{-iux}\hat{f}(k)dk\overline{g(x)}dx \\
&= \frac{1}{2\pi}\int_{-\infty}^{\infty} \hat{f}(k)\int_{-\infty}^{\infty} e^{-iux}\overline{g(x)}dxdk \\
&= \frac{1}{2\pi}\int_{-\infty}^{\infty} \hat{f}(k)\int_{-\infty}^{\infty} \overline{e^{iux}g(x)}dxdk \\
&= \frac{1}{2\pi}\int_{-\infty}^{\infty} \hat{f}(k)\overline{\hat{g}(k)}dk
\end{aligned}
$$

applying the Fubini-Tonello theorem where needed (cf. Bhattacharya and Waymire (2007), app. A). □

Definition 41 (Characteristic Function).   *Let a random variable X be distributed with pdf $q(x)$. The characteristic function $\hat{q}$ of X is the Fourier transform of its pdf*

$$
\hat{q}(u) \equiv \int_{-\infty}^{\infty} e^{iux}q(x)dx = \mathbf{E}^{Q}(e^{iuX})
$$

6.4 FOURIER-BASED OPTION PRICING

This section uses the tools developed so far to reproduce two popular, Fourier-based option pricing approaches.

6.4.1 Lewis (2001) Approach

Fourier-based option pricing is an application of Parseval's relation (6.2) to the risk-neutral pricing equation (6.1). Consider a European call option with payoff $C_T \equiv \max[e^s - K, 0]$ where $s \equiv \log S$.

Lemma 2 (Call Option Transform).   *For $u = u_r + iu_i$ with $u_i > 1$, the Fourier transform of C_T is*

$$
\hat{C}_T(u) = -\frac{K^{iu+1}}{u^2 - iu}
$$

Proof. By direct integration

$$
\begin{aligned}
\hat{C}_T(u) &= \int_{-\infty}^{\infty} e^{ius} \max[e^s - K, 0]ds \\
&= \int_{\log K}^{\infty} e^{ius}(e^s - K)ds
\end{aligned}
$$

$$
= \int_{\log K}^{\infty} (e^{(iu+1)s} - K e^{ius}) ds
$$

$$
= \left[\frac{e^{(iu+1)s}}{iu+1} - K \frac{e^{ius}}{iu} \right]_{\log K}^{\infty}
$$

$$
= -\frac{K^{iu+1}}{u^2 - iu}
$$

□

Fourier inversion gives

$$
C_T(s) = \frac{1}{2\pi} \int_{-\infty+iu_i}^{\infty+iu_i} e^{-ius} \widehat{C}_T(u) du
$$

Now

$$
C_0 = e^{-rT} \mathrm{E}_0^Q (C_T)
$$

$$
= \frac{e^{-rT}}{2\pi} \mathrm{E}_0^Q \left(\int_{-\infty+iu_i}^{\infty+iu_i} e^{-ius} \widehat{C}_T(u) du \right)
$$

$$
= \frac{e^{-rT}}{2\pi} \int_{-\infty+iu_i}^{\infty+iu_i} \mathrm{E}_0^Q (e^{i(-u)s}) \widehat{C}_T(u) du
$$

$$
= \frac{e^{-rT}}{2\pi} \int_{-\infty+iu_i}^{\infty+iu_i} \widehat{C}_T(u) \hat{q}(-u) du
$$

If $S_t \equiv S_0 e^{rt+X_t}$ with X_t a Lévy process and e^{X_t} a martingale with $X_0 = 0$, then $\hat{q}(-u) = e^{-iuy} \varphi(-u)$ where φ is the characteristic function of X_T. Here, $y \equiv \log S_0 + rT$. Now

$$
C_0 = \frac{e^{-rT}}{2\pi} \int_{-\infty+iu_i}^{\infty+iu_i} e^{-iuy} \widehat{C}(u) \varphi(-u) du
$$

Defining $k = \log(S_0/K) + rT$ and using the derived call option payoff transform yields

$$
C_0 = -\frac{K e^{-rT}}{2\pi} \int_{-\infty+iu_i}^{\infty+iu_i} e^{-iuk} \varphi(-u) \frac{du}{u^2 - ui} \tag{6.3}
$$

Proposition 6 (Lewis (2001)). *Assuming $u_i \in (0,1)$, the call option present value is*

$$
C_0 = S_0 - \frac{K e^{-rT}}{2\pi} \int_{-\infty+iu_i}^{\infty+iu_i} e^{-iuk} \varphi(-u) \frac{du}{u^2 - ui} \tag{6.4}
$$

Furthermore, setting $u_i = 0.5$ gives

$$
C_0 = S_0 - \frac{\sqrt{S_0 K} e^{-rT/2}}{\pi} \int_0^{\infty} \mathrm{Re}[e^{izk} \varphi(z - i/2)] \frac{dz}{z^2 + 1/4} \tag{6.5}
$$

where $\mathrm{Re}[x]$ denotes the real part of x.

Proof.   Equation (6.3) has two singularities at $u = i$ and $u = 0$. Residue calculus gives for the first

$$\mathbf{Res}(i) = \lim_{u \to i} \left((u - i) \left(-\frac{Ke^{-rT}}{2\pi} e^{-iuk} \frac{\varphi(-u)}{u(u - i)} \right) \right)$$

$$= -\frac{Ke^{-rT}}{2\pi} e^k \frac{\varphi(-i)}{i}$$

$$= \frac{S_0 i}{2\pi}$$

using $e^k = S_0/K \cdot e^{rT}$, $\varphi(-i) = 1$ and $i^{-1} = -i$ in the last equation. According to the residue theorem (cf. Rudin (1970), ch. 13), the call option value equals the integral along u_i minus $2\pi i \mathbf{Res}(i) = -S_0$ such that equation (6.4) follows immediately. Fixing $u_i = 0.5$

$$C_0 = S_0 - \frac{Ke^{-rT}}{2\pi} \int_{-\infty}^{\infty} e^{-i(u+i/2)k} \varphi(-(u + i/2)) \frac{du}{(u + i/2)^2 - (u + i/2)i}$$

Note that

$$e^{-i(u+i/2)k} = e^{-iuk} e^{k/2}$$

with

$$e^{k/2} = e^{(\log(S_0/K) + rT)/2}$$

so that

$$Ke^{-rT} e^{k/2} = e^{-rT/2} \sqrt{S_0 K}$$

Defining $u = z + i/2$ gives

$$(z - i/2)^2 - (z - i/2)i = z^2 - 2zi + 1/4$$

and

$$C_0 = S_0 - \frac{\sqrt{S_0 K} e^{-rT/2}}{\pi} \int_{-\infty}^{\infty} e^{-izk} \varphi(-z - i/2) \frac{dz}{z^2 - 2zi + 1/4}$$

For f integrable and real-valued, Fourier inversion and symmetry of the characteristic function around $u = 0$ yields (cf. Schmelzele (2010))

$$f(x) = \frac{1}{2\pi} \int_{-\infty}^{\infty} e^{-iux} \hat{f}(u) du$$

$$= \frac{1}{2\pi} \mathbf{Re} \left[\int_{-\infty}^{0} e^{-iux} \hat{f}(u) du \right] + \frac{1}{2\pi} \int_{0}^{\infty} \mathbf{Re}[e^{-iux} \hat{f}(u) du]$$

$$= \frac{1}{2\pi} \mathbf{Re} \left[\int_{0}^{\infty} \overline{e^{-iux} \hat{f}(u) du} \right] + \frac{1}{2\pi} \int_{0}^{\infty} \mathbf{Re}[e^{-iux} \hat{f}(u) du]$$

$$= \frac{1}{2\pi} \mathbf{Re} \left[2 \int_0^\infty e^{-iux} \hat{f}(u) du \right]$$

$$= \frac{1}{\pi} \mathbf{Re} \left[\int_0^\infty e^{-iux} \hat{f}(u) du \right]$$

Using this result leads to

$$C_0 = S_0 - \frac{\sqrt{S_0 K} e^{-rT/2}}{\pi} \int_0^\infty \mathbf{Re}[e^{-izk} \varphi(-z - i/2)] \frac{dz}{z^2 + 1/4}$$

By symmetry, the value of the integral remains unchanged if $e^{-izk} \varphi(-z - i/2)$ is replaced by $e^{izk} \varphi(z - i/2)$ proving equation (6.5). □

Valuation equation (6.5) can be evaluated by standard numerical integration methods, like numerical quadrature.

6.4.2 Carr-Madan (1999) Approach

Define the payoff of a European call option with strike price K at maturity T as $C_T \equiv \max[S_T - K, 0]$ where $K \equiv e^k$ and $S_T \equiv e^s$. The present value of the call option is

$$C_0 \equiv e^{-rT} \mathbf{E}_0^Q \left(\max[e^s - e^k, 0] \right)$$

$$= e^{-rT} \int_k^\infty (e^s - e^k) q(s) ds$$

where $q(s)$ is the risk-neutral pdf of s_T. To ensure integrability, define $c_0 \equiv e^{\alpha k} C_0$ with $\alpha > 0$. The Fourier transform of c_0 is

$$\psi(v) \equiv \int_{-\infty}^\infty e^{ivk} c_0 dk$$

while the inverse transform is

$$C_0 = \frac{e^{-\alpha k}}{\pi} \int_0^\infty e^{-ivk} \psi(v) dv \tag{6.6}$$

In-the-Money Options

Proposition 7 (Carr-Madan (1999)). *The call option value is given by (6.6) where*

$$\psi(v) = \frac{e^{-rT} \varphi(v - (\alpha + 1)i)}{\alpha^2 + \alpha - v^2 + i(2\alpha + 1)v} \tag{6.7}$$

with φ as characteristic function $\varphi(u) \equiv \mathbf{E}_0^Q (e^{ius_T})$ of $s_T \equiv \log S_T$.

Proof. Taking the Fourier transform, using risk-neutral valuation and applying the Fubini-Tonello theorem yields (cf. Schmelzele (2010))

$$
\psi(v) = \int_{-\infty}^{\infty} e^{ivk} c_0 dk
$$

$$
= \int_{-\infty}^{\infty} e^{ivk} e^{-rT} \left(\int_{-\infty}^{\infty} e^{\alpha k}(e^s - e^k)^+ q(s) ds \right) dk
$$

$$
= \int_{-\infty}^{\infty} e^{ivk} e^{-rT} \left(\int_{k}^{\infty} e^{\alpha k}(e^s - e^k) q(s) ds \right) dk
$$

$$
= \int_{-\infty}^{\infty} e^{-rT} q(s) \left(\int_{-\infty}^{s} e^{ivk} e^{\alpha k}(e^s - e^k) dk \right) ds
$$

The inner integral allows direct integration

$$
\int_{-\infty}^{s} e^{ivk} e^{\alpha k}(e^s - e^k) dk = e^s \int_{-\infty}^{s} e^{(iv+\alpha)k} dk - \int_{-\infty}^{s} e^{(iv+1+\alpha)k} dk
$$

$$
= \frac{e^s}{iv + \alpha} \left[e^{(iv+\alpha)k} \right]_{-\infty}^{s} - \frac{1}{iv + 1 + \alpha} \left[e^{(iv+1+\alpha)k} \right]_{-\infty}^{s}
$$

$$
= \frac{e^{(iv+1+\alpha)s}}{iv + \alpha} - \frac{e^{(iv+1+\alpha)s}}{iv + 1 + \alpha}
$$

$$
= \frac{e^{(iv+1+\alpha)s}}{(iv + \alpha)(iv + 1 + \alpha)}
$$

Rearranging $e^{(iv+1+\alpha)s} = e^{i(v-(\alpha+1))s}$, multiplying out the denominator and plugging back in yields the desired Fourier transform

$$
\psi(v) = \frac{e^{-rT} \varphi(v - (\alpha + 1)i)}{\alpha^2 + \alpha - v^2 + i(2\alpha + 1)v}
$$

$\square$

Consequently, knowledge of the characteristic function φ of the relevant process and therewith of ψ allows direct computation of C_0 via equation (6.6).

Out-of-the-Money Options For out-of-the-money options define z_0 to be the current price of a European put if $k < \log S_0$ and to be the price of a European call if $k > \log S_0$ where $S_0 \equiv 1$. In other words, consider time values only. After similar calculations and manipulations (see Carr and Madan (1999)) the Fourier transform of z_0 arises as

$$
\varsigma(v) = e^{-rT} \left(\frac{1}{1 + iv} - \frac{e^{rT}}{iv} - \frac{\varphi(v - i)}{v^2 - iv} \right)
$$

Due to the symmetry of z_0 around $k = 0$, dampen the function by $\sinh(\alpha k)$ to get a new transform

$$
\begin{aligned}
\gamma(v) &= \int_{-\infty}^{\infty} e^{ivk} \sinh(\alpha k) z_0 dk \\
&= \frac{\varsigma(v - i\alpha) - \varsigma(v + i\alpha)}{2}
\end{aligned}
$$

After inverting this new transform, the time value becomes

$$
z_0 = \frac{1}{\sinh(\alpha k)} \frac{1}{2\pi} \int_{-\infty}^{\infty} e^{-ivk} \gamma(v) dv \tag{6.8}
$$

6.5 NUMERICAL EVALUATION

This section illustrates the Fourier-based pricing approach by the means of more simple settings.

6.5.1 Fourier Series

We are now in a discrete setting.

Definition 42 (Fourier Series). *A Fourier series is an infinite sum of the form*

$$
\begin{aligned}
f(x) &= \sum_{n=0}^{\infty} (a_n \cos nx + b_n \sin nx) \\
&= a_0 + \sum_{n=1}^{\infty} (a_n \cos nx + b_n \sin nx)
\end{aligned}
$$

which is a 2π-periodic function, i.e. $f(x) = f(x + 2\pi)$.

If $f(x)$ is a known 2π-periodic function, then the coefficients of the series are according to the Euler formulas

$$
\begin{aligned}
a_0 &= \frac{1}{2\pi} \int_{-\pi}^{\pi} f(x) dx \\
a_n &= \frac{1}{\pi} \int_{-\pi}^{\pi} f(x) \cos nx dx \\
b_n &= \frac{1}{\pi} \int_{-\pi}^{\pi} f(x) \sin nx dx
\end{aligned}
$$

For an arbitrary interval $[-L, L]$, the formulas are

$$f(x) = a_0 + \sum_{n=1}^{\infty} \left(a_n \cos\left(\frac{n\pi}{L}x\right) + b_n \sin\left(\frac{n\pi}{L}x\right) \right)$$

$$a_0 = \frac{1}{2L} \int_{-L}^{L} f(x)dx$$

$$a_n = \frac{1}{L} \int_{-L}^{L} f(x) \cos\left(\frac{n\pi}{L}x\right) dx$$

$$b_n = \frac{1}{L} \int_{-L}^{L} f(x) \sin\left(\frac{n\pi}{L}x\right) dx$$

If u is complex with $u = u_r + iu_i$ then by Euler identity

$$e^{iux} = e^{u_r x} \cos(u_r x) + i e^{u_r x} \sin(u_i x)$$

so that

$$f(x) = \sum_{n=-\infty}^{\infty} c_n e^{i\frac{n\pi}{L}x} \qquad (6.9)$$

$$c_n = \frac{1}{2L} \int_{-L}^{L} f(x) e^{-i\frac{n\pi}{L}x} dx \qquad (6.10)$$

In a sense, the complex Fourier series (6.9) is the discrete equivalent of a Fourier transform. To see this, denote $k_n \equiv \frac{n\pi}{L}$, $\hat{c}(k_n) \equiv c_n$ and write

$$f(x) = \sum_{n=-\infty}^{\infty} \hat{c}(k_n) e^{ik_n x}$$

It holds $\Delta \frac{n\pi}{L} = \frac{\pi}{L}\Delta n$ with $\Delta n = 1$. So $\frac{L}{\pi}\Delta k_n = \frac{L}{\pi}\Delta \frac{n\pi}{L} = 1$. Multiplying with this unity factor gives

$$f(x) = \frac{L}{\pi} \sum_{n=-\infty}^{\infty} \hat{c}(k_n) e^{ik_n x} \Delta k_n$$

Now define $\hat{f}(k_n) \equiv \frac{L}{\pi}\hat{c}(k_n)$ yielding

$$f(x) = \sum_{n=-\infty}^{\infty} \hat{f}(k_n) e^{ik_n x} \Delta k_n$$

and

$$\hat{f}(k_n) = \frac{L}{\pi}\frac{1}{2L} \int_{-L}^{L} f(x) e^{-ik_n x} dx$$

using (6.10). Taking the limit $L \to \infty$ and dropping the n subscript, the sum becomes an integral yielding

$$f(x) = \int_{-\infty}^{\infty} \hat{f}(k) e^{ikx} dk$$

$$\hat{f}(k) = \frac{1}{2\pi} \int_{-\infty}^{\infty} e^{-ikx} f(x) dx$$

Changing the sign in the phase factor and multiplying $f(x)$ by 2π thus dividing $\hat{f}(x)$ by 2π leads to the Fourier transform pair as defined previously

$$\hat{f}(k) = \int_{-\infty}^{\infty} e^{ikx} f(x) dx$$

$$f(x) = \frac{1}{2\pi} \int_{-\infty}^{\infty} e^{-ikx} \hat{f}(k) dk$$

A simple numerical example shall illustrate how Fourier series can approximate functions.

Example 2 (Fourier Series). *Consider the function $f(x) = |x|$ over the interval $[-\pi, \pi]$. This function can be approximated by the Fourier series*

$$f(x) = \frac{\pi}{2} + \sum_{n=1}^{\infty} \left[\frac{2((-1)^n - 1)}{\pi n^2} \right] \cos nx$$

Sub-section 6.8.2 contains a Python script implementing and plotting the formula. Figure 6.1 shows the output for series of order 1 and 5—the better approximation of the higher order series is obvious.

6.5.2 Fast Fourier Transform

Fast Fourier Transform (FFT) is an efficient algorithm, dating back to Cooley (1965), to compute sums of type (cf. Carr and Madan (1999))

$$w(u) = \sum_{j=1}^{N} e^{-i\frac{2\pi}{N}(j-1)(u-1)} x(j), u = 1, \dots, N \tag{6.11}$$

Defining $v_j \equiv \eta(j-1)$ the integral (6.6) can be numerically approximated by the sum

$$C_0 \approx \frac{e^{-\alpha k}}{\pi} \sum_{j=1}^{N} e^{-iv_j k} \psi(v_j) \eta$$

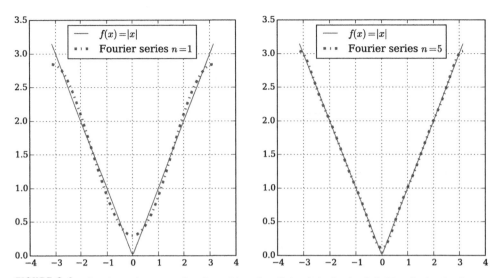

FIGURE 6.1 Fourier series approximation of function $f(x) = |x|$ of order 1 (left) and of order 5 (right)

Let ϵ be a regular spacing parameter and consider the sequence of log-strikes $k_u = -b + \epsilon(u-1)$ with $u = 1, \ldots, N$. With this spacing, the FFT algorithm returns N values for log-strikes ranging from $-b$ to b with $b = 0.5N\epsilon$. Then

$$C_0 \approx \frac{e^{-\alpha k_u}}{\pi} \sum_{j=1}^{N} e^{-iv_j(-b+\epsilon(u-1))} \psi(v_j)\eta, u = 1, \ldots, N$$

Substituting v_j yields

$$C_0 \approx \frac{e^{-\alpha k_u}}{\pi} \sum_{j=1}^{N} e^{-i\epsilon\eta(j-1)(u-1)} e^{ibv_j} \psi(v_j)\eta, u = 1, \ldots, N$$

Realizing that $\epsilon\eta = \frac{2\pi}{N}$ which implies that a small η increases ϵ and vice versa, introduce weightings according to Simpson's rule such that the call approximation finally takes on the form

$$C_0 \approx \frac{e^{-\alpha k_u}}{\pi} \sum_{j=1}^{N} e^{-i\frac{2\pi}{N}(j-1)(u-1)} e^{ibv_j} \psi(v_j)\frac{\eta}{3}(3 + (-1)^j - \diamond_{j-1}), u = 1, \ldots, N \quad (6.12)$$

with $\diamond_n$ being the Kronecker delta function which takes value one for $n = 0$ and zero otherwise. Equation (6.12) has a form similar enough to equation (6.11) to directly apply the FFT algorithm to it.

6.6 APPLICATIONS

This section applies the methods introduced in this chapter to different continuous and discrete market models.

6.6.1 Black-Scholes-Merton (1973) Model

To illustrate the usefulness of the transform method and the accuracy of formula (6.5) this example applies them alongside the FFT algorithm to the BSM model (the next sub-section and Chapter 8 do it for the Merton (1976) model and Chapter 9 for the Bakshi-Cao-Chen (1997) model). The characteristic function of the BSM model (without dividends) is given by

$$\varphi_0^{BSM}(u, T) = e^{((r-\sigma^2/2)iu - \sigma^2/2u^2)T}$$

The Python script in sub-section 6.8.1 implements this characteristic function and formula (11.12), which is a variant of (6.5), for a constant short rate r. In addition, it provides a FFT algorithm implementation for BSM and as a benchmark the standard analytical call option formula without dividends (cf. Wilmott et al. (1995), p. 48, or Chapter 5 of this book)

$$C_0 = S_0 \cdot N(d_1) - e^{-rT} \cdot K \cdot N(d_2)$$

$$d_1 \equiv \frac{\log \frac{S_0}{K} + \left(r + \frac{\sigma^2}{2}\right)T}{\sigma\sqrt{T}}$$

$$d_2 \equiv d_1 - \sigma\sqrt{T}$$

where N is the cumulative distribution function of a standard normal random variable. Figure 6.2 compares the accuracy of formula (6.5) against the analytical values for a range of strikes. Figure 6.3 does the same for FFT values where the same grid spacing is used as in CM99. While formula (6.5) is accurate up to 12 digits, the FFT approach is accurate "only" up to five digits (with this particular parametrization). In the calibration of the BCC97 model, we use formula (6.5) because it is more accurate.

In terms of speed one can say the following. Based on 5,000 valuations of the same call (with original CM99 parameters for the FFT routine), the analytical formula is the benchmark with a normalized time of 1 (which translates to 0.898 seconds on the author's notebook). FFT is slower by a factor of 7.9 and numerical integration by a factor of 15.1 such that FFT is about 1.9 times faster than numerical integration.

In the example, it is not taken into account that the FFT algorithm may in principle deliver call values for a number of different strikes with a single valuation run. However, the number of application areas for this particular feature of FFT seems sometimes a bit limited. Kahl (2007), for example, comments in this regard:

> "...when calibrating a model to quoted option prices one typically has quotes for just a couple of strikes and maturities. Using the FFT would require a uniform grid in the log-strike direction ... The strikes of the options to which we calibrate will typically not lie on this grid, so that an additional source of error is introduced when using the FFT: interpolation error."

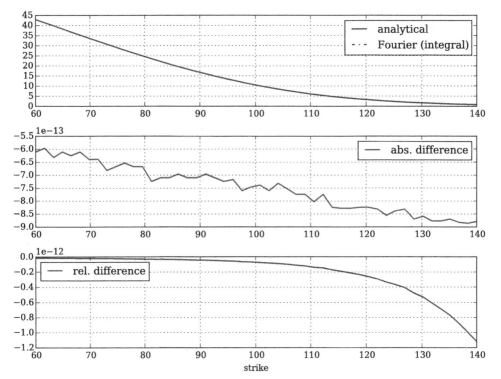

FIGURE 6.2 Valuation accuracy of Lewis' integral approach in comparison to BSM analytical formula; parameter values are $S_0 = 100, T = 1.0, r = 0.05, \sigma = 0.2$

Although it is quite nice to have an alternative pricing mechanism for BSM, the benefit is only marginal in this setup. This is different when considering more complex models, like Merton (1976) or Bakshi-Cao-Chen (1997). For these models, knowledge of the characteristic function makes European call option pricing as simple as in the BSM case.

6.6.2 Merton (1976) Model

Consider the continuous market model $\mathcal{M}^{M76}$ where the risk-neutral stock index dynamics are given by the jump diffusion of Merton (1976)

$$dS_t = (r - r_J)S_t dt + \sigma S_t dZ_t + J_t S_t dN_t \qquad (6.13)$$

r is the constant short rate, σ the constant volatility, Z_t a standard Brownian motion, N_t a Poisson process with intensity λ. Furthermore, J_t is the jump at date t with distribution

$$\log(1 + J_t) \approx \mathbf{N}\left(\log(1 + \mu_J) - \frac{\delta^2}{2}, \delta^2\right)$$

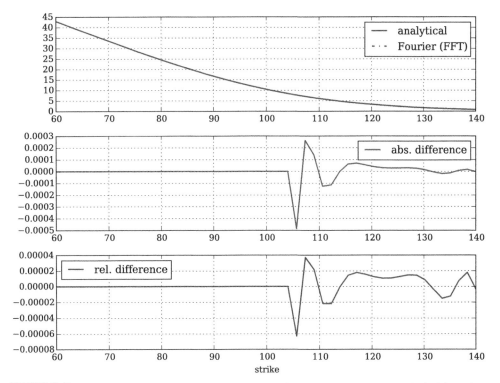

FIGURE 6.3 Valuation accuracy of CM99 FFT approach in comparison to BSM analytical formula; parameter values are $S_0 = 100, T = 1.0, r = 0.05, \sigma = 0.2, N = 4,096, \epsilon = 150^{-1}$

where **N** is the cumulative distribution function of a standardized normal random variable. Finally

$$r_J \equiv \lambda \cdot (e^{\mu_J + \delta^2/2} - 1)$$

The characteristic function of $\log S_T$ given stock index dynamics (6.13) is a well-known function

$$\varphi^{M76}(u) = \exp\left(\left(iu\omega - \frac{u^2\sigma^2}{2} + \lambda(e^{iu\mu_J - u^2\delta^2/2} - 1)\right)T\right) \tag{6.14}$$

where the risk-neutral drift term ω takes on the form

$$\omega = r - \frac{\sigma^2}{2} - \lambda(e^{\mu_J + \delta^2/2} - 1) \tag{6.15}$$

Valuation of a European call option then boils down to inserting (6.14)/(6.15) in either (6.5) and using an appropriate numerical integration scheme or (6.6)–(6.8) and applying FFT.

6.6.3 Discrete Market Model

Consider the discrete market model of Cox-Ross-Rubinstein with binomial representation of the index dynamics. Although not further needed, the application of Fourier-based option pricing to this type of model is rather instructive since it allows a "look behind the scenes". The exposition follows Černý (2004) rather closely.

Before attacking the valuation problem itself, some more notions have to be introduced.

Definition 43 (Root of Unity).   *The nth root of unity is*

$$z_n \equiv e^{-i\frac{2\pi}{n}}$$

Note that $(z_5)^0 = (z_5)^5 = (z_5)^{10} = (z_5)^{15} = \dots$ (anticlockwise rotation) and $(z_5)^0 = (z_5)^{-5} = (z_5)^{-10} = (z_5)^{-15} = \dots$ (clockwise rotation). We have

$$(z_n)^1 + (z_n)^2 + \dots (z_n)^{n-1} = 0$$

We also have

$$\left(z_n^k\right)^1 + \left(z_n^k\right)^2 + \dots + \left(z_n^k\right)^{n-1} = 0, k \neq 0, n, -n$$

and

$$\left(z_n^k\right)^1 + \left(z_n^k\right)^2 + \dots + \left(z_n^k\right)^{n-1} = n, k = 0, n, -n$$

Given a sequence of numbers $a = (a_0, a_1, \dots, a_{n-1})$, its reverse order is given by $\text{rev}(a) = (a_0, a_{n-1}, \dots, a_1)$. Given the sequence

$$z(k) = \left(\left(z_n^k\right)^0, \left(z_n^k\right)^1, \dots, \left(z_n^k\right)^{n-1}\right)$$

it can be shown that $\text{rev}(z(-k)) = z(k)$.

Figure 6.4 shows two series of roots of unity plotted as "spokes of a wheel", for $n = 5$ and $n = 30$. The Python script in sub-section 6.8.3 generates such plots.

Now, let a sequence $a = (a_0, a_1, \dots, a_{n-1})$ of n (complex) numbers be given.

Definition 44 (Discrete Fourier Transform).   *The discrete Fourier transform (DFT) of a is the sequence* $b = (b_0, b_1, \dots, b_{n-1})$ *where*

$$b_k = a_0 \left(z_n^k\right)^0 + a_1 \left(z_n^k\right)^1 + \dots + a_{n-1} \left(z_n^k\right)^{n-1}$$
$$= \sum_{j=0}^{n-1} a_j \left(z_n^k\right)^j$$

We write $\mathcal{T}(a) = b$.

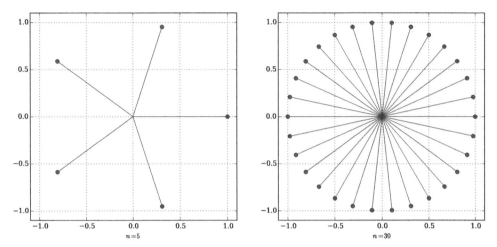

FIGURE 6.4 Series with roots of unity for $n = 5$ and $n = 30$ plotted in the imaginary plane

The discrete inverse Fourier transform of b is then the sequence $a = (a_0, a_1, \ldots, a_{n-1})$ where

$$a_l = \left(b_0 \left(z_n^{-l} \right)^0 + b_1 \left(z_n^{-l} \right)^1 + \cdots + b_{n-1} \left(z_n^{-l} \right)^{n-1} \right)$$

$$= \sum_{k=0}^{n-1} b_k \left(z_n^k \right)^{-l}$$

We write $a = \mathcal{T}^{-1}(b)$.

Consider next two sequences $a = (a_0, a_1, \ldots, a_{n-1})$ and $b = (b_0, b_1, \ldots, b_{n-1})$. The convolution c of the two sequences is denoted by $c = a \circ b$ and given element-wise by

$$c_j = \sum_{k=0}^{n-1} a_{j-k+n \cdot \mathbf{1}_{\{j-k<0\}}} \cdot b_k$$

The script in sub-section 6.8.4 implements this algorithm for two one-dimensional vectors.

Example 3 (Convolution). *Assume $n = 4$, then $c = a \circ b = (c_0, c_1, c_2, c_3)$ is given by*

$$c_0 = a_0 b_0 + a_3 b_1 + a_2 b_2 + a_1 b_3$$
$$c_1 = a_1 b_0 + a_0 b_1 + a_3 b_2 + a_2 b_3$$
$$c_2 = a_2 b_0 + a_1 b_1 + a_0 b_2 + a_3 b_3$$
$$c_3 = a_3 b_0 + a_2 b_1 + a_1 b_2 + a_0 b_3$$

We can apply convolutions to value European call options. To this end, remember the option pricing example of section 5.4 and revisit in particular Table 5.1. At time $t = 3\Delta t$ we have

$$C_{3\Delta t} = \begin{pmatrix} 36.23 \\ 11.76 \\ 0 \\ 0 \\ 0 \end{pmatrix}$$

Now define a probability vector by

$$qv = \begin{pmatrix} 0.5034 \\ 0.4966 \\ 0 \\ 0 \\ 0 \end{pmatrix}$$

We can now write

$$C_{2\Delta t} = e^{-r\Delta t} \cdot C_{3\Delta t} \mathrm{orev}(qv)$$

and so forth until we reach C_0. In Python, this takes on the form as presented in sub-section 6.8.6. The value the script derives equals exactly the one as reported in Table 5.1, namely 9.97. The Python script in sub-section 6.8.7 implements the algorithm in a general fashion (the script uses the parameters stored in the script of sub-section 6.8.5).

The next step is to use the DFT to value a European call option in the model. Consider two sequences $a = (a_0, a_1, \ldots, a_{n-1})$ and $b = (b_0, b_1, \ldots, b_{n-1})$. It holds

$$\mathcal{T}(aob) = \mathcal{T}(a) \cdot \mathcal{T}(b)$$
$$\mathcal{T}^{-1}(aob) = n \cdot \mathcal{T}^{-1}(a) \cdot \mathcal{T}^{-1}(b)$$

We now know that the present value of the call option is

$$C_0 = e^{-rT}(C_T \circ \underbrace{\mathrm{rev}(qv) \mathrm{orev}(qv) \mathrm{o} \ldots \mathrm{orev}(qv))}_{T/\Delta t \text{ times}}$$

Fourier inverting the last equation gives

$$\mathcal{T}^{-1}(C_0) = e^{-rT}\mathcal{T}^{-1}(C_T)((T/\Delta t + 1) \cdot \mathcal{T}^{-1}(\mathrm{rev}(qv)))^{T/\Delta t}$$

$(T/\Delta t + 1)$ is the dimension of C_T. Taking the DFT again, we get

$$C_0 = \mathcal{T}(e^{-rT}\mathcal{T}^{-1}(C_T)((T/\Delta t + 1) \cdot \mathcal{T}^{-1}(\mathrm{rev}(qv)))^{T/\Delta t})$$

With $(T/\Delta t + 1) \cdot \mathcal{T}^{-1}(\text{rev}(qv)) = \mathcal{T}(qv)$ one obtains

$$C_0 = \mathcal{T}(e^{-rT}\mathcal{T}^{-1}(C_T)\mathcal{T}(qv)^{T/\Delta t})$$

We also have

$$C_0 = \mathcal{T}^{-1}(e^{-rT}\mathcal{T}(C_T)\mathcal{T}(\text{rev}(qv))^{T/\Delta n})$$

The Python script in sub-section 6.8.8 implements three alternative formulas relying on DFT pricing in the binomial model. Equipped with these formulas we can now test both accuracy and speed of the approach. The BSM benchmark value for the example call option is 10.4506.

The DFT approach delivers the following results for 250 valuations including index level generations (cf. the script in sub-section 6.8.9). This accuracy is reached with $M = 5000$ time steps.

```
1   In [3]: run call_fft_speed.py
2   Value of European option is   10.4502
3   Number of Valuations                250
4   Duration in Seconds             11.1037
5   Time per Option in Seconds       0.0444
6
7   In [4]:
```

Reducing the number of time steps to $M = 500$, and thereby sacrificing a bit of accuracy, yields these results for 250 valuations:

```
1   In [4]: run call_fft_speed.py
2   Value of European option is   10.4466
3   Number of Valuations                250
4   Duration in Seconds              0.1865
5   Time per Option in Seconds       0.0007
6
7   In [5]:
```

Reducing the number of time steps by a factor of 10 reduces the time by a factor of more than 60. At this level of accuracy, one valuation takes less than 1 millisecond such that more than 1,000 options can be valued per second. These numbers are of course dependent on the system (hardware, operating system, etc.) used. However, they give a feeling for the trade-off between accuracy and speed. And they give a feeling for the advantage of Fourier-based option pricing.

6.7 CONCLUSIONS

Fourier-based option pricing combines generality of the risk-neutral valuation approach with the convenience of having a closed-form pricing formula as in the BSM setup. The two Fourier approaches presented in this chapter are widely applicable and quite fast when it comes to numerical valuations. In general, this is what makes them an indispensable tool for practical option pricing applications. Part III of the book will breathe life into these statements.

6.8 PYTHON SCRIPTS

6.8.1 BSM Call Valuation via Fourier Approach

```
#
# Valuation of European Call Options in BSM Model
# Comparison of Analytical, int_valueegral and FFT Approach
# 11_cal/BSM_option_valuation_FOU.py
#
# (c) Dr. Yves J. Hilpisch
# Derivatives Analytics with Python
#
import math
import numpy as np
from numpy.fft import fft
from scipy.integrate import quad
from scipy import stats
import matplotlib.pyplot as plt
import matplotlib as mpl
mpl.rcParams['font.family'] = 'serif'

#
# Model Parameters
#
S0 = 100.00  # initial index level
K = 100.00  # strike level
T = 1.  # call option maturity
r = 0.05  # constant short rate
sigma = 0.2  # constant volatility of diffusion

#
# Valuation by int_valueegration
#
### Analytical Formula
```

```
def BSM_call_value(S0, K, T, r, sigma):
    ''' Valuation of European call option in BSM Model.
    --> Analytical Formula.

    Parameters
    ==========
    S0: float
        initial stock/index level
    K: float
        strike price
    T: float
        time-to-maturity (for t=0)
    r: float
        constant risk-free short rate
    sigma: float
        volatility factor in diffusion term

    Returns
    =======
    call_value: float
        European call option present value

    '''
    d1 = (np.log(S0 / K) + (r + 0.5 * sigma ** 2) * T) \
                            / (sigma * np.sqrt(T))
    d2 = (np.log(S0 / K) + (r - 0.5 * sigma ** 2) * T) \
                            / (sigma * np.sqrt(T))
    BS_C = (S0 * stats.norm.cdf(d1, 0.0, 1.0)
            - K * np.exp(-r * T) * stats.norm.cdf(d2, 0.0, 1.0))
    return BS_C


#
# Fourier Transform with Numerical int_valueegration
#


def BSM_call_value_INT(S0, K, T, r, sigma):
    ''' Valuation of European call option in BSM model via Lewis (2001)
    --> Fourier-based approach (integral).

    Parameters
    ==========
    S0: float
        initial stock/index level
```

```
    K: float
        strike price
    T: float
        time-to-maturity (for t=0)
    r: float
        constant risk-free short rate
    sigma: float
        volatility factor in diffusion term

    Returns
    =======
    call_value: float
        European call option present value
    '''
    int_value = quad(lambda u:
            BSM_integral_function(u, S0, K, T, r, sigma), 0, 100)[0]
    call_value = max(0, S0 - np.exp(-r * T) * np.sqrt(S0 * K)
                                        / np.pi * int_value)
    return call_value


def BSM_integral_function(u, S0, K, T, r, sigma):
    ''' Valuation of European call option in BSM model via Lewis (2001)
    --> Fourier-based approach: integral function. '''
    cf_value = BSM_characteristic_function(u - 1j * 0.5, 0.0, T, r, sigma)
    int_value = 1 / (u ** 2 + 0.25) \
            * (np.exp(1j * u * np.log(S0 / K)) * cf_value).real
    return int_value


def BSM_characteristic_function(v, x0, T, r, sigma):
    '''  Valuation of European call option in BSM model via
    Lewis (2001) and Carr-Madan (1999)
    --> Fourier-based approach: characteristic function. '''
    cf_value = np.exp(((x0 / T + r - 0.5 * sigma ** 2) * 1j * v
                - 0.5 * sigma ** 2 * v ** 2) * T)
    return cf_value

#
# Fourier Transform with FFT
#


def BSM_call_value_FFT(S0, K, T, r, sigma):
    ''' Valuation of European call option in BSM model via Lewis (2001)
    --> Fourier-based approach (integral).
```

```
Parameters
==========
S0: float
    initial stock/index level
K: float
    strike price
T: float
    time-to-maturity (for t=0)
r: float
    constant risk-free short rate
sigma: float
    volatility factor in diffusion term

Returns
=======
call_value: float
    European call option present value

'''
k = np.log(K / S0)
x0 = np.log(S0 / S0)
g = 1  # factor to increase accuracy
N = g * 4096
eps = (g * 150.) ** -1
eta = 2 * np.pi / (N * eps)
b = 0.5 * N * eps - k
u = np.arange(1, N + 1, 1)
vo = eta * (u - 1)
# Modifications to Ensure int_valueegrability
if S0 >= 0.95 * K:  # ITM case
    alpha = 1.5
    v = vo - (alpha + 1) * 1j
    modcharFunc = np.exp(-r * T) * (BSM_characteristic_function(
                        v, x0, T, r, sigma) /
                        (alpha ** 2 + alpha
                          - vo ** 2 + 1j * (2 * alpha + 1) * vo))
else:          # OTM case
    alpha = 1.1
    v = (vo - 1j * alpha) - 1j
    modcharFunc1 = np.exp(-r * T) * (1 / (1 + 1j * (vo - 1j * alpha))
                        - np.exp(r * T) / (1j * (vo - 1j * alpha))
                        - BSM_characteristic_function(
                            v, x0, T, r, sigma) /
                            ((vo - 1j * alpha) ** 2
                          - 1j * (vo - 1j * alpha)))
    v = (vo + 1j * alpha) - 1j
```

```python
    modcharFunc2 = np.exp(-r * T) * (1 / (1 + 1j * (vo + 1j * alpha))
                         - np.exp(r * T) / (1j * (vo + 1j * alpha))
                         - BSM_characteristic_function(
                             v, x0, T, r, sigma) /
                           ((vo + 1j * alpha) ** 2
                         - 1j * (vo + 1j * alpha)))
    # Numerical FFT Routine
    delt = np.zeros(N, dtype=np.float)
    delt[0] = 1
    j = np.arange(1, N + 1, 1)
    SimpsonW = (3 + (-1) ** j - delt) / 3
    if S0 >= 0.95 * K:
        FFTFunc = np.exp(1j * b * vo) * modcharFunc * eta * SimpsonW
        payoff = (fft(FFTFunc)).real
        CallValueM = np.exp(-alpha * k) / np.pi * payoff
    else:
        FFTFunc = (np.exp(1j * b * vo)
                   * (modcharFunc1 - modcharFunc2)
                   * 0.5 * eta * SimpsonW)
        payoff = (fft(FFTFunc)).real
        CallValueM = payoff / (np.sinh(alpha * k) * np.pi)
    pos = int((k + b) / eps)
    CallValue = CallValueM[pos] * S0
    # klist = np.exp((np.arange(0, N, 1) - 1) * eps - b) * S0
    return CallValue #, klist[pos - 50:pos + 50]


def plot_val_differences(vtype='int'):
    k_list = np.linspace(S0 * 0.6, S0 * 1.4, 50)
    ana_values = BSM_call_value(S0, k_list, T, r, sigma)
    plt.figure(figsize=(8, 6))
    plt.subplot(311)
    plt.plot(k_list, ana_values, 'b', label='analytical', lw=1.5)
    if vtype == 'int':
        int_values = np.array([BSM_call_value_INT(S0, K, T, r, sigma)
                               for K in k_list])
        plt.plot(k_list, int_values, 'r-.', label='Fourier (integral)',
                 lw=1.5)
        diffs = int_values - ana_values
        rdiffs = (int_values - ana_values) / ana_values
    else:
        fft_values = np.array([BSM_call_value_FFT(S0, K, T, r, sigma)
                               for K in k_list])
        plt.plot(k_list, fft_values, 'r-.', label='Fourier (FFT)', lw=1.5)
        diffs = fft_values - ana_values
        rdiffs = (fft_values - ana_values) / ana_values
    plt.legend()
    plt.grid()
```

```
plt.subplot(312)
plt.plot(k_list, diffs, 'g', label='abs. difference', lw=1.5)
plt.legend(loc=0)
plt.grid()
plt.subplot(313)
plt.plot(k_list, rdiffs, 'r', label='rel. difference', lw=1.5)
plt.legend(loc=0)
plt.xlabel('strike')
plt.grid()
plt.tight_layout()
```

6.8.2 Fourier Series

```
#
# Fourier Series for f(x) = abs(x) for -pi <= x <= pi
# 06_fou/Fourier_series.py
#
# (c) Dr. Yves J. Hilpisch
# Derivatives Analytics with Python
#
import numpy as np
import matplotlib.pyplot as plt


#
# Fourier series function
#


def fourier_series(x, n):
    ''' Generate Fourier Series from vector x for f(x) = abs(x)
    of order n.

    Parameters
    ==========
    x:   float or array of floats
         input numbers
    n:   int
         order of Fourier series

    Returns
    =======
    fourier_values : float or array of floats
         numbers according to Fourier series approximation
    '''
    fourier_values = np.pi / 2
```

```python
    for i in range(1, n + 1):
        fourier_values += ((2 * ((-1) ** i - 1))
                        / (np.pi * i ** 2) * np.cos(i * x))
    return fourier_values

def plot_fourier_series():
    # Data Generation
    x = np.linspace(-np.pi, np.pi, 100)
    y1 = fourier_series(x, 1)
    y2 = fourier_series(x, 5)

    # Data Plotting
    plt.figure(figsize=(10, 5))
    plt.subplot(121)
    plt.plot(x, abs(x), 'b', label='$f(x) = |x|$')
    plt.plot(x, y1, 'r-.', lw=3.0, label='Fourier series $n=1$')
    plt.grid()
    plt.legend(loc=9)
    plt.subplot(122)
    plt.plot(x, abs(x), 'b', label='$f(x) = |x|$')
    plt.plot(x, y2, 'r-.', lw=3.0, label='Fourier series $n=5$')
    plt.grid()
    plt.legend(loc=9)
```

6.8.3 Roots of Unity

```python
#
# Plotting Spokes and Points on a Circle
# with Complex Numbers
# 06_fou/roots_of_unity.py
#
# (c) Dr. Yves J. Hilpisch
# Derivatives Analytics with Python
#
import numpy as np
import matplotlib.pyplot as plt

def generate_subplot(n):
    y = np.exp(1j * 2 * np.pi / n) ** np.arange(1, n + 1)
    for l in range(n):
        plt.plot(y[l].real, y[l].imag, 'ro')
        plt.plot((0, y[l].real), (0.0, y[l].imag), 'b')
    plt.axis([-1.1, 1.1, -1.1, 1.1])
    plt.xlabel('$n=%s$' % n)
    plt.grid()
```

```
def generate_plot():
    plt.figure(figsize=(10, 7))
    # first sub-plot for n=5
    plt.subplot(121)
    generate_subplot(n=5)

    # second sub-plot for n=30
    plt.subplot(122)
    generate_subplot(n=30)

    plt.subplots_adjust(left=0.05, bottom=0.2, top=0.8, right=1.0)
```

6.8.4 Convolution

```
#
# Circular convolution of two 1-dim vectors
# 06_fou/convolution.py
#
# (c) Dr. Yves J. Hilpisch
# Derivatives Analytics with Python
#
import numpy as np


#
# Function Definitions
#


def revpy(a):
    ''' Reversing the order of the vector's numbers (for loop). '''
    a = np.array(a)
    n = len(a)
    c = np.zeros(n, dtype=np.float)
    c[0] = a[0]
    for j in range(1, n):
        c[j] = a[n - j]
    return c


def revnp(a):
    ''' Reversing the order of the vector's numbers (NumPy version). '''
    b = a.copy()
    b[1:] = b[1:][::-1]
    return b
```

```python
def convolution(a, b):
    ''' Convolution of two vectors. '''
    if len(a) != len(b):
        raise ValueError(''Lengths of vectors do not match.'')
    n = len(a)
    c = np.zeros(n, dtype=np.float)
    for j in range(n):
        s = 0
        for k in range(n):
            if j - k >= 0:
                s += a[j - k] * b[k]
            else:
                s += a[j - k + n] * b[k]
        c[j] = s
    return c
```

6.8.5 Module with Parameters

```python
#
# Model Parameters for European Call Option
# in Binomial Model
# 06_fou/parameters.py
#
# (c) Dr. Yves J. Hilpisch
# Derivatives Analytics with Python
#
from math import exp, sqrt

# Model and Option Parameters
S0 = 100.0  # index level
K = 100.0  # option strike
T = 1.0  # maturity date
r = 0.05  # risk-less short rate
sigma = 0.2  # volatility

def get_binomial_parameters(M=100):
    # Time Parameters
    dt = T / M  # length of time interval
    df = exp(-r * dt)  # discount per interval

    # Binomial Parameters
    u = exp(sigma * sqrt(dt))  # up movement
    d = 1 / u  # down movement
    q = (exp(r * dt) - d) / (u - d)  # martingale branch probability
    return dt, df, u, d, q
```

6.8.6 Call Value by Convolution

```
#
# Call Option Pricing with Circular Convolution (Simple)
# 06_fou/call_convolution.py
#
# (c) Dr. Yves J. Hilpisch
# Derivatives Analytics with Python
#
import math
import numpy as np
from convolution import revnp, convolution

# Parameter Definitions
M = 4  # number of time steps
dt = 1.0 / M  # length of time interval
r = 0.05  # constant short rate
C = [49.18246976, 22.14027582, 0, 0, 0]  # call payoff at maturity
q = 0.537808372  # martingale probability
qv = np.array([q, 1 - q, 0, 0, 0])  # probabilitiy vector filled with zeros

# Calculation
V = np.zeros((M + 1, M + 1), dtype=np.float)
V[M] = C

for t in range(M - 1, -1, -1):
    V[t] = convolution(V[t + 1], revnp(qv)) * math.exp(-r * dt)

print "Value of the Call Option %8.3f" % V[0, 0]
```

6.8.7 Option Pricing by Convolution

```
#
# Call Option Pricing with Circular Convolution (General)
# 06_fou/call_convolution_general.py
#
# (c) Dr. Yves J. Hilpisch
# Derivatives Analytics with Python
#
import numpy as np
from convolution import revnp, convolution
from parameters import *
```

```python
# Parameter Adjustments
M = 3  # number of time steps
dt, df, u, d, q = get_binomial_parameters(M)

# Array Generation for Stock Prices
mu = np.arange(M + 1)
mu = np.resize(mu, (M + 1, M + 1))
md = np.transpose(mu)
mu = u ** (mu - md)
md = d ** md
S = S0 * mu * md

# Valuation
V = np.maximum(S - K, 0)
qv = np.zeros((M + 1), dtype=np.float)
qv[0] = q
qv[1] = 1 - q
for t in range(M - 1, -1, -1):
    V[:, t] = convolution(V[:, t + 1], revnp(qv)) * df

print "Value of the Call Option %8.3f" % V[0, 0]
```

6.8.8 Option Pricing by DFT

```python
#
# Call Option Pricing with Discrete Fourier Transforms (DFT/FFT)
# 06_fou/call_fft_pricing.py
#
# (c) Dr. Yves J. Hilpisch
# Derivatives Analytics with Python
#
import math
import numpy as np
from numpy.fft import fft, ifft
from convolution import revnp
from parameters import *

# Parameter Adjustments
M = 3  # number of time steps
dt, df, u, d, q = get_binomial_parameters(M)

# Array Generation for Stock Prices
mu = np.arange(M + 1)
mu = np.resize(mu, (M + 1, M + 1))
md = np.transpose(mu)
```

```
mu = u ** (mu - md)
md = d ** md
S = S0 * mu * md

# Valuation by fft
CT = np.maximum(S[:, -1] - K, 0)
qv = np.zeros(M + 1, dtype=np.float)
qv[0] = q
qv[1] = 1 - q
C0_a = fft(math.exp(-r * T) * ifft(CT) * ((M + 1) * ifft(revnp(qv))) ** M)
C0_b = fft(math.exp(-r * T) * ifft(CT) * fft(qv) ** M)
C0_c = ifft(math.exp(-r * T) * fft(CT) * fft(revnp(qv)) ** M)

# Results Output
print "Value of European option is %8.3f" % np.real(C0_a[0])
print "Value of European option is %8.3f" % np.real(C0_b[0])
print "Value of European option is %8.3f" % np.real(C0_c[0])
```

6.8.9   Speed Test of DFT

```
#
# Call Option Pricing with DFT/FFT Speed Test
# 06_fou/call_fft_speed.py
#
# (c) Dr. Yves J. Hilpisch
# Derivatives Analytics with Python
#
import math
import numpy as np
from numpy.fft import fft, ifft
from convolution import revnp
from parameters import *

def call_fft_value(M):
    # Parameter Adjustments
    dt, df, u, d, q = get_binomial_parameters(M)

    # Array Generation for Stock Prices
    mu = np.arange(M + 1)
    mu = np.resize(mu, (M + 1, M + 1))
    md = np.transpose(mu)
    mu = u ** (mu - md)
    md = d ** md
    S = S0 * mu * md
```

```
# Valuation by FFT
CT = np.maximum(S[:, -1] - K, 0)
qv = np.zeros(M + 1, dtype=np.float)
qv[0] = q
qv[1] = 1 - q
C0 = fft(math.exp(-r * T) * ifft(CT) * fft(qv) ** M)
```

## CHAPTER 7

Valuation of American Options by Simulation

7.1 INTRODUCTION

Monte Carlo simulation (MCS) is a flexible and powerful numerical method to value financial derivatives of any kind (cf. Glasserman (2004)). As a forward evolving technique, it is per se not suited to address the valuation of American or Bermudan options which are valued in general by backwards induction (cf. Kohler (2009)). However, Longstaff and Schwartz (2001) provide a numerically efficient method to solve this problem by what they call Least-Squares Monte Carlo (LSM).[1] Their approach approximates continuation values for American options in backwards steps by an ordinary least-squares regression. Equipped with such approximations, the option is exercised if the approximate continuation value is lower than the value of immediate exercise. Otherwise it is not exercised. The LSM leads to a *lower bound* for the option's value since the exercise decision is in any case sub-optimal (cf. Longstaff and Schwartz (2001)).

Haugh and Kogan (2004), among others, propose a dual formulation of the valuation problem for an American option which finally leads to a MCS estimator that represents an *upper bound* to the option's value. In some situations, it is very helpful to have an upper bound in addition to a lower bound since the LSM does not allow to assess "how much too low the value estimate is." Then, in the absence of alternative benchmarks, the accuracy of the LSM estimator cannot be judged.

This chapter proceeds as follows. Section 7.2 describes a financial model in the spirit of the Black-Scholes-Merton (BSM) economy. Section 7.3 introduces the primal and dual valuation problems for an American option and the respective MCS valuation algorithms. Section 7.4 presents valuation results for two different types of American options from a Python implementation of the MCS algorithms. Section 7.5 concludes.

---

[1]Cf. Tsitsiklis and Van Roy (2001) for a similar algorithm published at about the same time. Cf. Kohler (2009) for comparisons.

7.2 FINANCIAL MODEL

We consider the continuous market model of Black-Scholes-Merton

$$\mathcal{M}^{BSM} = \{(\Omega, \mathcal{F}, \mathbb{F}, P), T, (S, B)\}$$

with final date $T, 0 < T < \infty$. Uncertainty in the economy is represented by a filtered probability space $\{\Omega, \mathcal{F}, \mathbb{F}, P\}$. Ω denotes the continuous state space, $\mathcal{F}$ an σ-algebra, $\mathbb{F}$ a filtration and P the real or objective probability measure.

Against this background, we model for $0 \leq t \leq T$ the risk-neutral evolution of the relevant stock index S according to the stochastic differential equation (SDE)

$$\frac{dS_t}{S_t} = r dt + \sigma dZ_t \tag{7.1}$$

S_t denotes the index level at date t, r the constant risk-less short rate, σ the constant volatility of the index and Z_t a standard Brownian motion. The stochastic process generates the filtration $\mathbb{F}$, i.e. $\mathcal{F}_t \equiv \mathcal{F}(S_{0 \leq s \leq t})$. The differential equation a risk-less zero-coupon bond B satisfies is

$$\frac{dB_t}{B_t} = r dt \tag{7.2}$$

The time t value of a zero-coupon bond paying one unit of currency at T with $0 \leq t < T$ is $B_t(T) = e^{-r(T-t)}$.

To simulate the financial model, i.e. to generate numerical values for S_t, the SDE (7.1) has to be discretized. To this end, divide the given time interval $[0, T]$ in equidistant sub-intervals Δt such that now $t \in \{0, \Delta t, 2\Delta t, \dots, T\}$, i.e. there are $M + 1$ points in time with $M \equiv T/\Delta t$. A discrete version of the continuous time market model (7.1)–(7.2) is

$$\frac{S_t}{S_{t-\Delta t}} = e^{\left(r - \frac{\sigma^2}{2}\right)\Delta t + \sigma\sqrt{\Delta t}z_t} \tag{7.3}$$

$$\frac{B_t}{B_{t-\Delta t}} = e^{r\Delta t} \tag{7.4}$$

for $t \in \{\Delta t, \dots, T\}$ and standard normally distributed z_t. This scheme is a Euler discretization based on the log-dynamics of S_t which is known to be exact for the geometric Brownian motion (7.1) (cf. Glasserman (2004), pp. 93–94).

7.3 AMERICAN OPTION VALUATION

7.3.1 Problem Formulations

By the Fundamental Theorem of Asset Pricing, the time t value of an attainable[2] and $\mathcal{F}_T$-measurable contingent claim $V_T \equiv h_T(S_T) \geq 0$ (satisfying suitable integrability conditions) is given by arbitrage as

$$V_t = \mathbf{E}_t^Q \left(B_t(T) V_T \right)$$

---

[2]Recall that a contingent claim is *attainable* if it can be replicated via an admissible trading strategy in the index and a zero-coupon bond. A trading strategy is admissible if it is predictable and self-financing and if its value is at all times finite and bounded from below. See Chapter 4.

with $V_0 = \mathbf{E}_0^Q \left(B_0(T)V_T \right)$ as the important special case for valuation purposes. $\mathbf{E}$ denotes the expectation operator and Q the unique risk-neutral probability measure equivalent to the real world measure P.[3] $\mathbf{E}_t(\cdot)$ is short for the conditional expectation $\mathbf{E}(\cdot|\mathcal{F}_t)$.

The contingent claim could be a European call option maturing at T with payoff $h_T(S_T) \equiv \max[S_T - K, 0]$. It could also be a European put with payoff $h_T(S_T) \equiv \max[K - S_T, 0]$. In both cases, $K > 0$ is the fixed strike price of the option.

Primal Formulation The valuation of contingent claims with American exercise is more involved. In its *primal form*, this problem can be formulated as an optimal stopping problem (cf. Kohler (2009), p. 2)

$$V_0 = \sup_{\tau \in [0,T]} \mathbf{E}_0^Q (B_0(\tau) h_\tau(S_\tau)) \tag{7.5}$$

with V_0 being the present value of the American derivative, τ an $\mathbb{F}$-adapted stopping time, T the date of maturity, $B_0(\tau)$ the discount factor appropriate for stopping time τ, h_τ a non-negative, $\mathcal{F}_\tau$-measurable payoff function and S_τ the index level process stopped at $t = \tau$. The expectation is again taken under the risk-neutral measure Q. To value American options by MCS, the optimal stopping problem (7.5) also has to be discretized:

$$V_0 = \sup_{\tau \in \{0, \Delta t, 2\Delta t, \dots, T\}} \mathbf{E}_0^Q (B_0(\tau) h_\tau(S_\tau)) \tag{7.6}$$

The continuation value C_t at date t of the option, i.e. the value of not exercising the option at this date, is given under risk-neutrality as

$$C_t(s) = \mathbf{E}_t^Q (e^{-r\Delta t} V_{t+\Delta t}(S_{t+\Delta t})|S_t = s)$$

using the Markov property of S_t. Applying another important result in this context (cf. Kohler (2009), pp. 4–6), the value of the option at date t is then

$$V_t(s) = \max[h_t(s), C_t(s)] \tag{7.7}$$

i.e. the maximum of the payoff $h_t(s)$ of immediate exercise and the expected payoff $C_t(s)$ of not exercising.

The Python script in sub-section 7.6.1 implements this primal valuation problem in the context of the Cox-Ross-Rubinstein binomial model presented in Chapter 5. The adjustments to American exercise are quite simple in this context. The script values two different American options that are further analyzed in section 7.4.

Dual Formulation Let $\mathbb{M}$ be the set of all Q-martingales $Q_t, t \in \{0, \dots, T\}$, satisfying $Q_0 = 0$. For any such martingale and a stopping time $\tau \in \{\Delta t, \dots, T\}$ it holds (cf. Glasserman

---

[3]The defining characteristic of Q is that it makes the discounted index level process a martingale. Cf. Björk (2004), Theorems 8.3 and 10.17, for completeness of the BSM model (7.1)–(7.2) and uniqueness of the risk-neutral measure Q, respectively.

(2004), p. 471)

$$\mathbf{E}_0^Q(B_0(\tau)h_\tau(S_\tau)) = \mathbf{E}_0^Q(B_0(\tau)(h_\tau(S_\tau) - Q_\tau))$$

$$\leq \mathbf{E}_0^Q \left(\max_{t \in \{\Delta t, \dots, T\}} B_0(t)[h_t(S_t) - Q_t] \right) \tag{7.8}$$

The first equality follows by the optional sampling property of martingales (cf. Bhattacharya and Waymire (2007), Theorem 3.6). Since (7.8) holds for any martingale Q it also holds for the infimum taken over all $Q \in \mathbb{M}$

$$\mathbf{E}_0^Q(B_0(\tau)h_\tau(S_\tau)) \leq \inf_{Q \in \mathbb{M}} \mathbf{E}_0^Q \left(\max_{t \in \{\Delta t, \dots, T\}} B_0(t)[h_t(S_t) - Q_t] \right) \tag{7.9}$$

Finally, since (7.9) holds for any τ, it also holds for the supremum taken over all τ such that

$$V_0 = \sup_{\tau \in \{0, \Delta t, \dots, T\}} \mathbf{E}_0^Q(B_0(\tau)h_\tau(S_\tau))$$

$$\leq \inf_{Q \in \mathbb{M}} \mathbf{E}_0^Q \left(\max_{t \in \{\Delta t, \dots, T\}} B_0(t)[h_t(S_t) - Q_t] \right) \tag{7.10}$$

It can be proven that the last inequality holds with equality (cf. Kohler (2009), pp. 16–18). Therefore, the discrete *dual problem* of valuing an American option given the primal formulation (7.6) is

$$V_0 = \inf_{Q \in \mathbb{Q}} \mathbf{E}_0^Q \left(\max_{t \in \{0, \dots, T\}} B_0(t)[h_t(S_t) - Q_t] \right)$$

$$= \mathbf{E}_0^Q \left(\max_{t \in \{0, \dots, T\}} B_0(t)[h_t(S_t) - Q_t^*] \right) \tag{7.11}$$

with Q^* the martingale defined by (cf. Kohler (2009), p. 16)

$$Q_t^* = \sum_{u=\Delta t}^{t} \left(\max[h_u(S_u), C_u(S_u)] - \mathbf{E}^Q \left(\max[h_u(S_u), C_u(S_u)] \middle| \mathcal{F}_{u-\Delta t} \right) \right)$$

$$= \sum_{u=\Delta t}^{t} \left(V_u(S_u) - \mathbf{E}^Q \left(V_u(S_u) \middle| \mathcal{F}_{u-\Delta t} \right) \right) \tag{7.12}$$

7.3.2 Valuation Algorithms

This sub-section translates the basic theory into implementable algorithms.

LSM Algorithm The decision to exercise an American option or not is dependent on the continuation value. Consider a simulation with $M + 1$ points in time and I paths. Given a simulated index level $S_{t,i}, t \in \{0, \dots, T\}, i \in \{1, \dots, I\}$, what is the continuation value $C_{t,i}(S_{t,i})$, i.e. the *expected* payoff of not exercising the option? Of course, by simulation you know the *simulated* continuation value $Y_{t,i} \equiv e^{-r\Delta t} V_{t+\Delta t,i}$. However, using these quantities directly would translate into perfect foresight—something not seen in financial markets and therefore not acceptable for a valuation algorithm. In other words, using these quantities would lead to a *better-than-optimal* exercise policy and therewith to a consistently high biased estimator. On the other hand, estimating the continuation value through a nested MCS, for example, would lead to generally unacceptable computational times.[4]

The major insight of Longstaff-Schwartz is to estimate the continuation values $C_{t,i}$ by ordinary least-squares regression—hence the name *Least-Squares Monte Carlo* for their algorithm. They propose to regress the I continuation values $Y_{t,i}$ against the I simulated index levels $S_{t,i}$. Given D basis functions b with $b_1, \dots, b_D : \mathbb{R}^D \to \mathbb{R}$ for the regression, the continuation value $C_{t,i}$ is according to their approach approximated by

$$\hat{C}_{t,i} = \sum_{d=1}^{D} \alpha_{d,t}^* \cdot b_d(S_{t,i}) \tag{7.13}$$

The optimal regression parameters $\alpha_{d,t}^*$ are the result of the minimization

$$\min_{\alpha_{1,t},\dots,\alpha_{D,t}} \frac{1}{I} \sum_{i=1}^{I} \left(Y_{t,i} - \sum_{d=1}^{D} \alpha_{d,t} \cdot b_d(S_{t,i}) \right)^2 \tag{7.14}$$

In some circumstances, the quality of the regression can be improved upon when restricting the paths involved in the regression to those where the option is in-the-money. To apply the LSM, implement Algorithm 1.

Note that when updating option values $V_{t,i}$, the real continuation value $Y_{t,i}$ is to be taken and not the estimated one $\hat{C}_{t,i}$.

Sub-section 7.6.2 presents a Python script implementing the LSM primal algorithm. It uses the parametrization for the first option of table one in the seminal paper of Longstaff and Schwartz (2001) (see also the next section).

It is well-known that the LSM estimator (7.15)—for large enough I—provides a lower bound for the option's value. However, small I may lead to an in-sample bias of the regressions in the sense that the resulting exercise policy is better-than-optimal.[5] To avoid such a bias, the algorithm may be divided into two parts. To this end, one would simulate $I = I_1 + I_2$ paths and use the first I_1 paths for the derivation of the $\alpha_{d,t}^*$ and the remaining I_2 paths for the valuation of the American option given the $\alpha_{d,t}^*$.

Dual Algorithm   The algorithm to implement the dual approach to American option valuation (7.11) and (7.12) uses the optimal regression parameters $\alpha_{d,t}^*$ from the LSM algorithm. The dual algorithm is forward evolving and shown as Algorithm 2.

Note that when updating the $V_{t,i}$, the regression-based estimate for the continuation value is taken (in contrast to the LSM algorithm). Also note that for $t = T$ the $\hat{C}_{T,i,j}$ are zero by definition as well as formally due to the $\alpha_{d,T}^*$ being zero.

---

[4]Suppose the continuation value is also estimated with I paths through a nested MCS. Then the number of simulated index level values increases from $(M + 1) \cdot I$ to $(M + 1) \cdot I^2$.
[5]For $I = 1$ we again have the situation with perfect foresight. However, for small $I > 1$ the problem may nevertheless arise. Cf. Fries (2008).

Algorithm 1: Primal Algorithm

---

1 Divide the time interval $[0, T]$ into equidistant sub-intervals of length Δt

  for $t = 0, \Delta t, \ldots, T$ **do**

    for $i = 1, \ldots, I$ **do**

      if $t = 0$ **then**

2   Set $S_{t,i} = S_0$

      else

3   Draw a standard normally distributed pseudo-random number $z_{t,i}$

4   Simulate the index level value $S_{t,i}$ given $S_{t-\Delta t,i}$ and $z_{t,i}$

  for $t = T, T - \Delta t, \ldots, \Delta t, 0$ **do**

    if $t = T$ **then**

5   Set $V_{T,i} = h_T(S_{T,i})$

    if $T > t > 0$ **then**

6   Regress the $Y_{t,i}$ against the $S_{t,i}, i \in \{1, \ldots, I\}$, given D basis functions b

7   Approximate $C_{t,i}$ by $\hat{C}_{t,i}$ according to (7.13) given the optimal parameters $\alpha_{d,t}^*$ from (7.14)

8   According to (7.7) set

$$V_{t,i} = \begin{cases} h_t(S_{t,i}) & \text{if } h_t(S_{t,i}) > \hat{C}_{t,i} \\ Y_{t,i} & \text{if } h_t(S_{t,i}) \le \hat{C}_{t,i} \end{cases}$$

    if $t = 0$ **then**

9   With $V_{0,i} \equiv e^{-r\Delta t} V_{\Delta t,i}$, calculate the LSM estimator as

$$\hat{V}_0^{LSM} = \frac{1}{I} \sum_{i=1}^{I} V_{0,i} \tag{7.15}$$

7.4 NUMERICAL RESULTS

7.4.1 American Put Option

The first example is a simple American put option. It is the first non-trivial example in the seminal paper by Longstaff-Schwartz (2001) where the following assumptions are made:

- $S_0 = 36$
- $T = 1.0$
- $r = 0.06$
- $\sigma = 0.2$
- $h_t(s) = \max[40 - s, 0]$

Algorithm 2: Dual Algorithm

---

1 Divide the time interval $[0, T]$ into equidistant sub-intervals of length Δt

   for $t = 0, \Delta t, \dots, T$ **do**

      for $i = 1, \dots, I$ **do**

         if $t = 0$ **then**

2   Set $S_{t,i} = S_0$

         else

3   Draw a standard normally distributed pseudo-random number $z_{t,i}$

4   Simulate the index level value $S_{t,i}$ given $S_{t-\Delta t,i}$ and $z_{t,i}$

   for $t = 0, \Delta t, \dots, T$ **do**

      for $i = 1, \dots, I$ **do**

         if $t = 0$ **then**

5   initialize $Q_{0,i} = 0$ and $U_{0,i} = 0$

         if $0 < t < T$ **then**

6   Simulate J successors $S_{t,i,j}, j \in \{1, \dots, J\}$, for each $S_{t-\Delta t,i}$ by a nested MCS

7   According to (7.7) set $V_{t,i} = \max[h_t(S_{t,i}), \hat{C}_{t,i}(S_{t,i})]$ given the $\alpha^*_{d,t}$ from LSM and approximation (7.13)

8   Determine for all i,j the $\hat{V}_{t,i,j} = \max[h_t(S_{t,i,j}), \hat{C}_{t,i,j}(S_{t,i,j})]$ with the $\alpha^*_{d,t}$ and

             equation (7.13) to approximate $V_{t,i}$ by $\hat{V}_{t,i} = \frac{1}{J}\sum_{j=1}^{J} \hat{V}_{t,i,j}$

9   Set $Q_{t,i} = e^{r\Delta t}Q_{t-\Delta t,i} + (V_{t,i} - \hat{V}_{t,i})$

10   Update $U_{t,i} = \max[e^{r\Delta t}U_{t-\Delta t,i}, h_t(S_{t,i}) - Q_{t,i}]$

         if $t = T$ **then**

11   Update $U_{T,i} = \max[e^{r\Delta t}U_{T-\Delta t,i}, \hat{h}_T(S_{T,i}) - Q_{T,i}]$ where

$$\hat{h}_T(S_{T,i}) = \frac{1}{J}\sum_{j=1}^{J} h_T(S_{T,i,j})$$

12   Calculate the dual MCS estimator as

$$\hat{V}_0^{DUAL} = e^{-rT}\frac{1}{I}\sum_{i=1}^{I} U_{T,i} \tag{7.16}$$

    The true (theoretical) value of this option is 4.486 given a binomial valuation model with 500 time steps.

    The Python script in sub-section 7.6.3 implements the LSM algorithm with some additional features as well as the dual algorithm. As variance reduction techniques the implementation uses antithetic paths (cf. Glasserman (2004), sec. 4.2) and moment matching (cf. Glasserman (2004), sec. 4.5.). It is also possible to derive the optimal regression coefficients

TABLE 7.1 Valuation results from the LSM and DUAL algorithms for the American put option[a] from 25 different simulation runs with base case parametrization.

Algorithm	Value	$M = 25$	$M = 50$	$M = 75$
LSM	Maximum	4.526	4.529	4.544
	Mean	4.452	4.470	4.467
	Difference	−0.034	−0.016	−0.019
	Median	4.459	4.471	4.475
	Minimum	4.342	4.370	4.391
DUAL	Maximum	5.018	4.697	4.753
	Mean	4.651	4.595	4.598
	Difference	0.165	0.109	0.111
	Median	4.632	4.585	4.574
	Minimum	4.610	4.570	4.552
Spread	Absolute	0.199	0.125	0.131

[a]The true value of the American put option from a binomial model with 500 time steps is 4.486. Reported differences are absolute deviations of the mean values from the correct option value.

on the basis of in-the-money paths only. As regression functions, the implementation uses simple monomials, the number of which can be chosen freely.

We use the following simulation parameters as our base case to illustrate the valuation of the American put option:

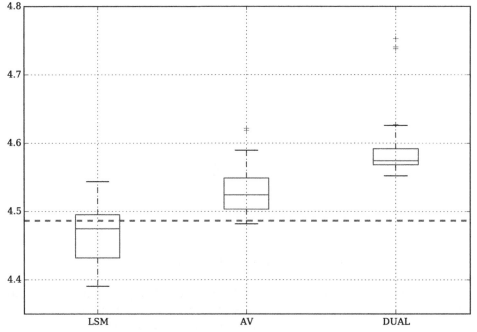

FIGURE 7.1 Valuation results for the American put option from 25 simulation runs with $M = 75$ time intervals; AV = average of primal (LSM) and dual (DUAL) values; dashed line = true value

- $M = 25$
- $I_1 = 4 \cdot 4096, I_2 = 1096$
- $J = 50$
- $D = 9$
- moment matching but no antithetic paths
- all paths are used for the regressions

Experience from a number of numerical experiments suggests that the value estimates do not become much more accurate when the path numbers I_1, I_2 or J are increased. The use of antithetic paths also does not contribute to accuracy. However, increasing the number of time steps M has a positive effect on the spread between the LSM and DUAL mean value as Table 7.1 illustrates. Figure 7.1 shows the main results for $M = 75$ as boxplots.

7.4.2 American Short Condor Spread

The second example is a so-called Short Condor Spread which is mainly a combination of long and short positions in vanilla options. This type of payoff is analyzed, for example, in Kohler (2009), sec. 8. The model assumptions now are:

- $S_0 = 100$
- $T = 1.0$
- $r = 0.05$
- $\sigma = 0.5$
- $h_t(s) = \min[40, \max(90 - s, 0) + \max(s - 110, 0)]$

This payoff is non-convex and therefore difficult to approximate via parametric regression with simple monomials. Therefore convergence of the LSM is generally weak and the availability of a high estimator quite useful. Table 7.2 reports results from different simulations for

TABLE 7.2 Valuation results from the LSM and DUAL algorithms for the Short Condor Spread[a] from 25 different simulation runs with base case parametrization.

Algorithm	Value	$M = 25$	$M = 50$	$M = 75$
LSM	Maximum	26.683	26.710	27.063
	Mean	25.977	26.027	26.308
	Difference	−1.000	−0.950	−0.669
	Median	25.946	25.989	26.294
	Minimum	25.181	25.564	25.521
DUAL	Maximum	33.462	45.401	32.416
	Mean	27.885	28.177	27.749
	Difference	0.908	1.200	0.772
	Median	27.493	27.479	27.569
	Minimum	27.221	27.230	27.282
Spread	Absolute	1.908	2.149	1.441

[a]The true value of the American put option from a binomial model with 500 time steps is 26.97705. Reported differences are absolute deviations of the mean values from the correct option value.

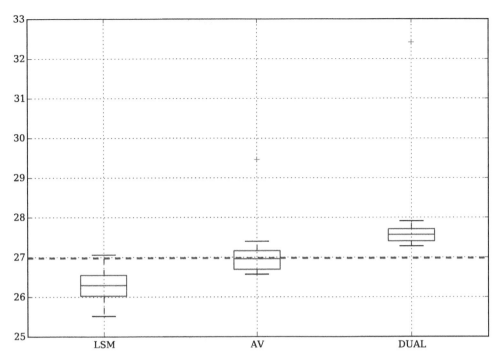

FIGURE 7.2 Valuation results for the American Short Condor Spread from 25 simulation runs with $M = 75$ time intervals; AV = average of primal (LSM) and dual (DUAL) values; dashed line = true value

this type of American derivative. Here, the increase of M has only a marginal effect on the spread between the LSM and DUAL mean value. However, the LSM estimate improves with increasing M. Figure 7.2 shows the valuation results graphically for the case $M = 75$.

7.5 CONCLUSIONS

The numerically efficient valuation of American options by MCS was almost impossible until Longstaff-Schwartz published their LSM algorithm in 2001. Although there have been different approaches available at about the same time (cf. Kohler (2009) or Glasserman (2004), ch. 8) we focus on the LSM because of its simplicity and popularity in practice. The LSM estimator for an option's value is known to be low biased with almost no means of judging *how much* too low it is in a practical situation.

We therefore also discuss a dual approach to American options pricing by MCS which leads to a high biased estimator. Taken together, the two approaches provide an interval in which the true option value lies. This is illustrated in this chapter by two examples: a typical American put option and a Short Condor Spread with non-convex payoff. The self-contained Python scripts accompanying this chapter allow experimentation with different parametrizations and the numerical analysis of the performance of the algorithms.

7.6 PYTHON SCRIPTS

7.6.1 Binomial Valuation

```python
#
# Valuation of American Options
# with the Cox-Ross-Rubinstein Model
# Primal Algorithm
# Case 1: American Put Option (APO)
# Case 2: Short Condor Spread (SCS)
# 07_amo/CRR_american_options.py
#
# (c) Dr. Yves J. Hilpisch
# Derivatives Analytics with Python
#
import math
import numpy as np

# General Parameters and Option Values
def set_parameters(otype, M):
    ''' Sets parameters depending on valuation case.

    Parameters
    ==========
    otype: int
        option type
        1 = American put option
        2 = Short Condor Spread
    '''
    if otype == 1:
        # Parameters -- American Put Option
        S0 = 36.  # initial stock level
        T = 1.0  # time-to-maturity
        r = 0.06  # short rate
        sigma = 0.2  # volatility

    elif otype == 2:
        # Parameters -- Short Condor Spread
        S0 = 100.  # initial stock level
        T = 1.0  # time-to-maturity
        r = 0.05  # short rate
        sigma = 0.5  # volatility

    else:
        raise ValueError('Option type not known.')

    # Numerical Parameters
```

```python
    dt = T / M  # time interval
    df = math.exp(-r * dt)  # discount factor
    u = math.exp(sigma * math.sqrt(dt))  # up-movement
    d = 1 / u  # down-movement
    q = (math.exp(r * dt) - d) / (u - d)  # martingale probability

    return S0, T, r, sigma, M, dt, df, u, d, q


def inner_value(S, otype):
    ''' Inner value functions for American put option and short condor spread
    option with American exercise.

    Parameters
    ==========
    otype: int
        option type
        1 = American put option
        2 = Short Condor Spread
    '''
    if otype == 1:
        return np.maximum(40. - S, 0)
    elif otype == 2:
        return np.minimum(40., np.maximum(90. - S, 0)
                        + np.maximum(S - 110., 0))
    else:
        raise ValueError('Option type not known.')


def CRR_option_valuation(otype, M=500):
    S0, T, r, sigma, M, dt, df, u, d, q = set_parameters(otype, M)
    # Array Generation for Stock Prices
    mu = np.arange(M + 1)
    mu = np.resize(mu, (M + 1, M + 1))
    md = np.transpose(mu)
    mu = u ** (mu - md)
    md = d ** md
    S = S0 * mu * md

    # Valuation by Backwards Induction
    h = inner_value(S, otype)  # innver value matrix
    V = inner_value(S, otype)  # value matrix
    C = np.zeros((M + 1, M + 1), dtype=np.float)  # continuation values
    ex = np.zeros((M + 1, M + 1), dtype=np.float)  # exercise matrix

    z = 0
    for i in range(M - 1, -1, -1):
```

```
        C[0:M - z, i] = (q * V[0:M - z, i + 1]
                      + (1 - q) * V[1:M - z + 1, i + 1]) * df
        V[0:M - z, i] = np.where(h[0:M - z, i] > C[0:M - z, i],
                      h[0:M - z, i], C[0:M - z, i])
        ex[0:M - z, i] = np.where(h[0:M - z, i] > C[0:M - z, i], 1, 0)
        z += 1
    return V[0, 0]
```

7.6.2 Monte Carlo Valuation with LSM

```
#
# Valuation of American Options
# with Least-Squares Monte Carlo
# Primal Algorithm
# American Put Option
# 07_amo/LSM_primal_valuation.py
#
# (c) Dr. Yves J. Hilpisch
# Derivatives Analytics with Python
#
import math
import numpy as np
np.random.seed(150000)

# Model Parameters
S0 = 36.  # initial stock level
K = 40.  # strike price
T = 1.0  # time-to-maturity
r = 0.06  # short rate
sigma = 0.2  # volatility

# Simulation Parameters
I = 25000
M = 50
dt = T / M
df = math.exp(-r * dt)

# Stock Price Paths
S = S0 * np.exp(np.cumsum((r - 0.5 * sigma ** 2) * dt
    + sigma * math.sqrt(dt) * np.random.standard_normal((M + 1, I)), axis=0))
S[0] = S0

# Inner Values
h = np.maximum(K - S, 0)

# Present Value Vector (Initialization)
V = h[-1]
```

```
# American Option Valuation by Backwards Induction
for t in xrange(M - 1, 0, -1):
    rg = np.polyfit(S[t], V * df, 5)
    C = np.polyval(rg, S[t])  # continuation values
    V = np.where(h[t] > C, h[t], V * df)
      # exercise decision
V0 = df * np.sum(V) / I  # LSM estimator

print "American put option value %5.3f" % V0
```

7.6.3 Primal and Dual LSM Algorithms

```
#
# Valuation of American Options
# with Least-Squares Monte Carlo
# Primal and Dual Algorithm
# Case 1: American Put Option (APO)
# Case 2: Short Condor Spread (SCS)
# 07_amo/LSM_primal_dual_valuation.py
#
# (c) Dr. Yves J. Hilpisch
# Derivatives Analytics with Python
#
import math
import numpy as np
import pandas as pd
from time import time
from datetime import datetime
import itertools as it
import warnings
warnings.simplefilter('ignore')

t0 = time()
np.random.seed(150000)  # seed for Python RNG

## Simulation Parameters
runs = 5
write = True
otype = [1, 2]  # option type
M = [10, 20]  # time steps
I1 = np.array([4, 6]) * 4096  # replications for regression
I2 = np.array([1, 2]) * 1024  # replications for valuation
J = [50, 75]  # replications for nested MCS
reg = [5, 9]  # no of basis functions
AP = [False, True]  # antithetic paths
MM = [False, True]  # moment matching of RN
ITM = [True, False]  # ITM paths for regression
```

```
results = pd.DataFrame()


#
# Function Definitions
#


def generate_random_numbers(I):
    ''' Function to generate I pseudo-random numbers. '''
    if AP:
            ran = np.random.standard_normal(I / 2)
            ran = np.concatenate((ran, -ran))
    else:
            ran = np.random.standard_normal(I)
    if MM:
        ran = ran - np.mean(ran)
        ran = ran / np.std(ran)
    return ran


def generate_paths(I):
    ''' Function to generate I stock price paths. '''
    S = np.zeros((M + 1, I), dtype=np.float)  # stock matrix
    S[0] = S0  # initial values
    for t in range(1, M + 1, 1):  # stock price paths
        ran = generate_random_numbers(I)
        S[t] = S[t - 1] * np.exp((r - sigma ** 2 / 2) * dt
                            + sigma * ran * math.sqrt(dt))
    return S


def inner_values(S):
    ''' Innver value functions for American put and Short Condor Spread. '''
    if otype == 1:
        return np.maximum(40. - S, 0)
    else:
        return np.minimum(40., np.maximum(90. - S, 0)
                            + np.maximum(S - 110., 0))


def nested_monte_carlo(St, J):
    ''' Function for nested Monte Carlo simulation.

    Parameters
    ==========
    St: float
        start value for S
    J:  int
        number of paths to simulate
```

```
    Returns
    =======
    paths : array
        simulated nested paths
    '''
    ran = generate_random_numbers(J)
    paths = St * np.exp((r - sigma ** 2 / 2) * dt
                        + sigma * ran * math.sqrt(dt))
    return paths


#
# Valuation
#
para = it.product(otype, M, I1, I2, J, reg, AP, MM, ITM)
count = 0
for pa in para:
    otype, M, I1, I2, J, reg, AP, MM, ITM = pa
    ## General Parameters and Option Values
    if otype == 1:
        ## Parameters -- American Put Option
        S0 = 36.  # initial stock level
        T = 1.0  # time-to-maturity
        r = 0.06  # short rate
        sigma = 0.2  # volatility
        V0_true = 4.48637  # American Put Option (500 steps bin. model)
    else:
        ## Parameters -- Short Condor Spread
        S0 = 100.  # initial stock level
        T = 1.0  # time-to-maturity
        r = 0.05  # short rate
        sigma = 0.5  # volatility
        V0_true = 26.97705  # Short Condor Spread (500 steps bin. model)
    dt = T / M  # length of time interval
    df = math.exp(-r * dt)  # discount factor per time interval
    for j in range(runs):
        count += 1
        # regression estimation
        S = generate_paths(I1)  # generate stock price paths
        h = inner_values(S)  # inner values
        V = inner_values(S)  # value matrix
        rg = np.zeros((M + 1, reg + 1), dtype=np.float)
            # regression parameter matrix

        itm = np.greater(h, 0)  # ITM paths
        for t in xrange(M - 1, 0, -1):
            if ITM:
                S_itm = np.compress(itm[t] == 1, S[t])
                V_itm = np.compress(itm[t] == 1, V[t + 1])
                if len(V_itm) == 0:
```

```
                rg[t] = 0.0
        else:
                rg[t] = np.polyfit(S_itm, V_itm * df, reg)
        else:
            rg[t] = np.polyfit(S[t], V[t + 1] * df, reg)
                # regression at time t
        C = np.polyval(rg[t], S[t])  # continuation values
        V[t] = np.where(h[t] > C, h[t], V[t + 1] * df)
            # exercise decision


## Simulation
Q = np.zeros((M + 1, I2), dtype=np.float)  # martingale matrix
U = np.zeros((M + 1, I2), dtype=np.float)  # upper bound matrix
S = generate_paths(I2)  # generate stock price paths
h = inner_values(S)  # inner values
V = inner_values(S)  # value matrix


## Primal Valuation
for t in xrange(M - 1, 0, -1):
    C = np.polyval(rg[t], S[t])  # continuation values
    V[t] = np.where(h[t] > C, h[t], V[t + 1] * df)
        # exercise decision
V0 = df * np.sum(V[1]) / I2  # LSM estimator


## Dual Valuation
for t in xrange(1, M + 1):
    for i in xrange(I2):
        Vt = max(h[t, i], np.polyval(rg[t], S[t, i]))
        # estimated value V(t,i)
        St = nested_monte_carlo(S[t - 1, i], J)  # nested MCS
        Ct = np.polyval(rg[t], St)  # cv from nested MCS
        ht = inner_values(St)  # iv from nested MCS
        VtJ = np.sum(np.where(ht > Ct, ht, Ct)) / len(St)
            # average of V(t,i,j)
        Q[t, i] = Q[t - 1, i] / df + (Vt - VtJ)  # "optimal" martingale
        U[t, i] = max(U[t - 1, i] / df, h[t, i] - Q[t, i])
            # high estimator values
        if t == M:
            U[t, i] = np.maximum(U[t - 1, i] / df,
                                 np.mean(ht) - Q[t, i])
U0 = np.sum(U[M]) / I2 * df ** M  # DUAL estimator
AV = (V0 + U0) / 2  # average of LSM and DUAL estimator


# output
print "%4d | %4.1f | %48s " % (count, (time() - t0) / 60, pa), \
        "| %6.3f | %6.3f | %6.3f" % (V0, U0, AV)
# results storage
results = results.append(pd.DataFrame({'otype': otype, 'runs': runs,
    'M': M, 'I1': I1, 'I2': I2, 'J': J, 'reg': reg, 'AP': AP,
```

```
                'MM': MM, 'ITM': ITM, 'LSM': V0, 'LSM_se': (V0 - V0_true) ** 2,
                'DUAL': U0, 'DUAL_se': (U0 - V0_true) ** 2, 'AV': AV,
                'AV_se': (AV - V0_true) ** 2}, index=[0,]), ignore_index=True)

t1 = time()
print "Total time in min %s" % ((t1 - t0) / 60)

if write:
    h5 = pd.HDFStore('results_%s_%s.h5' % (datetime.now().date(),
                                str(datetime.now().time())[:8]), 'w')
    h5['results'] = results
    h5.close()
```

Market-Based Valuation

Three

## CHAPTER 8

A First Example of Market-Based Valuation

8.1 INTRODUCTION

This chapter takes a hands-on approach and dives into a market-based valuation without paying too much attention to the theoretical and numerical foundations. It addresses all main steps of such a valuation: market modeling, European call valuation via Fourier techniques, calibration of a market model to European call option quotes and simulation of the calibrated model.

The exposition might seem a bit bumpy. However, all aspects are addressed and are made somewhat more precise later in this part of the book. Those with some background knowledge will find in this first example and the accompanying Python scripts a kind of sandbox in which first steps in other directions can be taken.

Section 8.2 introduces the market model. Section 8.3 addresses valuation via Fourier-based approaches. Section 8.4 calibrates the model to real market data. Finally, section 8.5 simulates the calibrated model and values a European call option by simulation.

8.2 MARKET MODEL

We consider the jump-diffusion model $\mathcal{M}^{M76}$ of Merton (cf. Merton (1976), M76) as already sketched out in section 6.6. The plan is to completely implement this specific model numerically and technically. The time horizon T is fixed, $0 < T < \infty$. In this continuous market model, the index level has risk-neutral dynamics of the form

$$dS_t = (r - r_J)S_t dt + \sigma S_t dZ_t + J_t S_t dN_t \tag{8.1}$$

The variables and parameters are defined as follows:

- S_t index level at date t
- r constant risk-less short rate
- $r_J \equiv \lambda \cdot (e^{\mu_J + \delta^2/2} - 1)$ drift correction for jump
- σ constant volatility of S
- Z_t standard Brownian motion

- J_t jump at date t with ...
  - ... distribution $\log(1 + J_t) \approx \mathbf{N}(\log(1 + \mu_J) - \frac{\delta^2}{2}, \delta^2)$ ...
  - ... and $\mathbf{N}$ as the cumulative distribution function of a standard normal random variable
- N_t Poisson process with intensity λ

At this moment, a full understanding of the details is not necessary.[1] It suffices to understand that these dynamics model a process with "generally" continuous paths which can jump at certain unforeseeable dates.

8.3 VALUATION

Applying Fourier techniques, one can value European call options in this model in semi-analytic form—a prerequisite for which is knowledge of the characteristic function for the stock price dynamics (8.1) in log terms. This is a well-known function of the form

$$\varphi_0^{M76}(u, T) = \exp\left(\left(iu\omega - \frac{u^2\sigma^2}{2} + \lambda(e^{iu\mu_J - u^2\delta^2/2} - 1)\right)T\right) \tag{8.2}$$

where the risk-neutral drift term ω takes on the form

$$\omega = r - \frac{\sigma^2}{2} - \lambda(e^{\mu_J + \delta^2/2} - 1) \tag{8.3}$$

This function may be found, for instance, in Gatheral (2006), pp. 57–58, where one has to include the non-zero short rate.

To value European call options in this model, we can apply both approaches introduced in Chapter 6. Sub-section 8.7.1 contains a Python script implementing the following valuation formula, which is due to Lewis (cf. Lewis (2001)), for the M76 setup and evaluating it via numerical integration.

$$C_0 = S_0 - \frac{\sqrt{S_0 K} e^{-rT/2}}{\pi} \int_0^\infty \mathbf{Re}\left[e^{izk}\varphi_0^{M76}(z - i/2, T)\right] \frac{dz}{z^2 + 1/4}$$

The value of a European call option on the index with strike K and maturity T is according to the Fourier-based approach of Carr-Madan (cf. Carr and Madan (1999)) given by

$$C_0 = \frac{e^{-\alpha k}}{\pi} \int_0^\infty e^{-ivk} \frac{e^{-rT} \varphi_0^{M76}(v - (\alpha + 1)i, T)}{\alpha^2 + \alpha - v^2 + i(2\alpha + 1)v} dv$$

with $k = \log K$. This integral has a form that allows the application of FFT. Sub-section 8.7.2 provides a Python script that implements FFT for the M76 model. For both approaches refer to section 6.4 for further details and derivations.

---

[1]Tankov and Voltchkova (2009) is a concise survey of jump-diffusion models and related techniques. Cont and Tankov (2004a) is a comprehensive textbook on this topic.

8.4 CALIBRATION

In simple terms, the—unfortunately ill-posed[2]—problem of *calibration* is to find parameters for the M76 model such that observed market quotes of liquidly traded plain vanilla options are replicated as closely as possible. To this end, one defines an error function that is to be minimized. Such a function could be the Root Mean Squared Error (RMSE). The task is then to solve the problem

$$\min_{\sigma, \lambda, \mu_J, \delta} \sqrt{\frac{1}{N} \sum_{n=1}^{N} \left(C_n^* - C_n^{M76}(\sigma, \lambda, \mu_J, \delta) \right)^2} \tag{8.4}$$

with the C_n^* being the market or input prices and the C_n^{M76} being the model or output prices for the options $n = 1, \dots, N$.

To gain a first impression of the calibration procedure, Appendix 8.7.3 provides a Python script that calibrates the M76 model to prices of European call options on the EURO STOXX 50 index from the Eurex in Frankfurt. All prices are from 30. September 2014. The script uses both *global* minimization in the form of a brute force algorithm and *local* minimization algorithm. The idea is first to roughly scan the error surface and then to dig deeper locally where it seems most promising. These two steps may be necessary since it cannot be excluded that there are multiple local minima in which a local minimization algorithm could be trapped.[3]

Figure 8.1 shows the result of a minimization run. It is obvious that the M76 model is not capable of perfectly replicating observed market quotes. The degrees of freedom are not sufficient to simultaneously accommodate both the different maturities and the different strike levels. This is a first hint at the fact that a realistic financial market model must be richer than M76.[4]

However, inspection of Figure 8.2 reveals that calibration of M76 to a small subset of the market quotes—i.e. to the market quotes for the shortest maturity options only—yields pretty good results. Appendix 8.7.4 contains the respective Python script which again combines global with local minimization. This script also uses the FFT approach. In fact, the role of the jump feature of the general market model will be to better replicate observed *short-term* option prices around the *at-the-money* strike level (while stochastic volatility is needed for longer maturities). In this calibration the final RMSE is about 0.17 only.

8.5 SIMULATION

To value a European call option with strike price K by MCS consider the simple discretization of the continuous time dynamics (8.1)

$$S_t = S_{t-\Delta t} \left(1 + (r - r_J)\Delta t + \sigma \sqrt{\Delta t} z_t^1 + (e^{\mu_J + \delta z_t^2} - 1)y_t \right) \tag{8.5}$$

---

[2]Galluccio and Le Cam (2008) discuss this aspect at considerable length. See also Chapter 11.
[3]Note that the error function definition in the calibration scripts includes a penalty routine which penalizes negative values for those parameters that are (economically) not allowed to become negative.
[4]Tankov and Voltchkova (2009) draw similar conclusions on the basis of another numerical example.

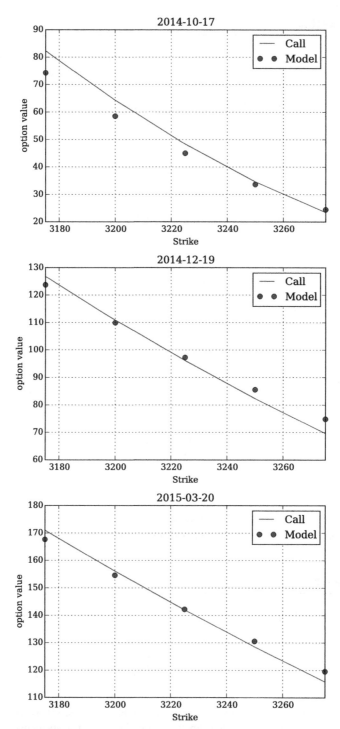

FIGURE 8.1   Results of the calibration of Merton's
jump-diffusion model to market quotes for three maturities; lines =
market quotes, dots = model prices

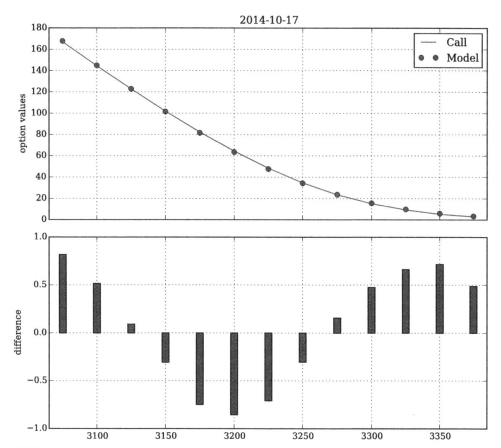

FIGURE 8.2 Results of the calibration of Merton's jump-diffusion model to a small subset of market quotes (i.e. a single maturity only; here: shortest maturity); line = market quotes, dots = model prices, bars = difference between model values and market quotes

with the z_t^n being standard normally distributed and the y_t being Poisson distributed with intensity λ.

An alternative discretization with generally better convergence properties is based on the log dynamics and takes the form

$$S_t = S_{t-\Delta t} \left(e^{(r-r_J - \sigma^2/2)\Delta t + \sigma \sqrt{\Delta t} z_t^1} + (e^{\mu_J + \delta z_t^2} - 1)y_t \right) \qquad (8.6)$$

To arrive at a value estimate for a European call option use Algorithm 3.

Appendix 8.7.5 provides a Python script that implements Algorithm 3 with both discretization alternatives (8.5) and (8.6). The script uses the optimal parameters (rounded) from the calibration to the short maturity option quotes. In addition, the script contains a routine to numerically compare the three valuation approaches for varying moneyness levels of the call option.

The values derived from the different approaches are shown in Figure 8.3. Although the figure suggests that all valuation results are equal, there are minor differences between the

---

Algorithm 3: Valuation Algorithm for Merton (1976)

---

1 Divide the time interval $[0, T]$ into equidistant sub-intervals of length Δt

for $t = 0, \Delta t, \dots, T$ **do**

    for $i = 1, \dots, I$ **do**

        if $t = 0$ **then**

2   Set $S_{t,i} = S_0$

        else

3   Draw standard normally distributed pseudo-random numbers $z_{t,i}^1, z_{t,i}^2$ and a Poission distributed pseudo-random number $y_{t,i}$

4   Simulate the index level value $S_{t,i}$ given $S_{t-\Delta t,i}$ and $z_{t,i}$ according to (8.5) or (8.6)

            if $t = T$ **then**

5   Determine the inner value $h_{T,i}$ of the call option at T as

$$h_{T,i}(S_T(i)) = \max[S_T(i) - K, 0]$$

6   Sum up the inner values, average and discount them back with the risk-less short rate:

$$C_0 \approx e^{-rT} \frac{1}{I} \sum_I h_T(S_T(i)) \tag{8.7}$$

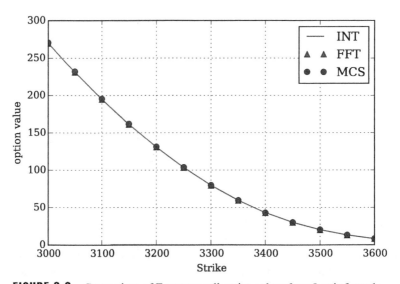

FIGURE 8.3 Comparison of European call option values from Lewis formula (line), from Carr-Madan formula (triangles) and Monte Carlo simulation (dots)

MCS estimates and the theoretical values according to the Lewis and Carr-Madan approaches. The detailed results are:

```
CALL STRIKE          3000.000
-------------------------
Call Value by Int     269.749
Call Value by FFT     269.733
Difference FFT/Int     -0.016
Call Value by MCS     270.503
Difference MCS/Int      0.754
-------------------------
CALL STRIKE          3050.000
-------------------------
Call Value by Int     231.142
Call Value by FFT     231.118
Difference FFT/Int     -0.025
Call Value by MCS     231.827
Difference MCS/Int      0.685
-------------------------
CALL STRIKE          3100.000
-------------------------
Call Value by Int     194.905
Call Value by FFT     194.890
Difference FFT/Int     -0.015
Call Value by MCS     195.531
Difference MCS/Int      0.625
-------------------------
CALL STRIKE          3150.000
-------------------------
Call Value by Int     161.340
Call Value by FFT     161.346
Difference FFT/Int      0.006
Call Value by MCS     161.905
Difference MCS/Int      0.565
-------------------------
CALL STRIKE          3200.000
-------------------------
Call Value by Int     130.761
Call Value by FFT     130.785
Difference FFT/Int      0.024
Call Value by MCS     131.247
Difference MCS/Int      0.486
-------------------------
CALL STRIKE          3250.000
-------------------------
Call Value by Int     103.466
Call Value by FFT     103.492
```

```
45 | Difference FFT/Int      0.026
46 | Call Value by MCS     103.823
47 | Difference MCS/Int      0.357
48 | -------------------------
49 | CALL STRIKE          3300.000
50 | -------------------------
51 | Call Value by Int      79.695
52 | Call Value by FFT      79.705
53 | Difference FFT/Int      0.010
54 | Call Value by MCS      79.906
55 | Difference MCS/Int      0.211
56 | -------------------------
57 | CALL STRIKE          3350.000
58 | -------------------------
59 | Call Value by Int      59.578
60 | Call Value by FFT      59.565
61 | Difference FFT/Int     -0.013
62 | Call Value by MCS      59.677
63 | Difference MCS/Int      0.099
64 | -------------------------
65 | CALL STRIKE          3400.000
66 | -------------------------
67 | Call Value by Int      43.104
68 | Call Value by FFT      43.076
69 | Difference FFT/Int     -0.028
70 | Call Value by MCS      43.161
71 | Difference MCS/Int      0.057
72 | -------------------------
73 | CALL STRIKE          3450.000
74 | -------------------------
75 | Call Value by Int      30.097
76 | Call Value by FFT      30.071
77 | Difference FFT/Int     -0.026
78 | Call Value by MCS      30.133
79 | Difference MCS/Int      0.036
80 | -------------------------
81 | CALL STRIKE          3500.000
82 | -------------------------
83 | Call Value by Int      20.232
84 | Call Value by FFT      20.224
85 | Difference FFT/Int     -0.008
86 | Call Value by MCS      20.288
87 | Difference MCS/Int      0.056
88 | -------------------------
89 | CALL STRIKE          3550.000
90 | -------------------------
91 | Call Value by Int      13.069
```

```
 92 │ Call Value by FFT      13.083
 93 │ Difference FFT/Int      0.015
 94 │ Call Value by MCS      13.161
 95 │ Difference MCS/Int      0.093
 96 │ --------------------------
 97 │ CALL STRIKE          3600.000
 98 │ --------------------------
 99 │ Call Value by Int       8.104
100 │ Call Value by FFT       8.132
101 │ Difference FFT/Int      0.028
102 │ Call Value by MCS       8.210
103 │ Difference MCS/Int      0.106
104 │ --------------------------
```

8.6 CONCLUSIONS

This chapter illustrates market-based valuation in the context of Merton's jump-diffusion model. In particular, the chapter provides:

1. **model**: a market model adding a jump component to the BSM setup
2. **vanilla valuation**: application of the Fourier-based option pricing approaches of Lewis and Carr-Madan to the market model
3. **calibration**: calibration of the model to a number of real market quotes; this is possible due to the inclusion of a jump component offering more degrees of freedom compared to BSM
4. **simulation**: discretization of the model and simulation of it for the purpose of getting European option values

These building blocks are the typical prerequisites for a market-based valuation of more complex derivatives. Subsequent chapters address all related aspects in more detail.

8.7 PYTHON SCRIPTS

8.7.1 Valuation by Numerical Integration

```
#
# Valuation of European Call Options
# in Merton's (1976) Jump Diffusion Model
# via Numerical Integration
# 08_m76/M76_valuation_INT.py
#
# (c) Dr. Yves J. Hilpisch
# Derivatives Analytics with Python
#
```

```
import math
import numpy as np
from scipy.integrate import quad

#
# Model Parameters
#
S0 = 100.0  # initial index level
K = 100.0  # strike level
T = 1.0  # call option maturity
r = 0.05  # constant short rate
sigma = 0.4  # constant volatility of diffusion
lamb = 1.0  # jump frequency p.a.
mu = -0.2  # expected jump size
delta = 0.1  # jump size volatility

#
# Valuation by Integration
#


def M76_value_call_INT(S0, K, T, r, sigma, lamb, mu, delta):
    ''' Valuation of European call option in M76 model via
    Lewis (2001) Fourier-based approach.

    Parameters
    ==========
    S0: float
        initial stock/index level
    K: float
        strike price
    T: float
        time-to-maturity (for t=0)
    r: float
        constant risk-free short rate
    sigma: float
        volatility factor in diffusion term
    lamb: float
        jump intensity
    mu: float
        expected jump size
    delta: float
        standard deviation of jump

    Returns
    =======
    call_value: float
```

```
            European call option present value
    '''
    int_value = quad(lambda u: M76_integration_function(u, S0, K, T, r,
                  sigma, lamb, mu, delta), 0, 50, limit=250)[0]
    call_value = S0 - np.exp(-r * T) * math.sqrt(S0 * K) / math.pi * int_value
    return call_value


def M76_integration_function(u, S0, K, T, r, sigma, lamb, mu, delta):
    ''' Valuation of European call option in M76 model via
    Lewis (2001) Fourier-based approach: integration function.

    Parameter definitions see function M76_value_call_INT. '''
    JDCF = M76_characteristic_function(u - 0.5 * 1j, T, r,
                            sigma, lamb, mu, delta)
    value = 1 / (u ** 2 + 0.25) * (np.exp(1j * u * math.log(S0 / K))
                        * JDCF).real
    return value


def M76_characteristic_function(u, T, r, sigma, lamb, mu, delta):
    ''' Valuation of European call option in M76 model via
    Lewis (2001) Fourier-based approach: characteristic function.

    Parameter definitions see function M76_value_call_INT. '''
    omega = r - 0.5 * sigma ** 2 - lamb * (np.exp(mu + 0.5 * delta ** 2) - 1)
    value = np.exp((1j * u * omega - 0.5 * u ** 2 * sigma ** 2 +
            lamb * (np.exp(1j * u * mu - u ** 2 * delta ** 2 * 0.5) - 1))  * T)
    return value

if __name__ == '__main__':
    print "Value of Call Option %8.3f" \
            % M76_value_call_INT(S0, K, T, r, sigma, lamb, mu, delta)
```

8.7.2 Valuation by FFT

```
#
# Valuation of European Call Options
# in Merton's (1976) Jump Diffusion Model
# via Fast Fourier Transform (FFT)
# 08_m76/M76_valuation_FFT.py
#
# (c) Dr. Yves J. Hilpisch
# Derivatives Analytics with Python
#
```

```python
import math
import numpy as np
from numpy.fft import *


#
# Model Parameters
#
S0 = 100.0  # initial index level
K = 100.0  # strike level
T = 1.0  # call option maturity
r = 0.05  # constant short rate
sigma = 0.4  # constant volatility of diffusion
lamb = 1.0  # jump frequency p.a.
mu = -0.2  # expected jump size
delta = 0.1  # jump size volatility


#
# M76 Characteristic Function
#


def M76_characteristic_function(u, x0, T, r, sigma, lamb, mu, delta):
    ''' Valuation of European call option in M76 model via
    Lewis (2001) Fourier-based approach: characteristic function.

    Parameter definitions see function M76_value_call_FFT. '''
    omega = x0 / T + r - 0.5 * sigma ** 2 \
                - lamb * (np.exp(mu + 0.5 * delta ** 2) - 1)
    value = np.exp((1j * u * omega - 0.5 * u ** 2 * sigma ** 2 +
            lamb * (np.exp(1j * u * mu - u ** 2 * delta ** 2 * 0.5) - 1))  * T)
    return value


#
# Valuation by FFT
#


def M76_value_call_FFT(S0, K, T, r, sigma, lamb, mu, delta):
    ''' Valuation of European call option in M76 model via
    Carr-Madan (1999) Fourier-based approach.

    Parameters
    ==========
    S0: float
        initial stock/index level
    K: float
        strike price
    T: float
```

```
        time-to-maturity (for t=0)
r: float
    constant risk-free short rate
sigma: float
    volatility factor in diffusion term
lamb: float
    jump intensity
mu: float
    expected jump size
delta: float
    standard deviation of jump

Returns
=======
call_value: float
    European call option present value
'''
k = math.log(K / S0)
x0 = math.log(S0 / S0)
g = 2  # factor to increase accuracy
N = g * 4096
eps = (g * 150.) ** -1
eta = 2 * math.pi / (N * eps)
b = 0.5 * N * eps - k
u = np.arange(1, N + 1, 1)
vo = eta * (u - 1)
# Modificatons to Ensure Integrability
if S0 >= 0.95 * K:  # ITM case
    alpha = 1.5
    v = vo - (alpha + 1) * 1j
    mod_char_fun = math.exp(-r * T) * M76_characteristic_function(
                        v, x0, T, r, sigma, lamb, mu, delta) \
            / (alpha ** 2 + alpha - vo ** 2 + 1j * (2 * alpha + 1) * vo)
else:  # OTM case
    alpha = 1.1
    v = (vo - 1j * alpha) - 1j
    mod_char_fun_1 = math.exp(-r * T) * (1 / (1 + 1j * (vo - 1j * alpha))
                        - math.exp(r * T) / (1j * (vo - 1j * alpha))
                        - M76_characteristic_function(
                            v, x0, T, r, sigma, lamb, mu, delta)
            / ((vo - 1j * alpha) ** 2 - 1j * (vo - 1j * alpha)))
    v = (vo + 1j * alpha) - 1j
    mod_char_fun_2 = math.exp(-r * T) * (1 / (1 + 1j * (vo + 1j * alpha))
                        - math.exp(r * T) / (1j * (vo + 1j * alpha))
                        - M76_characteristic_function(
                            v, x0, T, r, sigma, lamb, mu, delta)
            / ((vo + 1j * alpha) ** 2 - 1j * (vo + 1j * alpha)))
```

```python
    # Numerical FFT Routine
    delt = np.zeros(N, dtype=np.float)
    delt[0] = 1
    j = np.arange(1, N + 1, 1)
    SimpsonW = (3 + (-1) ** j - delt) / 3
    if S0 >= 0.95 * K:
        fft_func = np.exp(1j * b * vo) * mod_char_fun * eta * SimpsonW
        payoff = (fft(fft_func)).real
        call_value_m = np.exp(-alpha * k) / math.pi * payoff
    else:
        fft_func = (np.exp(1j * b * vo)
                    * (mod_char_fun_1 - mod_char_fun_2)
                    * 0.5 * eta * SimpsonW)
        payoff = (fft(fft_func)).real
        call_value_m = payoff / (np.sinh(alpha * k) * math.pi)
    pos = int((k + b) / eps)
    call_value = call_value_m[pos]
    return call_value * S0

if __name__ == '__main__':
    print "Value of Call Option %8.3f" \
        % M76_value_call_FFT(S0, K, T, r, sigma, lamb, mu, delta)
```

8.7.3 Calibration to Three Maturities

```python
#
# Calibration of Merton's (1976)
# Jump Diffusion Model
# via Fast Fourier Transform
# 08_m76/M76_calibration_FFT.py
#
# (c) Dr. Yves J. Hilpisch
# Derivatives Analytics with Python
#
import math
import numpy as np
np.set_printoptions(suppress=True,
                    formatter={'all': lambda x: '%5.3f' % x})
import pandas as pd
import scipy.optimize as sop
import matplotlib.pyplot as plt
import matplotlib as mpl
mpl.rcParams['font.family'] = 'serif'
from M76_valuation_FFT import M76_value_call_FFT
```

```
#
# Market Data from www.eurexchange.com
# as of 30. September 2014
#
h5 = pd.HDFStore('08_m76/option_data.h5', 'r')
data = h5['data']  # European call & put option data (3 maturities)
h5.close()
S0 = 3225.93  # EURO STOXX 50 level
r = 0.0005  # ECB base rate


# Option Selection
tol = 0.02
options = data[(np.abs(data['Strike'] - S0) / S0) < tol]


#
# Error Function
#


def M76_error_function_FFT(p0):
    ''' Error Function for parameter calibration in M76 Model via
    Carr-Madan (1999) FFT approach.

    Parameters
    ==========
    sigma: float
        volatility factor in diffusion term
    lamb: float
        jump intensity
    mu: float
        expected jump size
    delta: float
        standard deviation of jump

    Returns
    =======
    RMSE: float
        root mean squared error
    '''
    global i, min_RMSE
    sigma, lamb, mu, delta = p0
    if sigma < 0.0 or delta < 0.0 or lamb < 0.0:
        return 500.0
    se = []
    for row, option in options.iterrows():
        T = (option['Maturity'] - option['Date']).days / 365.
```

```python
        model_value = M76_value_call_FFT(S0, option['Strike'], T,
                                          r, sigma, lamb, mu, delta)
        se.append((model_value - option['Call']) ** 2)
    RMSE = math.sqrt(sum(se) / len(se))
    min_RMSE = min(min_RMSE, RMSE)
    if i % 50 == 0:
        print '%4d |' % i, np.array(p0), '| %7.3f | %7.3f' % (RMSE, min_RMSE)
    i += 1
    return RMSE


def generate_plot(opt, options):
    #
    # Calculating Model Prices
    #
    sigma, lamb, mu, delta = opt
    options['Model'] = 0.0
    for row, option in options.iterrows():
        T = (option['Maturity'] - option['Date']).days / 365.
        options.loc[row, 'Model'] = M76_value_call_FFT(S0, option['Strike'],
                                    T, r, sigma, lamb, mu, delta)

    #
    # Plotting
    #
    mats = sorted(set(options['Maturity']))
    options = options.set_index('Strike')
    for i, mat in enumerate(mats):
        options[options['Maturity'] == mat][['Call', 'Model']].\
                plot(style=['b-', 'ro'], title='%s' % str(mat)[:10])
        plt.ylabel('option value')
        plt.savefig('../images/08_m76/M76_calibration_3_%s.pdf' % i)


if __name__ == '__main__':
    #
    # Calibration
    #
    i = 0  # counter initialization
    min_RMSE = 100  # minimal RMSE initialization
    p0 = sop.brute(M76_error_function_FFT, ((0.075, 0.201, 0.025),
                    (0.10, 0.401, 0.1), (-0.5, 0.01, 0.1),
                    (0.10, 0.301, 0.1)), finish=None)

    # p0 = [0.15, 0.2, -0.3, 0.2]
    opt = sop.fmin(M76_error_function_FFT, p0,
                    maxiter=500, maxfun=750,
                    xtol=0.000001, ftol=0.000001)
```

8.7.4 Calibration to Short Maturity

```
#
# Calibration of Merton's (1976)
# Jump Diffusion Model
# to Short Maturity Data
# 08_m76/M76_calibration_single.py
#
# (c) Dr. Yves J. Hilpisch
# Derivatives Analytics with Python
#
import math
import numpy as np
np.set_printoptions(suppress=True,
                    formatter={'all': lambda x: '%5.3f' % x})
import pandas as pd
import scipy.optimize as sop
import matplotlib.pyplot as plt
import matplotlib as mpl
mpl.rcParams['font.family'] = 'serif'
from M76_valuation_FFT import M76_value_call_FFT


#
# Market Data from www.eurexchange.com
# as of 30. September 2014
#
h5 = pd.HDFStore('08_m76/option_data.h5', 'r')
data = h5['data']  # European call & put option data (3 maturities)
h5.close()
S0 = 3225.93  # EURO STOXX 50 level
r = 0.005  # assumption

# Option Selection
tol = 0.05
options = data[(np.abs(data['Strike'] - S0) / S0) < tol]
mats = sorted(set(options['Maturity']))
options = options[options['Maturity'] == mats[0]]

#
# Error Function
#


def M76_error_function_FFT(p0):
    ''' Error function for parameter calibration in M76 Model via
    Carr-Madan (1999) FFT approach.
```

```
    Parameters
    ==========
    sigma: float
        volatility factor in diffusion term
    lamb: float
        jump intensity
    mu: float
        expected jump size
    delta: float
        standard deviation of jump

    Returns
    =======
    RMSE: float
        root mean squared error
    '''
    global i, min_RMSE
    sigma, lamb, mu, delta = p0
    if sigma < 0.0 or delta < 0.0 or lamb < 0.0:
        return 500.0
    se = []
    for row, option in options.iterrows():
        T = (option['Maturity'] - option['Date']).days / 365.
        model_value = M76_value_call_FFT(S0, option['Strike'], T,
                                    r, sigma, lamb, mu, delta)
        se.append((model_value - option['Call']) ** 2)
    RMSE = math.sqrt(sum(se) / len(se))
    min_RMSE = min(min_RMSE, RMSE)
    if i % 50 == 0:
        print '%4d |' % i, np.array(p0), '| %7.3f | %7.3f' % (RMSE, min_RMSE)
    i += 1
    return RMSE


#
# Graphical Output
#
def generate_plot(opt, options):
    #
    # Calculating Model Prices
    #
    sigma, lamb, mu, delta = opt
    options['Model'] = 0.0
    for row, option in options.iterrows():
        T = (option['Maturity'] - option['Date']).days / 365.
        options.loc[row, 'Model'] = M76_value_call_FFT(S0, option['Strike'],
                                T, r, sigma, lamb, mu, delta)
```

```
#
# Plotting
#
options = options.set_index('Strike')
fig, ax = plt.subplots(2, sharex=True, figsize=(8, 7))
options[['Call', 'Model']].plot(style=['b-', 'ro'],
            title='%s' % str(option['Maturity'])[:10], ax=ax[0])
ax[0].set_ylabel('option values')
xv = options.index.values
ax[1] = plt.bar(xv - 5 / 2., options['Model'] - options['Call'],
            width=5)
plt.ylabel('difference')
plt.xlim(min(xv) - 10, max(xv) + 10)
plt.tight_layout()
plt.grid()


#
# Calibration
#
if __name__ == '__main__':
    i = 0
    min_RMSE = 100.
    p0 = sop.brute(M76_error_function_FFT, ((0.10, 0.201, 0.025),
                (0.1, 0.8, 0.1), (-0.4, 0.01, 0.1),
                (0.00, 0.121, 0.02)), finish=None)

    opt = sop.fmin(M76_error_function_FFT, p0, xtol=0.00001,
                ftol=0.00001, maxiter=750, maxfun=1500)
```

8.7.5 Valuation by MCS

```
#
# Valuation of European Call Options
# in Merton's (1976) Jump Diffusion Model
# via Monte Carlo Simulation
# 08_m76/M76_valuation_MCS.py
#
# (c) Dr. Yves J. Hilpisch
# Derivatives Analytics with Python
#
import math
import numpy as np
import pandas as pd
```

```python
from M76_valuation_FFT import M76_value_call_FFT
from M76_valuation_INT import M76_value_call_INT

#
# Model Parameters (from Calibration)
#
S0 = 3225.93  # EURO STOXX 50 level (30.09.2014)
T = 0.22  # shortest maturity
r = 0.005  # assumption

sigma, lamb, mu, delta = [0.113, 3.559, -0.075, 0.041]
  # from calibration


#
# Valuation by Simulation
#
seed = 100000  # seed value
M = 50  # time steps
I = 200000  # paths
disc = 2  # 1 = simple Euler; else = log Euler


def M76_generate_paths(S0, T, r, sigma, lamb, mu, delta, M, I):
    ''' Generate Monte Carlo Paths for M76 Model.
    Parameters
    ==========
    S0: float
        initial stock/index level
    K: float
        strike price
    T: float
        time-to-maturity (for t=0)
    r: float
        constant risk-free short rate
    sigma: float
        volatility factor in diffusion term
    lamb: float
        jump intensity
    mu: float
        expected jump size
    delta: float
        standard deviation of jump
    M: int
        number of time intervals
    I: int
        number of paths
```

```
    Returns
    =======
    S: array
        simulated paths
    '''
    dt = T / M
    rj = lamb * (math.exp(mu + 0.5 * delta ** 2) - 1)
    shape = (M + 1, I)
    S = np.zeros((M + 1, I), dtype=np.float)
    S[0] = S0

    np.random.seed(10000)
    rand1 = np.random.standard_normal(shape)
    rand2 = np.random.standard_normal(shape)
    rand3 = np.random.poisson(lamb * dt, shape)

    for t in xrange(1, M + 1, 1):
        if disc == 1:
            S[t] = S[t - 1] * ((1 + (r - rj) * dt) + sigma
                            * math.sqrt(dt) * rand1[t]
                            + (np.exp(mu + delta * rand2[t]) - 1)
                            * rand3[t])
        else:
            S[t] = S[t - 1] * (np.exp((r - rj - 0.5 * sigma ** 2) * dt
                            + sigma * math.sqrt(dt) * rand1[t])
                            + (np.exp(mu + delta * rand2[t]) - 1)
                            * rand3[t])
    return S

def M76_value_call_MCS(K):
    ''' Function to calculate the MCS estimator given K.

    Parameters
    ==========
    K: float
        strike price

    Returns
    =======
    call_mcs: float
        European call option Monte Carlo estimator
    '''
    return math.exp(-r * T) * np.sum(np.maximum(S[-1] - K, 0)) / I


if __name__ == '__main__':
```

```python
# Single Valuation
S = M76_generate_paths(S0, T, r, sigma, lamb, mu, delta, M, I)
print "Value of Call Option %8.3f" % M76_value_call_MCS(S0)

# Value Comparisons
strikes = np.arange(3000, 3601, 50)
values = np.zeros((3, len(strikes)), dtype=np.float)
z = 0
for k in strikes:
    print "CALL STRIKE        %10.3f" % k
    print "---------------------------"
    values[0, z] = M76_value_call_INT(S0, k, T, r, sigma,
                                      lamb, mu, delta)
    print "Call Value by Int %10.3f" % values[0, z]

    values[1, z] = M76_value_call_FFT(S0, k, T, r, sigma,
                                      lamb, mu, delta)
    print "Call Value by FFT %10.3f" % values[1, z]
    print "Difference FFT/Int%10.3f" % (values[1, z] - values[0, z])
    values[2, z] = M76_value_call_MCS(k)
    print "Call Value by MCS %10.3f" % values[2, z]
    print "Difference MCS/Int%10.3f" % (values[2, z] - values[0, z])
    print "---------------------------"
    z = z + 1

results = pd.DataFrame(values.T, index=strikes, columns=[
                                'INT', 'FFT', 'MCS'])
results.index.name = 'Strike'
```

## CHAPTER 9

General Model Framework

9.1 INTRODUCTION

Chapter 8 conducts a model calibration and market-based valuation with the jump-diffusion model of Merton (1976). The calibration effort reveals that a jump component alone is not capable of replicating a typical volatility surface. It is rather necessary to include at least a stochastic volatility component (as already pointed out in Chapter 3). In addition, we also need a stochastic short rate component to accommodate stylized facts of interest rate markets.

This chapter therefore introduces in section 9.2 the model framework of Bakshi, Cao and Chen (1997, BCC97, Bakshi et al. (1997)) that includes as special cases a number of popular financial models, like the Black-Scholes-Merton model. Section 9.3 briefly recaps the main statistical features a realistic market model should exhibit. That section also cites a number of empirical findings regarding the performance of the framework under different parametrizations. Section 9.5 then concerns itself with the valuation of European options in the general framework—a necessary prerequisite for an efficient calibration procedure.

9.2 THE FRAMEWORK

Given is a filtered probability space $(\Omega, \mathcal{F}, \mathbb{F}, P)$ representing uncertainty in the model economy $\mathcal{M}^{BCC97}$ with final date T where $0 < T < \infty$. Ω denotes the continuous state space, $\mathcal{F}$ a σ-algebra, $\mathbb{F}$ a filtration and P the real or objective probability measure. Traded securities are a risky stock index S and a risky unit zero-coupon bond B.

Together, we have the continuous market model

$$\mathcal{M}^{BCC97} = \{(\Omega, \mathcal{F}, \mathbb{F}, P), T, (S, B)\}$$

More specifically, the market model of Bakshi-Cao-Chen is characterized by stochastic volatility, jump risk and stochastic short rates. The risk-neutral dynamics of the stock index S are according to the stochastic volatility jump-diffusion model of Bates (1996, B96)

$$dS_t = (r_t - r_J)S_t dt + \sqrt{v_t}S_t dZ_t^1 + J_t S_t dN_t \tag{9.1}$$

$$dv_t = \kappa_v(\theta_v - v_t)dt + \sigma_v \sqrt{v_t}dZ_t^2 \tag{9.2}$$

The meanings of the variables and parameters are

- S_t index level at date t
- r_t risk-less short rate at date t
- $r_J \equiv \lambda \cdot (e^{\mu_J + \delta^2/2} - 1)$ drift correction for jump
- v_t variance at date t
- κ_v speed of adjustment of v_t to …
- … θ_v, the long-term average of the variance
- σ_v volatility coefficient of the index's variance
- Z_t^n standard Brownian motions
- N_t Poisson process with intensity λ
- J_t jump at date t with …
  - … distribution $\log(1 + J_t) \approx \mathbf{N}(\log(1 + \mu_J) - \frac{\delta^2}{2}, \delta^2)$ …
  - … and $\mathbf{N}$ as the cumulative distribution function of a standard normal random variable

Regarding the stochastic short rate, the model uses the setup of Cox, Ingersoll and Ross (1985, CIR85, Cox et al. (1985)) with the following dynamics for the short rate

$$dr_t = \kappa_r(\theta_r - r_t)dt + \sigma_r \sqrt{r_t}dZ_t^3 \tag{9.3}$$

The variables and the parameters of this square-root diffusion have, respectively, the meaning:

- r_t short rate at date t
- κ_r speed of adjustment of r_t to …
- … θ_r, the long-term average of the short rate
- σ_r volatility coefficient of the short rate
- Z_t^3 standard Brownian motion

All stochastic processes are adapted to the filtration $\mathbb{F}$. Moreover, instantaneous correlations are $dZ_t^1 dZ_t^2 \equiv \rho dt$, $dZ_t^1 dZ_t^3 \equiv dZ_t^2 dZ_t^3 \equiv 0$, N_t independent of Z_t^n, $n = 1, 2, 3$. The value of a zero-coupon bond paying one unit of currency at $T > t$ is

$$B_t(T) = \mathbf{E}_t^Q \left(\exp\left(-\int_t^T r_u du \right) \right)$$

with $\mathbf{E}$ being the expectation operator and Q a risk-neutral, P-equivalent probability measure which we assume to exist (i.e. we assume *no free lunches with vanishing risk* (NFLVR)). We define the set of uncertainties by $X_t \equiv (S_t, v_t, r_t)$—something needed occasionally.

9.3 FEATURES OF THE FRAMEWORK

A market model must, in order to be of any practical use, fulfill a minimum set of requirements.

- **statistical properties**: a fundamental requirement is that the model be able to replicate the most important statistical properties of the stock index and the interest rate to be modeled

- **price replication**: another important requirement is that a market model be able to replicate market prices from, for example, plain vanilla options like European puts and calls on indices and bonds or swaps
- **degrees of freedom**: from a formal perspective the market model has to offer sufficient degrees of freedom, i.e. parameters, to calibrate it to market prices or implied volatilities and the yield curve

Recall the results of Chapter 3. There it is shown that a realistic market model should ...

- ... take into account that index (implied) volatility
  - varies over time (stochasticity, mean reversion, clustering)
  - is negatively correlated with returns (leverage effect)
  - varies for different option strikes (volatility smile)
  - varies for different option maturities (volatility term structure)
- ... account for jumps in the index development
- ... take into account that interest rates
  - vary over time (positivity, stochasticity, mean reversion)
  - vary for different time horizons (term structure)

The general framework is capable, in principle, of fulfilling several or all of these requirements and of reproducing the statistical properties of stock indices sufficiently well. In a similar vein, it can also reproduce the most important characteristics of interest rates, like time-varying short rate or horizon-dependent yield (so-called yield curve). These statements will be substantiated in Chapter 11 where we will see that the general framework indeed reproduces the required statistical features sufficiently well. In addition, we will see that quotes from European call options will also be reproduced satisfactorily.

As a convenient fact, the framework of BCC97 encompasses as special cases the following widely applied option pricing models:

- **Black-Scholes-Merton (1973, BSM, Black and Scholes** (1973) **and Merton** (1973)): a model with geometric Brownian motion as the driving force and constant volatility as well as constant short rate (cf. Chapter 5)
- **Merton (1976, M76, Merton** (1976)): a model that enriches the model of BSM with a log-normally distributed jump component (cf. Chapter 8)
- **Heston (1993, H93, Heston** (1993)): one of the most popular models with stochastic volatility and constant short rate
- **Bates (1996, B96, Bates** (1996)) a model that adds a jump component to the stochastic volatility setting of H93

In addition, the general framework allows these special cases to be enriched by stochastic, instead of constant, short rates.

BCC97 conduct a number of empirical analyses for different parametrizations of their general model. Some major findings are:

- **quality of calibration**: "Our empirical evidence indicates that regardless of performance yardstick, taking stochastic volatility into account is of the first-order importance in improving upon the BS[M] formula."

- **quality of valuation**: "According to the out-of-sample pricing measures, adding the random jump feature to the [stochastic volatility] model can further improve its performance, especially in pricing short-term options; whereas modeling stochastic interest rates can enhance the fit of long-term options."
- **hedging performance**: "For hedging purposes, however, incorporating either the jump or the [stochastic interest rate] feature does not seem to improve the [stochastic volatility] model's performance further. The [stochastic volatility model] achieves the best hedging results among all the models studied, and its remaining hedging errors are generally quite small."[1]

As BCC97, p. 2009, point out, zero correlation between stock index and short rate might be counter-factual. However, when considering non-zero correlation they find no improvement upon the model with zero correlation:

"... when we implement this slightly more general model [with non-zero correlation], we find its pricing and hedging performance to be indistinguishable from that of the [stochastic volatility, stochastic interest rate] model studied in this article."

All in all, the framework of BCC97 seems well-suited to address the valuation and hedging of equity derivatives in an integrated manner. Fundamentally, it can be calibrated to observed market prices due to its sufficient degrees of freedom, it is capable of valuing derivative assets reasonably accurately and it provides hedging strategies that perform quite well. It also explicitly models all major market risks that affect equity derivatives, like index risk, volatility risk, jump risk and interest rate risk.

9.4 ZERO-COUPON BOND VALUATION

The discount factor $B_0(T)$ for discounting cash flows due at time T to time $t = 0$, i.e. the present value of a zero-coupon bond paying one unit of currency at T, in the CIR85 model takes the form (cf. Glasserman (2004), 128–129)

$$B_0(T) = b_1(T)e^{-b_2(T)r_0} \tag{9.4}$$

$$b_1(T) \equiv \left[\frac{2\gamma \exp((\kappa_r + \gamma)T/2)}{2\gamma + (\kappa_r + \gamma)(e^{\gamma T} - 1)} \right]^{\frac{2\kappa_r \theta_r}{\sigma_r^2}} \tag{9.5}$$

$$b_2(T) \equiv \frac{2(e^{\gamma T} - 1)}{2\gamma + (\kappa_r + \gamma)(e^{\gamma T} - 1)} \tag{9.6}$$

$$\gamma \equiv \sqrt{\kappa_r^2 + 2\sigma_r^2} \tag{9.7}$$

---

[1] All quotes from Bakshi et al. (1997), pp. 2042–2043.

The Python script of sub-section 9.7.2 implements formulas (9.4)–(9.7) for use in the European option valuation that follows.

9.5 EUROPEAN OPTION VALUATION

This section analyzes the valuation of European (call) options in the general framework. Three approaches are considered:

- **PDE method**: the traditional approach to derivative asset valuation is to solve a partial differential equation (PDE) that a derivative asset must satisfy given the dynamics of the underlying; this approach is sketched in Chapter 5 for the BSM model
- **Fourier-based pricing**: via Fourier transforms it is possible to derive for a number of models (semi-)analytical pricing formulas, i.e. integrals, for certain derivative assets, like European call options; Chapter 6 analyzes this approach in some detail
- **Monte Carlo simulation**: via discretizing the relevant risk-neutral processes and using (quasi- or pseudo-)random numbers one can generate random process evolutions and thereby values for the derivative asset under consideration at maturity or exercise; iterating sufficiently often, discounting the single option values at maturity or exercise back and averaging over all discounted option values then yields an estimate of the option value; Chapters 7 and 8 use this method

The valuation formulas obtained by the PDE approach or the transform method may then be evaluated via numerical integration or Fast Fourier Transform (FFT). However, no matter what valuation approach or numerical method is used, the general principle is that of *no arbitrage* pricing, which Chapter 4 explores comprehensively.

The PDE approach is quite powerful in addressing general valuation and hedging issues while the transform method is particularly appropriate for certain models and payoff structures. The advantage of the latter is, however, the form of the resulting (semi-)analytical valuation formulas that typically allow for fast numerical solutions. Monte Carlo simulation is most flexible in terms of models, payoff structures and other features (e.g. early exercise)—but generally also the slowest and least accurate alternative. For practical purposes, one therefore uses a mix of these approaches. When calibrating models to plain vanilla options, transforms are generally the method of choice. When valuing complex products with, for example, multiple underlyings, Asian or American features, Monte Carlo simulation often is the only practical choice.

Translated to the context of this book, the formulas from the transform method for plain vanilla options are used for calibration purposes while Monte Carlo simulation (based on the already calibrated model) yields numerical values for more complex equity derivatives.

9.5.1 PDE Approach

Omitting time indices, the value of a European call option on the stock index must satisfy—according to Itô's lemma (see section 9.7.1) and given the general market model—the PDE as reported in the following proposition.

Proposition 8 (BCC97 PDE). *A European call option $C(S, v, r, t)$ must satisfy in the general market model the PDE*

$$\frac{1}{2}vS^2\frac{\partial^2 C}{\partial S} + [r - r_J]S\frac{\partial C}{\partial S} + \rho\sigma_v vS\frac{\partial^2 C}{\partial S\partial v} +$$

$$+\frac{1}{2}\sigma_v^2\frac{\partial^2 C}{\partial v^2} + \kappa_v[\theta_v - v]\frac{\partial C}{\partial v} +$$

$$+\frac{1}{2}\sigma_r^2\frac{\partial^2 C}{\partial r^2} + \kappa_r[\theta_r - r]\frac{\partial C}{\partial r} + \frac{\partial C}{\partial t} - rC +$$

$$+\lambda\mathbf{E}^Q[C(K, T; (1 + J)S, v, r, t) - C(K, T; S, v, r, t_-)] = 0 \tag{9.8}$$

with suitable boundary conditions and in particular $C_T(S_T, K) = \max[S_T - K, 0]$ as the inner value of the call option at maturity T.

Proof. Consider a contingent claim $A(S, v, r, t)$ and apply proposition 9 to it

$$dA(S, v, r, t) = \frac{\partial A}{\partial S}(mdt + vdZ^1 + jdN) + \frac{\partial A}{\partial v}(\overline{m}dt + \overline{v}dZ^2)$$

$$+ \frac{\partial A}{\partial r}(\underline{m}dt + \underline{v}dZ^3) + \frac{\partial^2 A}{\partial S\partial v}v\overline{v}\rho dt$$

$$+ \frac{1}{2}\left(\frac{\partial^2 A}{\partial S^2}v^2 + \frac{\partial^2 A}{\partial v^2}\overline{v}^2 + \frac{\partial^2 A}{\partial r^2}\underline{v}^2 + \frac{\partial A}{\partial t}\right)dt$$

$$= \left(\frac{\partial A}{\partial S}m + \frac{\partial A}{\partial v}\overline{m} + \frac{\partial A}{\partial r}\underline{m} + \frac{1}{2}\frac{\partial^2 A}{\partial S^2}v^2\right.$$

$$+ \frac{1}{2}\frac{\partial^2 A}{\partial v^2}\overline{v}^2 + \frac{1}{2}\frac{\partial^2 A}{\partial r^2}\underline{v}^2 + \frac{\partial^2 A}{\partial S\partial v}v\overline{v}\rho + \frac{\partial A}{\partial t}\Bigg)dt$$

$$+ \frac{\partial A}{\partial S}vdZ^1 + \frac{\partial A}{\partial v}\overline{v}dZ^2 + \frac{\partial A}{\partial r}\underline{v}dZ^3$$

Next, replace drift, volatility and jump terms by their counterparts from BCC97 (omitting time subscripts)

$$m = (r - r_J)S$$
$$\overline{m} = \kappa_v(\theta_v - v)$$
$$\underline{m} = \kappa_r(\theta_r - r)$$
$$v = \sqrt{v}S$$
$$\overline{v} = \sigma_v\sqrt{v}$$
$$\underline{v} = \sigma_r\sqrt{r}$$
$$j = JS$$

The PDE (9.8) follows from taking expectation $\mathbf{E}^Q(dA)$ under the risk-neutral probability measure Q of the incremental change of the derivative asset's value

$$
\begin{aligned}
\mathbf{E}^{Q}(dA(S, v, r, t)) = \Bigg(&\frac{\partial A}{\partial S}(r - r_J)S + \lambda \mathbf{E}^{Q}(A((1 + J)S, t) - A(S, t_-)) \\
&+ \frac{\partial A}{\partial v}\kappa_v(\theta_v - v) + \frac{\partial A}{\partial r}\kappa_r(\theta_r - r) \\
&+ \frac{1}{2}\frac{\partial^2 A}{\partial S^2}vS^2 + \frac{1}{2}\frac{\partial^2 A}{\partial v^2}\sigma_v^2 v + \frac{1}{2}\frac{\partial^2 A}{\partial r^2}\sigma_r^2 r \\
&+ \frac{\partial^2 A}{\partial S \partial v}\sigma_v vS\rho + \frac{\partial A}{\partial t}\Bigg) dt
\end{aligned}
$$

and noting that under risk-neutrality $\mathbf{E}^{Q}(dA) = rAdt$ must hold. Dividing by dt, replacing A by C for the European call option and rearranging yields the PDE (9.8). □

A solution to the central equation (9.8) is

$$
C_t(K, T) = S_t \cdot \Pi_1(T; S, v, r, t) - B_t(T) \cdot K \cdot \Pi_2(T; S, v, r, t) \tag{9.9}
$$

where for $j = 1, 2$

$$
\Pi_j(T; S, v, r, t) = \frac{1}{2} + \frac{1}{\pi} \int_0^{\infty} \mathbf{Re}\left[\frac{e^{-iu \log(K)}\varphi_j(T; S, v, r, t; u)}{iu} \right] du
$$

The φ_j are characteristic functions as defined in the appendix of BCC97 and $\mathbf{Re}[x]$ gives the real part of x. In what follows, formula (9.9) plays essentially no role. It is nevertheless given here for reasons of completeness and its resemblance to the famous BSM formula—which is remarkable since the model of BCC97 is much richer.

9.5.2 Transform Methods

The key to the application of the Fourier transform methods of Lewis (2001) and Carr and Madan (1999) is knowledge of the characteristic function of the stochastic processes governing the evolution of the underlying. Chapter 8 illustrates this for the jump-diffusion model of M76 whose jump part is also a component of the general framework. However, the basic processes are those of H93.

The characteristic function φ_0^{H93} of the H93 stochastic volatility model is given by (cf. Heston (1993) or Gatheral (2006), ch. 2)

$$
\varphi_0^{H93}(u, T) = e^{H_1(u,T) + H_2(u,T)v_0} \tag{9.10}
$$

with the following definitions

$$
c_1 \equiv \kappa_v \theta_v
$$

$$
c_2 \equiv -\sqrt{(\rho \sigma_v ui - \kappa_v)^2 - \sigma_v^2(-ui - u^2)}
$$

$$
c_3 \equiv \frac{\kappa_v - \rho \sigma_v ui + c_2}{\kappa_v - \rho \sigma_v ui - c_2}
$$

$$H_1(u, T) \equiv r_{0,T}uiT + \frac{c_1}{\sigma_v^2}\left\{(\kappa_v - \rho\sigma_v ui + c_2)T - 2\log\left[\frac{1 - c_3 e^{c_2 T}}{1 - c_3}\right]\right\}$$

$$H_2(u, T) \equiv \frac{\kappa_v - \rho\sigma_v ui + c_2}{\sigma_v^2}\left[\frac{1 - e^{c_2 T}}{1 - c_3 e^{c_2 T}}\right]$$

and all variables as defined as before. In H_1 we set $r_{0,T} = -\log(B_0(T))/T$ where we get $B_0(T)$ from equations (9.4)–(9.7) for the CIR85 model.

For the M76 model we already know the characteristic function $\varphi_0^{M76}(u, T)$; see equations (6.14) and (6.15). These have to be adjusted since only the jump part (and not the diffusive part) is needed here:

$$\varphi_0^{M76J}(u, T) = \exp\left(\left(iu\omega + \lambda(e^{iu\mu_J - u^2\delta^2/2} - 1)\right)T\right) \tag{9.11}$$

where the risk-neutral drift term ω now takes the form

$$\omega = -\lambda(e^{\mu_J + \delta^2/2} - 1) \tag{9.12}$$

Due to zero correlation between the H93 index part and the index jump component, the characteristic function for the BCC97 model is obtained by simple multiplication as

$$\varphi_0^{BCC97}(u, T) = \varphi_0^{H93} \cdot \varphi_0^{M76J}(u, T) \tag{9.13}$$

Sub-section 9.7.3 provides a Python script that implements the Lewis formula (6.5) for the BCC97 model and the sub-models H93 and M76.

9.5.3 Monte Carlo Simulation

Monte Carlo simulation is a rather flexible valuation approach which is capable of much more than already seen in Chapters 7 and 8. It is applicable to almost any feature a financial product can exhibit: American and Bermudan exercise, Asian and lookback features (i.e. path dependency), multiple underlyings (i.e. a basket, for example) or simultaneous dependence on stock indices and interest rates (i.e. hybrid products). For a given financial model, Glasserman (2004), p. 30, gives the simplified recipe as replicated in Algorithm 4 for the risk-neutral valuation of a derivative asset with European exercise via Monte Carlo simulation.

Algorithm 4: General Monte Carlo Algorithm

---

1 replace the drift of the given dynamics (SDE) of the underlying with the risk-free short rate
2 discretize the risk-neutral continuous time dynamics to obtain difference equations in discrete time
3 simulate (sufficient) paths
4 determine the payoffs of the derivative asset for each path at maturity
5 discount the payoffs with the appropriate discount factor
6 calculate the average of the discounted payoffs over all paths

---

Subsequent chapters show how to apply this recipe to different parametrizations of the general framework. Previous chapters apply Monte Carlo simulation only to quite simple settings, i.e. BSM and M76, where exact discretizations are available in simple forms. However, as will become apparent, the simulation of the H93 model is a particularly tricky task with regard to the discretization step of Algorithm 4. Therefore, Chapter 10 devotes considerable attention to this topic. In that chapter, both European options and American options are valued for a number of different parametrizations for both the market model and the Monte Carlo simulation setup.

9.6 CONCLUSIONS

This chapter provides a general market model which is capable of addressing the major market risks affecting equity derivatives: index risk, volatility risk, jump risk and short rate risk. The following chapters will build on this foundation and will simulate the model, calibrate it and use it to value European and American options in a market-consistent manner. It will also be shown how to use numerical procedures to implement dynamic delta hedging strategies in this model.

9.7 PROOFS AND PYTHON SCRIPTS

9.7.1 Itô's Lemma

Proposition 9 (Itô's Lemma). *Let $f : \mathbb{R}^4 \to \mathbb{R}$ be a twice continuously differentiable function and S, v, r be (jump) diffusions*

$$dS_t = m_t dt + v_t dZ_t^1 + j_t dN_t \tag{9.14}$$

$$dv_t = \overline{m}_t dt + \overline{v}_t dZ_t^2 \tag{9.15}$$

$$dr_t = \underline{m}_t dt + \underline{v}_t dZ_t^3 \tag{9.16}$$

$$dZ_t^1 dZ_t^2 \equiv \rho dt$$

$$dZ_t^3 dZ_t^{n \neq 3} \equiv 0 \tag{9.17}$$

$$dN_t dZ_t^n \equiv 0 \tag{9.18}$$

with Z^n standard Brownian motions and N a Poisson process. Then for $f(S, v, r, t)$ the marginal change in time is (omitting time subscripts)

$$
\begin{aligned}
df(S, v, r, t) = {} & \frac{\partial f}{\partial S} dS + \frac{\partial f}{\partial v} dv + \frac{\partial f}{\partial r} dr \\
& + \frac{1}{2} \left(\frac{\partial^2 f}{\partial S^2} v^2 + \frac{\partial^2 f}{\partial v^2} \overline{v}^2 + \frac{\partial^2 f}{\partial r^2} \underline{v}^2 + 2 \frac{\partial f}{\partial t} \right) dt \\
& + \frac{\partial^2 f}{\partial S \partial v} v \overline{v} \rho \, dt
\end{aligned}
\tag{9.19}
$$

Proof. First, a Taylor series expansion up to second order yields (suppressing dt^2 terms and other terms of equal or smaller order as well as accounting for the respective zero correlations (9.17) and (9.18))

$$
\begin{aligned}
df(S, v, r, t) = {} & \frac{\partial f}{\partial S}dS + \frac{\partial f}{\partial v}dv + \frac{\partial f}{\partial r}dr + \frac{\partial f}{\partial t}dt \\
& + \frac{1}{2}\left(\frac{\partial^2 f}{\partial S^2}dS^2 + \frac{\partial^2 f}{\partial v^2}dv^2 + \frac{\partial^2 f}{\partial r^2}dr^2\right) \\
& + \frac{1}{2}\left(\frac{\partial^2 f}{\partial S\partial v}dSdv + \frac{\partial^2 f}{\partial v\partial S}dvdS\right)
\end{aligned}
\tag{9.20}
$$

Second, the assumptions about f ensure that the mixed partial derivatives are the same. Third, it holds

$$
\begin{aligned}
dS^2 &= v^2 dt \\
dv^2 &= \bar{v}^2 dt \\
dr^2 &= \underline{v}^2 dt \\
dSdv &= v\bar{v}\rho dt
\end{aligned}
$$

Substituting these terms and (9.14)–(9.16) in (9.20) gives (9.19) after rearranging. See also Brandimarte (2006), pp. 97–102. □

9.7.2 Python Script for Bond Valuation

```
#
# Valuation of Zero-Coupon Bonds
# in Cox-Ingersoll-Ross (1985) Model
# 09_gmm/CIR_zcb_valuation.py
#
# (c) Dr. Yves J. Hilpisch
# Derivatives Analytics with Python
#
import math
import numpy as np


#
# Example Parameters CIR85 Model
#
kappa_r, theta_r, sigma_r, r0, T = 0.3, 0.04, 0.1, 0.04, 1.0


#
# Zero-Coupon Bond Valuation Formula
#
```

```
def gamma(kappa_r, sigma_r):
    ''' Help Function. '''
    return math.sqrt(kappa_r ** 2 + 2 * sigma_r ** 2)


def b1(alpha):
    ''' Help Function. '''
    kappa_r, theta_r, sigma_r, r0, T = alpha
    g = gamma(kappa_r, sigma_r)
    return (((2 * g * math.exp((kappa_r + g) * T / 2)) /
            (2 * g + (kappa_r + g) * (math.exp(g * T) - 1)))
            ** (2 * kappa_r * theta_r / sigma_r ** 2))


def b2(alpha):
    ''' Help Function. '''
    kappa_r, theta_r, sigma_r, r0, T = alpha
    g = gamma(kappa_r, sigma_r)
    return ((2 * (math.exp(g * T) - 1)) /
            (2 * g + (kappa_r + g) * (math.exp(g * T) - 1)))


def B(alpha):
    ''' Function to value unit zero-coupon bonds in Cox-Ingersoll-Ross (1985)
    model.

    Parameters
    ==========
    r0: float
        initial short rate
    kappa_r: float
        mean-reversion factor
    theta_r: float
        long-run mean of short rate
    sigma_r: float
        volatility of short rate
    T: float
        time horizon/interval

    Returns
    =======
    zcb_value: float
        zero-coupon bond present value
    '''
    b_1 = b1(alpha)
    b_2 = b2(alpha)
    kappa_r, theta_r, sigma_r, r0, T = alpha
    return b_1 * math.exp(-b_2 * r0)
```

```
if __name__ == '__main__':
    #
    # Example Valuation
    #
    B0T = B([kappa_r, theta_r, sigma_r, r0, T])
        # discount factor, ZCB value
    print "ZCB Value   %10.4f" % B0T
```

9.7.3   Python Script for European Call Valuation

```
#
# Valuation of European Call and Put Options
# Under Stochastic Volatility and Jumps
# 09_gmm/BCC_option_valuation.py
#
# (c) Dr. Yves J. Hilpisch
# Derivatives Analytics with Python
#
import numpy as np
from scipy.integrate import quad
from CIR_zcb_valuation import B
import warnings
warnings.simplefilter('ignore')

#
# Example Parameters B96 Model
#
## H93 Parameters
kappa_v = 1.5
theta_v = 0.02
sigma_v = 0.15
rho = 0.1
v0 = 0.01

## M76 Parameters
lamb = 0.25
mu = -0.2
delta = 0.1
sigma = np.sqrt(v0)

## General Parameters
S0 = 100.0
K = 100.0
T = 1.0
r = 0.05
```

```
#
# Valuation by Integration
#


def BCC_call_value(S0, K, T, r, kappa_v, theta_v, sigma_v, rho, v0,
                        lamb, mu, delta):
    ''' Valuation of European call option in B96 Model via Lewis (2001)
    Fourier-based approach.

    Parameters
    ==========
    S0: float
        initial stock/index level
    K: float
        strike price
    T: float
        time-to-maturity (for t=0)
    r: float
        constant risk-free short rate
    kappa_v: float
        mean-reversion factor
    theta_v: float
        long-run mean of variance
    sigma_v: float
        volatility of variance
    rho: float
        correlation between variance and stock/index level
    v0: float
        initial level of variance
    lamb: float
        jump intensity
    mu: float
        expected jump size
    delta: float
        standard deviation of jump

    Returns
    =======
    call_value: float
        present value of European call option

    '''
    int_value = quad(lambda u: BCC_int_func(u, S0, K, T, r, kappa_v, theta_v,
                    sigma_v, rho, v0, lamb, mu, delta), 0, np.inf, limit=250)[0]
    call_value = max(0, S0 - np.exp(-r * T) * np.sqrt(S0 * K)
                            / np.pi * int_value)
    return call_value
```

```python
def H93_call_value(S0, K, T, r, kappa_v, theta_v, sigma_v, rho, v0):
    ''' Valuation of European call option in H93 model via Lewis (2001)
    Fourier-based approach.

    Parameters
    ==========
    S0: float
        initial stock/index level
    K: float
        strike price
    T: float
        time-to-maturity (for t=0)
    r: float
        constant risk-free short rate
    kappa_v: float
        mean-reversion factor
    theta_v: float
        long-run mean of variance
    sigma_v: float
        volatility of variance
    rho: float
        correlation between variance and stock/index level
    v0: float
        initial level of variance

    Returns
    =======
    call_value: float
        present value of European call option

    '''
    int_value = quad(lambda u: H93_int_func(u, S0, K, T, r, kappa_v,
                        theta_v, sigma_v, rho, v0), 0, np.inf, limit=250)[0]
    call_value = max(0, S0 - np.exp(-r * T) * np.sqrt(S0 * K)
                        / np.pi * int_value)
    return call_value


def M76_call_value(S0, K, T, r, v0, lamb, mu, delta):
    ''' Valuation of European call option in M76 model via Lewis (2001)
    Fourier-based approach.

    Parameters
    ==========
    S0: float
        initial stock/index level
    K: float
        strike price
```

```
    T: float
        time-to-maturity (for t=0)
    r: float
        constant risk-free short rate
    lamb: float
        jump intensity
    mu: float
        expected jump size
    delta: float
        standard deviation of jump

    Returns
    =======
    call_value: float
        present value of European call option
    '''
    sigma = np.sqrt(v0)
    int_value = quad(lambda u: M76_int_func_sa(u, S0, K, T, r,
                        sigma, lamb, mu, delta), 0, np.inf, limit=250)[0]
    call_value = max(0, S0 - np.exp(-r * T) * np.sqrt(S0 * K)
                        / np.pi * int_value)
    return call_value


#
# Integration Functions
#


def BCC_int_func(u, S0, K, T, r, kappa_v, theta_v, sigma_v, rho, v0,
                        lamb, mu, delta):
    ''' Valuation of European call option in BCC97 model via Lewis (2001)
    Fourier-based approach: integration function.

    Parameter definitions see function BCC_call_value.'''
    char_func_value = BCC_char_func(u - 1j * 0.5, T, r, kappa_v, theta_v,
                        sigma_v, rho, v0, lamb, mu, delta)
    int_func_value = 1 / (u ** 2 + 0.25) \
            * (np.exp(1j * u * np.log(S0 / K)) * char_func_value).real
    return int_func_value


def H93_int_func(u, S0, K, T, r, kappa_v, theta_v, sigma_v, rho, v0):
    ''' Valuation of European call option in H93 model via Lewis (2001)
    Fourier-based approach: integration function.

    Parameter definitions see function H93_call_value.'''
```

```python
    char_func_value = H93_char_func(u - 1j * 0.5, T, r, kappa_v,
                                    theta_v, sigma_v, rho, v0)
    int_func_value = 1 / (u ** 2 + 0.25) \
            * (np.exp(1j * u * np.log(S0 / K)) * char_func_value).real
    return int_func_value


def M76_int_func_sa(u, S0, K, T, r, sigma, lamb, mu, delta):
    ''' Valuation of European call option in M76 model via Lewis (2001)
    Fourier-based approach: integration function.

    Parameter definitions see function M76_call_value.'''
    char_func_value = M76_char_func_sa(u - 0.5 * 1j, T, r, sigma,
                                    lamb, mu, delta)
    int_func_value = 1 / (u ** 2 + 0.25) \
            * (np.exp(1j * u * np.log(S0 / K)) * char_func_value).real
    return int_func_value

#
# Characteristic Functions
#


def BCC_char_func(u, T, r, kappa_v, theta_v, sigma_v, rho, v0,
                  lamb, mu, delta):
    ''' Valuation of European call option in BCC97 model via Lewis (2001)
    Fourier-based approach: characteristic function.

    Parameter definitions see function BCC_call_value.'''
    BCC1 = H93_char_func(u, T, r, kappa_v, theta_v, sigma_v, rho, v0)
    BCC2 = M76_char_func(u, T, lamb, mu, delta)
    return BCC1 * BCC2


def H93_char_func(u, T, r, kappa_v, theta_v, sigma_v, rho, v0):
    ''' Valuation of European call option in H93 model via Lewis (2001)
    Fourier-based approach: characteristic function.

    Parameter definitions see function BCC_call_value.'''
    c1 = kappa_v * theta_v
    c2 = -np.sqrt((rho * sigma_v * u * 1j - kappa_v)
            ** 2 - sigma_v ** 2 * (-u * 1j - u ** 2))
    c3 = (kappa_v - rho * sigma_v * u * 1j + c2) \
            / (kappa_v - rho * sigma_v * u * 1j - c2)
    H1 = (r * u * 1j * T + (c1 / sigma_v ** 2)
            * ((kappa_v - rho * sigma_v * u * 1j + c2) * T
                - 2 * np.log((1 - c3 * np.exp(c2 * T)) / (1 - c3))))
```

```
        H2 = ((kappa_v - rho * sigma_v * u * 1j + c2) / sigma_v ** 2
                * ((1 - np.exp(c2 * T)) / (1 - c3 * np.exp(c2 * T)))))
        char_func_value = np.exp(H1 + H2 * v0)
        return char_func_value


def M76_char_func(u, T, lamb, mu, delta):
    ''' Valuation of European call option in M76 model via Lewis (2001)
    Fourier-based approach: characteristic function.

    Parameter definitions see function M76_call_value.'''
    omega = -lamb * (np.exp(mu + 0.5 * delta ** 2) - 1)
    char_func_value = np.exp((1j * u * omega + lamb
                * (np.exp(1j * u * mu - u ** 2 * delta ** 2 * 0.5) - 1)) * T)
    return char_func_value


def M76_char_func_sa(u, T, r, sigma, lamb, mu, delta):
    ''' Valuation of European call option in M76 model via Lewis (2001)
    Fourier-based approach: characteristic function "jump component".

    Parameter definitions see function M76_call_value.'''
    omega = r - 0.5 * sigma ** 2 - lamb * (np.exp(mu + 0.5 * delta ** 2) - 1)
    char_func_value = np.exp((1j * u * omega - 0.5 * u ** 2 * sigma ** 2
                    + lamb * (np.exp(1j * u * mu - u ** 2 * delta ** 2 * 0.5)
                        - 1)) * T)
    return char_func_value


if __name__ == '__main__':
    #
    # Example Parameters CIR85 Model
    #
    kappa_r, theta_r, sigma_r, r0, T = 0.3, 0.04, 0.1, 0.04, T
    B0T = B([kappa_r, theta_r, sigma_r, r0, T])  # discount factor
    r = -np.log(B0T) / T


    #
    # Example Values
    #
    print "M76 Value   %10.4f" \
        % M76_call_value(S0, K, T, r, v0, lamb, mu, delta)
    print "H93 Value   %10.4f" \
        % H93_call_value(S0, K, T, r, kappa_v, theta_v, sigma_v, rho, v0)
    print "BCC97 Value %10.4f" \
        % BCC_call_value(S0, K, T, r, kappa_v, theta_v,
                            sigma_v, rho, v0, lamb, mu, delta)
```

## CHAPTER 10

Monte Carlo Simulation

10.1 INTRODUCTION

Monte Carlo simulation is among the most important numerical algorithms of the 20th century (cf. Cipra (2000)) and obviously will remain so in the 21st century as well. Its importance for financial applications stems from the fact that it is most flexible in terms of financial products that can be valued. First applied to European option pricing in 1977 by Phelim Boyle (cf. Boyle (1977)), it took until the 21st century for the problem of valuing American options by Monte Carlo simulation to be satisfactorily solved by Francis Longstaff and Eduardo Schwartz (cf. Longstaff and Schwartz (2001)) and others (cf. Chapter 7). Glasserman (2004) provides a comprehensive introduction to Monte Carlo methods for financial engineering and is a standard reference. Kohler (2009) is a survey article of regression-based valuation approaches for American options.

Although quite flexible, Monte Carlo simulation is generally not very fast (relative to alternative approaches) since millions of computations are necessary to value a single option. Consider a simulation run with 100 time intervals (=100 exercise dates) and 100,000 paths for an American put option on a single stock with constant volatility and constant short rate. You need 10 million random numbers, several arrays (i.e. matrices) of size 101 times 100,000 and you have to estimate 100 least-squares regressions over 100,000 pairs of numbers as well as discounting 100 times 100,000 numbers. If you enrich the financial model to include, for example, stochastic volatility and stochastic interest rates the number of necessary calculations further increases substantially.

For practical purposes, it is important to have available efficient, i.e. accurate and fast, algorithms to value options and other derivatives by Monte Carlo simulation. This chapter therefore analyzes in detail the simulation of financial models of type (9.1)–(9.3) as presented in the previous chapter. The simulation of equation (9.1) turns out be straightforward since an exact discretization is easily found. However, this is not the case for the two square-root diffusions (9.2) and (9.3).

The chapter proceeds as follows. Section 10.2 values zero-coupon bonds in the CIR85 model by Monte Carlo simulation. Here, we only need to consider a single square-root diffusion. Section 10.3 values European options by Monte Carlo simulation in the H93 stochastic volatility model with constant short rate and without jumps. Section 10.4 then adds stochastic short rates of CIR85 type to the H93 setting to value American put options by Monte Carlo simulation. Section 10.5 summarizes the major findings.

10.2 VALUATION OF ZERO-COUPON BONDS

In this section, we consider the stochastic short rate model $\mathcal{M}^{CIR85}$ of Cox-Ingersoll-Ross (cf. Cox et al. (1985)) which is given by the SDE (9.3). We repeat the SDE for convenience:

$$dr_t = \kappa_r(\theta_r - r_t)dt + \sigma_r\sqrt{r_t}dZ_t$$

To simulate the short rate model, it has to be discretized. To this end, we again divide the given time interval $[0, T]$ in equidistant sub-intervals of length Δt such that now $t \in \{0, \Delta t, 2\Delta t, ..., T\}$, i.e. there are $M + 1$ points in time with $M \equiv T/\Delta t$.

The exact transition law of the square-root diffusion is known. The article by Broadie and Kaya (2006) provides an in-depth analysis of this topic. Consider the general square-root diffusion process

$$dx_t = \kappa(\theta - x_t)dt + \sigma\sqrt{x_t}dZ_t \tag{10.1}$$

In Broadie and Kaya (2006) it is shown that x_t, given x_s with $s = t - \Delta t$, is distributed according to

$$x_t = \frac{\sigma^2\left(1 - e^{-\kappa\Delta t}\right)}{4\kappa}\chi_d'^2\left(\frac{4\kappa e^{-\kappa\Delta t}}{\sigma^2(1 - e^{-\kappa\Delta t})}x_s\right)$$

where $\chi_d'^2$ denotes a non-central chi-squared distributed random variable with

$$d = \frac{4\theta\kappa}{\sigma^2}$$

degrees of freedom and non-centrality parameter

$$l = \frac{4\kappa e^{-\kappa\Delta t}}{\sigma^2(1 - e^{-\kappa\Delta t})}x_s$$

For implementation purposes, it may be convenient to sample a chi-squared distributed random variable χ_d^2 instead of a non-central chi-squared one, $\chi_d'^2$. If $d > 1$, the following relationship holds true

$$\chi_d'^2(l) = \left(z + \sqrt{l}\right)^2 + \chi_{d-1}^2$$

where z is an independent standard normally distributed random variable. Similarly, if $d \leq 1$, one has

$$\chi_d'^2(l) = \chi_{d+2N}^2$$

where N is now a Poisson-distributed random variable with intensity $l/2$. For an algorithmic representation of this simulation scheme refer to Glasserman (2004), p. 124.

The exactness comes with a relatively high computational burden which may, however, be justified by higher accuracy due to faster convergence. In other words, although the computational burden per simulated value of x_t may be relatively high with the exact scheme, the possible reduction in necessary time steps and simulation paths may more than compensate for this. However, Andersen, Jäckel and Kahl argue in Andersen et al. (2010)—referring to the exact simulation approach of Broadie and Kaya (2006)—that

> "One might think that the existence of an exact simulation-scheme ... would settle once and for all the question of how to generate paths of the square-root process...., it seems [nevertheless] reasonable to also investigate the application of simpler simulation algorithms. These will typically exhibit a bias for finite values of [M], but convenience and speed may more than compensate for this, ..."

We therefore also consider a Euler discretization of the square-root diffusion (10.1). A possible discretization is given by

$$\tilde{x}_t = \tilde{x}_s + \kappa(\theta - \max[0, \tilde{x}_s])\Delta t + \sigma\sqrt{\max[0, \tilde{x}_s]}\sqrt{\Delta t}z_t \qquad (10.2)$$

$$x_t = \max[0, \tilde{x}_s] \qquad (10.3)$$

with z_t standard normal (this scheme is usually called *Full Truncation*, see below). While x_t cannot reach zero with the exact scheme if the Feller condition $2\kappa\theta > \sigma^2$ is met, this is not the case with the Euler scheme. Therefore, the maximum function is applied several times.[1]

The plan now is as follows. We simulate the CIR85 model and derive Monte Carlo simulation estimates for Zero-Coupon Bond (ZCB) values at different points in time. Since we know these values in closed form in the CIR85 model, we have a natural benchmark to check the accuracy of the Monte Carlo simulation implementation. Chapter 9 presents the respective formula for the present value of the ZCB, i.e. for $t = 0$. Sub-section 10.6.1 contains a Python implementation which allows us to freely choose $0 < t \le T$. Two adjustments are made:

1. The final date T is replaced by time-to-maturity $T - t$
2. The initial rate r_0 is replaced by the expectation

$$\mathbf{E}(r_t) = \theta_r + e^{-\kappa_r t}(r_0 - \theta_r)$$

Figure 10.1 shows 20 simulated paths for the short rate process of CIR85 and for the example parameters of the Python script of sub-section 10.6.2. A Monte Carlo simulation estimator for the value of the ZCB at t is derived as follows. Consider a certain path i of the I simulated paths for the short rate process with time grid $t \in \{0, \Delta t, 2\Delta t, ..., T\}$. We discount

---

[1] There are number of alternative Euler schemes available which section 10.3 presents and compares with regard to their performance, i.e. accuracy and speed.

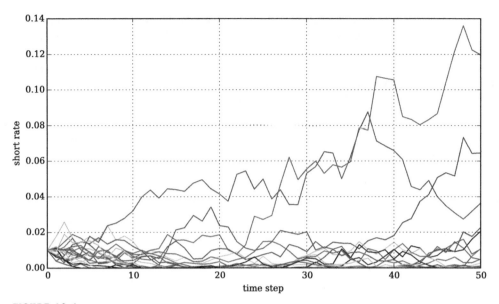

FIGURE 10.1   Twenty simulated paths for the CIR85 short rate process

the terminal value of the ZCB, i.e. 1.0, step by step backwards. For $t < T$ and $s \equiv t - \Delta t$ we have

$$B_{s,i} = B_{t,i} e^{-\frac{r_t + r_s}{2} \Delta t}$$

The Monte Carlo simulation estimator of the ZCB value at t then is

$$B_t^{MCS} = \frac{1}{I} \sum_{i=1}^{I} B_{t,i}$$

Figures 10.2 and 10.3 present valuation results for both the exact scheme and the Euler scheme compared, respectively, to the analytical values for a ZCB maturing at $T = 2$. The figures illustrate that with $M = 50$ time steps and $I = 50{,}000$ paths both schemes deliver Monte Carlo simulation estimates really close to the analytical values. However, the Euler scheme shows a systematically low bias in this particular case. The errors for the exact scheme are not only smaller but also negative as well as positive.

In terms of speed, the Euler scheme is indeed much faster. The generation of $I = 50{,}000$ sample paths with $M = 50$ time steps takes only about one-quarter of the time with the Euler scheme compared to the exact scheme. As a consequence, one could, for example, double the number of time steps to $M = 100$ to increase accuracy of the Euler scheme.

These numbers and comparisons are illustrative only. They are by no means a "proof" that the exact scheme easily outperforms a Euler scheme. The subsequent section revisits this issue in the context of the stochastic volatility model of H93—in this case we need to correlate the square-root diffusion with a second process which introduces a new problem area.

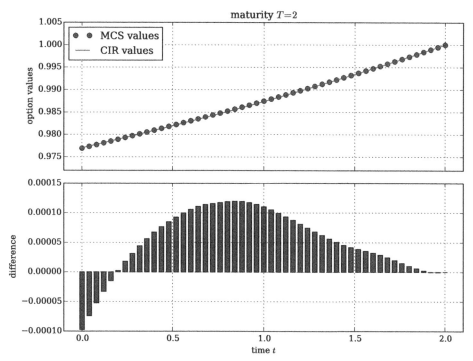

FIGURE 10.2 Values for a ZCB maturing at $T = 2$; line = analytical values, dots = Monte Carlo simulation estimates from the exact scheme for $M = 50$ and $I = 50,000$

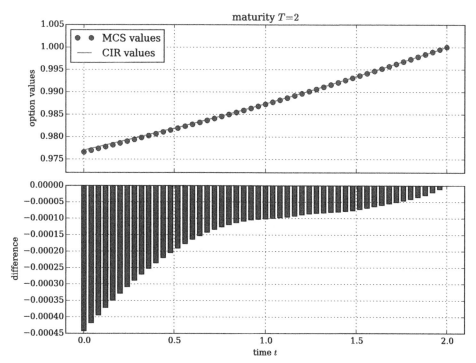

FIGURE 10.3 Values for a ZCB maturing at $T = 2$; line = analytical values, dots = Monte Carlo simulation estimates from the Euler scheme for $M = 50$ and $I = 50,000$

10.3 VALUATION OF EUROPEAN OPTIONS

As the next special case of the general framework $\mathcal{M}^{BCC97}$ with risk-neutral dynamics given by (9.1)–(9.3), we consider the H93 stochastic volatility model $\mathcal{M}^{H93}$ with constant short rate. This section values European call and put options in this model by Monte Carlo simulation. As for the ZCB values, we also have available a (semi-analytical) pricing formula which generates natural benchmark values against which to compare the Monte Carlo simulation estimates.

For $0 \leq t \leq T$, the risk-neutral dynamics of the index in the H93 stochastic volatility model are given by

$$dS_t = rS_t dt + \sqrt{v_t} S_t dZ_t^1 \tag{10.4}$$

with the variance following the square-root diffusion

$$dv_t = \kappa_v(\theta_v - v_t)dt + \sigma_v \sqrt{v_t} dZ_t^2 \tag{10.5}$$

The two Brownian motions are instantaneously correlated with $dZ_t^1 dZ_t^2 = \rho$. This correlation introduces a new problem dimension into the discretization for simulation purposes (cf. Broadie and Kaya (2006)). To avoid problems arising from correlating normally distributed increments (of S) with chi-squared distributed increments (of v), we consider in the following only Euler schemes for both the S and v processes. This has the advantage that the increments of v become normally distributed as well and can therefore be easily correlated with the increments of S.

In total, we consider *two* discretization schemes for S and seven discretization schemes for v. For S, we consider the exact **log** Euler scheme with

$$S_t = S_s e^{(r-v_t/2)\Delta t + \sqrt{v_t}\sqrt{\Delta t}z_t^1} \tag{10.6}$$

where $s \equiv t - \Delta t$ and z_t^1 standard normal. This scheme is obtained by considering the dynamics of log S_t and applying Itô's lemma to it. For illustration purposes, we also consider the **naive** Euler discretization (with $s \equiv t - \Delta t$)

$$S_t = S_s \left(e^{r\Delta t} + \sqrt{v_t}\sqrt{\Delta t}z_t^1 \right) \tag{10.7}$$

These schemes can be combined with any of the following Euler schemes for the square-root diffusion.[2]

■ **Full Truncation**

$$\tilde{x}_t = \tilde{x}_s + \kappa(\theta - \tilde{x}_s^+)\Delta t + \sigma\sqrt{\tilde{x}_s^+}\sqrt{\Delta t}z_t$$
$$x_t = \tilde{x}_t^+$$

---

[2]In the following, x^+ is notation for max$[x, 0]$.

- **Partial Truncation**

$$\tilde{x}_t = \tilde{x}_s + \kappa(\theta - \tilde{x}_s)\Delta t + \sigma\sqrt{\tilde{x}_s^+}\sqrt{\Delta t}z_t$$
$$x_t = \tilde{x}_t^+$$

- **Truncation**

$$x_t = \max[0, x_s + \kappa(\theta - x_s)\Delta t + \sigma\sqrt{x_s}\sqrt{\Delta t}z_t]$$

- **Reflection**

$$\tilde{x}_t = |\tilde{x}_s| + \kappa(\theta - |\tilde{x}_s|)\Delta t + \sigma\sqrt{|\tilde{x}_s|}\sqrt{\Delta t}z_t$$
$$x_t = |\tilde{x}_t|$$

- **Higham-Mao**

$$\tilde{x}_t = \tilde{x}_s + \kappa(\theta - \tilde{x}_s)\Delta t + \sigma\sqrt{|\tilde{x}_s|}\sqrt{\Delta t}z_t$$
$$x_t = |\tilde{x}_t|$$

- **Simple Reflection**

$$x_t = \left| x_s + \kappa(\theta - x_s)\Delta t + \sigma\sqrt{x_s}\sqrt{\Delta t}z_t \right|$$

- **Absorption**

$$\tilde{x}_t = \tilde{x}_s^+ + \kappa(\theta - \tilde{x}_s^+)\Delta t + \sigma\sqrt{\tilde{x}_s^+}\sqrt{\Delta t}z_t$$
$$x_t = \tilde{x}_t^+$$

This list contains only Euler schemes and is not exhaustive with regard to discretization schemes for the square-root diffusion (cf. Andersen et al. (2010), Andersen (2008), Broadie and Kaya (2006), Glasserman (2004) and Haastrecht and Pelsser (2010)). However, all these schemes share the convenient feature that correlation of the variance square-root diffusion with the index process is easily accomplished.

In the literature, there are a lot of tests and numerical studies available that compare efficiency of different discretization schemes. But since the approach of this book is a practical one, we want to implement our own test and comparison procedures. Moreover, we want to use Python in combination with the data management and analysis library pandas to automate our tests.

For our tests, we take four different parametrizations for the H93 model as found in Medvedev and Scaillet (2010), table 3. In these four model economies, we value the following:

- **options**: European call and put options
- **maturities**: we take $T \in \{\frac{1}{12}, 1, 2\}$
- **strikes**: we take $K \in \{90, 100, 110\}$ for $S_0 = 100$
- **time steps**: we take $M \in \{25, 50\}$ steps per year

- **paths**: we take $I \in \{25{,}000, 50{,}000, 75{,}000, 100{,}000\}$
- **discretization**: we combine all schemes (two for index with seven for variance = 14 schemes)

This makes a total of 36 option values per option type. In view of the empirical results about option spreads and tick sizes, as presented in section 3.5, we say that a valuation is accurate if

1. the absolute value difference is smaller than **2.5 cents or**
2. the absolute value difference is smaller than **1.5%**

To improve upon valuation accuracy, we use both moment matching and antithetic paths for our Python implementation found in sub-section 10.6.3. This script writes all results into a pandas DataFrame object and saves this in HDF5 format to disk (e.g. for later usage and analysis).

To generate antithetic paths (cf. Glasserman (2004), sec. 4.2), we use both the pseudo-random number $z_{t,i}$ and its negative value $-z_{t,i}$ (where we generate only $I/2$ random numbers). With regard to moment matching (cf. Glasserman (2004), sec. 4.5.), we correct the first two moments of the pseudo-random numbers delivered by Python. The respective code for both antithetic paths and moment matching looks like this:

```python
def random_number_generator(M, I):
    if antipath:
        rand = np.random.standard_normal((2, M + 1, I / 2))
        rand = np.concatenate((rand, -rand), 2)
    else:
        rand = np.random.standard_normal((2, M + 1, I))
    if momatch:
        rand = rand / np.std(rand)
        rand = rand - np.mean(rand)
    return rand
```

Depending on the time interval Δt used, the drift of the index level process may also show a non-negligible bias (even after correction of the random numbers). We can correct the first moment of the index level process in a fashion similar to the pseudo-random numbers:

```python
for t in range(1, M + 1, 1):
    ran = np.dot(CM, rand[:, t])
    if momatch:
        bias = np.mean(np.sqrt(v[t]) * ran[row] * sdt)
    if s_disc == 'Log':
        S[t] = S[t - 1] * np.exp((r - 0.5 * v[t]) * dt +
            np.sqrt(v[t]) * ran[row] * sdt - bias)
    elif s_disc == 'Naive':
        S[t] = S[t - 1] * (math.exp(r * dt) +
            np.sqrt(v[t]) * ran[row] * sdt - bias)
```

TABLE 10.1 Valuation results for European call and put options in H93 model for parametrizations from Medvedev and Scaillet (2010) and $M_0 = 50, I = 100,000$. Performance yardsticks are $PY_1 = 0.025$ and $PY_1 = 0.015$.[a]

OT	R	I	ID	XD	MM	AP	#ER	#OP	AE	MSE
CALL	5	100,000	L	A	False	False	146	180	0.07670	3.74152
CALL	5	100,000	L	A	False	True	146	180	0.07288	3.75574
CALL	5	100,000	L	A	True	False	3	180	0.00633	0.00136
CALL	5	100,000	L	A	True	True	3	180	0.00468	0.00149
CALL	5	100,000	L	F	False	False	146	180	0.03556	3.63164
CALL	5	100,000	L	F	False	True	148	180	0.03462	3.62426
CALL	5	100,000	L	F	True	False	1	180	−0.01659	0.00113
CALL	5	100,000	L	F	True	True	1	180	−0.01299	0.00090
CALL	5	100,000	L	P	False	False	144	180	0.03942	3.68678
CALL	5	100,000	L	P	False	True	145	180	0.04079	3.64441
CALL	5	100,000	L	P	True	False	1	180	−0.01474	0.00108
CALL	5	100,000	L	P	True	True	1	180	−0.01128	0.00111
CALL	5	100,000	L	T	False	False	147	180	0.07196	3.72847
CALL	5	100,000	L	T	False	True	145	180	0.07256	3.74803
CALL	5	100,000	L	T	True	False	3	180	0.00340	0.00155
CALL	5	100,000	L	T	True	True	3	180	0.01147	0.00162
PUT	5	100,000	L	A	False	False	143	180	0.04343	0.93155
PUT	5	100,000	L	A	False	True	141	180	0.04284	0.93065
PUT	5	100,000	L	A	True	False	14	180	0.00445	0.00110
PUT	5	100,000	L	A	True	True	20	180	0.00657	0.00149
PUT	5	100,000	L	F	False	False	141	180	0.03198	0.94487
PUT	5	100,000	L	F	False	True	142	180	0.03797	0.94874
PUT	5	100,000	L	F	True	False	9	180	−0.01349	0.00068
PUT	5	100,000	L	F	True	True	10	180	−0.01379	0.00083
PUT	5	100,000	L	P	False	False	143	180	0.03593	0.96873
PUT	5	100,000	L	P	False	True	141	180	0.03330	0.94941
PUT	5	100,000	L	P	True	False	3	180	−0.00881	0.00041
PUT	5	100,000	L	P	True	True	5	180	−0.00987	0.00056
PUT	5	100,000	L	T	False	False	143	180	0.04830	0.92206
PUT	5	100,000	L	T	False	True	142	180	0.04231	0.92051
PUT	5	100,000	L	T	True	False	10	180	0.00687	0.00111
PUT	5	100,000	L	T	True	True	10	180	0.00445	0.00117

[a]Monte Carlo simulation values benchmarked against semi-analytical values from Fourier-based pricing approach. The columns report the following values: **OT** = the option type (call or put), **R** = number of valuation runs, **I** = number of paths per single option valuation, **ID** = (first letter of) discretization scheme for index process, **XD** = (first letter of) discretization scheme for variance process, **MM** = moment matching, **AP** = antithetic paths, **#ER** = number of errors out of #OP, **#OP** = number of options valued, **AE** = average error over all valuations, **MSE** = mean squared error of all valuations.

Table 10.1 reports valuation results for European call and put options with $M_0 = 50$ and $I = 100,000$. Here, M_0 means steps per year. For example, if time-to-maturity is 2 years, we set $M = 2 \cdot M_0 = 100$. The table uses the exact scheme for the index process and combines this with four different schemes for the variance process (Full Truncation, Partial Truncation, Truncation and Absorption). It is evident that variance reduction techniques are indispensable

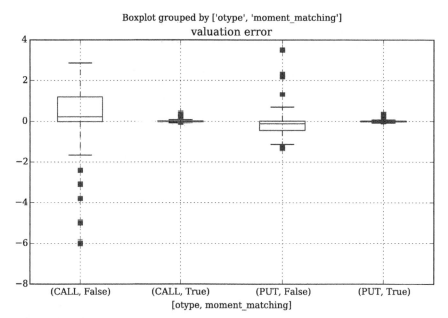

FIGURE 10.4 Boxplot of Monte Carlo valuation errors without and with moment matching

in this setting. While antithetic paths have no noticeable influence ceteris paribus, moment matching significantly increases accuracy of the valuation process. Using moment matching (with or without antithetic paths) the Full Truncation scheme shows the best overall performance. However, for some configurations the Absorption scheme, for example, also performs quite well. The average absolute valuation errors for the total set of 180 options when using moment matching mainly range between 0.5 cents and 1 cent. The good performance of the Full Truncation scheme is in line with results obtained in Lord et al. (2006) who name this particular scheme as their winner.

Figure 10.4 illustrates the importance of moment matching techniques in this context. The correction effect moment matching has for Monte Carlo valuation is impressively illustrated in that figure.

Table 10.2 presents further valuation results. This time all possible combinations of the discretization schemes are considered. Again, the Full Truncation scheme generates good valuation results—and, which may come as a surprise, the naive discretization scheme for the index process also performs relatively well throughout.

10.4 VALUATION OF AMERICAN OPTIONS

We now turn to American (put) options which are a little bit harder to value efficiently, i.e. accurately and fast, by Monte Carlo simulation.[3] The setup for this section is the H93 stochastic

---

[3]This section is mainly based on a 2011 working paper by the author titled "Fast Monte Carlo Valuation of American Options under Stochastic Volatility and Interest Rates." The results of the paper were presented at the EuroScipy 2011 conference in Paris.

TABLE 10.2 Valuation results for European call and put options in H93 model for parametrizations from Medvedev and Scaillet (2010) and $M_0 = 50, I = 100,000$. Performance yardsticks are $PY_1 = 0.025$ and $PY_1 = 0.015$.[a]

OT	R	I	ID	XD	MM	AP	#ER	#OP	AE	MSE
CALL	5	100,000	L	A	True	True	3	180	0.00468	0.00149
CALL	5	100,000	L	F	True	True	1	180	−0.01299	0.00090
CALL	5	100,000	L	H	True	True	4	180	0.01169	0.00175
CALL	5	100,000	L	P	True	True	1	180	−0.01128	0.00111
CALL	5	100,000	L	R	True	True	5	180	0.01208	0.00253
CALL	5	100,000	L	S	True	True	13	180	0.02979	0.00659
CALL	5	100,000	L	T	True	True	3	180	0.01147	0.00162
CALL	5	100,000	N	A	True	True	1	180	0.00805	0.00101
CALL	5	100,000	N	F	True	True	2	180	−0.01566	0.00104
CALL	5	100,000	N	H	True	True	4	180	0.00545	0.00226
CALL	5	100,000	N	P	True	True	4	180	−0.01526	0.00120
CALL	5	100,000	N	R	True	True	6	180	0.01221	0.00279
CALL	5	100,000	N	S	True	True	11	180	0.03020	0.00549
CALL	5	100,000	N	T	True	True	3	180	0.00692	0.00174
PUT	5	100,000	L	A	True	True	20	180	0.00657	0.00149
PUT	5	100,000	L	F	True	True	10	180	−0.01379	0.00083
PUT	5	100,000	L	H	True	True	14	180	0.00808	0.00157
PUT	5	100,000	L	P	True	True	5	180	−0.00987	0.00056
PUT	5	100,000	L	R	True	True	18	180	0.01005	0.00207
PUT	5	100,000	L	S	True	True	29	180	0.02747	0.00592
PUT	5	100,000	L	T	True	True	10	180	0.00445	0.00117
PUT	5	100,000	N	A	True	True	16	180	0.00084	0.00123
PUT	5	100,000	N	F	True	True	9	180	−0.01466	0.00075
PUT	5	100,000	N	H	True	True	13	180	0.00402	0.00176
PUT	5	100,000	N	P	True	True	7	180	−0.01529	0.00070
PUT	5	100,000	N	R	True	True	17	180	0.00987	0.00217
PUT	5	100,000	N	S	True	True	30	180	0.02535	0.00556
PUT	5	100,000	N	T	True	True	11	180	0.00622	0.00106

[a]Monte Carlo simulation values benchmarked against semi-analytical values from Fourier-based pricing approach. For the meaning of column headings refer to Table 10.1.

volatility (SV) model in combination with the CIR85 stochastic short rate (SI) model. This model $\mathcal{M}^{SVSI}$ is a special case of the general market model $\mathcal{M}^{BCC97}$ and exhibits risk-neutral dynamics as follows:

$$dS_t = r_t S_t dt + \sqrt{v_t} S_t dZ_t^1$$
$$dv_t = \kappa_v(\theta_v - v_t)dt + \sigma_v \sqrt{v_t} dZ_t^2$$
$$dr_t = \kappa_r(\theta_r - r_t)dt + \sigma_r \sqrt{r_t} dZ_t^3$$

The major algorithm we apply is the LSM of Longstaff-Schwartz (Longstaff and Schwartz, 2001). However, in addition to moment matching and antithetic variates, we introduce a further variance reduction technique: control variates.

The LSM estimator (7.15) provides us with an estimate for an American option's value. We correct this estimator by the simulated differences gained from a control variate. Consider that we have simulated I paths of $X_t = (S_t, v_t, r_t)$ to value an American put option with maturity T and strike K. Then there are also I simulated present values of the corresponding European put option. They are given by $P_{0,i} = B_0(T)h_T(X_{T,i})$, $i \in \{1, ..., I\}$, with $h_T(x) \equiv \max[K - x, 0]$. The correction for the estimator (7.15) is as follows

$$\hat{V}_0^{CV} = \frac{1}{I} \sum_{i=1}^{I} \left(V_{0,i} - \lambda \cdot (P_{0,i} - P_0^{H93}) \right) \tag{10.8}$$

For λ one can use the statistical correlation between the simulated European and American option present values. However, results from a number of numerical experiments indicate that simply setting $\lambda \equiv 1$ yields more accurate results in the test cases covered in this section.

10.4.1 Numerical Results

This sub-section presents numerical results from the simulation study based on American put options as implemented in the Python script of sub-section 10.6.4.

Parametrized Financial Model   We consider all model parametrizations for the H93 and the CIR85 parts of the financial model from table 3 in Medvedev and Scaillet (2010). These are four different parameter sets for the financial model.

Per parameter set, American put options for three different maturities and moneyness levels, respectively, are valued:

- $T \in \left\{ \frac{1}{12}, \frac{1}{4}, \frac{1}{2} \right\}$
- $K \in \{90, 100, 110\}$

All parameter sets and all values for the single options (for a total of 36 option values) are included in the Python script provided in sub-section 10.6.4. The script uses all seven discretization schemes for the square-root diffusions. With respect to the index process, it relies on an additive version of the log Euler scheme. The script implements the LSM algorithm with certain options to alter algorithm features (like control variates, moment matching or antithetic paths).

To measure accuracy, we consider the absolute difference between our script's values and the benchmark values from Medvedev and Scaillet (2010). As benchmark values we take their LSM estimates obtained by simulations with 50 exercise dates, 500 time steps and 1,000,000 paths. We say that our value estimates are accurate if the absolute difference is either smaller than 2.5 cents or 1.5% (i.e. we take the same yardsticks as for the European options).

Medvedev and Scaillet (2010) derive in their paper approximations for American option values under stochastic volatility (of H93 type) and stochastic interest rates (of CIR85 type) which can be evaluated very fast. They write on page 16:

"To give an idea of the computational advantage of our method, a Matlab code implementing the algorithm of Longstaff and Schwartz (2001) takes dozens of minutes to compute a single option price while our approximation takes roughly a tenth of a second."

Apart from accuracy, we therefore want to take a look at how fast we can value options accurately with our Python implementation. This obviously is an important issue since "dozens of minutes" per single option price are of course unacceptable for practical applications.

Example Results from Simulation   A numerical experiment with 10 simulation runs—for a total of 360 American put option values—yielded the following results (using control variate, moment matching and antithetic paths techniques):

- **discretization**: Full Truncation
- **time steps**: 20
- **paths**: 20,000
- **simulation runs**: 10
- **number of options**: 360
- **number of errors**: 13
- **average error**: −0.00096
- **total time**: 29.18 seconds
- **time per option**: 0.08 seconds

Three hundred and forty-seven out of 360 American put options are valued accurately given our yardsticks. The average valuation error is about −0.001 cents and therewith well below 1 cent in absolute value. The average relative error is not quite representative since the relative error for option values of about 0.01 cents easily reaches 100% and more. Nevertheless, it is only about +4%. Average time per option is about 0.08 seconds—which has to be compared with the "dozens of minutes" reported in Medvedev and Scaillet (2010). Our approach seems to be 1,000+ times faster (if we assume a 'single' dozen of minutes) with an accurateness that is consistent with a typical market microstructure.

Simulation Results   Table 10.3 shows simulation results for different configurations of the LSM algorithm. Each of the 36 options is valued five times making for a total of 180 option valuations per configuration.

Interpretation of Results   What are the reasons for the combination of reasonable accuracy and valuation speed of the Python script? Actually, there are a number of reasons:

- **implementation**: the LSM algorithm has been implemented in Python using the fast numerical library NumPy which runs at the speed of C code for certain operations; for some applications this may be faster than Matlab or other domain-specific environments like R
- **discretization**: we only use Euler discretization schemes which provide "sufficient" accuracy at a high speed; we let the simulated index level paths according to (10.4) drift step-by-step by the average of the two relevant short rate values
- **control variates**: the use of European put options as control variates (cf. Glasserman (2004), sec. 4.1) is of high or even highest importance for variance reduction and accuracy of the LSM estimator
- **moment matching**: we correct the set of standard normal pseudo-random numbers generated by Python to match the first two moments correctly (cf. Glasserman (2004), sec. 4.5),

TABLE 10.3   Valuation results for American put options in H93 and CIR85 model for parametrizations from Medvedev and Scaillet (2010). Performance yardsticks are $PY_1 = 0.025$ and $PY_1 = 0.015$.[a]

R	M	I	XD	CV	MM	AP	#ER	#OP	AE	MSE
5	20	25,000	A	True	True	True	1	180	−0.00117	0.00064
5	20	25,000	F	True	True	True	1	180	−0.00105	0.00042
5	20	25,000	H	True	True	True	5	180	0.00043	0.00046
5	20	25,000	P	True	True	True	4	180	−0.00379	0.00047
5	20	25,000	R	True	True	True	5	180	−0.00187	0.00058
5	20	25,000	S	True	True	True	3	180	−0.00290	0.00044
5	20	25,000	T	True	True	True	2	180	0.00072	0.00062
5	20	35,000	A	True	True	True	1	180	−0.00836	0.00050
5	20	35,000	F	True	True	True	1	180	−0.00289	0.00043
5	20	35,000	H	True	True	True	5	180	−0.00205	0.00057
5	20	35,000	P	True	True	True	4	180	−0.00328	0.00039
5	20	35,000	R	True	True	True	4	180	−0.00543	0.00051
5	20	35,000	S	True	True	True	2	180	−0.00408	0.00044
5	20	35,000	T	True	True	True	2	180	−0.00283	0.00035
5	25	25,000	A	True	True	True	2	180	−0.00171	0.00045
5	25	25,000	F	True	True	True	1	180	0.00126	0.00039
5	25	25,000	H	True	True	True	2	180	−0.00177	0.00043
5	25	25,000	P	True	True	True	1	180	−0.00083	0.00037
5	25	25,000	R	True	True	True	2	180	−0.00016	0.00059
5	25	25,000	S	True	True	True	4	180	0.00044	0.00050
5	25	25,000	T	True	True	True	3	180	−0.00173	0.00054
5	25	35,000	A	True	True	True	2	180	−0.00162	0.00043
5	25	35,000	F	True	True	True	1	180	−0.00135	0.00045
5	25	35,000	H	True	True	True	2	180	−0.00166	0.00041
5	25	35,000	P	True	True	True	1	180	−0.00199	0.00036
5	25	35,000	R	True	True	True	0	180	−0.00436	0.00028
5	25	35,000	S	True	True	True	5	180	−0.00429	0.00048
5	25	35000	T	True	True	True	1	180	−0.00144	0.00045

[a]Monte Carlo simulation estimates benchmarked against LSM values from Medvedev and Scaillet (2010). The columns report the following values: **R** = number of valuation runs, **M** = number of time steps, **I** = number of paths per single option valuation, **XD** = (first letter of) discretization scheme for square-root diffusions, **CV** = control variates, **MM** = moment matching, **AP** = antithetic paths, **#OP** = number of options valued, **#ER** = number of errors out of #OP, **AE** = average error over all valuations, **MSE** = mean squared error of all valuations.

   i.e. the mean is adjusted to 0.0 and the standard deviation to 1.0; we also correct the first moment of the simulated index level paths according to (10.4) step by step to account for some remaining errors

▪ **antithetic paths**: as a general variance reduction technique we generate, as in Medvedev and Scaillet (2010), antithetic paths (cf. Glasserman (2004), sec. 4.2) such that convergence of the algorithm may improve somewhat

- **use of paths**: we use only in-the-money paths such that both the estimation of the regressions becomes faster (in particular for out-of-the-money options) and convergence of the algorithm may improve
- **basis functions**: we use all in all ten different basis functions for the regressions in the LSM implementation
- **exercise at** $t = 0$: we allow for exercise at $t = 0$ such that we get at least the inner value as the option price for the in-the-money cases
- **paths**: our LSM implementation allows a significant reduction in the number of discretization intervals (25 instead of 500 as in Medvedev and Scaillet (2010)) and paths (35,000 instead of 1,000,000); our approach reduces the number of necessary simulated values by a factor of more than 500 and halves the number of regressions (25 exercise dates instead of 50)
- **recycling**: we use the same set of random numbers for the 36 options to be valued per simulation run; we also use the same simulated processes for each of the three options per time-to-maturity
- **hardware**: of course, hardware also plays a role; the computational times reported for the script are from a server with Intel Xeon CPU E3-1231 v3 @ 3.40GHz; Python 2.7 and NumPy ran on a Linux 64 bit operating system; however, better hardware or parallelization techniques could further speed up calculations

Importance of Algorithm Features   In this sub-section, we report further simulation results for variants of the LSM algorithm implementation. The aim is to identify those features of the implementation that indeed contribute to accuracy. Using the same seed value for the Python pseudo-random number generator, we replicate the 180 American option valuations several times—changing, respectively, features of the algorithm implementation. Table 10.4 shows the results.

It is obvious that the use of control variates is of paramount importance for accuracy. By contrast, moment matching and antithetic variates may be beneficial or not (if at all, then on a small scale). In view of the rather small additional computational time needed to include control variates they should be used whenever possible in such a context.

10.4.2   Higher Accuracy vs. Lower Speed

In some circumstances, our yardsticks used to assess accuracy may be too lax. Even if only for theoretical reasons, one might be interested in the LSM estimator (corrected with the help of a control variate) being even closer to the true (i.e. theoretical) option value. To this end, we set the performance yardsticks now to $PY_1 \equiv 0.01$ currency units (i.e. 1%) and $PY_2 \equiv 0.01$ (i.e. 1 percent). In particular, the 1 cent threshold is reasonable since it represents the smallest currency unit in general. Therefore it is often used to judge accuracy. For example, Longstaff and Schwartz (2001), p. 127, write: "Of the 20 differences shown in Table 1, 16 are less than or equal to one cent in absolute value."

To better meet the new yardsticks, we increase the number of time intervals to 50 as well as the number of paths to 100,000 and 200,000, respectively. As the results in Table 10.5 show, there are six valuation errors for the 180 options in the case of 50 time steps, 100,000 paths

TABLE 10.4 Valuation results for American put options in H93 and CIR85 model for parametrizations from Medvedev and Scaillet (2010). Performance yardsticks are $PY_1 = 0.025$ and $PY_1 = 0.015$.[a]

R	M	I	XD	CV	MM	AP	#ER	#OP	AE	MSE
5	20	35,000	A	False	False	False	54	180	−0.01504	0.00412
5	20	35,000	A	False	False	True	42	180	−0.01279	0.00365
5	20	35,000	A	False	True	False	43	180	−0.01126	0.00368
5	20	35,000	A	False	True	True	42	180	−0.01366	0.00351
5	20	35,000	A	True	False	False	0	180	−0.00319	0.00041
5	20	35,000	A	True	False	True	2	180	−0.00594	0.00046
5	20	35,000	A	True	True	False	1	180	−0.00364	0.00037
5	20	35,000	A	True	True	True	0	180	−0.00499	0.00045
5	20	35,000	F	False	False	False	44	180	−0.00894	0.00394
5	20	35,000	F	False	False	True	43	180	−0.01226	0.00379
5	20	35,000	F	False	True	False	42	180	−0.01283	0.00374
5	20	35,000	F	False	True	True	46	180	−0.01179	0.00422
5	20	35,000	F	True	False	False	4	180	−0.00525	0.00059
5	20	35,000	F	True	False	True	3	180	−0.00366	0.00038
5	20	35,000	F	True	True	False	2	180	−0.00416	0.00046
5	20	35,000	F	True	True	True	2	180	−0.00618	0.00042
5	20	35,000	P	False	False	False	45	180	−0.01272	0.00432
5	20	35,000	P	False	False	True	44	180	−0.01313	0.00407
5	20	35,000	P	False	True	False	42	180	−0.01241	0.00371
5	20	35,000	P	False	True	True	41	180	−0.01339	0.00385
5	20	35,000	P	True	False	False	3	180	−0.00337	0.00046
5	20	35,000	P	True	False	True	4	180	−0.00540	0.00047
5	20	35,000	P	True	True	False	1	180	−0.00322	0.00036
5	20	35,000	P	True	True	True	3	180	−0.00154	0.00045
5	20	35,000	T	False	False	False	53	180	−0.01329	0.00431
5	20	35,000	T	False	False	True	40	180	−0.01140	0.00374
5	20	35,000	T	False	True	False	42	180	−0.01210	0.00400
5	20	35,000	T	False	True	True	42	180	−0.01345	0.00367
5	20	35,000	T	True	False	False	1	180	−0.00513	0.00050
5	20	35,000	T	True	False	True	1	180	−0.00530	0.00042
5	20	35,000	T	True	True	False	3	180	−0.00479	0.00042
5	20	35,000	T	True	True	True	2	180	−0.00446	0.00039

[a]Monte Carlo simulation estimates benchmarked against LSM values from Medvedev and Scaillet (2010). For the meaning of column headings refer to Table 10.3.

and the Full Truncation scheme. The average valuation error in this case is around −0.5 cents. However, further increasing the number of paths to 200,000 ceteris paribus does not guarantee better valuation results, as is also illustrated in Table 10.5.

These results illustrate the trade-off between valuation accuracy and speed quite well. By increasing the number of time intervals and paths per simulation, you can get closer to the true (theoretical) value—just as the convergence results of Clément et al. (2002) imply. Longer valuation times are the price to pay.

TABLE 10.5   Valuation results for American put options in H93 and CIR85 model for parametrizations from Medvedev and Scaillet (2010). Performance yardsticks are $PY_1 = 0.01$ and $PY_1 = 0.01$.[a]

R	M	I	XD	CV	MM	AP	#ER	#OP	AE	MSE
5	20	35,000	A	True	True	True	10	180	−0.00417	0.00038
5	20	35,000	F	True	True	True	11	180	−0.00241	0.00043
5	20	35,000	P	True	True	True	10	180	−0.00323	0.00051
5	20	35,000	T	True	True	True	15	180	−0.00318	0.00051
5	20	100,000	A	True	True	True	14	180	−0.00928	0.00048
5	20	100,000	F	True	True	True	15	180	−0.00857	0.00033
5	20	100,000	P	True	True	True	20	180	−0.00855	0.00047
5	20	100,000	T	True	True	True	15	180	−0.00981	0.00047
5	20	200,000	A	True	True	True	17	180	−0.00966	0.00040
5	20	200,000	F	True	True	True	19	180	−0.01116	0.00044
5	20	200,000	P	True	True	True	15	180	−0.01055	0.00043
5	20	200,000	T	True	True	True	16	180	−0.01032	0.00041
5	50	35,000	A	True	True	True	12	180	−0.00211	0.00040
5	50	35,000	F	True	True	True	16	180	−0.00004	0.00048
5	50	35,000	P	True	True	True	14	180	0.00020	0.00043
5	50	35,000	T	True	True	True	15	180	−0.00258	0.00047
5	50	100,000	A	True	True	True	7	180	−0.00478	0.00031
5	50	100,000	F	True	True	True	6	180	−0.00536	0.00028
5	50	100,000	P	True	True	True	7	180	−0.00657	0.00032
5	50	100,000	T	True	True	True	9	180	−0.00591	0.00034
5	50	200,000	A	True	True	True	7	180	−0.00783	0.00034
5	50	200,000	F	True	True	True	7	180	−0.00720	0.00038
5	50	200,000	P	True	True	True	3	180	−0.00709	0.00029
5	50	200,000	T	True	True	True	9	180	−0.00743	0.00032

[a]Monte Carlo simulation values benchmarked against LSM values from Medvedev and Scaillet (2010). For the meaning of column headings refer to Table 10.3.

10.5   CONCLUSIONS

Monte Carlo simulation is an indispensable tool for the valuation of non-vanilla equity derivatives and for risk management purposes. However, even valuing simple products correctly by simulation in more complex models—like the ones of CIR85, H93 or BCC97—is already a daunting task. This chapter first shows how to correctly discretize the square-root diffusion in the CIR85 model and value zero-coupon bonds numerically. It then proceeds and values European call and put options in the H93 model where the variance process is discretized by a Euler scheme—a total of seven schemes is implemented to allow for numerical comparisons.

Section 4 then adds the CIR85 short rate model to the H93 model to value American put options by Monte Carlo simulation and the LSM algorithm. We show that our Python implementation allows for quite fast valuations in this context—the script needs only about a tenth of a second for a single option valuation. This is, among others, accomplished by the use of three variance reduction techniques: control variates, moment matching and antithetic paths. In this context, control variates play a dominant role in increasing valuation accuracy.

10.6   PYTHON SCRIPTS

10.6.1   General Zero-Coupon Bond Valuation

```python
#
# Valuation of Zero-Coupon Bonds
# in Cox-Ingersoll-Ross (1985) Model
# 09_gmm/CIR_zcb_valuation_gen.py
#
# (c) Dr. Yves J. Hilpisch
# Derivatives Analytics with Python
#
import math
import numpy as np


#
# Example Parameters CIR85 Model
#
r0, kappa_r, theta_r, sigma_r, t, T = 0.04, 0.3, 0.04, 0.1, 0.5, 5.0


#
# Zero-Coupon Bond Valuation Formula
#


def gamma(kappa_r, sigma_r):
    ''' Help Function. '''
    return np.sqrt(kappa_r ** 2 + 2 * sigma_r ** 2)


def b1(alpha):
    ''' Help Function. '''
    r0, kappa_r, theta_r, sigma_r, t, T = alpha
    g = gamma(kappa_r, sigma_r)
    return (((2 * g * np.exp((kappa_r + g) * (T - t) / 2)) /
            (2 * g + (kappa_r + g) * (np.exp(g * (T - t)) - 1)))
            ** (2 * kappa_r * theta_r / sigma_r ** 2))


def b2(alpha):
    ''' Help Function. '''
    r0, kappa_r, theta_r, sigma_r, t, T = alpha
    g = gamma(kappa_r, sigma_r)
    return ((2 * (np.exp(g * (T - t)) - 1)) /
            (2 * g + (kappa_r + g) * (np.exp(g * (T - t)) - 1)))
```

```
def B(alpha):
    ''' Function to value unit zero-coupon bonds in CIR85 Model.

    Parameters
    ==========
    r0: float
        initial short rate
    kappa_r: float
        mean-reversion factor
    theta_r: float
        long-run mean of short rate
    sigma_r: float
        volatility of short rate
    t: float
        valuation date
    T: float
        time horizon/interval

    Returns
    =======
    zcb_value: float
        value of zero-coupon bond
    '''
    b_1 = b1(alpha)
    b_2 = b2(alpha)
    r0, kappa_r, theta_r, sigma_r, t, T = alpha
    E_rt = theta_r + np.exp(-kappa_r * t) * (r0 - theta_r)
        # expected value of r_t
    zcb_value = b_1 * np.exp(-b_2 * E_rt)
    return zcb_value

if __name__ == '__main__':
    #
    # Example Valuation
    #
    BtT = B([r0, kappa_r, theta_r, sigma_r, t, T])
        # discount factor, ZCB value for t & T
    print "ZCB Value    %10.4f" % BtT
```

10.6.2   CIR85 Simulation and Valuation

```
#
# Valuation of Zero-Coupon Bonds by Monte Carlo Simulation
# in Cox-Ingersoll-Ross (1985) Model
```

```python
# 10_mcs/CIR_zcb_simulation.py
#
# (c) Dr. Yves J. Hilpisch
# Derivatives Analytics with Python
#
import math
import numpy as np
from CIR_zcb_valuation_gen import B
import matplotlib.pyplot as plt
import matplotlib as mpl
mpl.rcParams['font.family'] = 'serif'
from time import time


#
# Simulation of Square Root Diffusion
#


def CIR_generate_paths(x0, kappa, theta, sigma, T, M, I, x_disc='exact'):
    ''' Function to simulate Square-Root Difussion (SRD/CIR) process.

    Parameters
    ==========
    x0: float
        initial value
    kappa: float
        mean-reversion factor
    theta: float
        long-run mean
    sigma: float
        volatility factor
    T: float
        final date/time horizon
    M: int
        number of time steps
    I: int
        number of paths

    Returns
    =======
    x: NumPy array
        simulated paths
    '''
    dt = T / M
    x = np.zeros((M + 1, I), dtype=np.float)
    x[0] = x0
    xh = np.zeros_like(x)
```

```python
    xh[0] = x0
    ran = np.random.standard_normal((M + 1, I))

    if x_disc is 'exact':
        # exact discretization
        d = 4 * kappa * theta / sigma ** 2
        c = (sigma ** 2 * (1 - math.exp(-kappa * dt))) / (4 * kappa)
        if d > 1:
            for t in xrange(1, M + 1):
                l = x[t - 1] * math.exp(-kappa * dt) / c
                chi = np.ramdom.chisquare(d - 1, I)
                x[t] = c * ((ran[t] + np.sqrt(l)) ** 2 + chi)
        else:
            for t in xrange(1, M + 1):
                l = x[t - 1] * math.exp(-kappa * dt) / c
                N = np.random.poisson(l / 2, I)
                chi = np.random.chisquare(d + 2 * N, I)
                x[t] = c * chi

    else:
        # Euler scheme (full truncation)
        for t in xrange(1, M + 1):
            xh[t] = (xh[t - 1] + kappa * (theta - np.maximum(0, xh[t - 1]))
                     * dt + np.sqrt(np.maximum(0, xh[t - 1]))
                     * sigma * ran[t] * math.sqrt(dt))
            x[t] = np.maximum(0, xh[t])
    return x


#
# Graphical Output of Simulated Paths
#
def plot_paths():
    plt.figure(figsize=(9, 5))
    plt.plot(range(len(r)), r[:, :20])
    plt.grid()
    plt.xlabel('time step')
    plt.ylabel('short rate')


#
# Valuation of ZCB
#
def zcb_estimator(M=50, x_disc='exact'):
    dt = T / M
    r = CIR_generate_paths(r0, kappa_r, theta_r, sigma_r, T, M, I, x_disc)
    zcb = np.zeros((M + 1, I), dtype=np.float)
    zcb[-1] = 1.0  # final value
```

```
    for t in range(M, 0, -1):
        zcb[t - 1] = zcb[t] * np.exp(-(r[t] + r[t - 1]) / 2 * dt)
    return np.sum(zcb, axis=1) / I


#
# Graphical Value Comparison
#
def graphical_comparison(M=50, x_disc='exact'):
    MCS_values = zcb_estimator(M, x_disc)
    CIR_values = []
    dt = T / M
    t_list = np.arange(0.0, T + 0.001, dt)  # dates of interest
    for t in t_list:
        alpha = r0, kappa_r, theta_r, sigma_r, t, T
        CIR_values.append(B(alpha))
          # CIR model values given date list

    fig, ax = plt.subplots(2, sharex=True, figsize=(8, 6))
    ax[0].plot(t_list, MCS_values, 'ro', label='MCS values')
    ax[0].plot(t_list, CIR_values, 'b', label='CIR values')
    ax[0].legend(loc=0)
    ax[0].grid()
    ax[0].set_ylim(min(CIR_values) - 0.005, max(CIR_values) + 0.005)
    ax[0].set_ylabel('option values')
    ax[0].set_title('maturity $T=2$')
    ax[1].bar(t_list - 0.025 / 2., MCS_values - CIR_values,
                    width=0.025)
    plt.ylabel('difference')
    plt.xlim(min(t_list) - 0.1, max(t_list) + 0.1)
    plt.xlabel('time $t$')
    plt.tight_layout()
    plt.grid()


if __name__ == '__main__':
    #
    # Model Parameters
    #
    r0, kappa_r, theta_r, sigma_r = [0.01, 0.1, 0.03, 0.2]
    T = 2.0  # time horizon
    M = 50  # time steps
    dt = T / M
    I = 50000  # number of MCS paths
    np.random.seed(50000)  # seed for RNG

    r = CIR_generate_paths(r0, kappa_r, theta_r, sigma_r, T, M, I)
```

10.6.3 Automated Valuation of European Options by Monte Carlo Simulation

```
#
# Valuation of European Options
# Under Heston (1993) Stochastic Volatility Model
# Comparison of Fourier-based Value and MCS Estimator
# 10_mcs/H93_european_mcs.py
#
# (c) Dr. Yves J. Hilpisch
# Derivatives Analytics with Python
#
import sys
sys.path.append('09_gmm/')
import math
import string
import numpy as np
np.set_printoptions(precision=3)
import pandas as pd
import itertools as it
from datetime import datetime
from time import time
from BCC_option_valuation import H93_call_value

# Fixed Short Rate
r = 0.05

# Heston (1993) Parameters
# from MS (2009), table 3
para = np.array(((0.01, 1.5, 0.15, 0.1),   # panel 1
            # (v0,kappa_v,sigma_v,rho)
               (0.04, 0.75, 0.3, 0.1),   # panel 2
               (0.04, 1.50, 0.3, 0.1),   # panel 3
               (0.04, 1.5, 0.15, -0.5)))  # panel 4

theta_v = 0.02  # long-term variance level
S0 = 100.0  # initial index level

# General Simulation Parameters
write = True
verbose = False
option_types = ['CALL', 'PUT']  # option types
steps_list = [25, 50]  # time steps p.a.
paths_list = [25000, 50000, 75000, 100000]   # number of paths per valuation
s_disc_list = ['Log', 'Naive']  # Euler scheme: log vs. naive
x_disc_list = ['Full Truncation', 'Partial Truncation', 'Truncation',
```

```
                    'Absorption', 'Reflection', 'Higham-Mao', 'Simple Reflection']
                    # discretization schemes for SRD process

anti_paths = [False, True]
  # antithetic paths for variance reduction
moment_matching = [False, True]
  # random number correction (std + mean + drift)

t_list = [1.0 / 12, 1.0, 2.0]  # maturity list
k_list = [90, 100, 110]        # strike list
PY1 = 0.025  # performance yardstick 1: abs. error in currency units
PY2 = 0.015  # performance yardstick 2: rel. error in decimals
runs = 5  # number of simulation runs
np.random.seed(250000)  # set RNG seed value


#
# Function for Short Rate and Volatility Processes
#


def SRD_generate_paths(x_disc, x0, kappa, theta, sigma,
                       T, M, I, rand, row, cho_matrix):
    ''' Function to simulate Square-Root Diffusion (SRD/CIR) process.

    Parameters
    ==========
    x0: float
        initial value
    kappa: float
        mean-reversion factor
    theta: float
        long-run mean
    sigma: float
        volatility factor
    T: float
        final date/time horizon
    M: int
        number of time steps
    I: int
        number of paths
    row: int
        row number for random numbers
    cho_matrix: NumPy array
        Cholesky matrix

    Returns
    =======
```

```
x: NumPy array
    simulated variance paths
'''
dt = T / M
x = np.zeros((M + 1, I), dtype=np.float)
x[0] = x0
xh = np.zeros_like(x)
xh[0] = x0
sdt = math.sqrt(dt)
for t in xrange(1, M + 1):
    ran = np.dot(cho_matrix, rand[:, t])
    if x_disc == 'Full Truncation':
        xh[t] = (xh[t - 1] + kappa * (theta -
            np.maximum(0, xh[t - 1])) * dt +
            np.sqrt(np.maximum(0, xh[t - 1])) * sigma * ran[row] * sdt)
        x[t] = np.maximum(0, xh[t])
    elif x_disc == 'Partial Truncation':
        xh[t] = (xh[t - 1] + kappa * (theta - xh[t - 1]) * dt +
            np.sqrt(np.maximum(0, xh[t - 1])) * sigma * ran[row] * sdt)
        x[t] = np.maximum(0, xh[t])
    elif x_disc == 'Truncation':
        x[t] = np.maximum(0, x[t - 1]
            + kappa * (theta - x[t - 1]) * dt +
            np.sqrt(x[t - 1]) * sigma * ran[row] * sdt)
    elif x_disc == 'Reflection':
        xh[t] = (xh[t - 1]
            + kappa * (theta - abs(xh[t - 1])) * dt +
            np.sqrt(abs(xh[t - 1])) * sigma * ran[row] * sdt)
        x[t] = abs(xh[t])
    elif x_disc == 'Higham-Mao':
        xh[t] = (xh[t - 1] + kappa * (theta - xh[t - 1]) * dt +
            np.sqrt(abs(xh[t - 1])) * sigma * ran[row] * sdt)
        x[t] = abs(xh[t])
    elif x_disc == 'Simple Reflection':
        x[t] = abs(x[t - 1] + kappa * (theta - x[t - 1]) * dt +
            np.sqrt(x[t - 1]) * sigma * ran[row] * sdt)
    elif x_disc == 'Absorption':
        xh[t] = (np.maximum(0, xh[t - 1])
            + kappa * (theta - np.maximum(0, xh[t - 1])) * dt +
            np.sqrt(np.maximum(0, xh[t - 1])) * sigma * ran[row] * sdt)
        x[t] = np.maximum(0, xh[t])
    else:
        print x_disc
        print "No valid Euler scheme."
        sys.exit(0)
return x
```

```python
#
# Function for Heston Index Process
#

def H93_generate_paths(S0, r, v, row, cho_matrix):
    ''' Simulation of Heston (1993) index process.

    Parameters
    ==========
    S0: float
        initial value
    r: float
        constant short rate
    v: NumPy array
        simulated variance paths
    row: int
        row/matrix of random number array to use
    cho_matrix: NumPy array
        Cholesky matrix

    Returns
    =======
    S: NumPy array
        simulated index level paths
    '''
    S = np.zeros((M + 1, I), dtype=np.float)
    S[0] = S0
    bias = 0.0
    sdt = math.sqrt(dt)
    for t in xrange(1, M + 1, 1):
        ran = np.dot(cho_matrix, rand[:, t])
        if momatch:
            bias = np.mean(np.sqrt(v[t]) * ran[row] * sdt)
        if s_disc == 'Log':
            S[t] = S[t - 1] * np.exp((r - 0.5 * v[t]) * dt +
                    np.sqrt(v[t]) * ran[row] * sdt - bias)
        elif s_disc == 'Naive':
            S[t] = S[t - 1] * (math.exp(r * dt) +
                    np.sqrt(v[t]) * ran[row] * sdt - bias)
        else:
            print "No valid Euler scheme."
            exit(0)
    return S


def random_number_generator(M, I):
    ''' Function to generate pseudo-random numbers.
```

```
        Parameters
        ==========
        M: int
            time steps
        I: int
            number of simulation paths

        Returns
        =======
        rand: NumPy array
            random number array
        '''
        if antipath:
            rand = np.random.standard_normal((2, M + 1, I / 2))
            rand = np.concatenate((rand, -rand), 2)
        else:
            rand = np.random.standard_normal((2, M + 1, I))
        if momatch:
            rand = rand / np.std(rand)
            rand = rand - np.mean(rand)
        return rand


#
# Valuation
#

t0 = time()

results = pd.DataFrame()

tmpl_1 = '%4s | %3s | %6s | %6s | %6s | %6s | %5s | %5s' \
            % ('T', 'K', 'V0', 'V0_MCS', 'err', 'rerr', 'acc1', 'acc2')
tmpl_2 = '%4.3f | %3d | %6.3f | %6.3f | %6.3f | %6.3f | %5s | %5s'

if __name__ == '__main__':

    for alpha in it.product(option_types, steps_list, paths_list, s_disc_list,
                        x_disc_list, anti_paths, moment_matching):
        print '\n\n', alpha, '\n'
        option, M0, I, s_disc, x_disc, antipath, momatch = alpha
        for run in range(runs):
            for panel in range(4):
                # Correlation Matrix
                v0, kappa_v, sigma_v, rho = para[panel]
                covariance_matrix = np.zeros((2, 2), dtype=np.float)
                covariance_matrix[0] = [1.0, rho]
                covariance_matrix[1] = [rho, 1.0]
```

```
cho_matrix = np.linalg.cholesky(covariance_matrix)
if verbose:
    print "nResults for Panel %dn" % (panel + 1)
    print tmpl_1
for T in t_list:  # maturity list
    # memory clean-up
    v, S, rand, h = 0.0, 0.0, 0.0, 0.0
    M = int(M0 * T)  # number of total time steps
    dt = T / M  # time interval in years
    # random numbers
    rand = random_number_generator(M, I)
    # volatility process paths
    v = SRD_generate_paths(x_disc, v0, kappa_v, theta_v,
                sigma_v, T, M, I, rand, 1, cho_matrix)
    # index level process paths
    S = H93_generate_paths(S0, r, v, 0, cho_matrix)
    for K in k_list:
        # European option values
        B0T = math.exp(-r * T)  # discount factor
        # European call option value (semi-analytical)
        C0 = H93_call_value(S0, K, T, r, kappa_v,
                            theta_v, sigma_v, rho, v0)
        P0 = C0 + K * B0T - S0
        if option is 'PUT':
            # benchmark value
            V0 = P0
            # inner value matrix put
            h = np.maximum(K - S, 0)
        elif option is 'CALL':
            # benchmark value
            V0 = C0
            # inner value matrix call
            h = np.maximum(S - K, 0)
        else:
            print "No valid option type."
            sys.exit(0)
        pv = B0T * h[-1]  # present value vector
        V0_MCS = np.sum(pv) / I   # MCS estimator
        SE = np.std(pv) / math.sqrt(I)
          # standard error
        error = V0_MCS - V0
        rel_error = (V0_MCS - V0) / V0
        PY1_acc = abs(error) < PY1
        PY2_acc = abs(rel_error) < PY2
        res = pd.DataFrame({'timestamp': datetime.now(),
            'otype': option, 'runs': runs, 'steps': M0,
            'paths': I, 'index_disc': s_disc,
            'var_disc': x_disc, 'anti_paths': antipath,
```

```
                              'moment_matching': momatch, 'panel': panel,
                              'maturity': T, 'strike': K, 'value': V0,
                              'MCS_est': V0_MCS, 'SE': SE, 'error': error,
                              'rel_error': rel_error, 'PY1': PY1, 'PY2': PY2,
                              'PY1_acc': PY1_acc, 'PY2_acc': PY2_acc,
                              'PY_acc': PY1_acc or PY2_acc},
                              index=[0,])

                    if verbose:
                        print tmpl_2 % (T, K, V0, V0_MCS, error,
                                   rel_error, PY1_acc, PY2_acc)

                    results = results.append(res, ignore_index=True)

        if write:
            d = str(datetime.now().replace(microsecond=0))
            d = d.translate(string.maketrans("-:", "__"))
            h5 = pd.HDFStore('10_mcs/mcs_european_%s_%s.h5'
                             % (d[:10], d[11:]), 'w')
            h5['results'] = results
            h5.close()

        print "Total time in minutes %8.2f" % ((time() - t0) / 60)
```

10.6.4 Automated Valuation of American Put Options by Monte Carlo Simulation

```
#
# Script for American Put Option Valuation by MCS/LSM
# in H93 and CIR85 model
#
# Examples from Medvedev & Scaillet (2010):
# "Pricing American Options Under Stochastic Volatility
# and Stochastic Interest Rates."
#
# 10_mcs/SVSI_american_mcs.py
#
# (c) Dr. Yves J. Hilpisch
# Derivatives Analytics with Python
#
import gc
import sys
sys.path.append('09_gmm/')
import math
import string
```

```
import numpy as np
import pandas as pd
import itertools as it
from datetime import datetime
from BCC_option_valuation import H93_call_value
from H93_european_mcs import SRD_generate_paths
from CIR_zcb_valuation_gen import B
from time import time

# 'True' American Options Prices by Monte Carlo
# from MS (2009), table 3
benchmarks = np.array((((0.0001, 1.0438, 9.9950, 0.0346, 1.7379, 9.9823,
                0.2040, 2.3951, 9.9726),        # panel 1
                (0.0619, 2.1306, 10.0386, 0.5303, 3.4173, 10.4271,
                1.1824, 4.4249, 11.0224),       # panel 2
                (0.0592, 2.1138, 10.0372, 0.4950, 3.3478, 10.3825,
                1.0752, 4.2732, 10.8964),       # panel 3
                (0.0787, 2.1277, 10.0198, 0.6012, 3.4089, 10.2512,
                1.2896, 4.4103, 10.6988)))      # panel 4

# Cox, Ingersoll, Ross (1985) Parameters
# from MS (2009), table 3, panel 1
r0 = 0.04
kappa_r = 0.3
theta_r = 0.04
sigma_r = 0.1

# Heston (1993) Parameters
# from MS (2009), table 3
para = np.array((((0.01, 1.50, 0.15, 0.10),  # panel 1
            # (v0, kappa_v, sigma_v, rho)
            (0.04, 0.75, 0.30, 0.10),   # panel 2
            (0.04, 1.50, 0.30, 0.10),    # panel 3
            (0.04, 1.50, 0.15, -0.50)))  # panel 4

theta_v = 0.02  # long-term variance level
S0 = 100.0  # initial index level
D = 10  # number of basis functions

# General Simulation Parameters
write = True
verbose = False

py_list = [(0.025, 0.015)] # , (0.01, 0.01)]
    # combinations of performance yardsticks (absolute, relative)
    # performance yardstick 1: abs. error in currency units
    # performance yardstick 2: rel. error in decimals
```

```
m_list = [20, 25]  # number of time intervals
paths_list = [25000, 35000]  # number of paths per valuation

x_disc_list = ['Full Truncation', 'Partial Truncation', 'Truncation',
               'Absorption', 'Reflection', 'Higham-Mao', 'Simple Reflection']
               # discretization schemes for SRD process

control_variate = [False, True]
  # use of control variate
anti_paths = [False, True]
  # antithetic paths for variance reduction
moment_matching = [False, True]
  # random number correction (std + mean + drift)

t_list = [1.0 / 12, 0.25, 0.5]  # maturity list
k_list = [90., 100., 110.]       # strike list

runs = 5  # number of simulation runs

np.random.seed(250000)  # set RNG seed value



#
# Function for Heston Index Process
#


def H93_index_paths(S0, r, v, row, cho_matrix):
    ''' Simulation of the Heston (1993) index process.

    Parameters
    ==========
    S0: float
        initial value
    r: NumPy array
        simulated short rate paths
    v: NumPy array
        simulated variance paths
    row: int
        row/matrix of random number array to use
    cho_matrix: NumPy array
        Cholesky matrix

    Returns
    =======
    S: NumPy array
```

```
        simulated index level paths
    '''
    sdt = math.sqrt(dt)
    S = np.zeros((M + 1, I), dtype=np.float)
    S[0] = math.log(S0)
    for t in xrange(1, M + 1, 1):
        ran = np.dot(cho_matrix, rand[:, t])
        S[t] += S[t - 1]
        S[t] += ((r[t] + r[t - 1]) / 2 - v[t] / 2) * dt
        S[t] += np.sqrt(v[t]) * ran[row] * sdt
        if momatch is True:
            S[t] -= np.mean(np.sqrt(v[t]) * ran[row] * sdt)
    return np.exp(S)


def random_number_generator(M, I):
    ''' Function to generate pseudo-random numbers.

    Parameters
    ==========
    M: int
        time steps
    I: int
        number of simulation paths

    Returns
    =======
    rand: NumPy array
        random number array
    '''
    if antipath:
        rand = np.random.standard_normal((3, M + 1, I / 2))
        rand = np.concatenate((rand, -rand), 2)
    else:
        rand = np.random.standard_normal((3, M + 1, I))
    if momatch:
        rand = rand / np.std(rand)
        rand = rand - np.mean(rand)
    return rand

#
# Valuation
#
t0 = time()

results = pd.DataFrame()
```

```
tmpl_1 = '%5s | %3s | %6s | %6s | %6s | %6s | %6s | %6s | %6s | %5s | %5s'
tmpl_2 = '%4.3f | %3d ' + 7 * '| %6.3f ' + '| %5s | %5s'

for alpha in it.product(py_list, x_disc_list, m_list, paths_list,
                        control_variate, anti_paths, moment_matching):
    print '\n\n', alpha, '\n'
    (PY1, PY2), x_disc, M, I, convar, antipath, momatch = alpha
    for run in xrange(runs):  # simulation runs
        for panel in xrange(4):  # panels
            if verbose:
                print "\nResults for Panel %d\n" % (panel + 1)
                print tmpl_1 % ('T', 'K', 'V0', 'V0_LSM', 'V0_CV', 'P0',
                    'P0_MCS', 'err', 'rerr', 'acc1', 'acc2')
            # correlation matrix, cholesky decomposition
            v0, kappa_v, sigma_v, rho = para[panel]
            correlation_matrix = np.zeros((3, 3), dtype=np.float)
            correlation_matrix[0] = [1.0, rho, 0.0]
            correlation_matrix[1] = [rho, 1.0, 0.0]
            correlation_matrix[2] = [0.0, 0.0, 1.0]
            cho_matrix = np.linalg.cholesky(correlation_matrix)

            z = 0  # option counter
            S, r, v, h, V, matrix = 0, 0, 0, 0, 0, 0
            gc.collect()
            for T in t_list:  # times-to-maturity
                # discount factor
                B0T = B([r0, kappa_r, theta_r, sigma_r, 0.0, T])
                # average constant short rate/yield
                ra = -math.log(B0T) / T
                # time interval in years
                dt = T / M
                # pseudo-random numbers
                rand = random_number_generator(M, I)
                # short rate process paths
                r = SRD_generate_paths(x_disc, r0, kappa_r, theta_r,
                                sigma_r, T, M, I, rand, 0, cho_matrix)
                # volatility process paths
                v = SRD_generate_paths(x_disc, v0, kappa_v, theta_v,
                                sigma_v, T, M, I, rand, 2, cho_matrix)
                # index level process paths
                S = H93_index_paths(S0, r, v, 1, cho_matrix)
                for K in k_list:  # strikes
                    # inner value matrix
                    h = np.maximum(K - S, 0)
                    # value/cash flow matrix
                    V = np.maximum(K - S, 0)
```

```
for t in xrange(M - 1, 0, -1):
    df = np.exp(-(r[t] + r[t + 1]) / 2 * dt)
    # select only ITM paths
    itm = np.greater(h[t], 0)
    relevant = np.nonzero(itm)
    rel_S = np.compress(itm, S[t])
    no_itm = len(rel_S)
    if no_itm == 0:
        cv = np.zeros((I), dtype=np.float)
    else:
        rel_v = np.compress(itm, v[t])
        rel_r = np.compress(itm, r[t])
        rel_V = (np.compress(itm, V[t + 1])
                    * np.compress(itm, df))
        matrix = np.zeros((D + 1, no_itm), dtype=np.float)
        matrix[10] = rel_S * rel_v * rel_r
        matrix[9] = rel_S * rel_v
        matrix[8] = rel_S * rel_r
        matrix[7] = rel_v * rel_r
        matrix[6] = rel_S ** 2
        matrix[5] = rel_v ** 2
        matrix[4] = rel_r ** 2
        matrix[3] = rel_S
        matrix[2] = rel_v
        matrix[1] = rel_r
        matrix[0] = 1
        reg = np.linalg.lstsq(matrix.transpose(), rel_V)
        cv = np.dot(reg[0], matrix)
    erg = np.zeros((I), dtype=np.float)
    np.put(erg, relevant, cv)
    V[t] = np.where(h[t] > erg, h[t], V[t + 1] * df)

# final discounting step
df = np.exp(-(r[0] + r[1]) / 2 * dt)

## European Option Values
C0 = H93_call_value(S0, K, T, ra, kappa_v,
                    theta_v, sigma_v, rho, v0)

P0 = C0 + K * B0T - S0
P0_MCS = B0T * np.sum(h[-1]) / I

x = B0T * h[-1]
y = V[1] * df

## Control Variate Correction
if convar is True:
```

```
                    # statistical correlation
                    b = (np.sum((x - np.mean(x)) * (y - np.mean(y)))
                      / np.sum((x - np.mean(x)) ** 2))
                    # correction
                    y_cv = y - 1.0 * (B0T * h[-1] - P0)
                        # set b instead of 1.0
                        # to use stat. correlation
                else:
                    y_cv = y
                # standard error
                SE = np.std(y_cv) / math.sqrt(I)
                # benchmark value
                V0 = benchmarks[panel, z]
                # LSM control variate
                V0_CV = max(np.sum(y_cv) / I, h[0, 0])
                # pure LSM
                V0_LSM = max(np.sum(y) / I, h[0, 0])

                ## Errors
                error = V0_CV - V0
                rel_error = error / V0
                PY1_acc = abs(error) < PY1
                PY2_acc = abs(rel_error) < PY2
                res = pd.DataFrame({'timestamp': datetime.now(),
                    'runs': runs, 'PY1': PY1, 'PY2': PY2,
                    'var_disc': x_disc, 'steps': M, 'paths': I,
                    'control_variate': convar, 'anti_paths': antipath,
                    'moment_matching': momatch, 'panel': panel,
                    'maturity': T, 'strike': K, 'benchmark': V0,
                    'V0_euro': P0, 'MCS_euro': P0_MCS,
                    'LSM_pure': V0_LSM, 'LSM_convar': V0_CV,
                    'SE': SE, 'error': error, 'rel_error': rel_error,
                    'PY1_acc': PY1_acc, 'PY2_acc': PY2_acc,
                    'PY_acc': PY1_acc or PY2_acc},
                    index=[0,])

                z += 1 # option counter

                if verbose:
                    print tmpl_2 % (T, K, V0, V0_LSM, V0_CV, P0,
                        P0_MCS, error, rel_error, PY1_acc, PY2_acc)

                results = results.append(res, ignore_index=True)

    if write:
        d = str(datetime.now().replace(microsecond=0))
        d = d.translate(string.maketrans("-:", "__"))
```

```
    h5 = pd.HDFStore('10_mcs/mcs_american_%s_%s.h5' % (d[:10], d[11:]), 'w')
    h5['results'] = results
    h5.close()

print "Total time in minutes %8.2f" % ((time() - t0) / 60)
```

CHAPTER 11

Model Calibration

11.1 INTRODUCTION

Historically, *theoretical valuation* has been seen as a process where a number of input parameters of a model or formula determine the price/value of a derivative instrument. The fundamental assumption behind this reasoning is that you can observe, in principle, anything in the markets that finally determines the price/value of a security—markets should be, after all, *informationally efficient*. A major example is the Black-Scholes-Merton formula which takes as input six variables—initial price level of the underlying, the underlying's volatility, the strike price of the option at hand, time-to-maturity, short rate and maybe dividends paid by the underlying. If you put in numerical values for the six variables, the formula returns a value for the option at hand.

However, if "the market is always right", what does a model price/value mean which deviates from an observable market value? As earlier chapters discuss, market-based valuation refers to the process where more complex derivatives are valued "in consistency" with observed market prices of plain vanilla derivatives. Therefore, today's *valuation practice* requires in the first place that valuation models be capable of replicating observed market values of vanilla products sufficiently well.

This chapter is concerned with the calibration of the general market model to observed market quotes for such vanilla products, i.e. European call options in particular. In comparison to the historical approach, instrument prices/values are not the objective of the effort in the first place. The objective is rather to get a parameter set for a certain model that leads to market-consistent values for vanilla products. In that sense, the whole theoretical valuation procedure is turned upside down.

Section 11.2 concerns itself with some fundamental questions in the context of model calibration (like which market data to use). Section 11.3 calibrates the CIR85 short rate model to the Euribor term structure. Finally, section 11.4 implements a calibration procedure for the equity component of the BCC97 model, based on EURO STOXX 50 European call option quotes. As before, a complete set of self-contained Python scripts is provided.

11.2 GENERAL CONSIDERATIONS

In Chapter 8 calibration is done "ad hoc". However, when calibrating a financial market model, fundamental questions arise that have to be carefully addressed. This sub-section briefly discusses the most important ones against the background of the book's main objectives.

11.2.1   Why Calibration at All?

In a *narrow* sense (i.e. in the theory of continuous processes), market incompleteness implies that a given derivative asset cannot be replicated perfectly by trading in its underlying(s) (cf. Björk (2004), ch. 8 and ch. 15). In a *wider* sense (i.e. in the theory of processes with jumps), market incompleteness implies that a given derivative asset cannot be replicated perfectly even if trading in all available (derivative) assets is allowed (cf. Cont and Tankov (2004a), ch. 9 and ch. 10).

Regarding the special cases of the general market model $\mathcal{M}^{BCC97}$, one can say the following. The model of BSM is complete. The model of H93 is incomplete in a narrow sense but complete in a wider sense since a derivative asset generally can be replicated by trading in both the underlying and another derivative asset.[1] The model of M76 is incomplete even in a wider sense which is due to the jump component having stochastic jump size. To hedge jump risk perfectly, an over-countably infinite number of traded assets would be necessary; of course something not found, neither in practice nor in theory. As Tankov and Voltchkova (2009), p. 16, point out:

> "Since typically the jump size is not known in advance, the risk associated to jumps cannot be hedged away completely: we are in an incomplete market. In this setting, the hedging becomes an approximation problem: instead of *replicating* an option, one tries to *minimize* the residual hedging error."

As a consequence, the model of BCC97 is incomplete in a wider sense, implying that perfect hedges are not possible. Formally speaking, incompleteness leads to non-uniqueness of the risk-neutral probability measure Q and to multiple prices of derivative assets consistent with the absence of arbitrage. A simple example illustrates this insight.

Example 4 (Incomplete Market).   *Consider a simple financial market with two dates $t \in \{0, 1\}$ and three states of the economy tomorrow, i.e. at $t = 1$, which occur with equal probability. There are two assets. First, a risk-less bond B_t which pays tomorrow $B_1 = 10$ units of currency for sure and whose price today is $B_0 = 10 = (1 + r)^{-1} \cdot B_1$ such that $r = 0.0$. Second, a risky security, called the index, which costs $S_0 = 10$ today and pays tomorrow*

$$S_1 = \begin{pmatrix} 20 \\ 10 \\ 0 \end{pmatrix}$$

By standard results from linear algebra, the financial market is incomplete (in a narrow sense) since not every payoff at $t = 1$ can be replicated via trading in the available securities.[2]

---

[1] Roughly speaking, there are two sources of risk in H93—index risk and volatility risk—such that one needs (at least) two instruments to hedge away all risk.

[2] Two linearly independent vectors are not enough to form a basis of the $\mathbb{R}^3$. At least three are necessary.

Consider now the derivative asset

$$A_1 = \begin{pmatrix} 16 \\ 4 \\ 0 \end{pmatrix}$$

which should be valued. Simple calculations show that perfect replication is not possible. However, absence of arbitrage must hold such that there exists by the Fundamental Theorem of Asset Pricing (cf. Theorem 1 in Chapter 4 or Björk (2004), p. 29) a martingale measure Q such that

$$\mathbf{E}_0^Q(S_1 t) = S_0$$
$$\Rightarrow q^1 \cdot 20 + q^2 \cdot 10 + q^3 \cdot 0 = 10$$
$$\Leftrightarrow q^2 = 1 - 2 \cdot q^1$$

with $q^s > 0$ and $q^1 + q^2 + q^3 = 1$ for Q to be a (risk-neutral) probability measure. One gets

$$q^1 + (1 - 2 \cdot q^1) + q^3 = 1$$
$$\Leftrightarrow q^3 = q^1$$

As a consequence, every risk-neutral probability measure from the set

$$\mathbb{Q} = \left\{ Q \in \mathbb{R}^3_{++} : \begin{pmatrix} q^1 \\ q^2 \\ q^3 \end{pmatrix} \equiv \begin{pmatrix} v \\ 1 - 2v \\ v \end{pmatrix}, 0 < v < \frac{1}{4} \right\}$$

makes the index a martingale consistent with the absence of arbitrage. Also, every price A_0 of the derivative asset A_1 which lies in the open interval $]\underline{A_0}, \overline{A_0}[$ with

$$\underline{A_0} \equiv \mathbf{E}^{Q(v=0)}[A_1] = 4.0$$

and

$$\overline{A_0} \equiv \mathbf{E}^{Q(v=0.25)}[A_1] = 1 + 8 = 9.0$$

is consistent with the absence of arbitrage.

Market incompleteness leaves one with the unsatisfactory situation that there are multiple prices for derivative assets. To resolve this problem, calibration comes into play. Because there is, in general, no simple criterion to choose among the possible risk-neutral probability measures, one has to ask the market for the right one—this is what calibration is about. Or as Björk (2004), p. 221, puts it: "Question: Who chooses the martingale measure? ... Answer: The market!"

Therefore, calibration yields the *market-consistent* risk-neutral probability measure in the sense that (i) liquidly traded plain vanilla options are priced correctly and (ii) other (exotic) derivatives are priced such that prices are both consistent with the absence of arbitrage and indeed unique.

11.2.2 Which Role Do Different Model Components Play?

Formally speaking, calibration means to find parameters for a given model such that it is market-consistent as explained before. Chapter 8 shows that the model of M76 is not capable of perfectly replicating prices for multiple strikes and maturities. However, for the short maturity and a subset of option prices the fit is pretty good. Therefore, the jump component of the general model of BCC97 will take care of short-term option prices. On the other hand, it is well-known (cf. Gatheral (2006), ch. 3) that the model of H93 is capable of replicating option prices of longer maturities pretty well. Therefore, when calibrating a financial market model simultaneously to short as well as longer maturities one needs both a jump component and stochastic volatility. Gallucio and Le Cam (2008), p. 9, conclude:

> "… no matter how parameters are chosen, it is impossible to make a pure [stochastic volatility] or jumps model consistent with the observed shape of the smile … This further reinforces the view that option markets are consistent with the simultaneous presence of both jumps and stochastic volatility in the asset dynamics."

The model of B96 is one of the simplest to accommodate both jumps and stochastic volatility.[3] Its attractiveness further stems from the fact that the two sub-models, H93 and M76, are well understood and widely applied in theory and practice.

What about stochastic short rates? It is well-known that the impact of short rate volatility is almost negligible when calibrating models to short maturity option prices (cf. Bakshi et al. (1997)). However, the longer the maturities become the more important becomes short rate volatility such that it obviously cannot be neglected in the context of equity derivatives—which can have pretty long maturities.[4]

Stochastic short rates play a dual role in the general market model. First, they are important factors in the risk-neutral valuation and hedging of derivative assets in general. Second, they are central for determining present values of deterministic cash flows, like, for instance, liabilities or cash flows from bonds. Again, the model of CIR85 is well understood and widely applied (cf. Björk (2004), ch. 22, or Brigo and Mercurio (2006)) and therefore an obvious choice.

The short rate model is to be calibrated to the term structure of interest rates such that it is replicated reasonably well and short rate sensitive instruments, like bonds, options on bonds or swaptions are correctly priced. Due to the zero correlation between the short rate and the index model, the task of calibrating the general model can be separated in two independent procedures.

---

[3]There exist richer models that allow, among others, for time-dependent parameters (cf. Galluccio and Le Cam (2008)), jumps in the volatility process (cf. Duffie et al. (2000)) or generalizations of the H93 volatility process (cf. Grzelak et al. (2012)).

[4]Many life insurance products, like variable annuities with guarantee components, have features that resemble typical equity derivatives. This requires that they be valued/priced accordingly as well as hedged like equity derivatives by the insurance company. Such products tend to have relatively long maturities typically well beyond 10 years and up to 30 years.

11.2.3 What Objective Function?

To calibrate a financial market model, one needs a performance yardstick for the quality of the calibration—formally, an objective or error function which is to be minimized. In general, model selection and selection of an objective or error function are treated as separate tasks. However, as Christoffersen and Jacobs (2004), pp. 314–315, point out:

"The key is that one should stop thinking of the specification of a theoretical model as separate from the choice of the loss function. When operationalizing a determin- istic theoretical model, whether for estimation or evaluation purposes, one has to impose a statistical structure. This statistical structure is an integral part of empirical model specification, and the choice of loss function is a major part of the statistical structure."

A multitude of candidate objective functions is available, three of which Christoffersen and Jacobs analyze in detail:

- mean squared error (MSE) of the price differences in currency units
- MSE of the relative price differences
- MSE of the implied volatility differences

They identify these to be among the most commonly used in the literature. The first one takes on the form

$$\min_p \frac{1}{N} \sum_{n=1}^{N} \left(C_n^* - C_n^{mod}(p) \right)^2 \tag{11.1}$$

with the C_n^* being the market or input prices and the C_n^{mod} being the model or output prices for options $n = 1, \ldots, N$ given parameter vector p. For example, Bakshi et al. (1997) and Reinsberg (2006) use this particular function for the calibration. The second one is similar but includes a scaling term

$$\min_p \frac{1}{N} \sum_{n=1}^{N} \left(\frac{C_n^* - C_n^{mod}(p)}{C_n^*} \right)^2 \tag{11.2}$$

Finally, the third one resembles the first one with the option prices replaced by the implied volatilities

$$\min_p \frac{1}{N} \sum_{n=1}^{N} \left(\sigma_n^* - \sigma_n^{mod}(p) \right)^2 \tag{11.3}$$

Here, σ_n^* is the volatility that gives a BSM option value equal to C_n^* and σ_n^{mod} analogous. These values are called *market* and *model implied volatilities*, respectively.

Christoffersen and Jacobs (2004) stress that the choice of an objective function for calibration purposes should take into account the specific objective itself (e.g. valuation, hedging, speculation). Although they do not favor one function over another, they find that their "... results indicate that the $MSE estimates perform the best across different loss functions. The $MSE may thus serve as a good general-purpose loss function in option valuation applications" (p. 316). By $MSE they mean function (11.1).

Regarding functions (11.1)–(11.3) it is not uncommon to include a square root to obtain RMSE instead of MSE (cf. Chapter 8 function (8.4); Schoutens et al. (2004) also use RMSE alongside other candidate functions). Also, some authors include weighting terms (like vega, bid-ask spread or implied volatility of the respective option), cf. Cont and Tankov (2004b) and Detlefsen (2005), to avoid biases due to the error function specification.[5] Additionally, it cannot be excluded that the function to be minimized has multiple local minima such that it is not assured that—depending on the optimization algorithm—the global minimum is identified. Some regularization procedure might be necessary in such a case (cf. Cont and Tankov (2004b), Galluccio and Le Cam (2008)).

Often the implied volatilities are the target of the calibration procedure. This chapter illustrates this approach as well, making use of a variant of function (11.3). In particular, we use the following error function specification:

$$\min_p \frac{1}{N} \sum_{n=1}^{N} \left(\left(\sigma_n^* - \sigma_n^{mod}(p) \right) \cdot \frac{\partial C_n^{BSM}}{\partial \sigma_n^*} \right)^2 \tag{11.4}$$

Here, the differences between the model and market implied volatilities are respectively weighted by the *vega of the Black-Scholes-Merton option price at the market implied volatility*. This approach takes into account how sensitive vanilla options are with respect to changes in volatility for different strikes and maturities. A look at Figure 5.7 in Chapter 5 reveals that vega in general increases with closeness to the ATM strike level and with longer maturities. This error function specification therefore gives, for example, less weight to implied volatility differences for short-term far ITM or OTM options.

In this chapter, function (11.1) is used throughout for the calibration to market quotes since this specification is in line with the main objective "valuation" and since corresponding numerical results are accurate enough in view of the chapter's general scope.[6] When calibrating to implied volatilites—with the main objective, for example, being "hedging"—function (11.4) is used.

11.2.4 What Market Data?

The first question regarding market data of course is what the relevant index is when analyzing equity index derivatives. This generally is pretty easy to answer; S&P 500, EURO STOXX 50, DAX or SMI could be candidates. The second is also relatively easy: which interest rates, yields, bond prices, etc. to use for the calibration of the short rate model. The third— more difficult to answer—question is about the concrete option quotes to be included in the

---

[5]For example, in function (11.1) options with high prices possibly gain too much weight while in function (11.2) this is the case for options with prices near zero; cf. Bakshi et al. (1997), p. 2016.

[6]Numerical experiments conducted with a Python script regarding the two functions RMSE (8.4) and MSE (11.1) suggest that there are, if at all, only negligible differences in terms of optimization speed or accuracy.

calibration. If one has decided upon the option provider itself—say, for example, the Eurex for the EURO STOXX 50 index—the decision is about the option maturities and strikes to be included. In addition, there are different quotes per option, like bid, ask, last and settlement price. For discussions in this regard refer to Bakshi et al. (1997) or Detlefsen (2005). There is also no guarantee that market prices are arbitrage-free such that the need to adjust raw market data may arise (cf. Fries (2008), Kahale (2004)).

Section 11.4 implements an approach similar to the one of Galluccio and Le Cam (2008) who propose to use (at least) three different options per maturity. They choose the at-the-money (ATM) option, one in-the-money (ITM) option and one out-of-the-money (OTM) option because "[t]his is the minimal number of instruments to calibrate ATM volatility level, smile slope and convexity for a given maturity" (p. 20). For the ITM and OTM option strike levels they propose $K^{ITM} = K^{ATM} + \sigma^{ATM}\sqrt{T}$ and $K^{OTM} = K^{ATM} - \sigma^{ATM}\sqrt{T}$, respectively.

Somewhat deviating from the suggestions in Galluccio and Le Cam (2008), we use a set of 15 market quotes for European call options as follows:

- **maturities**: three maturities (all shorter than 1 year)
- **strikes**: five strikes per maturity

In summary, since the subsequent analysis focuses on equity derivatives on the EURO STOXX 50 index, the following market data is used for calibration of the BCC97 model (all data from 30. September 2014):

- **short rate component** (section 11.3): Eonia rate and Euribor rates (up to 1 year)[7]
- **equity component** (section 11.4): European call options on the EURO STOXX 50 offered by the Eurex in Frankfurt

11.2.5 What Optimization Algorithm?

The calibration in Chapter 8 uses a two-step procedure: global minimization (i.e. brute force) followed by local minimization. In what follows, this approach is augmented by another, higher ranking four-step procedure. First, the stochastic short rate model is calibrated. Second, the H93 stocahstic volatility model is calibrated via global and local optimization. Third, taking as input the results from the stochastic volatility calibration, the jump component of the general market model BCC97 is calibrated—first via global and then via local optimization. Lastly, the stochastic volatility component of BCC97 is calibrated—via local optimization, taking as input the results of all other calibrations. During the last step, the jump parameters are, however, freed again to attain a better overall fit.[8]

---

[7]Cf. Hull and White (2013) for an in-depth discussion of the appropriate risk-free discounting rate for derivative instruments. As in Filipović (2009), p. 8, Euribor rates are considered risk-free rates in this book.

[8]Note that this procedure is only possible since the general market model assumes zero correlation between the short rate and the equity component. In principle, the general market model could be calibrated in a single step, at the cost of having a high dimensional parameter space leading to a pretty high computational burden for the single step.

Regarding global and local optimization algorithms there are a number of candidates available. Detlefsen (2005) and Mikhailov and Nögel (2003) discuss this topic in the context of option model calibration. Liberti (2008) offers a more general and more comprehensive discussion of alternative optimization algorithms.

11.3 CALIBRATION OF SHORT RATE COMPONENT

This section provides the required tool set to calibrate the CIR85 short rate model to market rates.

11.3.1 Theoretical Foundations

The short rate model of CIR85 is widely applied in theory and practice. This section does not treat it in its full richness but concentrates rather on the calibration procedure for which only several standard results are needed.[9] Recall the CIR85 stochastic differential equation (9.3)

$$dr_t = \kappa_r(\theta_r - r_t)dt + \sigma_r \sqrt{r_t}dZ_t$$

The task of calibration is to minimize, for all considered times t and a parameter set $\alpha = (\kappa_r, \theta_r, \sigma_r, r_0)$, simultaneously the differences

$$\Delta f(0, t) \equiv f(0, t) - f^{CIR85}(0, t; \alpha)$$

where $f(0, t)$ is the current market implied forward rate for time t and $f^{CIR85}(0, t; \alpha)$ is the current model implied forward rate for time t given parameter set α. If $B_t(T), t < T$, denotes the time t price of a zero-coupon bond maturing at time T and paying one unit of currency at that date, then the (instantaneous) forward rate at time t for time T is defined by

$$f(t, T) \equiv -\frac{\partial B_t(T)}{\partial T} \tag{11.5}$$

with $f(0, t)$ as an obvious special case. Furthermore, the short rate at time t follows from $r_t = f(t, t)$. The other way round (cf. Björk (2004), p. 305) zero-coupon bond prices are uniquely determined by the forward rate curve

$$B_t(T) = \exp\left(-\int_t^T f(t, s)ds\right)$$

---

[9]Svoboda (2002) provides a detailed account of the CIR85 model and a number of alternative short rate models. For a comprehensive overview of interest models in general refer to Brigo and Mercurio (2006).

With this background knowledge, the usefulness of the following formula for the forward rates in the CIR85 short rate model becomes clear[10]

$$f^{CIR85}(0, t; \alpha) = \frac{\kappa_r \theta_r (e^{\gamma t} - 1)}{2\gamma + (\kappa_r + \gamma)(e^{\gamma t} - 1)}$$

$$+ r_0 \frac{4\gamma^2 e^{\gamma t}}{(2\gamma + (\kappa_r + \gamma)(e^{\gamma t} - 1))^2} \tag{11.6}$$

where

$$\gamma \equiv \sqrt{\kappa_r^2 + 2\sigma_r^2}$$

with the parameters and variables as defined in section 9.2.

The time t price a of zero-coupon bond maturing at time T and paying one unit of currency is given by the affine formula[11]

$$B_t(T) = a(t, T)e^{-b(t,T)\mathbf{E}_0^{\mathbf{Q}}(r_t)} \tag{11.7}$$

where

$$a(t, T) \equiv \left[\frac{2\gamma \exp(0.5(\kappa_r + \gamma)(T - t))}{2\gamma + (\kappa_r + \gamma)(e^{\gamma(T-t)} - 1)} \right]^{\frac{2\kappa_r \theta_r}{\sigma_r^2}} \tag{11.8}$$

and

$$b(t, T) \equiv \frac{2(e^{\gamma(T-t)} - 1)}{2\gamma + (\kappa_r + \gamma)(e^{\gamma(T-t)} - 1)} \tag{11.9}$$

For the expectation value of r_t it holds $\mathbf{E}_0^{\mathbf{Q}}(r_t) = \theta_r + e^{-\kappa_r t}(r_0 - \theta_r)$.

This completes the tool set for the calibration of the CIR85 model.[12]

11.3.2 Calibration to Euribor Rates

Forward rates are seldom quoted directly in the market. However, what is generally publicly available is yields, reference or swap rates, like US Treasury yields, German Bund yields, LIBOR, Euribor, OIS or Eonia spot rates and respective swap rates, for different maturities.

---

[10]The formula presented is from London (2005), pp. 542 and 433. Heath, Jarrow and Morton (Heath et al., 1992), pioneered the approach of taking the forward rate curve as initial input for the modeling of interest rates.

[11]In general, it is a desirable feature of short rate models to be affine. This is due to the fact that such models yield essentially closed-form expressions for zero-coupon bond prices. Cf. Dai and Singleton (2000).

[12]Refer to Svoboda (2002) for a detailed derivation of the bond formula (11.7) with (11.8) and (11.9) from which the forward rate formula (11.6) follows via (11.5).

There is a one-to-one correspondence between zero-coupon bond yields for different maturities and forward rates via (cf. Baxter and Rennie (1996), p. 134)

$$f(0, T) = Y(0, T) + \frac{\partial Y(0, T)}{\partial T} \cdot T \tag{11.10}$$

with $Y(0, T)$ as the yield today of a bond maturing at T. The (continuous) yield for a zero-coupon bond solves the equation

$$B_T(T) = B_0(T)e^{Y(0,T) \cdot T}$$
$$\Leftrightarrow Y(0, T) = \frac{\log B_T(T) - \log B_0(T)}{T}$$

With the final value of the bond normalized to 1, one has

$$Y(0, T) = -\frac{\log(B_0(T))}{T}$$

The same relationship holds true for continuous Euribor rates analogously. For coupon bonds, the formula is not as simple because the single coupon payments up to maturity have to be accounted for (cf. Filipović (2009), ch. 3).

Unfortunately, spot rates and bond yields are generally only quoted for selected, discrete maturities so that the need arises to interpolate between the single data points. With a continuously differentiable interpolating function—e.g. from a cubic splines regression (cf. Brandimarte (2006), pp. 183–188)—one can derive the partial derivative in (11.10) and therewith forward rates for arbitrary times T.

Euribor rates are quoted on a 30/360 day count basis. For what follows, Euribor rates therefore have to be transformed into continuous rates (continuous yield of a unit zero-coupon bond). As an example, take the 6-month Euribor rate which is 0.043%. The corresponding factor is

$$f_s^{6m} = 1 + 180/360 \cdot 0.00043$$

The equivalent annualized continuous rate then is

$$f_c^{6m} = 360/180 \cdot \log(f_s^{6m})$$

This ensures that

$$1 + 180/360 \cdot f_s^{6m} = e^{180/360 \cdot f_c^{6m}}$$

holds.

The Python script in sub-section 11.6.1 implements this transformation and the necessary interpolation for the Euribor term structure from 30. September 2014. The Euribor data set is complemented by the Eonia rate as the time $t = 0$ short rate ("maturity of one day") from 01. October 2014.

Figure 11.1 shows the spot rates for different maturities, the interpolated rate curve and its first derivative.

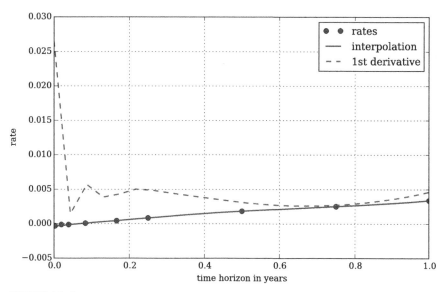

FIGURE 11.1 Euribor term structure up to 12 months (incl. Eonia rate); points = market quotes from 30. September 2014, line = interpolated curve, dashed line = 1st derivative of term structure curve

To calibrate the CIR85 model to the forward rates, the MSE of the market implied and model implied forward rate curve at selected discrete points in time is minimized. Given a fixed r_0 and an equidistant spacing of $[0, T]$ by Δt with $M \equiv T/\Delta t$, the task is to

$$\min_{\alpha} \frac{1}{M} \sum_{m=0}^{M} (f(0, m\Delta t) - f^{CIR85}(0, m\Delta t; \alpha))^2 \tag{11.11}$$

A respective algorithm is found in the Python script of sub-section 11.6.1. The results of the calibration are shown graphically in Figure 11.2.[13]

Finally, Figure 11.3 shows values for a unit zero-coupon bonds maturing 2 years out according to the bond valuation formula for the CIR85 model as provided in (11.7) and given the calibration results.

11.4 CALIBRATION OF EQUITY COMPONENT

This section now deals with the required tools and approaches to calibrate the BCC97 market model to market observed option quotes.

---

[13]Using a deterministic-shift approach, one can make the calibration of the model perfect while preserving the affine structure. Cf. Brigo and Mercurio (2001).

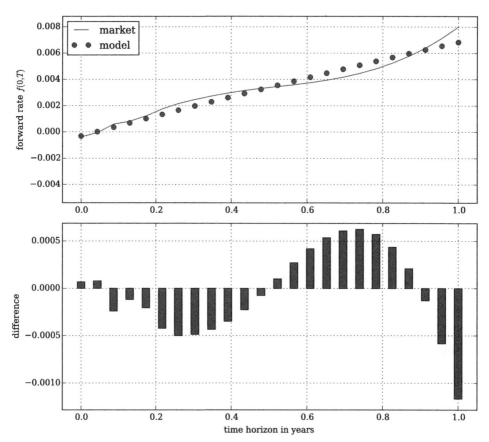

FIGURE 11.2 Market and model implied forward rates for Euribor; line = market forward rates from 30. September 2014, dots = model implied forward rates; bars = the difference between the model and market forward rates

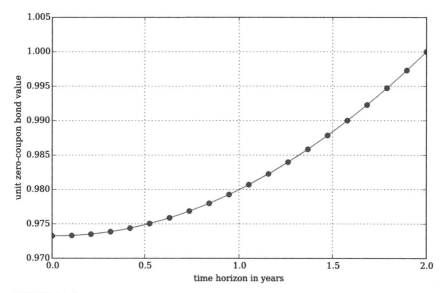

FIGURE 11.3 Unit zero-coupon bond values at time t maturing at time $T = 2$

11.4.1 Valuation via Fourier Transform Method

The previous section provides a calibrated short rate model so that market consistent short rates are now available for the valuation of plain vanilla European call options. This is the major prerequisite for the calibration of the general market model in terms of the equity component. This section applies the Fourier transform method and makes heavy use of the following formula for call options

$$C_0(K, T) = S_0 - B_0(T)\sqrt{S_0 K}\frac{1}{\pi}$$
$$\cdot \int_0^\infty \text{Re}[e^{-iuk}\phi_0(u - i/2, T)]\frac{du}{u^2 + 1/4} \tag{11.12}$$

with $k \equiv \log(S_0/K)$ and φ_0 the characteristic function of the model at hand—in our case $\mathcal{M}^{BCC97}$. $B_0(T)$ is the appropriate discount factor, i.e. bond present value, for the option maturity from the calibrated CIR85 model. The related Python scripts work with a constant short rate where a value $\bar{r}$ is used that solves the equation $B_0(T) = e^{-\bar{r}T}$. This is made for simplicity and is possible because of European exercise. Sub-section 9.7.3 offers Python implementations for the BCC97 model and the special cases of M76 and H93.

The script in sub-section 9.7.3 provides characteristic function implementations for M76 (on a stand-alone basis), for H93 (on a stand-alone basis) and for BCC97 (combination of H93 and jump component of M76). The characteristic function of the BCC97 model with constant short rate is simply the product of the characteristic function of the M76 jump component (see also equations (6.14) and (6.15))

$$\varphi_0^{M76J}(u, T) = \exp((iu\omega + \lambda(e^{iu\mu_J - u^2\delta^2/2} - 1))T) \tag{11.13}$$

where the risk-neutral drift (correction) term ω takes now on the form

$$\omega \equiv -\lambda(e^{\mu_J + \delta^2/2} - 1) \tag{11.14}$$

and the characteristic function of the H93 model[14]

$$\varphi_0^{H93}(u, T) = e^{H_1(u,T) + H_2(u,T)v_0} \tag{11.15}$$

with the following definitions

$$c_1 \equiv \kappa_v \theta_v$$
$$c_2 \equiv -\sqrt{(\rho\sigma_v ui - \kappa_v)^2 - \sigma_v^2(-ui - u^2)}$$
$$c_3 \equiv \frac{\kappa_v - \rho\sigma_v ui + c_2}{\kappa_v - \rho\sigma_v ui - c_2}$$
$$H_1(u, T) \equiv r_{0,T}uiT + \frac{c_1}{\sigma_v^2}\left\{(\kappa_v - \rho\sigma_v ui + c_2)T - 2\log\left[\frac{1 - c_1 e^{c_3 T}}{1 - c_3}\right]\right\}$$
$$H_2(u, T) \equiv \frac{\kappa_v - \rho\sigma_v ui + c_2}{\sigma_v^2}\left[\frac{1 - e^{c_2 T}}{1 - c_3 e^{c_2 T}}\right]$$

---

[14]See Cherubini et al. (2009), app. G, Gatheral (2006), ch. 2, or Heston (1993).

and all variables as defined as before. In H_1 we set $r_{0,T} = -\log(B_0(T))/T$ where we get $B_0(T)$ from equations (9.4)–(9.7) for the CIR85 model.

Therefore, the characteristic function for BCC97 with constant short rate is the product of (11.15) and (11.13)

$$\varphi_0^{BCC97}(u, T) = \varphi_0^{H93} \cdot \varphi_0^{M76J}(u, T) \tag{11.16}$$

This completes the necessary ingredients for the calibration of the equity component.

11.4.2   Calibration to EURO STOXX 50 Option Quotes

To have a small but still meaningful subset of market prices in terms of maturities, the subsequent analysis considers *three maturities*:

- 17. October 2014 (17 days)
- 19. December 2014 (80 days)
- 20. March 2015 (171 days)

Maturity day generally is the third Friday of the month if this is a business day.

Per maturity, we consider *five different strikes*: 3,000, 3,100, 3,200, 3,300, 3,400—given a spot closing level of 3,225.93 of the EURO STOXX 50 on 30. September 2014.

The calibration is done for the EURO STOXX 50 index and on the basis of European call options from the Eurex.[15] The calibration takes a total of 15 European call option quotes into account.

Before proceeding, the right short rates have to be derived from the calibrated CIR85 model since the Fourier transform pricing formula is for constant short rates only. One can recover the right short rate for option maturity T in knowledge of the bond price $B_0(T)$ via

$$\bar{r}^*(T) = -\frac{\log B_0(T)}{T}$$

which is equivalent to the continuous yield of the respective zero-coupon bond. This approach is used in the calibration scripts to derive equivalent constant short rates for each maturity, respectively.

11.4.3   Calibration of H93 Model

Before going on to the general market model BCC97, we look first at a model calibration of the H93 stochastic volatility model without jump component. Sub-section 11.6.2 contains the Python script for the model calibration.

Figure 11.4 shows the results of the calibration which are already quite good. The MSE of this calibration is 0.307 and the optimal parameters are as follows:

- $\kappa_v = 18.447$
- $\theta_v = 0.026$

---

[15]Reinsberg (2006), for example, is an empirical study of option pricing models similar to Bakshi et al. (1997) and also with the EURO STOXX 50 as the benchmark index.

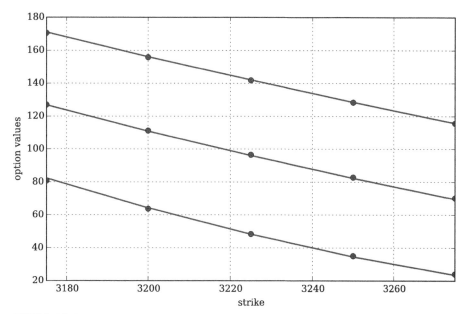

FIGURE 11.4 Results of H93 model calibration to EURO STOXX 50 option quotes; line = market quotes from 30. September 2014, red dots = model values after calibration

- $\sigma_v = 0.978$
- $\rho = -0.821$
- $v_0 = 0.035$

Figure 11.5 shows the resulting model implied volatilities compared to the market implied volatilities—including absolute differences. The figures are generated with the Python script in sub-section 11.6.3. The implied volatility fit is also quite good.

11.4.4 Calibration of Jump Component

It is well-known that the problem of calibrating a jump-diffusion model—and in particular the M76 one—suffers from two major problems (cf. the in-depth discussion in Galluccio and Le Cam (2008)):

- **degeneracy**: different parameter combinations may yield the same values for the error function
- **indeterminacy**: the error function is not strictly convex and may exhibit many local minima

This so-called ill-posedness is of importance when calibrating models for the first time but in particular when re-calibrating them. Practitioners look for stable parameters in calibrations[16]

---

[16]This is mainly due to the fact that in general hedging programs depend on the parameters of the model used. Strongly varying parameters could therefore lead to highly oscillating hedge positions.

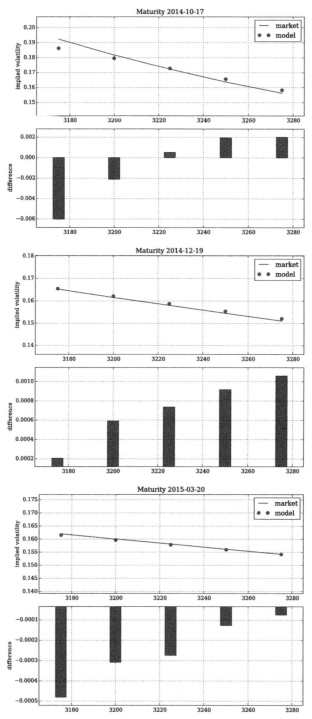

FIGURE 11.5 Implied volatilities from H93 model calibration to EURO STOXX 50 option quotes from 30. September 2014

and with degeneracy and indeterminacy parameters might "jump" significantly when re-calibrating models. A solution to this is the regularization of the error function—where MSE is used in the following—via, for example, Tikhonov regularization. To this end, the error function used for the local optimization is enhanced by a penalty term of the form (cf. Cherubini et al. (2009))

$$Penalty(p) \equiv \sqrt{(p_0 - p)^2} \qquad (11.17)$$

where p_0 is the initial input parameter vector for the local optimization (here coming from the global optimization) and p the current parameter vector. Term (11.17) penalizes deviations from the initial inputs—and thereby avoids unjustifiable deviations from the preliminary global optimum and undesired jumps of parameter values.

The problem of calibrating the BCC97 model therefore is (cf. equation (11.1)) in its general form, including the penalty term

$$\min_p \frac{1}{N} \sum_{n=1}^{N} \left(C_n^* - C_n^{BCC97}(p) \right)^2 + w \cdot Penalty(p)$$

with the C_n^* being the market or input prices and the C_n^{BCC97} being the model or output prices given parameter vector p. w is a weighting parameter which can be used to give the penalty more influence if necessary.

Sub-section 11.6.4 contains the Python script that implements the second part of the equity component calibration. Here the jump part of the equity component is calibrated to the five options with the shortest maturity, first via global then via local optimization using Tikhonov regularization. The script uses the results of the H93 calibration for the stochastic volatility parametrization. The calibration yields the following optimal results:

- $\lambda = 0.008$
- $\mu = -0.600$
- $\delta = 0.001$

Figure 11.6 shows the calibration results graphically. The fit for the shortest maturity has an MSE of 0.558.

11.4.5 Complete Calibration of BCC97 Model

In the third part of the equity component calibration, the results from the H93 model calibration and from the jump component calibration are taken as input parameters ($\kappa_v, \theta_v, \sigma_v, \rho, v_0, \lambda, \mu, \delta$) for the local optimization procedure. The Python script in sub-section 11.6.5 calibrates the BCC97 model to all options and simultaneously derives—via local optimization—optimal values for all parameters of BCC97 (with constant but maturity-dependent short rate). The MSE decreases to a rather low 0.104 and the optimal parameters are:

- $\kappa_v = 22.212$
- $\theta_v = 0.025$
- $\sigma_v = 0.952$

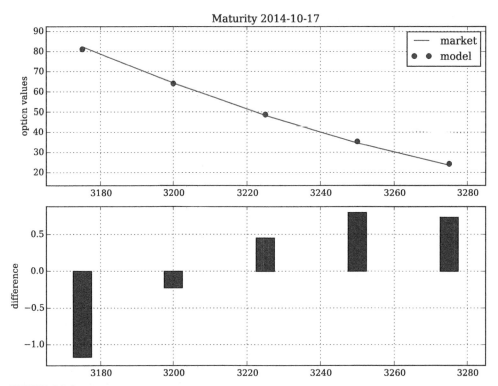

FIGURE 11.6 Results of BCC97 jump-diffusion part calibration to five European call options on the EURO STOXX 50 with 17 days maturity; market quotes from 30. September 2014

- $\rho = -0.999$
- $v_0 = 0.036$
- $\lambda = 0.008$
- $\mu = -0.501$
- $\delta = 0.000$

Figure 11.7 compares the market quotes with the option values generated by the calibrated BCC97 model.

Finally, Figure 11.8 compares the market implied volatilities with the model implied volatilities after calibration of the BCC97 model.

11.4.6 Calibration to Implied Volatilities

Depending on the specific purpose of the calibration a good implied volatility fit may be more important than a good price fit. This final sub-section, therefore, calibrates the BCC97 model to market implied volatilities directly. To this end, one needs to calculate market implied volatilities first and model implied volatilities per iteration of local optimization runs.

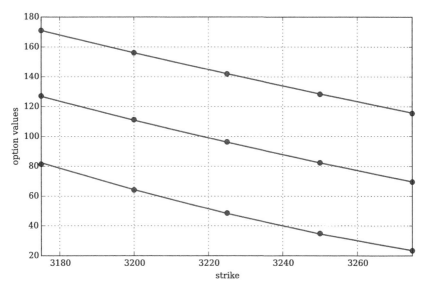

FIGURE 11.7 Results of simultaneous BCC97 jump-diffusion and stochastic volatility part calibration to 15 European call options on the EURO STOXX 50 with 17, 80 and 171 days maturity, respectively; quotes from 30. September 2014

The Python script in sub-section 11.6.6 implements a local calibration procedure in this regard, taking the optimal parameters from the previous BCC97 model calibration (to market quotes) as starting values. The major difference is the specification of the error function according to (11.4). The vega-weighted MSE in this case is pretty low with 0.083 for the following optimal parameters:

- $\kappa_v = 28.473$
- $\theta_v = 0.025$
- $\sigma_v = 1.175$
- $\rho = -0.953$
- $v_0 = 0.039$
- $\lambda = 0.007$
- $\mu = -0.600$
- $\delta = 0.000$

Figure 11.9 shows the resulting model values compared to the market quotes of the EURO STOXX 50 call options. Although not the direct target of the optimization, the value fits are again quite good.

Figure 11.10 shows the resulting model implied volatilities compared to the market implied volatilities. Here, it is important to recall that the error function (11.4) gives less weight to errors for (far) OTM/ITM options and more weight to errors for options with longer maturities ceteris paribus.

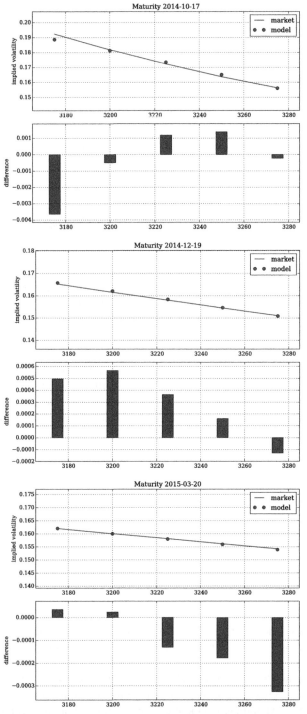

FIGURE 11.8 Implied volatilities from BCC97 model calibration to EURO STOXX 50 option quotes from 30. September 2014

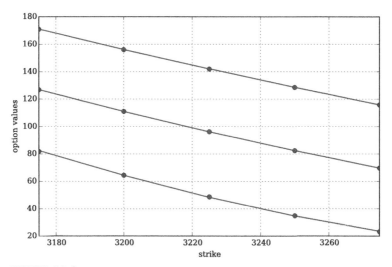

FIGURE 11.9 Results of BCC97 calibration to 15 market implied volatilities of EURO STOXX 50 European call options with 17, 80 and 171 days maturity, respectively; market quotes from 30. September 2014

11.5 CONCLUSIONS

"The market is always right." This is the credo of this chapter. In this sense, the chapter takes market interest rates and market quotes for plain vanilla instruments as given and tries to find—by global and local optimization—those parameters for the BCC97 model that best replicate the observed option quotes.

A central question in this context is to what market data one should try to calibrate the model. This question cannot be answered with any generality. The answer depends, in a complex fashion, on the task at hand and on the particular products one wishes to trade, price/value or hedge.

However, the chapter illustrates that the model of BCC97 is rich enough to replicate observed yields and option quotes as well as implied volatilities of quoted options reasonably well. Equipped with a market-calibrated model, the next two chapters can now proceed with the market-based valuation and hedging of equity derivatives, respectively.

11.6 PYTHON SCRIPTS FOR COX-INGERSOLL-ROSS MODEL

11.6.1 Calibration of CIR85

```
#
# Calibration of CIR85 model
# to Euribor Rates from 30. September 2014
# 11_cal/CIR_calibration.py
#
```

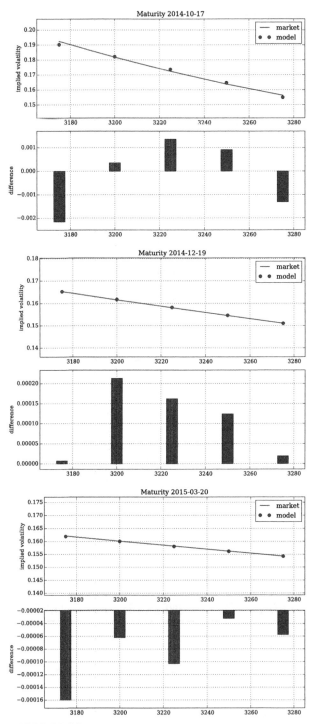

FIGURE 11.10 Implied volatilities from BCC97 model calibration to EURO STOXX 50 implied volatilities from 30. September 2014

```
# (c) Dr. Yves J. Hilpisch
# Derivatives Analytics with Python
#
import sys
sys.path.append('10_mcs')
import math
import numpy as np
np.set_printoptions(suppress=True,
                    formatter={'all': lambda x: '%7.6f' % x})
import matplotlib.pyplot as plt
import matplotlib as mpl
mpl.rcParams['font.family'] = 'serif'
import scipy.interpolate as sci
from scipy.optimize import fmin
from CIR_zcb_valuation_gen import B


#
# Market Data: Eonia rate (01.10.2014) + Euribor rates
# Source: http://www.emmi-benchmarks.eu
# on 30. September 2014
#
t_list = np.array((1, 7, 14, 30, 60, 90, 180, 270, 360)) / 360.
r_list =  np.array((-0.032, -0.013, -0.013, 0.007, 0.043,
                    0.083, 0.183, 0.251, 0.338)) / 100

factors = (1 + t_list * r_list)
zero_rates = 1 / t_list * np.log(factors)


r0 = r_list[0]


#
# Interpolation of Market Data
#


tck = sci.splrep(t_list, zero_rates, k=3)  # cubic splines
tn_list = np.linspace(0.0, 1.0, 24)
ts_list = sci.splev(tn_list, tck, der=0)
de_list = sci.splev(tn_list, tck, der=1)

f = ts_list + de_list * tn_list
  # forward rate transformation

def plot_term_structure():
    plt.figure(figsize=(8, 5))
    plt.plot(t_list, r_list, 'ro', label='rates')
    plt.plot(tn_list, ts_list, 'b', label='interpolation', lw=1.5)
      # cubic splines
```

```
        plt.plot(tn_list, de_list, 'g--', label='1st derivative', lw=1.5)
            # first derivative
        plt.legend(loc=0)
        plt.xlabel('time horizon in years')
        plt.ylabel('rate')
        plt.grid()


#
# Model Forward Rates
#
def CIR_forward_rate(opt):
    ''' Function for forward rates in CIR85 model.

    Parameters
    ==========
    kappa_r: float
        mean-reversion factor
    theta_r: float
        long-run mean
    sigma_r: float
        volatility factor

    Returns
    =======
    forward_rate: float
        forward rate
    '''
    kappa_r, theta_r, sigma_r = opt
    t = tn_list
    g = np.sqrt(kappa_r ** 2 + 2 * sigma_r ** 2)
    sum1 = ((kappa_r * theta_r * (np.exp(g * t) - 1)) /
            (2 * g + (kappa_r + g) * (np.exp(g * t) - 1)))
    sum2 = r0 * ((4 * g ** 2 * np.exp(g * t)) /
            (2 * g + (kappa_r + g) * (np.exp(g * t) - 1)) ** 2)
    forward_rate = sum1 + sum2
    return forward_rate


#
# Error Function
#
def CIR_error_function(opt):
    ''' Error function for CIR85 model calibration. '''
    kappa_r, theta_r, sigma_r = opt
    if 2 * kappa_r * theta_r < sigma_r ** 2:
        return 100
    if kappa_r < 0 or theta_r < 0 or sigma_r < 0.001:
```

```
        return 100
    forward_rates = CIR_forward_rate(opt)
    MSE = np.sum((f - forward_rates) ** 2) / len(f)
    # print opt, MSE
    return MSE


#
# Calibration Procedure
#
def CIR_calibration():
    opt = fmin(CIR_error_function, [1.0, 0.02, 0.1],
            xtol=0.00001, ftol=0.00001,
            maxiter=300, maxfun=500)
    return opt


#
# Graphical Results Output
#
def plot_calibrated_frc(opt):
    ''' Plots market and calibrated forward rate curves. '''
    forward_rates = CIR_forward_rate(opt)
    plt.figure(figsize=(8, 7))
    plt.subplot(211)
    plt.grid()
    plt.ylabel('forward rate $f(0,T)$')
    plt.plot(tn_list, f, 'b', label='market')
    plt.plot(tn_list, forward_rates, 'ro', label='model')
    plt.legend(loc=0)
    plt.axis([min(tn_list) - 0.05, max(tn_list) + 0.05,
        min(f) - 0.005, max(f) * 1.1])
    plt.subplot(212)
    plt.grid(True)
    wi = 0.02
    plt.bar(tn_list - wi / 2, forward_rates - f, width=wi)
    plt.xlabel('time horizon in years')
    plt.ylabel('difference')
    plt.axis([min(tn_list) - 0.05, max(tn_list) + 0.05,
        min(forward_rates - f) * 1.1, max(forward_rates - f) * 1.1])
    plt.tight_layout()


def plot_zcb_values(p0, T):
    ''' Plots unit zero-coupon bond values (discount factors). '''
    t_list = np.linspace(0.0, T, 20)
    r_list = B([r0, p0[0], p0[1], p0[2], t_list, T])
    plt.figure(figsize=(8, 5))
    plt.plot(t_list, r_list, 'b')
```

```
    plt.plot(t_list, r_list, 'ro')
    plt.xlabel('time horizon in years')
    plt.ylabel('unit zero-coupon bond value')
    plt.grid()
```

11.6.2 Calibration of H93 Stochastic Volatility Model

```
#
# Calibration of Bakshi, Cao and Chen (1997)
# Stoch Vol Jump Model to EURO STOXX Option Quotes
# Data Source: www.eurexchange.com
# via Numerical Integration
# 11_cal/BCC97_calibration_2.py
#
# (c) Dr. Yves J. Hilpisch
# Derivatives Analytics with Python
#
import sys
sys.path.append('09_gmm')
import math
import numpy as np
np.set_printoptions(suppress=True,
                    formatter={'all': lambda x: '%5.3f' % x})
import pandas as pd
from scipy.optimize import brute, fmin, minimize
import matplotlib as mpl
mpl.rcParams['font.family'] = 'serif'
from BCC_option_valuation import H93_call_value
from CIR_calibration import CIR_calibration, r_list
from CIR_zcb_valuation import B


#
# Calibrate Short Rate Model
#
kappa_r, theta_r, sigma_r = CIR_calibration()


#
# Market Data from www.eurexchange.com
# as of 30. September 2014
#
h5 = pd.HDFStore('08_m76/option_data.h5', 'r')
data = h5['data']  # European call & put option data (3 maturities)
h5.close()
S0 = 3225.93  # EURO STOXX 50 level 30.09.2014
r0 = r_list[0]  # initial short rate
```

```
#
# Option Selection
#
tol = 0.02  # percent ITM/OTM options
options = data[(np.abs(data['Strike'] - S0) / S0) < tol]

# options = data[data['Strike'].isin([3100, 3150, 3225, 3300, 3350])]

#
# Adding Time-to-Maturity and Short Rates
#
for row, option in options.iterrows():
    T = (option['Maturity'] - option['Date']).days / 365.
    options.ix[row, 'T'] = T
    B0T = B([kappa_r, theta_r, sigma_r, r0, T])
    options.ix[row, 'r'] = -math.log(B0T) / T

#
# Calibration Functions
#
i = 0
min_MSE = 500
def H93_error_function(p0):
    ''' Error function for parameter calibration in BCC97 model via
    Lewis (2001) Fourier approach.

    Parameters
    ==========
    kappa_v: float
        mean-reversion factor
    theta_v: float
        long-run mean of variance
    sigma_v: float
        volatility of variance
    rho: float
        correlation between variance and stock/index level
    v0: float
        initial, instantaneous variance

    Returns
    =======
    MSE: float
        mean squared error
    '''
    global i, min_MSE
    kappa_v, theta_v, sigma_v, rho, v0 = p0
```

```python
    if kappa_v < 0.0 or theta_v < 0.005 or sigma_v < 0.0 or \
            rho < -1.0 or rho > 1.0:
        return 500.0
    if 2 * kappa_v * theta_v < sigma_v ** 2:
        return 500.0
    se = []
    for row, option in options.iterrows():
        model_value = H93_call_value(S0, option['Strike'], option['T'],
                            option['r'], kappa_v, theta_v, sigma_v, rho, v0)
        se.append((model_value - option['Call']) ** 2)
    MSE = sum(se) / len(se)
    min_MSE = min(min_MSE, MSE)
    if i % 25 == 0:
        print '%4d |' % i, np.array(p0), '| %7.3f | %7.3f' % (MSE, min_MSE)
    i += 1
    return MSE


def H93_calibration_full():
    ''' Calibrates H93 stochastic volatility model to market quotes. '''
    # first run with brute force
    # (scan sensible regions)
    p0 = brute(H93_error_function,
                ((2.5, 10.6, 5.0),   # kappa_v
                (0.01, 0.041, 0.01),  # theta_v
                (0.05, 0.251, 0.1),  # sigma_v
                (-0.75, 0.01, 0.25),  # rho
                (0.01, 0.031, 0.01)),  # v0
                finish=None)

    # second run with local, convex minimization
    # (dig deeper where promising)
    opt = fmin(H93_error_function, p0,
                xtol=0.000001, ftol=0.000001,
                maxiter=750, maxfun=900)
    np.save('11_cal/opt_sv', np.array(opt))
    return opt


def H93_calculate_model_values(p0):
    ''' Calculates all model values given parameter vector p0. '''
    kappa_v, theta_v, sigma_v, rho, v0 = p0
    values = []
    for row, option in options.iterrows():
        model_value = H93_call_value(S0, option['Strike'], option['T'],
                            option['r'], kappa_v, theta_v, sigma_v, rho, v0)
        values.append(model_value)
    return np.array(values)
```

11.6.3 Comparison of Implied Volatilities

```
#
# Black-Scholes-Merton Implied Volatilities of
# of Calibrated BCC97 Model
# Data Source: www.eurexchange.com, 30. September 2014
# 11_cal/plot_implied_volatilities.py
#
# (c) Dr. Yves J. Hilpisch
# Derivatives Analytics with Python
#
import sys
sys.path.extend(['03_stf', '09_gmm'])
import math
import pandas as pd
import matplotlib.pyplot as plt
import matplotlib as mpl
mpl.rcParams['font.family'] = 'serif'
from BSM_imp_vol import call_option
from CIR_zcb_valuation import B
from H93_calibration import S0, r0, kappa_r, theta_r, sigma_r


#
# Calibration Results
#

def calculate_implied_volatilities(filename):
    ''' Calculates market and model implied volatilities. '''
    h5 = pd.HDFStore(filename, 'r')
    options = h5['options']
    h5.close()
    for row, option in options.iterrows():
        T = (option['Maturity'] - option['Date']).days / 365.
        B0T = B([kappa_r, theta_r, sigma_r, r0, T])
        r = -math.log(B0T) / T
        call = call_option(S0, option['Strike'], option['Date'],
                           option['Maturity'], option['r'], 0.1)
        options.ix[row, 'market_iv'] = call.imp_vol(option['Call'], 0.15)
        options.ix[row, 'model_iv'] = call.imp_vol(option['Model'], 0.15)
    return options

def plot_implied_volatilities(options, model):
    ''' Plots market implied volatilities against model implied ones. '''
    mats = sorted(set(options.Maturity))
    for mat in mats:
        opts = options[options.Maturity == mat]
```

```
plt.figure(figsize=(8, 6))
plt.subplot(211)
plt.grid()
plt.ylabel('implied volatility')
plt.plot(opts.Strike, opts.market_iv, 'b', label='market', lw=1.5)
plt.plot(opts.Strike, opts.model_iv, 'ro', label='model')
plt.legend(loc=0)
plt.axis([min(opts.Strike) - 10, max(opts.Strike) + 10,
        min(opts.market_iv) - 0.015, max(opts.market_iv) + 0.015])
plt.title('Maturity %s' % str(mat)[:10])
plt.subplot(212)
plt.grid(True)
wi = 5.0
diffs = opts.model_iv.values - opts.market_iv.values
plt.bar(opts.Strike - wi / 2, diffs, width=wi)
plt.ylabel('difference')
ymi = min(diffs) - (max(diffs) - min(diffs)) * 0.1
yma = max(diffs) + (max(diffs) - min(diffs)) * 0.1
plt.axis([min(opts.Strike) - 10, max(opts.Strike) + 10, ymi, yma])
plt.tight_layout()
plt.savefig('../images/11_cal/%s_calibration_iv_%s.pdf'
                % (model, str(mat)[:10]))
```

11.6.4 Calibration of Jump-Diffusion Part of BCC97

```
#
# Calibration of Bakshi, Cao and Chen (1997)
# Stoch Vol Jump Model to EURO STOXX Option Quotes
# Data Source: www.eurexchange.com
# via Numerical Integration
# 11_cal/BCC97_calibration_short.py
#
# (c) Dr. Yves J. Hilpisch
# Derivatives Analytics with Python
#
import sys
sys.path.append('09_gmm')
import math
import numpy as np
np.set_printoptions(suppress=True,
                formatter={'all': lambda x: '%5.3f' % x})
import pandas as pd
from scipy.optimize import brute, fmin
import matplotlib.pyplot as plt
```

```
import matplotlib as mpl
mpl.rcParams['font.family'] = 'serif'
from BCC_option_valuation import BCC_call_value
from CIR_calibration import CIR_calibration, r_list
from CIR_zcb_valuation import B
from H93_calibration import options


#
# Calibrate Short Rate Model
#
kappa_r, theta_r, sigma_r = CIR_calibration()


#
# Market Data from www.eurexchange.com
# as of 30. September 2014
#
S0 = 3225.93  # EURO STOXX 50 level
r0 = r_list[0]  # initial short rate
#
# Option Selection
#
mats = sorted(set(options['Maturity']))
options = options[options['Maturity'] == mats[0]]
  # only shortest maturity


#
# Initial Parameter Guesses
#
kappa_v, theta_v, sigma_v, rho, v0 = np.load('11_cal/opt_sv.npy')
    # from H93 model calibration



#
# Calibration Functions
#
i = 0
min_MSE = 5000.0
local_opt = False
def BCC_error_function(p0):
    ''' Error function for parameter calibration in M76 Model via
    Carr-Madan (1999) FFT approach.

    Parameters
    ==========
    lamb: float
        jump intensity
```

```
    mu: float
        expected jump size
    delta: float
        standard deviation of jump

    Returns
    =======
    MSE: float
        mean squared error
    '''
    global i, min_MSE, local_opt, opt1
    lamb, mu, delta = p0
    if lamb < 0.0 or mu < -0.6 or mu > 0.0 or delta < 0.0:
        return 5000.0
    se = []
    for row, option in options.iterrows():
        model_value = BCC_call_value(S0, option['Strike'], option['T'],
                            option['r'], kappa_v, theta_v, sigma_v, rho, v0,
                            lamb, mu, delta)
        se.append((model_value - option['Call']) ** 2)
    MSE = sum(se) / len(se)
    min_MSE = min(min_MSE, MSE)
    if i % 25 == 0:
        print '%4d |' % i, np.array(p0), '| %7.3f | %7.3f' % (MSE, min_MSE)
    i += 1
    if local_opt:
        penalty = np.sqrt(np.sum((p0 - opt1) ** 2)) * 1
        return MSE + penalty
    return MSE

#
# Calibration
#

def BCC_calibration_short():
    ''' Calibrates jump component of BCC97 model to market quotes. '''
    # first run with brute force
    # (scan sensible regions)
    opt1 = 0.0
    opt1 = brute(BCC_error_function,
                ((0.0, 0.51, 0.1),   # lambda
                (-0.5, -0.11, 0.1),  # mu
                (0.0, 0.51, 0.25)),  # delta
                finish=None)

    # second run with local, convex minimization
    # (dig deeper where promising)
```

```
        local_opt = True
        opt2 = fmin(BCC_error_function, opt1,
                    xtol=0.0000001, ftol=0.0000001,
                    maxiter=550, maxfun=750)
        np.save('11_cal/opt_jump', np.array(opt2))
        return opt2


def BCC_jump_calculate_model_values(p0):
    ''' Calculates all model values given parameter vector p0. '''
    lamb, mu, delta = p0
    values = []
    for row, option in options.iterrows():
        T = (option['Maturity'] - option['Date']).days / 365.
        B0T = B([kappa_r, theta_r, sigma_r, r0, T])
        r = -math.log(B0T) / T
        model_value = BCC_call_value(S0, option['Strike'], T, r,
                            kappa_v, theta_v, sigma_v, rho, v0,
                            lamb, mu, delta)
        values.append(model_value)
    return np.array(values)


#
# Graphical Results Output
#
def plot_calibration_results(p0):
    options['Model'] = BCC_jump_calculate_model_values(p0)
    plt.figure(figsize=(8, 6))
    plt.subplot(211)
    plt.grid()
    plt.title('Maturity %s' % str(options['Maturity'].iloc[0])[:10])
    plt.ylabel('option values')
    plt.plot(options.Strike, options.Call, 'b', label='market')
    plt.plot(options.Strike, options.Model, 'ro', label='model')
    plt.legend(loc=0)
    plt.axis([min(options.Strike) - 10, max(options.Strike) + 10,
              min(options.Call) - 10, max(options.Call) + 10])
    plt.subplot(212)
    plt.grid(True)
    wi = 5.0
    diffs = options.Model.values - options.Call.values
    plt.bar(options.Strike - wi / 2, diffs, width=wi)
    plt.ylabel('difference')
    plt.axis([min(options.Strike) - 10, max(options.Strike) + 10,
              min(diffs) * 1.1, max(diffs) * 1.1])
    plt.tight_layout()
```

11.6.5 Calibration of Complete Model of BCC97

```python
#
# Calibration of Bakshi, Cao and Chen (1997)
# Stoch Vol Jump Model to EURO STOXX Option Quotes
# Data Source: www.eurexchange.com
# via Numerical Integration
# 11_cal/BCC97_calibration_full.py
#
# (c) Dr. Yves J. Hilpisch
# Derivatives Analytics with Python
#
import sys
sys.path.append('09_gmm')
import math
import numpy as np
np.set_printoptions(suppress=True,
                    formatter={'all': lambda x: '%5.3f' % x})
import pandas as pd
from scipy.optimize import brute, fmin, minimize
import matplotlib as mpl
mpl.rcParams['font.family'] = 'serif'
from BCC_option_valuation import BCC_call_value
from CIR_calibration import CIR_calibration, r_list
from CIR_zcb_valuation import B
from H93_calibration import options


#
# Calibrate Short Rate Model
#
kappa_r, theta_r, sigma_r = CIR_calibration()

#
# Market Data from www.eurexchange.com
# as of 30. September 2014
#
S0 = 3225.93  # EURO STOXX 50 level
r0 = r_list[0]  # initial short rate
#
# Parameters from H93 & jump calibrations
#
kappa_v, theta_v, sigma_v, rho, v0 = np.load('11_cal/opt_sv.npy')
lamb, mu, delta = np.load('11_cal/opt_jump.npy')
p0 = [kappa_v, theta_v, sigma_v, rho, v0, lamb, mu, delta]


#
# Calibration Functions
```

```
#
i = 0
min_MSE = 5000.0
def BCC_error_function(p0):
    ''' Error function for parameter calibration in BCC97 model via
    Lewis (2001) Fourier approach.

    Parameters
    ==========
    kappa_v: float
        mean-reversion factor
    theta_v: float
        long-run mean of variance
    sigma_v: float
        volatility of variance
    rho: float
        correlation between variance and stock/index level
    v0: float
        initial, instantaneous variance
    lamb: float
        jump intensity
    mu: float
        expected jump size
    delta: float
        standard deviation of jump

    Returns
    =======
    MSE: float
        mean squared error
    '''
    global i, min_MSE
    kappa_v, theta_v, sigma_v, rho, v0, lamb, mu, delta = p0
    if kappa_v < 0.0 or theta_v < 0.005 or sigma_v < 0.0 or \
        rho < -1.0 or rho > 1.0 or v0 < 0.0 or lamb < 0.0 or \
        mu < -.6 or mu > 0.0 or delta < 0.0:
        return 5000.0
    if 2 * kappa_v * theta_v < sigma_v ** 2:
        return 5000.0
    se = []
    for row, option in options.iterrows():
        model_value = BCC_call_value(S0, option['Strike'], option['T'],
                            option['r'], kappa_v, theta_v, sigma_v, rho, v0,
                            lamb, mu, delta)
        se.append((model_value - option['Call']) ** 2)
    MSE = sum(se) / len(se)
    min_MSE = min(min_MSE, MSE)
```

```
    if i % 25 == 0:
        print '%4d |' % i, np.array(p0), '| %7.3f | %7.3f' % (MSE, min_MSE)
    i += 1
    return MSE


def BCC_calibration_full():
    ''' Calibrates complete BCC97 model to market quotes. '''
    # local, convex minimization for all parameters
    opt = fmin(BCC_error_function, p0,
                xtol=0.000001, ftol=0.000001,
                maxiter=450, maxfun=650)
    np.save('11_cal/opt_full', np.array(opt))
    return opt


def BCC_calculate_model_values(p0):
    ''' Calculates all model values given parameter vector p0. '''
    kappa_v, theta_v, sigma_v, rho, v0, lamb, mu, delta = p0
    values = []
    for row, option in options.iterrows():
        model_value = BCC_call_value(S0, option['Strike'], option['T'],
                            option['r'], kappa_v, theta_v, sigma_v, rho, v0,
                            lamb, mu, delta)
        values.append(model_value)
    return np.array(values)
```

11.6.6   Calibration of BCC97 Model to Implied Volatilities

```
#
# Calibration of Bakshi, Cao and Chen (1997)
# Stoch Vol Jump Model to EURO STOXX Option Quotes
# Data Source: www.eurexchange.com
# via Numerical Integration
# 11_cal/BCC97_calibration_iv.py
#
# (c) Dr. Yves J. Hilpisch
# Derivatives Analytics with Python
#
import sys
sys.path.append('09_gmm')
import math
import numpy as np
np.set_printoptions(suppress=True,
                    formatter={'all': lambda x: '%5.3f' % x})
import pandas as pd
from scipy.optimize import brute, fmin, minimize
```

```
import matplotlib as mpl
mpl.rcParams['font.family'] = 'serif'
from BSM_imp_vol import call_option
from BCC_option_valuation import BCC_call_value
from CIR_calibration import CIR_calibration, r_list
from CIR_zcb_valuation import B
from H93_calibration import options


#
# Calibrate Short Rate Model
#
kappa_r, theta_r, sigma_r = CIR_calibration()


#
# Market Data from www.eurexchange.com
# as of 30. September 2014
#
S0 = 3225.93  # EURO STOXX 50 level 30.09.2014
r0 = r_list[0]  # initial short rate


#
# Market Implied Volatilities
#
for row, option in options.iterrows():
    call = call_option(S0, option['Strike'], option['Date'],
                        option['Maturity'], option['r'], 0.15)
    options.ix[row, 'Market_IV'] = call.imp_vol(option['Call'], 0.15)


#
# Calibration Functions
#
i = 0
min_MSE = 5000.0
def BCC_iv_error_function(p0):
    ''' Error function for parameter calibration in BCC97 model via
    Lewis (2001) Fourier approach.

    Parameters
    ==========
    kappa_v: float
        mean-reversion factor
    theta_v: float
        long-run mean of variance
    sigma_v: float
        volatility of variance
    rho: float
        correlation between variance and stock/index level
```

```
    v0: float
        initial, instantaneous variance
    lamb: float
        jump intensity
    mu: float
        expected jump size
    delta: float
        standard deviation of jump

    Returns
    =======
    MSE: float
        mean squared error
    '''
    global i, min_MSE
    kappa_v, theta_v, sigma_v, rho, v0, lamb, mu, delta = p0
    if kappa_v < 0.0 or theta_v < 0.005 or sigma_v < 0.0 or \
        rho < -1.0 or rho > 1.0 or v0 < 0.0 or lamb < 0.0 or \
        mu < -.6 or mu > 0.0 or delta < 0.0:
        return 5000.0
    if 2 * kappa_v * theta_v < sigma_v ** 2:
        return 5000.0
    se = []
    for row, option in options.iterrows():
        call = call_option(S0, option['Strike'], option['Date'],
                            option['Maturity'], option['r'],
                            option['Market_IV'])
        model_value = BCC_call_value(S0, option['Strike'], option['T'],
                            option['r'], kappa_v, theta_v, sigma_v, rho, v0,
                            lamb, mu, delta)
        model_iv = call.imp_vol(model_value, 0.15)
        se.append(((model_iv - option['Market_IV']) * call.vega()) ** 2)
    MSE = sum(se) / len(se)
    min_MSE = min(min_MSE, MSE)
    if i % 25 == 0:
        print '%4d |' % i, np.array(p0), '| %7.3f | %7.3f' % (MSE, min_MSE)
    i += 1
    return MSE

def BCC_iv_calibration_full():
    ''' Calibrates complete BCC97 model to market implied volatilities. '''

    p0 = np.load('11_cal/opt_full.npy')

    # local, convex minimization
    opt = fmin(BCC_iv_error_function, p0,
               xtol=0.000001, ftol=0.000001,
```

```
                    maxiter=450, maxfun=650)
    np.save('11_cal/opt_iv', opt)
    return opt

def BCC_calculate_model_values(p0):
    ''' Calculates all model values given parameter vector p0. '''
    kappa_v, theta_v, sigma_v, rho, v0, lamb, mu, delta = p0
    values = []
    for row, option in options.iterrows():
        model_value = BCC_call_value(S0, option['Strike'], option['T'],
                            option['r'], kappa_v, theta_v, sigma_v, rho, v0,
                            lamb, mu, delta)
        values.append(model_value)
    return np.array(values)
```

## CHAPTER 12

Simulation and Valuation in the General Model Framework

12.1 INTRODUCTION

Monte Carlo simulation (MCS) is an efficient and flexible method to evaluate financial models and derivative pricing formulas numerically. The first step when valuing derivative instruments via MCS is to discretize the stochastic differential equations (SDE) that govern the dynamics of a given model. The correct and efficient discretization of SDEs is all but trivial and there is a large body of literature that deals with this particular topic. Chapter 10 addresses this topic in detail and introduces a number of correct and approximate discretization schemes for both the index process and the square-root diffusions of the general model framework $\mathcal{M}^{BCC97}$.

The didactical approach of this book is to illustrate the translation of theoretical models into executable Python scripts. Therefore, the exposition in this chapter only applies one discretization scheme for the index and the other processes, respectively.

Section 12.2 simulates the calibrated model $\mathcal{M}^{BCC97}$ of the previous chapter. Apart from being calibrated, the model now includes the jump component—a topic not addressed in Chapter 10. Section 12.3 then proceeds by valuing European and American options in this set-up by means of MCS.

12.2 SIMULATION OF BCC97 MODEL

Given is the general market model $\mathcal{M}^{BCC97}$ of Chapter 9. To begin with, divide the time interval $[0, T]$ in equidistant sub-intervals of length Δt such that one has $t \in \{0, \Delta t, 2\Delta t, \ldots, T\}$, i.e. $M + 1$ discrete points in time with $M \equiv T/\Delta t$. A discretization of the general market model (9.1), (9.2) and (9.3) then looks like (with $s \equiv t - \Delta t$)

$$S_t = S_s \left(e^{(\tilde{r}_t - r_J - v_t/2)\Delta t + \sqrt{v_t}\sqrt{\Delta t}z_t^1} + \left(e^{\mu_J + \delta^2 z_t^4} - 1 \right) y_t \right) \tag{12.1}$$

$$\tilde{v}_t = \tilde{v}_s + \kappa_v(\theta_v - \tilde{v}_s^+)\Delta t + \sigma_v\sqrt{\tilde{v}_s^+}\sqrt{\Delta t}z_t^2 \tag{12.2}$$

$$v_t = \tilde{v}_t^+$$

$$\tilde{r}_t = \tilde{r}_s + \kappa_r(\theta_r - \tilde{r}_s^+)\Delta t + \sigma_r\sqrt{\tilde{r}_s^+}\sqrt{\Delta t}z_t^3$$

$$r_t = \tilde{r}_t^+ \tag{12.3}$$

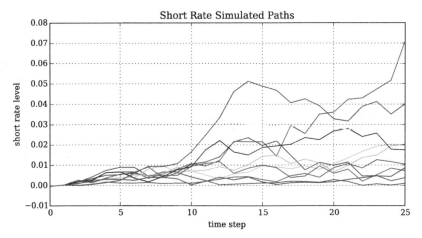

FIGURE 12.1 Ten simulated short rate paths from calibrated CIR85 model for a time horizon of 1 year (starting 30. September 2014) and 25 time intervals

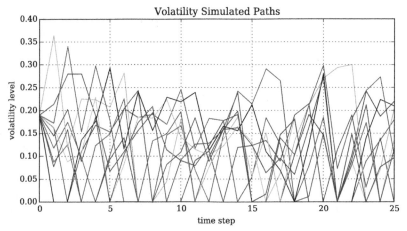

FIGURE 12.2 Ten simulated volatility paths from calibrated BCC97 model for a time horizon of 1 year (starting 30. September 2014) and 25 time intervals

for $t \in \{\Delta t, \ldots, T\}$ with $\bar{r}_t \equiv (r_t + r_s)/2$, the z_t^n being standard normally distributed and the y_t being Poisson distributed with intensity λ. Here, the z_t^1 and z_t^2 are correlated with ρ while all other random variables are uncorrelated.[1] x^+ is notation for $\max[x, 0]$.[2]

Sub-section 12.5.1 contains a Python script for numerically generating discrete processes according to equations (12.1)–(12.3). From an implementation point of view, the v_t and the r_t have to be calculated first because they represent input factors for the calculation of the S_t.

To make MCS more efficient, there are a number of so-called variance reduction techniques available. Among them are *control variates*, *antithetic paths* and *importance sampling*

---

[1] However, the script implementing the scheme allows for arbitrary correlations.

[2] This discretization scheme is usually called *Full Truncation*, cf. Lord et al. (2006) and Chapter 10.

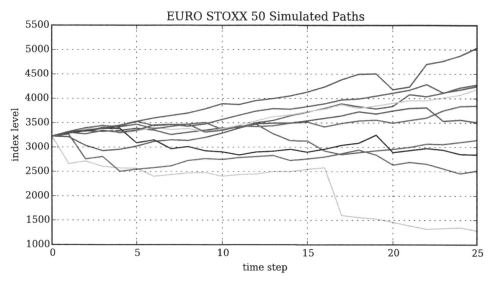

FIGURE 12.3 Ten simulated EURO STOXX 50 level paths from calibrated BCC97 model for a time horizon of 1 year (starting 30. September 2014) and 25 time intervals

(cf. Glasserman (2004), ch. 4). The script in sub-section 12.5.1 implements with optionality antithetic paths and moment matching—simple forms of generic variance reduction techniques. However, as Glasserman (2004), ch. 4 points out, the most efficient techniques in this regard are those which exploit problem-specific features—something illustrated in Chapter 10 by the use of control variates.

Figures 12.1–12.4 show simulation results from the Python script. Figure 12.3 exhibits some large jumps which finally lead to a significant deviation of the EURO STOXX 50 level frequency distribution from log-normality (see Figure 12.4).

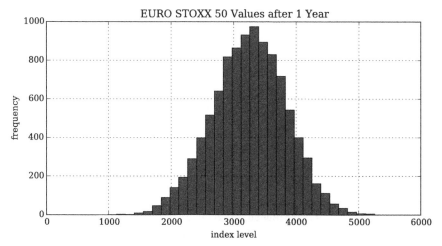

FIGURE 12.4 Histogram of simulated EURO STOXX 50 levels from calibrated BCC97 model after a time period of 1 year (i.e. on 30. September 2015)

12.3 VALUATION OF EQUITY OPTIONS

12.3.1 European Options

Equipped with a Python script for the simulation of the BCC97 model, valuation of European options is only one additional step away. As in the most simple case, we "just" simulate end-of-period index levels and calculate the MCS estimator as

$$C_0^{MCS} = B_0(T)\frac{1}{I} \sum_{i=1}^{I} \max[S_{T,i} - K, 0]$$

The Python script in sub-section 12.5.2 uses the simulation functions from the simulation script and scales the number of time steps with the time horizon T. The script yields, for instance, the results as listed below (with wall times). The first parametrization—50 time steps p.a. and 50,000 paths—leads to a systematic valuation bias with MCS estimators much too high in general.

```
In [1]: %time compare_values(M0=50, I=50000)
     T |      K |       C0 |      MCS |     DIFF
 0.083 |   3050 |  193.692 |  195.584 |    1.892
 0.083 |   3225 |   62.147 |   64.162 |    2.016
 0.083 |   3400 |    1.967 |    2.544 |    0.577
 0.500 |   3050 |  259.126 |  272.960 |   13.834
 0.500 |   3225 |  146.891 |  164.333 |   17.443
 0.500 |   3400 |   67.142 |   85.330 |   18.188
 1.000 |   3050 |  321.419 |  344.280 |   22.861
 1.000 |   3225 |  216.227 |  243.415 |   27.188
 1.000 |   3400 |  133.950 |  162.403 |   28.453
 1.500 |   3050 |  378.978 |  407.035 |   28.057
 1.500 |   3225 |  276.942 |  309.251 |   32.309
 1.500 |   3400 |  193.333 |  227.887 |   34.554
 2.000 |   3050 |  435.337 |  470.659 |   35.322
 2.000 |   3225 |  335.010 |  374.315 |   39.305
 2.000 |   3400 |  250.314 |  291.888 |   41.574
 3.000 |   3050 |  549.127 |  594.413 |   45.287
 3.000 |   3225 |  450.522 |  499.873 |   49.350
 3.000 |   3400 |  364.049 |  416.300 |   52.252
CPU times: user 5.77 s, sys: 164 ms, total: 5.93 s
Wall time: 5.93 s
```

Increasing the number of paths does not really help with valuation accuracy in this case.

```
In [2]: %time compare_values(M0=50, I=200000)
     T |      K |       C0 |      MCS |     DIFF
 0.083 |   3050 |  193.692 |  195.870 |    2.178
 0.083 |   3225 |   62.147 |   64.609 |    2.462
```

```
5    0.083 |   3400 |   1.967 |   2.606 |   0.639
6    0.500 |   3050 | 259.126 | 273.046 |  13.920
7    0.500 |   3225 | 146.891 | 164.698 |  17.807
8    0.500 |   3400 |  67.142 |  85.852 |  18.710
9    1.000 |   3050 | 321.419 | 342.696 |  21.277
10   1.000 |   3225 | 216.227 | 241.375 |  25.148
11   1.000 |   3400 | 133.950 | 160.706 |  26.756
12   1.500 |   3050 | 378.978 | 407.341 |  28.363
13   1.500 |   3225 | 276.942 | 309.124 |  32.182
14   1.500 |   3400 | 193.333 | 227.473 |  34.140
15   2.000 |   3050 | 435.337 | 470.323 |  34.986
16   2.000 |   3225 | 335.010 | 373.940 |  38.930
17   2.000 |   3400 | 250.314 | 291.583 |  41.268
18   3.000 |   3050 | 549.127 | 597.571 |  48.444
19   3.000 |   3225 | 450.522 | 503.362 |  52.840
20   3.000 |   3400 | 364.049 | 420.019 |  55.970
21   CPU times: user 23.2 s, sys: 848 ms, total: 24.1 s
22   Wall time: 24.1 s
```

However, increasing the number of time steps used for the discretization has a huge impact.

```
1    In [3]: %time compare_values(M0=200, I=50000)
2         T |     K |     C0 |    MCS |   DIFF
3    0.083 |   3050 | 193.692 | 193.241 |  -0.450
4    0.083 |   3225 |  62.147 |  61.595 |  -0.552
5    0.083 |   3400 |   1.967 |   2.581 |   0.614
6    0.500 |   3050 | 259.126 | 259.140 |   0.014
7    0.500 |   3225 | 146.891 | 149.090 |   2.199
8    0.500 |   3400 |  67.142 |  71.122 |   3.980
9    1.000 |   3050 | 321.419 | 322.117 |   0.697
10   1.000 |   3225 | 216.227 | 219.528 |   3.301
11   1.000 |   3400 | 133.950 | 139.285 |   5.335
12   1.500 |   3050 | 378.978 | 377.499 |  -1.479
13   1.500 |   3225 | 276.942 | 278.276 |   1.334
14   1.500 |   3400 | 193.333 | 197.137 |   3.804
15   2.000 |   3050 | 435.337 | 435.067 |  -0.270
16   2.000 |   3225 | 335.010 | 337.597 |   2.587
17   2.000 |   3400 | 250.314 | 255.541 |   5.227
18   3.000 |   3050 | 549.127 | 552.842 |   3.715
19   3.000 |   3225 | 450.522 | 457.774 |   7.252
20   3.000 |   3400 | 364.049 | 374.340 |  10.291
21   CPU times: user 21.8 s, sys: 914 ms, total: 22.7 s
22   Wall time: 22.7 s
23
```

Too few time steps obviously lead to a systematic valuation bias. Increasing the number of paths does not really help—however, increasing the number of time steps leads to significant accuracy improvements with valuation errors being much smaller and both positive as well as negative. This makes clear that using Euler discretization schemes makes a large number of time steps necessary to achieve sufficient accuracy with such complex models.

12.3.2 American Options

Now we can add the LSM algorithm to the script—see sub-section 12.5.3—to value put options with American, i.e. early, exercise feature. The script generates, for instance, the following results, illustrating the early exercise premium for American put options vs. their European counterparts (for longer maturities):

```
In [4]: %time lsm_compare_values(M0=150, I=50000)
     T |      K |      P0 |     LSM |    DIFF
  0.083 |   3050 |  17.681 |  17.431 |  -0.250
  0.083 |   3225 |  61.131 |  61.001 |  -0.130
  0.083 |   3400 | 175.947 | 181.565 |   5.619
  0.500 |   3050 |  77.963 |  84.277 |   6.314
  0.500 |   3225 | 140.428 | 149.270 |   8.842
  0.500 |   3400 | 235.379 | 246.148 |  10.769
  1.000 |   3050 | 124.220 | 136.155 |  11.934
  1.000 |   3225 | 192.808 | 207.958 |  15.149
  1.000 |   3400 | 284.311 | 302.051 |  17.740
  1.500 |   3050 | 155.970 | 174.835 |  18.865
  1.500 |   3225 | 226.234 | 250.278 |  24.044
  1.500 |   3400 | 314.923 | 344.215 |  29.292
  2.000 |   3050 | 177.841 | 206.460 |  28.619
  2.000 |   3225 | 247.834 | 282.910 |  35.077
  2.000 |   3400 | 333.458 | 376.640 |  43.182
  3.000 |   3050 | 201.032 | 249.858 |  48.826
  3.000 |   3225 | 267.549 | 328.487 |  60.937
  3.000 |   3400 | 346.197 | 421.464 |  75.267
CPU times: user 37.1 s, sys: 935 ms, total: 38 s
Wall time: 38 s
```

Obviously, the early exercise premium rises with an increase in time-to-maturity.

12.4 CONCLUSIONS

This chapter illustrates how to numerically evaluate the general market model—based on the calibrated model parameters—by the means of Monte Carlo simulation. It also values

European as well as American call options by simulation. In a sense, it merely glues together the single pieces worked out in previous chapters to finally arrive at a market-based valuation of European and American index options.

12.5 PYTHON SCRIPTS

12.5.1 Simulating the BCC97 Model

```
#
# Monte Carlo Simulation of BCC97 Model
# 12_val/BCC97_simulation.py
#
# (c) Dr. Yves J. Hilpisch
# Derivatives Analytics with Python
#
import sys
sys.path.append('11_cal')
import math
import numpy as np
import matplotlib as mpl
mpl.rcParams['font.family'] = 'serif'
import matplotlib.pyplot as plt
from H93_calibration import S0, kappa_r, theta_r, sigma_r, r0


#
# Model Parameters
#
opt = np.load('11_cal/opt_full.npy')
kappa_v, theta_v, sigma_v, rho, v0, lamb, mu, delta = opt



#
# Simulation Parameters
#
T = 1.0  # time horizon
M = 25  # time steps
I = 10000  # number of replications per valuation
anti_paths = True  # antithetic paths for variance reduction
moment_matching = True  # moment matching for variance reduction
np.random.seed(100000)  # seed value for random number generator



#
# Random Number Generation
#
```

```python
def generate_cholesky(rho):
    ''' Function to generate Cholesky matrix.

    Parameters
    ==========
    rho: float
        correlation between index level and variance

    Returns
    =======
    matrix: NumPy array
        Cholesky matrix
    '''
    rho_rs = 0  # correlation between index level and short rate
    covariance = np.zeros((4, 4), dtype=np.float)
    covariance[0] = [1.0, rho_rs, 0.0, 0.0]
    covariance[1] = [rho_rs, 1.0, rho, 0.0]
    covariance[2] = [0.0, rho, 1.0, 0.0]
    covariance[3] = [0.0, 0.0, 0.0, 1.0]
    cho_matrix = np.linalg.cholesky(covariance)
    return cho_matrix


def random_number_generator(M, I, anti_paths, moment_matching):
    ''' Function to generate pseudo-random numbers.

    Parameters
    ==========
    M: int
        time steps
    I: int
        number of simulation paths
    anti_paths: bool
        flag for antithetic paths
    moment_matching: bool
        flag for moment matching

    Returns
    =======
    rand: NumPy array
        random number array
    '''
    if anti_paths:
        rand = np.random.standard_normal((4, M + 1, I / 2))
        rand = np.concatenate((rand, -rand), 2)
    else:
        rand = np.random.standard_normal((4, M + 1, I))
```

```
    if moment_matching:
        for a in range(4):
            rand[a] = rand[a] / np.std(rand[a])
            rand[a] = rand[a] - np.mean(rand[a])
    return rand


#
# Function for Short Rate and Volatility Processes
#

def SRD_generate_paths(x0, kappa, theta, sigma, T, M, I,
                        rand, row, cho_matrix):
    ''' Function to simulate Square-Root Difussion (SRD/CIR) process.

    Parameters
    ==========
    x0: float
        initial value
    kappa: float
        mean-reversion factor
    theta: float
        long-run mean
    sigma: float
        volatility factor
    T: float
        final date/time horizon
    M: int
        number of time steps
    I: int
        number of paths
    row: int
        row number for random numbers
    cho_matrix: NumPy array
        Cholesky matrix

    Returns
    =======
    x: NumPy array
        simulated variance paths
    '''
    dt = T / M
    x = np.zeros((M + 1, I), dtype=np.float)
    x[0] = x0
    xh = np.zeros_like(x)
    xh[0] = x0
    sdt = math.sqrt(dt)
    for t in range(1, M + 1):
```

```
            ran = np.dot(cho_matrix, rand[:, t])
            xh[t] = (xh[t - 1] + kappa * (theta -
                    np.maximum(0, xh[t - 1]))) * dt +
                    np.sqrt(np.maximum(0, xh[t - 1])) * sigma * ran[row] * sdt)
            x[t] = np.maximum(0, xh[t])
        return x


#
# Function for B96 Index Process
#

def B96_generate_paths(S0, r, v, lamb, mu, delta, rand, row1, row2,
                        cho_matrix, T, M, I, moment_matching):
    ''' Simulation of Bates (1996) index process.

    Parameters
    ==========
    S0: float
        initial value
    r: NumPy array
        simulated short rate paths
    v: NumPy array
        simulated variance paths
    lamb: float
        jump intensity
    mu: float
        expected jump size
    delta: float
        standard deviation of jump
    rand: NumPy array
        random number array
    row1, row2: int
        rows/matrices of random number array to use
    cho_matrix: NumPy array
        Cholesky matrix
    T: float
        time horizon, maturity
    M: int
        number of time intervals, steps
    I: int
        number of paths to simulate
    moment_matching: bool
        flag for moment matching

    Returns
    =======
    S: NumPy array
        simulated index level paths
```

```
    '''
    S = np.zeros((M + 1, I), dtype=np.float)
    S[0] = S0
    dt = T / M
    sdt = math.sqrt(dt)
    ranp = np.random.poisson(lamb * dt, (M + 1, I))
    rj = lamb * (math.exp(mu + 0.5 * delta ** 2) - 1)
    bias = 0.0
    for t in xrange(1, M + 1, 1):
        ran = np.dot(cho_matrix, rand[:, t, :])
        if moment_matching:
            bias = np.mean(np.sqrt(v[t]) * ran[row1] * sdt)
        S[t] = S[t - 1] * (np.exp(((r[t] + r[t -1]) / 2 - 0.5 * v[t]) * dt +
                    np.sqrt(v[t]) * ran[row1] * sdt - bias)
                + (np.exp(mu + delta * ran[row2]) - 1) * ranp[t])
    return S


if __name__ == '__main__':
    #
    # Simulation
    #
    cho_matrix = generate_cholesky(rho)
    rand = random_number_generator(M, I, anti_paths, moment_matching)
    r = SRD_generate_paths(r0, kappa_r, theta_r, sigma_r, T, M, I,
                        rand, 0, cho_matrix)
    v = SRD_generate_paths(v0, kappa_v, theta_v, sigma_v, T, M, I,
                        rand, 2, cho_matrix)
    S = B96_generate_paths(S0, r, v, lamb, mu, delta, rand, 1, 3,
                        cho_matrix, T, M, I, moment_matching)


def plot_rate_paths(r):
    plt.figure(figsize=(8, 4))
    plt.plot(r[:, :10])
    plt.xlabel('time step')
    plt.ylabel('short rate level')
    plt.title('Short Rate Simulated Paths')
    plt.grid()


def plot_volatility_paths(v):
    plt.figure(figsize=(8, 4))
    plt.plot(np.sqrt(v[:, :10]))
    plt.xlabel('time step')
    plt.ylabel('volatility level')
    plt.title('Volatility Simulated Paths')
    plt.grid()
```

```
def plot_index_paths(S):
    plt.figure(figsize=(8, 4))
    plt.plot(S[:, :10])
    plt.xlabel('time step')
    plt.ylabel('index level')
    plt.title('EURO STOXX 50 Simulated Paths')
    plt.grid()

def plot_index_histogram(S):
    plt.figure(figsize=(8, 4))
    plt.hist(S[-1], bins=30)
    plt.xlabel('index level')
    plt.ylabel('frequency')
    plt.title('EURO STOXX 50 Values after 1 Year')
    plt.grid()
```

12.5.2 Valuation of European Call Options by MCS

```
#
# Valuation of European Options in BCC97 Model
# by Monte Carlo Simulation
# 12_val/BCC97_valuation_comparison.py
#
# (c) Dr. Yves J. Hilpisch
# Derivatives Analytics with Python
#
import sys
sys.path.extend(['09_gmm', '10_mcs'])
import math
from BCC_option_valuation import *
from CIR_zcb_valuation_gen import B
from BCC97_simulation import *

#
# Parameters
#
t_list = [1 / 12., 0.5, 1.0, 1.5, 2.0, 3.0]
k_list = [3050, 3225, 3400]

#
# Valuation for Different Strikes & Maturities
#
def compare_values(M0=50, I=50000):
    results = []
    for T in t_list:
```

```
#
# Simulation
#
M = int(M0 * T)
cho_matrix = generate_cholesky(rho)
rand = random_number_generator(M, I, anti_paths, moment_matching)
r = SRD_generate_paths(r0, kappa_r, theta_r, sigma_r, T, M, I,
                       rand, 0, cho_matrix)
v = SRD_generate_paths(v0, kappa_v, theta_v, sigma_v, T, M, I,
                       rand, 2, cho_matrix)
S = B96_generate_paths(S0, r, v, lamb, mu, delta, rand, 1, 3,
                       cho_matrix, T, M, I, moment_matching)
for K in k_list:
    #
    # Valuation
    #
    h = np.maximum(S[-1] - K, 0)
    B0T = B([r0, kappa_r, theta_r, sigma_r, 0.0, T])
    V0_mcs = B0T * np.sum(h) / I # MCS estimator
    #
    # European Call Option via Fourier
    #
    ra = -math.log(B0T) / T  # average short rate/yield
    C0 = BCC_call_value(S0, K, T, ra, kappa_v, theta_v, sigma_v,
                        rho, v0, lamb, mu, delta)

    results.append((T, K, C0, V0_mcs, V0_mcs - C0))

print " %6s | %6s | %7s | %7s | %7s" % ('T', 'K', 'C0', 'MCS', 'DIFF')
for res in results:
    print " %6.3f | %6d | %7.3f | %7.3f | %7.3f" % res
```

12.5.3 Valuation of American Call Options by MCS

```
#
# Valuation of American Options in BCC97 Model
# by Least-Squares Monte Carlo Algorithm
# 12_val/BCC97_american_valuation.py
#
# (c) Dr. Yves J. Hilpisch
# Derivatives Analytics with Python
#
import sys
sys.path.extend(['09_gmm', '10_mcs'])
import math
from BCC_option_valuation import *
```

```python
from CIR_zcb_valuation_gen import B
from BCC97_simulation import *
#
# Additional Parameters
#
D = 10  # number of basis functions
t_list = [1 / 12., 0.5, 1.0, 1.5, 2.0, 3.0]
k_list = [3050, 3225, 3400]


#
# LSM Valuation Function
#
def BCC97_lsm_valuation(S, r, v, K, T, M, I):
    ''' Function to value American put options by LSM algorithm.

    Parameters
    ==========
    S: NumPy array
        simulated index level paths
    r: NumPy array
        simulated short rate paths
    v: NumPy array
        simulated variance paths
    K: float
        strike of the put option
    T: float
        final date/time horizon
    M: int
        number of time steps
    I: int
        number of paths

    Returns
    =======
    LSM_value: float
        LSM Monte Carlo estimator of American put option value
    '''
    dt = T / M
    # inner value matrix
    h = np.maximum(K - S, 0)
    # value/cash flow matrix
    V = np.maximum(K - S, 0)
    for t in xrange(M - 1, 0, -1):
        df = np.exp(-(r[t] + r[t + 1]) / 2 * dt)
        # select only ITM paths
        itm = np.greater(h[t], 0)
        relevant = np.nonzero(itm)
```

```
        rel_S = np.compress(itm, S[t])
        no_itm = len(rel_S)
        if no_itm == 0:
            cv = np.zeros((I), dtype=np.float)
        else:
            rel_v = np.compress(itm, v[t])
            rel_r = np.compress(itm, r[t])
            rel_V = (np.compress(itm, V[t + 1])
                        * np.compress(itm, df))
            matrix = np.zeros((D + 1, no_itm), dtype=np.float)
            matrix[10] = rel_S * rel_v * rel_r
            matrix[9] = rel_S * rel_v
            matrix[8] = rel_S * rel_r
            matrix[7] = rel_v * rel_r
            matrix[6] = rel_S ** 2
            matrix[5] = rel_v ** 2
            matrix[4] = rel_r ** 2
            matrix[3] = rel_S
            matrix[2] = rel_v
            matrix[1] = rel_r
            matrix[0] = 1
            reg = np.linalg.lstsq(matrix.transpose(), rel_V)
            cv = np.dot(reg[0], matrix)
        erg = np.zeros((I), dtype=np.float)
        np.put(erg, relevant, cv)
        V[t] = np.where(h[t] > erg, h[t], V[t + 1] * df)
            # exercise decision
    df = np.exp(-((r[0] + r[1]) / 2) * dt)
    LSM_value = max(np.sum(V[1, :] * df) / I, h[0, 0])   # LSM estimator
    return LSM_value


#
# Valuation for Different Strikes & Maturities
#
def lsm_compare_values(M0=50, I=50000):
    results = []
    for T in t_list:
        #
        # Simulation
        #
        M = int(M0 * T)
        cho_matrix = generate_cholesky(rho)
        rand = random_number_generator(M, I, anti_paths, moment_matching)
        r = SRD_generate_paths(r0, kappa_r, theta_r, sigma_r, T, M, I,
                                rand, 0, cho_matrix)
        v = SRD_generate_paths(v0, kappa_v, theta_v, sigma_v, T, M, I,
                                rand, 2, cho_matrix)
```

```
    S = B96_generate_paths(S0, r, v, lamb, mu, delta, rand, 1, 3,
                            cho_matrix, T, M, I, moment_matching)
for K in k_list:
    #
    # Valuation
    #
    h = np.maximum(S[-1] - K, 0)
    B0T = B([r0, kappa_r, theta_r, sigma_r, 0.0, T])
    V0_lsm = BCC97_lsm_valuation(S, r, v, K, T, M, I)
        # LSM estimator
    #
    # European Call Option via Fourier
    #
    ra = -math.log(B0T) / T  # average short rate/yield
    C0 = BCC_call_value(S0, K, T, ra, kappa_v, theta_v, sigma_v,
                        rho, v0, lamb, mu, delta)
    P0 = C0 + K * B0T - S0

    results.append((T, K, P0, V0_lsm, V0_lsm - P0))

print " %6s | %6s | %7s | %7s | %7s" % ('T', 'K', 'P0', 'LSM', 'DIFF')
for res in results:
    print " %6.3f | %6d | %7.3f | %7.3f | %7.3f"  % res
```

## CHAPTER 13

Dynamic Hedging

13.1 INTRODUCTION

In a friction-less market, *dynamic delta hedging* is a perfect method to hedge against price changes of a derivative instrument when the underlying of the option is the only source of risk, its price paths are continuous and volatility is constant. This is, for example, the case in the benchmark model of Black-Scholes-Merton (BSM, cf. Wilmott et al. (1995), ch. 3). In fact, it is one approach—another one being an equilibrium argument—to come up with the famous analytical formula of BSM. Independent of the particular model at hand, the *delta* of, for example, a put option P is defined by the first derivative of the option's value with respect to the value of the underlying S

$$\Delta_t^P \equiv \frac{\partial P_t}{\partial S_t}$$

Delta hedging the put P then says that adding $-\Delta_t^P$ units of the underlying at time t to the put option completely neutralizes the price changes in the put option due to changes in the underlying. One then has for all t that

$$dP_t - \Delta_t^P dS_t = 0$$

Investment banks are also often interested in replicating the payoff of such a put (or another option). This is accomplished by setting up a replication portfolio consisting of Δ_t^P units of the underlying and $\gamma_t \equiv P_t - \Delta_t^P S_t$ units of the risk-less bond B_t such that the resulting portfolio value equals the option value at any time t

$$P_t = \Delta_t^P S_t + \gamma_t B_t$$

or

$$dP_t = \Delta_t^P dS_t + \gamma_t dB_t$$

For a plain vanilla put option this generally implies being short the underlying ($\Delta_t^P < 0$) and long the bond. For a call option ($\Delta_t^C > 0$) this implies the opposite.

A replication strategy $(\Delta_t^P, \gamma_t), t \in \{0, ..., \tau - \Delta t\}$, is called *self-financing* if for $t > 0$ and τ being the exercise date (i.e. $\tau = T$ for a European option)

$$\Delta_t^P S_t + \gamma_t B_t = \Delta_{t-\Delta t}^P S_t + \gamma_{t-\Delta t} B_t$$

By the means of two simulation studies, this chapter implements the idea of dynamic delta hedging in the BSM model (section 13.2) and the general market model of BCC97 (section 13.3), respectively. While the strategy works quite well in the BSM framework, jumps allow us to break down the strategy frequently in the BCC97 model.

13.2 HEDGING STUDY FOR BSM MODEL

This section illustrates dynamic replication of an American put option in the BSM model. The example is taken from the seminal paper on the LSM by Longstaff and Schwartz (2001). We use an approximative method based on the LSM algorithm to numerically derive option deltas. The approach comprises two parts, an initial one and one that is replicated as often as necessary.[1] These are:

- **initial delta**: the initial delta Δ_0^P is estimated via a difference quotient of the form

$$\Delta_0^P \equiv \frac{P_0^{LSM}(S_0 + 0.01) - P_0^{LSM}(S_0)}{0.01} \tag{13.1}$$

    where the two option values are derived from two separate LSM valuations of the put, changing the starting value of the underlying as indicated
- **subsequent deltas**: all other deltas $\Delta_t^P, t \in \{\Delta t, ..., \tau - \Delta t\}$, with τ being the exercise time, are estimated via the regression function available at each time step using the same difference quotient as before

$$\Delta_t^P \equiv \frac{\hat{V}_t(\hat{S}_t + 0.01) - \hat{V}_t(\hat{S}_t)}{0.01} \tag{13.2}$$

here, $\hat{V}_t$ is the LSM regression estimate of the American put option value at date t given the simulated index level $\hat{S}_t$

The Python script in sub-section 13.5.1 implements this simple, approximative algorithm for the American put option in the BSM setting.[2] In the script, the replicating portfolio is

---

[1] Cf. Wallner and Wystup (2004) for the numerical estimation of price sensitivities for options with American exercise. The method introduced here is a so-called *first order approximation*.
[2] The approach presented here is similar in spirit to that of Wang and Calfisch (2010) but is even "more simple and approximative".

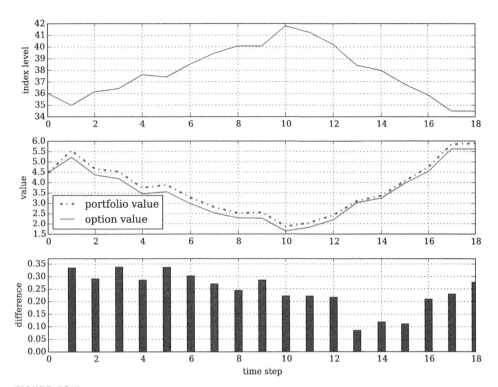

FIGURE 13.1 Dynamic replication of American put option in BSM model with profit at exercise

considered to be self-financing which implies that there are neither cash inflows nor outflows after $t = 0$. The respective values of the portfolio are benchmarked against an out-of-sample valuation[3] of the American put option given time t and the then current level of the underlying S_t.

Figure 13.1 illustrates a replicating strategy for a randomly chosen path from the original valuation. In this particular run, the replicating strategy has over-replicated the option's payoff leading to a positive difference, i.e. a profit, at the exercise date.

Figure 13.2 shows another path where the replicating strategy underperforms, leading to a significant loss at the exercise date. Two aspects are noteworthy. First, the regression coefficients are estimated only once at the beginning and used for every time step up to exercise or maturity. Second, the performance of the second delta hedging program is quite good on average in the short run but becomes worse the longer the option remains alive. With a constant reassessment of the regression coefficients the performance of the hedge program could be improved. In practical applications, this is what one would do at least on a daily basis.

[3]This is to make sure that there is not an in-sample bias of the replicating strategy which would make the calculated profit and loss (P&L) too optimistic.

The single position adjustments for a particular dynamic hedge might look as follows:

```
1    DYNAMIC HEDGING OF PUT
2    ---------------------------
3    Initial Hedge
4    Stocks              -0.587
5    Bonds               25.585
6    Cost                 4.469
7
8    Regular Rehedges
9    ----------------------------------------------------------------------------
```

step	S_t	Port	Put	Diff	Stock	Bond	Cost
1	37.509	3.615	3.535	0.079	-0.450	20.483	3.615
2	38.126	3.362	3.186	0.176	-0.477	21.566	3.362
3	38.338	3.287	3.074	0.212	-0.481	21.730	3.287
4	37.493	3.719	3.551	0.168	-0.554	24.483	3.719
5	36.652	4.214	4.048	0.166	-0.657	28.278	4.214
6	36.894	4.089	3.897	0.192	-0.616	26.802	4.089
7	37.780	3.576	3.390	0.186	-0.557	24.603	3.576
8	39.197	2.817	2.664	0.153	-0.474	21.401	2.817
9	39.449	2.723	2.545	0.178	-0.461	20.912	2.723
10	39.621	2.669	2.471	0.198	-0.433	19.829	2.669
11	38.791	3.052	2.853	0.199	-0.501	22.493	3.052
12	39.174	2.887	2.673	0.214	-0.473	21.409	2.887
13	39.432	2.791	2.563	0.227	-0.434	19.910	2.791
14	37.930	3.467	3.298	0.169	-0.567	24.979	3.467
15	37.582	3.694	3.481	0.213	-0.598	26.153	3.694
16	38.677	3.071	2.915	0.157	-0.516	23.024	3.071
17	37.774	3.565	3.373	0.191	-0.595	26.033	3.565
18	39.876	2.346	2.373	-0.027	-0.426	19.323	2.346
19	40.624	2.050	2.078	-0.028	-0.370	17.072	2.050
20	40.949	1.951	1.959	-0.008	-0.349	16.245	1.951
21	40.166	2.243	2.248	-0.004	-0.408	18.646	2.243
22	39.944	2.356	2.341	0.015	-0.410	18.724	2.356
23	39.836	2.423	2.383	0.040	-0.418	19.066	2.423
24	40.601	2.127	2.079	0.048	-0.360	16.738	2.127
25	39.229	2.640	2.653	-0.013	-0.502	22.331	2.640
26	39.436	2.564	2.564	-0.000	-0.494	22.050	2.564
27	38.928	2.841	2.797	0.044	-0.538	23.785	2.841
28	38.055	3.339	3.218	0.121	-0.626	27.144	3.339
29	38.333	3.198	3.075	0.123	-0.604	26.369	3.198
30	38.445	3.162	3.010	0.152	-0.598	26.157	3.162
31	39.784	2.392	2.406	-0.014	-0.466	20.944	2.392
32	40.044	2.296	2.299	-0.002	-0.447	20.205	2.296
33	39.356	2.628	2.588	0.040	-0.516	22.935	2.628
34	38.360	3.170	3.047	0.123	-0.626	27.200	3.170
35	36.726	4.226	3.969	0.257	-0.781	32.916	4.226
36	37.156	3.930	3.705	0.225	-0.745	31.611	3.930
37	36.722	4.291	3.976	0.314	-0.794	33.447	4.291

```
48   MSE                  0.023
49   Average Error        0.118
50   Total P&L            4.485
```

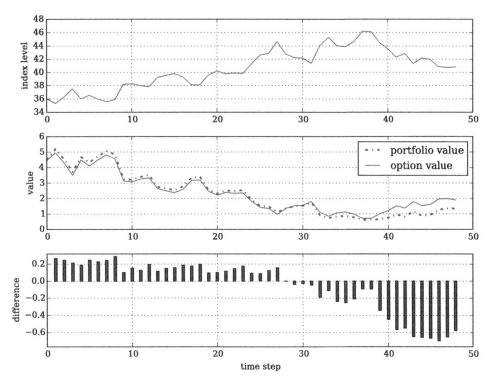

FIGURE 13.2 Dynamic replication of American put option in BSM model with loss at exercise

Finally, Figure 13.3 shows the frequency distribution of the discounted P&L at exercise of 10,000 dynamic replications for this case (see the Python script in sub-section 13.5.2). This simulation is based on 50 time steps for the discretization and 10,000 paths. Summary statistics are:

```
 1    SUMMARY STATISTICS FOR P&L
 2    --------------------------------
 3    Dynamic Replications        10000
 4    Time Steps                     50
 5    Paths for Valuation         10000
 6    Maximum                     5.447
 7    Average                     0.041
 8    Median                      0.036
 9    Minimum                   -11.475
10    --------------------------------
11    CPU times: user 19 s, sys: 4 ms, total: 19 s
12    Wall time: 19 s
```

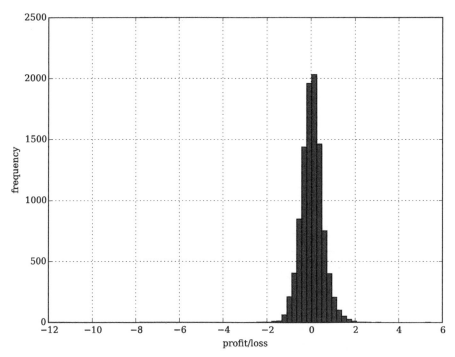

FIGURE 13.3 Frequency distribution of (discounted) P&L at exercise date of 10,000 dynamic replications of American put option in BSM model

The average hedge error is 0.4 cents only which is not too bad given the simplicity of the approach. The highest loss is −11.37 and the highest profit +5.446 (as very exceptions).

The hedge errors (i.e. the P&L) can be controlled for by increasing both the number of time steps and paths. This is illustrated in Figure 13.4 and by the following summary statistics based on 200 time steps and 150,000 paths.

```
1   SUMMARY STATISTICS FOR P&L
2   --------------------------------
3   Dynamic Replications         10000
4   Time Steps                     200
5   Paths for Valuation         150000
6   Maximum                      2.118
7   Average                      0.003
8   Median                       0.016
9   Minimum                     -1.328
10  --------------------------------
11  CPU times: user 45.3 s, sys: 208 ms, total: 45.6 s
12  Wall time: 45.5 s
```

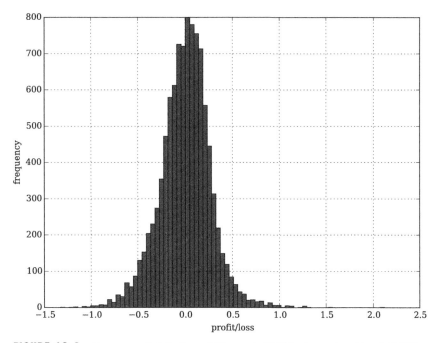

FIGURE 13.4 Frequency distribution of (discounted) P&L at exercise date of 10,000 dynamic replications of American put option in BSM model with more time steps and paths used

In this case, the average hedge error is 0.1 cents only while the maximum profit is 1.35 and the maximum loss is reduced to -3.66.

13.3 HEDGING STUDY FOR BCC97 MODEL

The previous section introduces a simple, approximative algorithm to delta hedge an American option—the major advantage of it being the low computational burden which results from recycling the regression coefficients from an initial LSM simulation run. This section now applies this algorithm with a second order approximation formula to dynamically replicate an American index put option in the calibrated BCC97 setting.

For $0 \leq a \leq 2$ and $\Delta_t^S > 0$, the deltas are approximated along an index level path through the following difference quotients:[4]

- **initial delta**: the initial delta Δ_0^P is estimated via a difference quotient of the form

$$\Delta_0^P \equiv \frac{P_0^{LSM}\left(S_0 + (2-a)\cdot\Delta_0^S\right) - P_0^{LSM}\left(S_0 - a\cdot\Delta_0^S\right)}{2\cdot\Delta_0^S} \tag{13.3}$$

---

[4]Refer to Wallner and Wystup (2004) for this kind of *second order approximation* to option sensitivities.

where the two option values are derived from two separate LSM valuations of the put, changing the starting value of the underlying as indicated
- **subsequent deltas**: all other deltas $\Delta_t^P, t \in \{\Delta t, ..., \tau - \Delta t\}$, with τ being the exercise time, are estimated via the regression function available at each time step using a similar difference quotient as before

$$\Delta_t^P \equiv \frac{\hat{V}_t\left(\hat{S}_t + (2-a) \cdot \Delta_t^S \left| \hat{X}_t \right.\right)^+ - \hat{V}_t\left(\hat{S}_t - a \cdot \Delta_t^S \left| \hat{X}_t \right.\right)^+}{2 \cdot \Delta_t^S} \qquad (13.4)$$

here, $\hat{V}_t$ is the LSM regression estimate of the American put option value[5] using all (simulated) state variables $\hat{X}_t = (\hat{S}_t, \hat{v}_t, \hat{r}_t)$, i.e. the index level, the variance level and the short rate at date t

By varying a and Δ_t^S one can fine-tune the approximations. In particular, it is important to adjust Δ_t^S such that it reflects the initial index level S_0 and the later index levels S_t. Therefore, we set for $0 \leq t < T$

$$\Delta_t^S = 0.01 \cdot \hat{S}_t$$

Figure 13.5 shows a delta hedging procedure along a specific simulated EURO STOXX 50 index level path (sub-section 13.5.3 provides the Python script for the valuation of the American put and the dynamic delta hedging, respectively). Here, the hedge strategy super-replicates the option, i.e. it produces a profit at maturity. In comparison, Figure 13.6 illustrates that losses can also accumulate in significant amounts, with the portfolio value even ending in the negatives. Finally, Figure 13.7 (cf. sub-section 13.5.4 for the script) shows the discounted P&L of 10,000 dynamic replications. Summary statistics are:

```
 1   SUMMARY STATISTICS FOR P&L
 2   ---------------------------------
 3   Dynamic Replications          10000
 4   Time Steps                      150
 5   Paths for Valuation          150000
 6   Maximum                     143.354
 7   Average                       4.343
 8   Median                       15.136
 9   Minimum                   -1014.275
10   ---------------------------------
11   CPU times: user 42.6 s, sys: 887 ms, total: 43.4 s
12   Wall time: 43.4 s
```

---

[5]Note that simple evaluation of the regression function could generate negative values for the option price such that the formula truncates the estimates below zero.

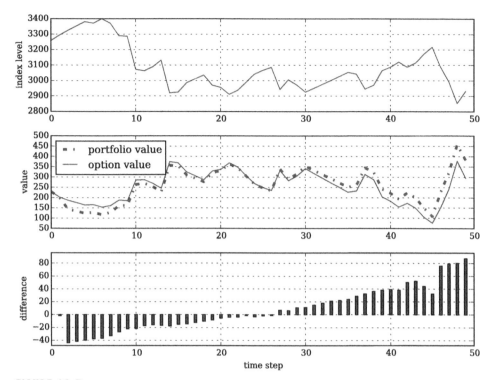

FIGURE 13.5   Dynamic replication of American put option in BCC97 with profit at maturity

On average, the dynamic hedging strategy for the American put option yields a discounted profit of 4.34 so that its application to a large options book might be justified. In that sense, this analysis illustrates Merton's (1976) original assumption that jump risk can (almost) be *diversified* away—instead of being completely *hedged* away which is impossible here.

It is worthwhile emphasizing that in general a pure delta hedging strategy in such a context cannot perform as well as for a European option in a more simple model. A major reason for this is that delta hedging cannot account for jumps or other risk factors apart from index risk. Figure 13.8 shows a case where a delta hedging strategy performs reasonably well until a jump in the EURO STOXX 50 index level occurs and the option is exercised right afterwards. As a consequence of the jump, the dynamic hedging strategy breaks down since the replication portfolio payoff after the jump is insufficient to account for the steep increase in the put option's value (cf. Tankov and Voltchkova (2009) for a similar numerical example).

In summary, with regard to a single option, delta hedging is obviously not sufficient—at least if one takes the terms "hedging" and "replication" seriously. What one rather needs is the static or dynamic addition of other (plain vanilla) options on the same underlying to the hedge portfolio.[6]

---

[6] Again, refer to Tankov and Voltchkova (2009) for this insight as well as to Cont et al. (2007) for the implementation of hedging strategies with options in the presence of jumps.

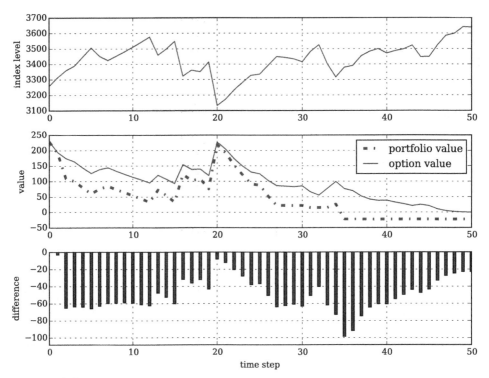

FIGURE 13.6   Dynamic replication of American put option in BCC97 with loss at maturity

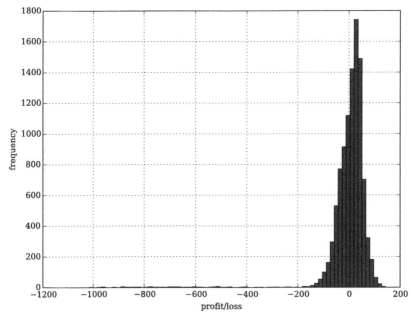

FIGURE 13.7   Frequency distribution of (discounted) P&L at exercise date of
10,000 dynamic replications of American put option in general market model BCC97

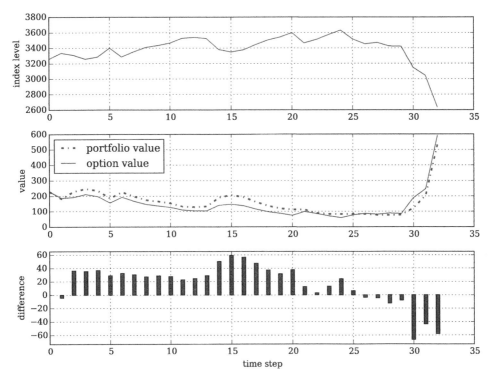

FIGURE 13.8 Dynamic replication of American put option in BCC97 with large loss at exercise due to an index jump

13.4 CONCLUSIONS

This chapter analyzes the market-based dynamic hedging and replication of American index options. As it turns out, delta hedging works quite well in the benchmark model of BSM. However, delta hedging may break down in the general market model of BCC97 since jumps make this model incomplete in a wider sense leading to the impossibility of perfectly replicating options by trading in the available underlyings (or even other options to this end).

13.5 PYTHON SCRIPTS

13.5.1 LSM Delta Hedging in BSM (Single Path)

```
#
# Dynamic Hedging of American Put Option in BSM Model
# with Least Squares Monte Carlo
# 13_dyh/BSM_lsm_hedging_algorithm.py
#
# (c) Dr. Yves J. Hilpisch
```

```
# Derivatives Analytics with Python
#
import math
import numpy as np
import warnings
warnings.simplefilter('ignore')
import matplotlib as mpl
mpl.rcParams['font.family'] = 'serif'
import matplotlib.pyplot as plt


#
# Parameters
#
S0 = 36.0  # initial stock value
K = 40.0  # strike price
T = 1.0  # time to maturity
r = 0.06  # risk-less short rate
sigma = 0.20  # volatility of stock value
M = 50  # number of time steps
I = 50000  # number of paths


#
# Valuation
#
D = 9  # number of regression functions


def BSM_lsm_put_value(S0, M, I):
    ''' Function to value an American put option by LSM algorithm.

    Parameters
    ==========
    S0: float
        initial index level
    M: int
        number of time steps

    Returns
    =======
    V0: float
        LSM Monte Carlo estimator of American put option value
    S: NumPy array
        simulated index level paths
    ex: NumPy array
        exercise matrix
    rg: NumPy array
        regression coefficients
```

```
    h: NumPy array
        inner value matrix
    dt: float
        length of time interval
    '''
    rand = np.random.standard_normal((M + 1, I))   # random numbers
    dt = T / M   # length of time interval
    df = math.exp(-r * dt)  # discount factor
    S = np.zeros((M + 1, I), dtype=np.float)  # stock price matrix
    S[0] = S0  # initial values
    for t in xrange(1, M + 1, 1):  # stock price at t
        S[t] = S[t - 1] * (np.exp((r - sigma ** 2 / 2) * dt
                            + sigma * math.sqrt(dt) * rand[t]))
    h = np.maximum(K - S, 0)   # inner values
    V = np.maximum(K - S, 0)   # value matrix
    ex = np.zeros((M + 1, I), dtype=np.float)    # exercise matrix
    C = np.zeros((M + 1, I), dtype=np.float)    # continuation value matrix
    rg = np.zeros((M + 1, D + 1), dtype=np.float)
      # matrix for reg. coefficients
    for t in range(M - 1, 0, -1):
        rg[t] = np.polyfit(S[t], V[t + 1] * df, D)
        # regression in step i
        C[t] = np.polyval(rg[t], S[t])
        # estimated continuation values
        C[t] = np.where(C[t] < 0, 0., C[t])
        # correction for neg C
        V[t] = np.where(h[t] >= C[t],
                    h[t], V[t + 1] * df)  # exercise decision
        ex[t] = np.where(h[t] >= C[t], 1, 0)
        # exercise decision (yes=1)
    V0 = np.sum(V[1]) / I * df
    return V0, S, ex, rg, h, dt

def BSM_hedge_run(p=0):
    ''' Implements delta hedging for a single path. '''
    np.random.seed(50000)
    #
    # Initial Delta
    #
    ds = 0.01
    V_1, S, ex, rg, h, dt = BSM_lsm_put_value(S0 + ds, M, I)
    V_2 = BSM_lsm_put_value(S0, M, I)[0]
    del_0 = (V_1 - V_2) / ds


    #
    # Dynamic Hedging
    #
```

```python
delt = np.zeros(M + 1, dtype=np.float)  # vector for deltas
print
print "APPROXIMATION OF FIRST ORDER "
print "----------------------------"
print " %7s | %7s | %7s " % ('step', 'S_t', 'Delta')
for t in xrange(1, M, 1):
    if ex[t, p] == 0:  # if option is alive
        St = S[t, p]  # relevant index level
        diff = (np.polyval(rg[t], St + ds) -
                np.polyval(rg[t], St))
                # numerator of difference quotient
        delt[t] = diff / ds  # delta as difference quotient
        print " %7d | %7.2f | %7.2f" % (t, St, delt[t])
        if (S[t, p] - S[t - 1, p]) * (delt[t] - delt[t - 1]) < 0:
            print "          wrong"
    else:
        break

delt[0] = del_0
print
print "DYNAMIC HEDGING OF AMERICAN PUT (BSM)"
print "-------------------------------------"
po = np.zeros(t, dtype=np.float)  # vector for portfolio values
vt = np.zeros(t, dtype=np.float)  # vector for option values
vt[0] = V_1
po[0] = V_1
bo = V_1 - delt[0] * S0  # bond position value
print "Initial Hedge"
print "Stocks           %8.3f" % delt[0]
print "Bonds            %8.3f" % bo
print "Cost             %8.3f" % (delt[0] * S0 + bo)

print
print "Regular Rehedges "
print 68 * "-"
print "step|" + 7 * " %7s|" % ('S_t', 'Port', 'Put',
                    'Diff', 'Stock', 'Bond', 'Cost')
for j in range(1, t, 1):
    vt[j] = BSM_lsm_put_value(S[j, p], M - j, I)[0]
    po[j] = delt[j - 1] * S[j, p] + bo * math.exp(r * dt)
    bo = po[j] - delt[j] * S[j, p]  # bond position value
    print "%4d|" % j + 7 * " %7.3f|" % (S[j, p], po[j], vt[j],
                    (po[j] - vt[j]), delt[j], bo, delt[j] * S[j, p] + bo)

errs = po - vt  # hedge errors
print "MSE             %7.3f" % (np.sum(errs ** 2) / len(errs))
print "Average Error   %7.3f" % (np.sum(errs) / len(errs))
```

```
    print "Total P&L       %7.3f" % np.sum(errs)
    return S[:, p], po, vt, errs, t

def plot_hedge_path(S, po, vt, errs, t):
    #
    # Graphical Output
    #
    tl = np.arange(t)
    plt.figure(figsize=(8, 6))
    plt.subplot(311)
    plt.grid(True)
    plt.plot(tl, S[tl], 'r')
    plt.ylabel('index level')
    plt.subplot(312)
    plt.grid(True)
    plt.plot(tl, po[tl], 'r-.', label='portfolio value', lw=2)
    plt.plot(tl, vt[tl], 'b', label='option value', lw=1)
    plt.ylabel('value')
    plt.legend(loc=0)
    ax = plt.axis()
    plt.subplot(313)
    plt.grid(True)
    wi = 0.3
    diffs = po[tl] - vt[tl]
    plt.bar(tl - wi / 2, diffs, color='b', width=wi)
    plt.ylabel('difference')
    plt.xlabel('time step')
    plt.axis([ax[0], ax[1], min(diffs) * 1.1, max(diffs) * 1.1])
    plt.tight_layout()
```

13.5.2 LSM Delta Hedging in BSM (Multiple Paths)

```
#
# Dynamic Hedging of American Put Option in BSM Model
# with Least Squares Monte Carlo -- Histogram
# 13_dyh/BSM_lsm_hedging_histogram.py
#
# (c) Dr. Yves s. Hilpisch
# Derivatives Analytics with Python
#
from BSM_lsm_hedging_algorithm import *

def BSM_dynamic_hedge_mcs(M=50, I=10000):
    ''' Monte Carlo simulation of dynamic hedging paths
    for American put option in BSM model. '''
```

```
#
# Initial Delta
#
ds = 0.01
V_1, S, ex, rg, h, dt = BSM_lsm_put_value(S0 + ds, M, I)
V_2 = BSM_lsm_put_value(S0, M, I)[0]
del_0 = (V_1 - V_2) / ds

print"Value of American Put Option is %8.3f" % V_2
print"Delta t=0 is                      %8.3f" % del_0
#
# Dynamic Hedging Runs
#
pl_list = []
run = 0
runs = min(I, 10000)
for run in xrange(runs):
    p = run
    run += 1
    delta = np.zeros(M + 1, dtype=np.float)  # vector for deltas
    for t in xrange(0, M, 1):
        if ex[t - 1, p] == 0:  # if option is alive
            St = S[t, p]  # relevant index level
            diff = (np.polyval(rg[t, :], St + ds)
                  - np.polyval(rg[t, :], St))
                    # numerator of difference quotient
            delta[t] = diff / ds  # delta as difference quotient
        else:
            break
    delta[0] = del_0
    po = np.zeros(t, dtype=np.float)  # vector for portfolio values
    vt = np.zeros(t, dtype=np.float)  # vector for option values
    vt[0] = V_2  # initial option value
    po[0] = V_2  # initial portfolio value
    bo = V_2 - delta[0] * S0  # initial bond position value
    for s in range(1, t, 1):  # for all times up to i-1
        po[s] = delta[s - 1] * S[s, p] + bo * math.exp(r * dt)
            # portfolio payoff
        bo = po[s] - delta[s] * S[s, p]  # bond position value
        if s == t - 1:  # at exercise/expiration date
            vt[s] = h[s, p]  # option value equals inner value
            pl = (po[s] - vt[s]) * math.exp(-r * t * dt)
              # discounted difference between option and portfolio value
            if run % 1000 == 0:
                print "run %5d   p/l %8.3f" % (run, pl)
            pl_list.append(pl)  # collect all differences
pl_list = np.array(pl_list)
```

```
#
# Summary Results Output
#
print "\nSUMMARY STATISTICS FOR P&L"
print "---------------------------------"
print "Dynamic Replications %12d" % runs
print "Time Steps            %12d" % M
print "Paths for Valuation   %12d" % I
print "Maximum               %12.3f" % max(pl_list)
print "Average               %12.3f" % np.mean(pl_list)
print "Median                %12.3f" % np.median(pl_list)
print "Minimum               %12.3f" % min(pl_list)
print "---------------------------------"

return pl_list

def plot_hedge_histogram(pl_list):
    ''' Plot of P/L histogram. '''
    #
    # Graphical Output
    #
    plt.figure(figsize=(8, 6))
    plt.grid()
    plt.hist(pl_list, 75)
    plt.xlabel('profit/loss')
    plt.ylabel('frequency')
```

13.5.3 LSM Algorithm for American Put in BCC97

```
#
# Delta Hedging an American Put Option in BCC97
# via Least Squares Monte Carlo (Multiple Replications)
# 13_dyh/BCC97_lsm_hedging_algorithm.py
#
# (c) Dr. Yves J. Hilpisch
# Derivatives Analytics with Python
#
import sys
sys.path.extend(['09_gmm', '11_cal', '12_val'])
import math
import numpy as np
import warnings
warnings.simplefilter('ignore')
```

```python
import matplotlib as mpl
mpl.rcParams['font.family'] = 'serif'
import matplotlib.pyplot as plt
from H93_calibration import S0, kappa_r, theta_r, sigma_r, r0
from BCC97_simulation import *
from BSM_lsm_hedging_algorithm import plot_hedge_path

#
# Model Parameters
#
opt = np.load('11_cal/opt_full.npy')
kappa_v, theta_v, sigma_v, rho, v0, lamb, mu, delta = opt

#
# Simulation
#
K = S0
T = 1.0
M = 50
I = 50000
a = 1.0  # a from the interval [0.0, 2.0]
dis = 0.01  # change of S[t] in percent to estimate derivative
dt = T / M
moment_matching = True

def BCC97_lsm_put_value(S0, K, T, M, I):
    ''' Function to value American put options by LSM algorithm.

    Parameters
    ==========
    S0: float
        intial index level
    K: float
        strike of the put option
    T: float
        final date/time horizon
    M: int
        number of time steps
    I: int
        number of paths

    Returns
    =======
    V0: float
        LSM Monte Carlo estimator of American put option value
    S: NumPy array
        simulated index level paths
```

```
    r: NumPy array
        simulated short rate paths
    v: NumPy array
        simulated variance paths
    ex: NumPy array
        exercise matrix
    rg: NumPy array
        regression coefficients
    h: NumPy array
        inner value matrix
    dt: float
        length of time interval
    '''
    dt = T / M
    # Cholesky Matrix
    cho_matrix = generate_cholesky(rho)
    # Random Numbers
    rand = random_number_generator(M, I, anti_paths, moment_matching)
    # Short Rate Process Simulation
    r = SRD_generate_paths(r0, kappa_r, theta_r, sigma_r, T, M, I,
                            rand, 0, cho_matrix)
    # Variance Process Simulation
    v = SRD_generate_paths(v0, kappa_v, theta_v, sigma_v, T, M, I,
                            rand, 2, cho_matrix)
    # Index Level Process Simulation
    S = B96_generate_paths(S0, r, v, lamb, mu, delta, rand, 1, 3,
                            cho_matrix, T, M, I, moment_matching)
    h = np.maximum(K - S, 0)   # inner value matrix
    V = np.maximum(K - S, 0)   # value/cash flow matrix
    ex = np.zeros_like(V)   # exercise matrix
    D = 10   # number of regression functions
    rg = np.zeros((M + 1, D + 1), dtype=np.float)
      # matrix for regression parameters
    for t in xrange(M - 1, 0, -1):
        df = np.exp(-(r[t] + r[t + 1]) / 2 * dt)
        # select only ITM paths
        itm = np.greater(h[t], 0)
        relevant = np.nonzero(itm)
        rel_S = np.compress(itm, S[t])
        no_itm = len(rel_S)
        if no_itm == 0:
            cv = np.zeros((I), dtype=np.float)
        else:
            rel_v = np.compress(itm, v[t])
            rel_r = np.compress(itm, r[t])
            rel_V = (np.compress(itm, V[t + 1])
                    * np.compress(itm, df))
```

```
            matrix = np.zeros((D + 1, no_itm), dtype=np.float)
            matrix[10] = rel_S * rel_v * rel_r
            matrix[9] = rel_S * rel_v
            matrix[8] = rel_S * rel_r
            matrix[7] = rel_v * rel_r
            matrix[6] = rel_S ** 2
            matrix[5] = rel_v ** 2
            matrix[4] = rel_r ** 2
            matrix[3] = rel_S
            matrix[2] = rel_v
            matrix[1] = rel_r
            matrix[0] = 1
            rg[t] = np.linalg.lstsq(matrix.transpose(), rel_V)[0]
            cv = np.dot(rg[t], matrix)
        erg = np.zeros((I), dtype=np.float)
        np.put(erg, relevant, cv)
        V[t] = np.where(h[t] > erg, h[t], V[t + 1] * df)
            # value array
        ex[t] = np.where(h[t] > erg, 1, 0)
            # exercise decision
    df = np.exp(-((r[0] + r[1]) / 2) * dt)
    V0 = max(np.sum(V[1, :] * df) / I, h[0, 0])    # LSM estimator
    return V0, S, r, v, ex, rg, h, dt


def BCC97_hedge_run(p):
    ''' Implements delta hedging for a single path. '''
    #
    # Initializations
    #
    np.random.seed(50000)
    po = np.zeros(M + 1, dtype=np.float)  # vector for portfolio values
    vt = np.zeros(M + 1, dtype=np.float)  # vector for option values
    delt = np.zeros(M + 1, dtype=np.float)  # vector for deltas
    # random path selection ('real path')
    print
    print "DYNAMIC HEDGING OF AMERICAN PUT (BCC97)"
    print "---------------------------------------"
    ds = dis * S0
    V_1, S, r, v, ex, rg, h, dt = BCC97_lsm_put_value(S0 + (2 - a) * ds,
                                            K, T, M, I)
    # 'data basis' for delta hedging
    V_2 = BCC97_lsm_put_value(S0 - a * ds, K, T, M, I)[0]
    delt[0] = (V_1 - V_2) / (2 * ds)
    V0LSM = BCC97_lsm_put_value(S0, K, T, M, I)[0]
      # initial option value for S0
    vt[0] = V0LSM  # initial option values
    po[0] = V0LSM  # initial portfolio values
    bo = V0LSM - delt[0] * S0  # initial bond position value
```

```
print "Initial Hedge"
print "Stocks              %8.3f" % delt[0]
print "Bonds               %8.3f" % bo
print "Cost                %8.3f" % (delt[0] * S0 + bo)

print
print "Regular Rehedges "
print 82 * "-"
print "step|" + 7 * " %9s|" % ('S_t', 'Port', 'Put',
                      'Diff', 'Stock', 'Bond', 'Cost')
for t in range(1, M + 1, 1):
    if ex[t, p] == 0:
        df = math.exp((r[t, p] + r[t - 1, p]) / 2 * dt)
        if t != M:
            po[t] = delt[t - 1] * S[t, p] + bo * df
            vt[t] = BCC97_lsm_put_value(S[t, p], K, T - t * dt,
                                  M - t, I)[0]
        ds = dis * S[t, p]
        sd = S[t, p] + (2 - a) * ds  # disturbed index level
        stateV_A = [sd * v[t, p] * r[t, p],
                    sd * v[t, p],
                    sd * r[t, p],
                    v[t, p] * r[t, p],
                    sd ** 2,
                    v[t, p] ** 2,
                    r[t, p] ** 2,
                    sd,
                    v[t, p],
                    r[t, p],
                    1]
                    # state vector for S[t, p] + (2.0 - a) * dis
        stateV_A.reverse()
        V0A = max(0, np.dot(rg[t], stateV_A))
        # print V0A
        # revaluation via regression
        sd = S[t, p] - a * ds  # disturbed index level
        stateV_B = [sd * v[t, p] * r[t, p],
                    sd * v[t, p],
                    sd * r[t, p],
                    v[t, p] * r[t, p],
                    sd ** 2,
                    v[t, p] ** 2,
                    r[t, p] ** 2,
                    sd,
                    v[t, p],
                    r[t, p],
                    1]
                    # state vector for S[t, p] - a * dis
```

```
                    stateV_B.reverse()
                    V0B = max(0, np.dot(rg[t], stateV_B))
                    # print V0B
                    # revaluation via regression
                    delt[t] = (V0A - V0B) / (2 * ds)
                    bo = po[t] - delt[t] * S[t, p]  # bond position value
                else:
                    po[t] = delt[t - 1] * S[t, p] + bo * df
                    vt[t] = h[t, p]
                    # inner value at final date
                    delt[t] = 0.0
                print "%4d|" % t + 7 * " " %9.3f|" % (S[t, p], po[t], vt[t],
                            (po[t] - vt[t]), delt[t], bo, delt[t] * S[t, p] + bo)
        else:
            po[t] = delt[t - 1] * S[t, p] + bo * df
            vt[t] = h[t, p]
            break
    errs = po - vt  # hedge errors
    print "MSE              %7.3f" % (np.sum(errs ** 2) / len(errs))
    print "Average Error    %7.3f" % (np.sum(errs) / len(errs))
    print "Total P&L        %7.3f" % np.sum(errs)
    return S[:, p], po, vt, errs, t
```

13.5.4 LSM Delta Hedging in BCC97 (Single Path)

```
#
# Delta Hedging an American Put Option in BCC97
# via Least Squares Monte Carlo (Multiple Replications)
# 13_dyh/BCC97_lsm_hedging_histogram.py
#
# (c) Dr. Yves s. Hilpisch
# Derivatives Analytics with Python
#
from BCC97_lsm_hedging_algorithm import *
from CIR_zcb_valuation_gen import B
from BSM_lsm_hedging_histogram import plot_hedge_histogram


#
# Simulation
#
T = 1.0
a = 1.0  # a from the interval [0.0, 2.0]
dis = 0.05  # change of S[t] in percent to estimate derivative
dt = T / M
np.random.seed(50000)
def BCC97_hedge_simulation(M=50, I=10000):
```

```
''' Monte Carlo simualtion of dynamic hedging paths
for American put option in BSM model. '''
#
# Initializations
#
po = np.zeros(M + 1, dtype=np.float)  # vector for portfolio values
delt = np.zeros(M + 1, dtype=np.float)  # vector for deltas
ds = dis * S0
V_1, S, r, v, ex, rg, h, dt = BCC97_lsm_put_value(S0 + (2 - a) * ds,
                                                  K, T, M, I)
# 'data basis' for delta hedging
V_2 = BCC97_lsm_put_value(S0 - a * ds, K, T, M, I)[0]
delt[0] = (V_1 - V_2) / (2 * ds)
V0LSM = BCC97_lsm_put_value(S0, K, T, M, I)[0]  # initial option value for S0
po[0] = V0LSM  # initial portfolio values


#
# Hedge Runs
#
pl_list = []
runs = min(I, 10000)
for run in range(runs):
    bo = V0LSM - delt[0] * S0  # initial bond position value
    p = run
    run += 1
    for t in range(1, M + 1, 1):
        if ex[t, p] == 0:
            df = math.exp((r[t, p] + r[t - 1, p]) / 2 * dt)
            if t != M:
                po[t] = delt[t - 1] * S[t, p] + bo * df  # portfolio payoff
                ds = dis * S[t, p]
                sd = S[t, p] + (2 - a) * ds  # disturbed index level
                stateV_A = [sd * v[t, p] * r[t, p],
                            sd * v[t, p],
                            sd * r[t, p],
                            v[t, p] * r[t, p],
                            sd ** 2,
                            v[t, p] ** 2,
                            r[t, p] ** 2,
                            sd,
                            v[t, p],
                            r[t, p],
                            1]
                    # state vector for S[t, p] + (2.0 - a) * ds
                stateV_A.reverse()
                V0A = max(0, np.dot(rg[t], stateV_A))
                # revaluation via regression
                sd = S[t, p] - a * ds  # disturbed index level
                stateV_B = [sd * v[t, p] * r[t, p],
```

```
                            sd * v[t, p],
                            sd * r[t, p],
                            v[t, p] * r[t, p],
                            sd ** 2,
                            v[t, p] ** 2,
                            r[t, p] ** 2,
                            sd,
                            v[t, p],
                            r[t, p],
                            1]
                    # state vector for S[t, p] - a * ds
                stateV_B.reverse()
                V0B = max(0, np.dot(rg[t], stateV_B))
                # revaluation via regression
                delt[t] = (V0A - V0B) / (2 * ds)
            else:
                po[t] = delt[t - 1] * S[t, p] + bo * df
                delt[t] = 0.0
            bo = po[t] - delt[t] * S[t, p]
        else:
            po[t] = delt[t - 1] * S[t, p] + bo * df
            break
    alpha_t = [kappa_r, theta_r, sigma_r, r0, 0.0, t * dt]
    pl = (po[t] - h[t, p]) * B(alpha_t)
    if run % 1000 == 0:
        print "run %5d   p/l %8.3f" % (run, pl)
    pl_list.append(pl)
pl_list = np.array(pl_list)


#
# Results Output
#
print "\nSUMMARY STATISTICS FOR P&L"
print "-------------------------------"
print "Dynamic Replications %12d" % runs
print "Time Steps           %12d" % M
print "Paths for Valuation  %12d" % I
print "Maximum              %12.3f" % max(pl_list)
print "Average              %12.3f" % np.mean(pl_list)
print "Median               %12.3f" % np.median(pl_list)
print "Minimum              %12.3f" % min(pl_list)
print "-------------------------------"

return pl_list
```

## CHAPTER 14

Executive Summary

This book is about the market-based valuation of European and American stock index options. It is a discipline of particular interest in derivatives analytics. To this end, it introduces—among a number of basic tools and approaches—the general market model from Bakshi-Cao-Chen (cf. Bakshi et al. (1997)) as a framework to accomplish the following goals:

- **modeling market risks**: the model should account for market risks generally affecting index options, like index level risk, volatility risk, jump risk and interest rate risk
- **efficient valuation of vanilla options**: as a major requirement, the market model should be able to value plain vanilla options, like European puts or calls on an index, in an efficient manner; as it turns out, the Fourier transform method in combination with numerical integration or Fast Fourier Transforms (FFT) offers a convenient approach to accomplish this
- **calibration of model parameters**: equipped with efficient techniques for the valuation of plain vanilla options, the model can then be calibrated to observed market quotes of such instruments in order to derive a single martingale measure for the valuation of other (exotic) index derivatives
- **valuation by simulation**: in general, numerical methods are necessary to value the majority of (exotic) equity derivatives; Monte Carlo simulation (MCS) is the most flexible one with the Least-Squares Monte Carlo (LSM) algorithm (cf. Longstaff and Schwartz (2001)) allowing for the incorporation of early exercise features
- **dynamic delta hedging**: relying on the LSM algorithm, it is possible to numerically estimate deltas for (exotic) equity derivatives even with American exercise; however, due to market incompleteness (e.g. because of jumps) delta hedging on a stand-alone basis is generally insufficient to hedge or replicate equity derivatives sufficiently well in the general market model of Bakshi-Cao-Chen (1997)

The whole exposition is accompanied by a self-contained set of Python scripts which allows the easy replication of the results and graphics presented throughout the book. All Python codes and additional IPython Notebooks are provided on the Quant Platform under http://wiley.quant-platform.com. For further resources see also http://derivatives-analytics-with-python.com.

Python in a Nutshell

This appendix introduces into the Python language mainly by the means of simple interactive examples and some shorter code snippets (i.e. modules and scripts). It cannot replace any kind of proper training in this programming language or more comprehensive treatments in book form.

By reading this appendix, you will NOT learn how to code in general or learn Python from scratch to black belt level. However, for someone coming with C++ experience, for example, the appendix illustrates fundamental aspects of Python that are useful for derivatives analytics and financial engineering in general. For someone who starts out in these areas, the topics covered provide a first glimpse at coding in general and for derivatives analytics in particular. For this group, the appendix may act as a starting point for digging deeper into areas of further interest.

The best Python foundation for this book can be gained by reading the recent book by the same author (Hilpisch, 2014). That book focuses on teaching Python for finance and covers many topics of interest in this area on more than 600 pages. Another useful book is McKinney (2012) which introduces in detail the main data analysis tools and libraries needed for the applications presented in this book (in particular NumPy and pandas). For general introductions to Python from a scientific point of view, you can consult either the book by Langtangen (2009) or the freely available lecture notes of Haenel et al. (2013).

A.1 PYTHON FUNDAMENTALS

This first section is about some important, fundamental topics when it comes to Python usage.

A.1.1 Installing Python Packages

No matter what operating system you use, make sure to install at least current versions of the following Python packages/libraries:

- Python 2.7.x (www.python.org): the basic Python interpreter
- NumPy (http://numpy.scipy.org): library to efficiently handle (large) arrays at high speed
- SciPy (www.scipy.org): library with many useful scientific functions

- matplotlib (http://matplotlib.sourceforge.net): the standard 2d and 3d plotting library
- pandas (http://pandas.sourceforge.net): efficient and fast data analysis, for example, of financial time series
- PyTables (www.pytables.org): handling of HDF5 database files for high performance I/O operations
- IPython (www.ipython.org): interactive analytics and development environment (shell, browser-based)
- xlrd, xlwt (www.python-excel.org): functions to work with Microsoft Excel spreadsheet files

Having installed these packages/libraries (and maybe additional ones on which these particular ones are dependent) allows to use all modules and scripts provided in the book and to follow this appendix. However, installing single packages and libraries might sometimes prove too time consuming and inefficient. It is therefore recommended to work on the Quant Platform (cf. http://wiley.quant-platform.com) or to at least install a complete Python distribution which comes in general with the most important libraries in those versions that are compatible with each other.

For example, Anaconda is a distribution of a Python base system in combination with quite a large number of useful libraries and tools for scientific purposes. It is pretty well suited for financial application building and interactive financial analytics. The website www.continuum.io provides current downloads and further information. It is available for all popular operating systems. Installing a complete distribution like Anaconda is generally relatively easy and fast. It also greatly simplifies the updating of single libraries and the interpreter itself.

One might wonder why Python version 2.7.x is used in this book and not the newest generation of Python which is already 3.4 at the time of this writing. There are two reasons. First, Python 2.7.x is current (at the end of 2014) and still maintained by the Open Source community. Second, some syntax has changed in 3.x such that the versions are not fully compatible—and most code in the financial ecosystem and documentation available is still based on Python 2.7.x. On the other hand, the majority of the code presented in this book is either executable with a Python 3.4 interpreter without any changes or relatively easy to adjust for this version.

A.1.2 First Steps with Python

After starting IPython, a popular and powerful interactive shell for Python, you should see something like this on your screen:

```
1   yhilpisch@ONE:~$ ipython
2   Python 2.7.8 |Anaconda 2.0.1 (64-bit)| (default, Aug 21 2014, 18:22:21)
3   Type "copyright", "credits" or "license" for more information.
4
5   IPython 2.3.0 -- An enhanced Interactive Python.
6   Anaconda is brought to you by Continuum Analytics.
7   Please check out: http://continuum.io/thanks and https://binstar.org
8   ?         -> Introduction and overview of IPython's features.
```

```
9    %quickref -> Quick reference.
10   help        -> Python's own help system.
11   object?    -> Details about 'object', use 'object??' for extra details.
12
13   In [1]:
```

Before a first *module* (something that can be imported) or *script* (something that can be executed stand-alone) is implemented, some first and simple exercises on the shell with the interpreter may serve as a warm-up.

```
1    In [1]: 3 + 4
2    Out[1]: 7
3
4    In [2]: 3 / 4
5    Out[2]: 0
6
7    In [3]:
```

Addition seems to work well, but division apparently not. This is due to Python interpreting 3 and 4 as integers such that division gives 0 instead of 0.75. Putting a dot behind either 3 or 4 or both does the trick (i.e. one tells Python that one is working with floats).[1]

```
1    In [3]: 3.0 / 4
2    Out[3]: 0.75
3
4    In [4]:
```

Obviously, types are important with Python. One has to be careful since Python is a dynamically typed language which means that there are default types which are used given a specific context. In C++, for example, you would have to assign a certain static type to a variable before using it. Variable names (more general: reference pointers) are defined in Python with the $=$ sign:

```
1    In [4]: a = 3
2
3    In [5]: b = 4
4
5    In [6]: a / b
6    Out[6]: 0
7
```

---

[1]In Python 3.x, the float division is the default setting while in Python 2.x it is the floor or integer division. In Python 3.x, you have the following syntax for both types of division: 3 / 4 for float division and 3 // 4 for floor division.

```
8    In [7]: a = 3.0
9
10   In [8]: a / b
11   Out[8]: 0.75
12
13   In [9]:
```

Even if the Python interpreter has already built in lots of functionality, most of it is stored in modules or whole packages of different modules which have to be imported before usage. An example is the math module which comes with the so-called *standard library* and contains, among others, trigonometric functions.

```
1    In [1]: a = 3.0
2
3    In [2]: sin(a)
4    ---------------------------------------------------------------------
5    NameError                                 Traceback (most recent call last)
6    <ipython-input-3-66bf5e82d1e2> in <module>()
7    ----> 1 sin(a)
8
9    NameError: name 'sin' is not defined
10
11   In [3]: from math import sin
12
13   In [4]: sin(a)
14   Out[4]: 0.1411200080598672
15
16   In [5]:
```

If you want to indicate that the sin function is from the math module (which is recommended), you have to import the module/library itself and not the functions that are contained therein.

```
1    In [5]: b = 4
2
3    In [6]: import math
4
5    In [7]: math.sin(b)
6    Out[7]: -0.7568024953079282
7
8    In [8]:
```

You can easily define functions by yourself.

```
In [8]: def f(x):
    ...:       return x ** 3 + x ** 2 - 2 + math.sin(x)

In [9]: f(2)
Out[9]: 10.909297426825681

In [10]: f(a)
Out[10]: 34.141120008059865

In [11]:
```

Here, x ** 3 stands for x^3. Generally, if you are doing something useful which you would like to store for later use you would not work with a command line interpreter or a shell. Rather, you would open a new file (module/script), store the function in it and save it on disk. Python modules/scripts are characterized by the .py suffix. A new module can be generated with a dedicated Python editor or with the most simple text editor. In fact, Python modules/scripts are nothing more or less than text files.

In such a file, say with name a_first_program.py, you could store the previous code like this:

```
#
# First Program with Python
# A_pyt/a_first_program.py
#
import math

# Variable Definition
a = 3.0
b = 4

# Function Definition


def f(x):
    ''' Mathematical Function. '''
    return x ** 3 + x ** 2 - 2 + math.sin(x)

# Calculation
f_a = f(a)
f_b = f(b)

# Output
print "f(a) = %6.3f" % f_a
print "f(b) = %6.3f" % f_b
```

The # sign allows the inclusion of comments in your code that are ignored by the Python interpreter. Make sure when saving Python modules to always include the suffix .py. Now you can run the script from IPython which should produce the following output:

```
In [12]: %run a_first_program.py
f(a) = 34.141
f(b) = 77.243

In [13]:
```

This should be enough for some very first steps with Python. This sub-section showed how to calculate, how to evaluate a numerical expression, how to define a function and how to write a script containing the function that can be executed.

A.1.3 Array Operations

NumPy is a powerful library that allows efficient array manipulations (linear algebra) in a compact form and at high speed. The speed comes from the implementation of main parts of the library in C. So you have the convenience of Python combined with the speed of C when doing array operations.

```
In [1]: import numpy as np

In [2]: a = np.arange(0.0, 20.0, 1.0)   # (start, end, step)

In [3]: a
Out[3]:
array([  0.,   1.,   2.,   3.,   4.,   5.,   6.,   7.,   8.,   9.,  10.,
        11.,  12.,  13.,  14.,  15.,  16.,  17.,  18.,  19.])

In [4]: a.resize(4, 5)

In [5]: a
Out[5]:
array([[  0.,   1.,   2.,   3.,   4.],
       [  5.,   6.,   7.,   8.,   9.],
       [ 10.,  11.,  12.,  13.,  14.],
       [ 15.,  16.,  17.,  18.,  19.]])

In [6]: a[0]  # first row
Out[6]: array([ 0.,  1.,  2.,  3.,  4.])

In [7]: a[3]  # fourth (=last) row
Out[7]: array([ 15.,  16.,  17.,  18.,  19.])
```

```
25 | In [8]: a[1, 4]  # second row, 5th (=last) element
26 | Out[8]: 9.0
27 |
28 | In [9]: a[1, 2:4]  # second row, third & forth element
29 | Out[9]: array([ 7.,  8.])
30 |
31 | In [10]:
```

The first examples of array definition and manipulation should be self-explanatory. Care is to be taken with the conventions regarding array indices. The best way to learn these is to play with arrays. In particular, note that zero-based numbering is used and that slicing (see input prompt 9) excludes the last value in the output.

With NumPy, array operations are as easy to implement as operations on integers or floats. This is mainly due to the fact that it provides powerful *vectorization and broadcasting* capabilities (cf. chapter 4 in Hilpisch (2014)).

```
 1 | In [10]: a * 0.5
 2 | Out[10]:
 3 | array([[ 0. ,  0.5,  1. ,  1.5,  2. ],
 4 |        [ 2.5,  3. ,  3.5,  4. ,  4.5],
 5 |        [ 5. ,  5.5,  6. ,  6.5,  7. ],
 6 |        [ 7.5,  8. ,  8.5,  9. ,  9.5]])
 7 |
 8 | In [11]: a ** 2
 9 | Out[11]:
10 | array([[   0.,    1.,    4.,    9.,   16.],
11 |        [  25.,   36.,   49.,   64.,   81.],
12 |        [ 100.,  121.,  144.,  169.,  196.],
13 |        [ 225.,  256.,  289.,  324.,  361.]])
14 |
15 | In [12]: a + a
16 | Out[12]:
17 | array([[  0.,   2.,   4.,   6.,   8.],
18 |        [ 10.,  12.,  14.,  16.,  18.],
19 |        [ 20.,  22.,  24.,  26.,  28.],
20 |        [ 30.,  32.,  34.,  36.,  38.]])
21 |
22 | In [13]:
```

One can also use the previously defined function f with NumPy arrays—one change is necessary, however: one has to now use the universal functions that NumPy provides instead of those of the math module.

```
1 | In [13]: def f(x):
2 |     ...:     return x ** 3 + x ** 2 - 2 + np.sin(x)
```

```
In [14]: f(a)
Out[14]:
array([[ -2.00000000e+00,    8.41470985e-01,    1.09092974e+01,
           3.41411200e+01,    7.72431975e+01],
        [  1.47041076e+02,    2.49720585e+02,    3.90656987e+02,
           5.74989358e+02,    8.08412118e+02],
        [  1.09745598e+03,    1.44900001e+03,    1.86946343e+03,
           2.36442017e+03,    2.93899061e+03],
        [  3.59865029e+03,    4.34971210e+03,    5.19903860e+03,
           6.15324901e+03,    7.21814988e+03]])

In [15]:
```

Here, the syntax e+03 is for 10^3. Sometimes you need to loop over arrays to check something or to do some calculation. Looping is also quite intuitive in Python.

```
In [15]: for i in xrange(5):
   ....:         print i
   ....:
0
1
2
3
4

In [16]: b = np.arange(0.0, 100.0, 1.0)

In [17]: for i in range(100):
   ...:         if b[i] == 50.0:
   ...:                 print "50.0 at index no. %d" % i
   ...:
50.0 at index no. 50

In [18]:
```

Note that there is a difference between range and xrange: the first generates in one step a list object containing all the numbers while the latter instantiates a generator object which generates and returns values one by one (when called/needed). Like with array indexing note the zero-based numbering and the fact that the last value is not included in the results (i.e. xrange(5) starts at 0 and ends at 4).

The difference between arange and range is that the first can produce arrays with elements of float type while the latter can only generate list objects containing integers; and indices of arrays are always integers which is why the loop is over integers and not over floats or something else.[2]

In the iteration you will find something called *string replacement*. %d indicates that at the very place where it is found in the string the value of i should be shown—instead of %d. It is convenient, for example, to "parametrize" larger strings in this way. String replacement is also helpful when it comes to formatting:

```
In [18]: print "%d divided by %d gives %6.3f" % (1000, 17, 1000./17)
1000 divided by 17 gives 58.824

In [19]:
```

%6.3f in the string is replaced by a 6 digit long float object (including the decimal point) with 3 decimals.

A.1.4 Random Numbers

Derivatives analytics cannot live without random numbers, be they either pseudo-random or quasi-random. NumPy has built in convenient functions for the generation of pseudo-random numbers in the sub-module random.[3]

```
In [1]: import numpy as np

In [2]: b = np.random.standard_normal((4, 5))

In [3]: b
Out[3]:
array([[ 0.73262022, -0.32977027, -0.63735777,  0.29651912,  0.92829732],
       [ 0.06622625,  1.68082578,  0.47302614, -0.44214276,  0.54175322],
       [-0.66753795, -0.82754659,  0.3837979 ,  0.45688461,  0.44984762],
       [-0.60468346,  1.84658194, -0.35433689,  0.50973071,  0.11169662]])

In [4]: np.sum(b)
Out[4]: 4.6144317809306132

In [5]: np.mean(b)
Out[5]: 0.23072158904653067

In [6]: np.std(b)
Out[6]: 0.7190698353463989

In [7]:
```

[2]On data types and structures in Python see Chapter 4 of Hilpisch (2014).
[3]Refer to Chapter 10 of Hilpisch (2014) for more background on generating pseudo-random numbers and simulating random variables as well as stochastic processes.

A.1.5 Plotting

In interactive financial analytics, one often wants to visualize results from calculations or simulations. The library matplotlib is quite powerful when it comes to 2d visualizations of any kind—but also for 3d plotting. The most important types of graphics for derivatives analytics are line and dot plots as well as bar charts and histograms.

```
In [8]: import matplotlib.pyplot as plt

In [9]: plt.plot(np.cumsum(b))
Out[9]: [<matplotlib.lines.Line2D at 0x37c1890>]

In [10]: plt.xlabel('x axis')
Out[10]: <matplotlib.text.Text at 0x343a210>

In [11]: plt.ylabel('y axis')
Out[11]: <matplotlib.text.Text at 0x343ec10>

In [12]: plt.grid(True)

In [13]: plt.show()

In [14]:
```

cumsum calculates the running cumulative sum over an array. In this case it also flattens the two-dimensional array to a one-dimensional vector. Figure A.1 shows the output.

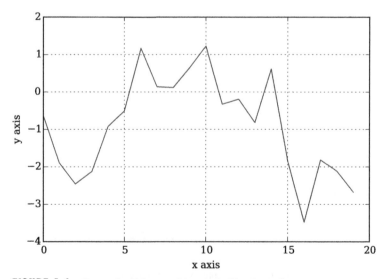

FIGURE A.1 Example of figure with matplotlib—here: line

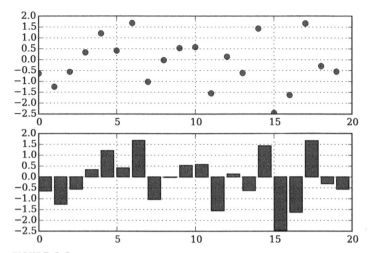

FIGURE A.2 Example of figure with matplotlib—here: dots and bars

The next example combines a dot sub-plot with a bar sub-plot the result of which is shown in Figure A.2. Here, due to resizing of the array there is only a one-dimensional set of numbers (i.e. the array b is flattened again).

```
In [15]: c = np.resize(b, 20)

In [16]: plt.figure()
Out[16]: <matplotlib.figure.Figure at 0x420a710>

In [17]: plt.subplot(211)
Out[17]: <matplotlib.axes.AxesSubplot at 0x47b2c10>

In [18]: plt.plot(c, 'ro')   # red dots
Out[18]: [<matplotlib.lines.Line2D at 0x4935490>]

In [19]: plt.grid(True)

In [20]: plt.subplot(212)
Out[20]: <matplotlib.axes.AxesSubplot at 0x4935850>

In [21]: plt.bar(range(len(c)), c)
Out[21]: <Container object of 20 artists>

In [22]: plt.grid(True)

In [23]: plt.show()

In [24]:
```

This is already all one needs to implement the different European option pricing algorithms in the next section. What may be missing will be added on the fly.

A.2 EUROPEAN OPTION PRICING

This section now illustrates Python usage by the means of specific financial algorithms. In particular, it implements the Black-Scholes-Merton analytical option pricing formula, the binomial option pricing model as well as a Monte Carlo valuation algorithm.

A.2.1 Black-Scholes-Merton Approach

The seminal model $\mathcal{M}^{BSM}$ of Black-Scholes-Merton (cf. Black and Scholes (1973) and Merton (1973)) is still a benchmark for the pricing of European options on stocks and stock indices.[4] The analytical call option formula without dividends is

$$C_0(K, T) = S_0 \cdot \mathbf{N}(d_1) - e^{-rT} \cdot K \cdot \mathbf{N}(d_2)$$

$$d_1 \equiv \frac{\log \frac{S_0}{K} + \left(r + \frac{\sigma^2}{2}\right) T}{\sigma \sqrt{T}}$$

$$d_2 \equiv d_1 - \sigma \sqrt{T}$$

where $\mathbf{N}$ is the cumulative distribution function (cdf) of a standard normal random variable. The single variables have the following meaning, respectively:

- C_0 call option value today
- S_0 index level today
- K strike price of the option
- T time-to-maturity of the call option
- r risk-less short rate
- σ volatility of index level (standard deviation of its returns)

All we need additionally to implement the formula is the cdf for a standard normal variable. We get this from the scipy library which contains a sub-library called stats.

```
#
# Valuation of European Call Option
# in Black-Scholes-Merton Model
# A_pyt/b_BSM_valuation.py
#
from scipy import stats
import math
```

---

[4] See Chapter 5 for details.

```
# Option Parameters
S0 = 105.00  # initial index level
K = 100.00  # strike price
T = 1.  # call option maturity
r = 0.05  # constant short rate
vola = 0.25  # constant volatility factor of diffusion

# Analytical Formula

def BSM_call_value(S0, K, T, r, vola):
    ''' Analytical European call option value for Black-Scholes-Merton (1973).

    Parameters
    ==========
    S0: float
        initial index level
    K: float
        strike price
    T: float
        time-to-maturity
    r: float
        constant short rate
    vola: float
        constant volatility factor

    Returns
    =======
    call_value: float
        European call option present value
    '''
    S0 = float(S0)  # make sure to have float type
    d1 = (math.log(S0 / K) + (r + 0.5 * vola ** 2) * T) / (vola * math.sqrt(T))
    d2 = d1 - vola * math.sqrt(T)
    call_value = (S0 * stats.norm.cdf(d1, 0.0, 1.0)
            - K * math.exp(-r * T) * stats.norm.cdf(d2, 0.0, 1.0))
    return call_value

# Output
print "Value of European call option is %8.3f" \
    % BSM_call_value(S0, K, T, r, vola)
```

The function BSM_call_value gives us a benchmark value for the European call option with the parameters as defined in the Python script:

```
1   In [3]: run b_BSM_valuation.py
2   Value of European call option is   15.655
3
4   In [4]:
```

A.2.2   Cox-Ross-Rubinstein Approach

To better understand how to implement the binomial option pricing model $\mathcal{M}^{CRR}$ of Cox-Ross-Rubinstein (Cox et al., 1979), a little background seems helpful.[5]

There are two securities traded in the model: a risky stock index and a risk-less zero-coupon bond. The time horizon $[0, T]$ is divided into equidistant time intervals Δt so that one gets $M + 1$ points in time $t \in \{0, \Delta t, 2\Delta t, ..., T\}$ with $M \equiv T/\Delta t$. The zero-coupon bond grows p.a. in value with the risk-less short rate r, $B_t = B_0 e^{rt}$ where $B_0 > 0$.

Starting from a strictly positive, fixed stock index level of S_0 at $t = 0$, the stock index evolves according to the law

$$S_{t+\Delta t} \equiv S_t \cdot m$$

where m is selected randomly from $\{u, d\}$. Here, $0 < d < e^{r\Delta t} < u \equiv e^{\sigma\sqrt{\Delta t}}$ as well as $u \equiv \frac{1}{d}$ as a simplification which leads to a recombining tree.

Assuming risk-neutral valuation holds, the following relationship can be derived

$$\begin{aligned} S_t &= e^{-r\Delta t} \cdot \mathbf{E}_t^Q[S_{t+\Delta t}] \\ &= e^{-r\Delta t} \cdot (q \cdot u \cdot S_t + (1 - q) \cdot d \cdot S_t) \end{aligned}$$

Against this background, the risk-neutral (or martingale) probability is

$$q = \frac{e^{r\Delta t} - d}{u - d}$$

The value of a European call option C_0 is then obtained by discounting the final payoffs $C_T(S_T, K) \equiv \max[S_T - K, 0]$ at $t = T$ to $t = 0$:

$$C_0 = e^{-rT} \cdot \mathbf{E}_0^Q[C_T]$$

The discounting can be done step-by-step and node-by-node backwards starting at $t = T - \Delta t$.

From an algorithmical point of view, one has to first generate the index level values, then determine the final payoffs of the call option and finally discount them back. This is what we will do now, starting with a somewhat "naive" implementation. But before we do it, we generate a Python module which contains all parameters that we will need for different implementations afterwards. All parameters can be imported by using the import command and the respective filename without the suffix .py (i.e. the filename is c_parameters.py and the module name is c_parameters).

---

[5]See also Chapter 5 for more details.

```
#
# Model Parameters for European Call Option
# and Binomial Model
# A_pyt/c_parameters.py
#
import math

# Option Parameters
S0 = 105.0  # initial index level
K = 100.0  # strike price
T = 1.  # call option maturity
r = 0.05  # constant short rate
vola = 0.25  # constant volatility factor of diffusion

# Time Parameters
M = 3  # time steps
dt = T / M  # length of time interval
df = math.exp(-r * dt)  # discount factor per time interval

# Binomial Parameters
u = math.exp(vola * math.sqrt(dt))  # up-movement
d = 1 / u  # down-movement
q = (math.exp(r * dt) - d) / (u - d)  # martingale probability
```

Here is the first version of the implemented binomial model which uses nested loop structures extensively (as would be the case, for example, in C or C++).

```
#
# Valuation of European Call Option in CRR1979 Model
# Loop Version (= C-like Iterations)
# A_pyt/d_CRR1979_loop.py
#
import numpy as np
from c_parameters import *

# Array Initialization for Index Levels
S = np.zeros((M + 1, M + 1), dtype=np.float)  # index level array
S[0, 0] = S0
z = 0
for j in xrange(1, M + 1, 1):
    z += 1
    for i in xrange(z + 1):
        S[i, j] = S[0, 0] * (u ** j) * (d ** (i * 2))

# Array Initialization for Inner Values
iv = np.zeros((M + 1, M + 1), dtype=np.float)  # inner value array
```

```
z = 0
for j in xrange(0, M + 1, 1):
    for i in xrange(z + 1):
        iv[i, j] = round(max(S[i, j] - K, 0), 8)
    z += 1


# Valuation by Risk-Neutral Discounting
pv = np.zeros((M + 1, M + 1), dtype=np.float)  # present value array
pv[:, M] = iv[:, M]  # initialize last time step
z = M + 1
for j in xrange(M - 1, -1, -1):
    z -= 1
    for i in xrange(z):
        pv[i, j] = (q * pv[i, j + 1] + (1 - q) * pv[i + 1, j + 1]) * df


# Result Output
print "Value of European call option is %8.3f" % pv[0, 0]
```

The command np.zeros((i, j), dtype=np.float) initializes a NumPy array object with shape $i \times j$ where each number is of the double float type. The execution of the script gives the following output and arrays where one can follow the three steps easily (index levels, inner values, discounting):

```
 1  In [3]: run d_CRR1979_Naive.py
 2  Value of European call option is    16.293
 3
 4  In [4]: S
 5  Out[4]:
 6  array([[ 105.         ,  121.30377267,  140.13909775,  161.89905958],
 7         [   0.         ,   90.88752771,  105.         ,  121.30377267],
 8         [   0.         ,    0.         ,   78.67183517,   90.88752771],
 9         [   0.         ,    0.         ,    0.         ,   68.09798666]])
10
11  In [5]: iv
12  Out[5]:
13  array([[   5.         ,   21.30377267,   40.13909775,   61.89905958],
14         [   0.         ,    0.         ,    5.         ,   21.30377267],
15         [   0.         ,    0.         ,    0.         ,    0.         ],
16         [   0.         ,    0.         ,    0.         ,    0.         ]])
17
18  In [6]: pv
19  Out[6]:
20  array([[  16.29293245,   26.59599847,   41.79195237,   61.89905958],
21         [   0.         ,    5.61452766,   10.93666406,   21.30377267],
22         [   0.         ,    0.         ,    0.         ,    0.         ],
23         [   0.         ,    0.         ,    0.         ,    0.         ]])
```

```
24
25   In [7]:
```

Our alternative version makes more use of the *vectorization* capabilities of NumPy—the consequence is more compact code even if it is not so easy to read initially.

```
#
# Valuation of European Call Option in CRR1979 Model
# Vectorized Version (= NumPy-level Iterations)
# A_pyt/e_CRR1979_vectorized.py
#
import numpy as np
from c_parameters import *

# Array Initialization for Index Levels
mu = np.arange(M + 1)
mu = np.resize(mu, (M + 1, M + 1))
md = np.transpose(mu)
mu = u ** (mu - md)
md = d ** md
S = S0 * mu * md

# Valuation by Risk-Neutral Discounting
pv = np.maximum(S - K, 0)  # present value array initialized with inner values
z = 0
for i in xrange(M - 1, -1, -1):  # backwards induction
    pv[0:M - z, i] = (q * pv[0:M - z, i + 1]
                     + (1 - q) * pv[1:M - z + 1, i + 1]) * df
    z += 1

# Result Output
print "Value of European call option is %8.3f" % pv[0, 0]
```

The valuation result is, as expected, the same for the parameter definitions from before. However, three time intervals are of course not enough to come close to the Black-Scholes-Merton benchmark of 15.6547. With 1,000 time intervals, however, the algorithms come quite close to it:

```
1   In [7]: run e_CRR1979_vectorized.py
2   Value of European call option is   15.654
3
4   In [8]:
```

The major difference between the two algorithms is execution time. The second implementation which avoids Python iterations as much as possible is about 10 times faster than the first one (for 1,000 time steps). You should make this a principle for your own coding efforts:

whenever possible avoid necessary iterations (e.g. nested loops) on the Python interpreter level and delegate them to NumPy where they are executed by optimized C code in general. Apart from time savings, you generally also get more compact and readable code. A direct comparison illustrates this point:

```
#
# Loop Version --- Iterations in Python
#
# Array Initialization for Inner Values
iv = np.zeros((M + 1, M + 1), dtype=np.float)
z = 0
for j in xrange(0, M + 1, 1):
    for i in xrange(z + 1):
        iv[i, j] = max(S[i, j] - K, 0)
    z += 1


#
# Vectorized Version --- Iterations on NumPy Level
#
# Array Initialization for Inner Values
iv = maximum(S - K, 0)
```

To conclude this section, the Fast Fourier Transform (FFT) algorithm is applied to the binomial model. Nowadays, this numerical routine plays an important role in derivatives analytics. It is used regularly for plain vanilla option pricing in productive environments in investment banks or hedge funds. In general, however, it is not applied to a binomial model but the application in this case is straightforward and therefore a quick win.[6]

```
#
# Valuation of European Call Option in CRR1979 Model
# FFT Version
# A_pyt/f_CRR1979_fft.py
#
import numpy as np
from numpy.fft import fft, ifft
from c_parameters import *

# Array Generation for Index Levels
md = np.arange(M + 1)
mu = np.resize(md[-1], M + 1)
mu = u ** (mu - md)
md = d ** md
S = S0 * mu * md
```

---

[6]Cf. Černý (2004) for details of this method and its application to the binomial model. See also Chapter 6.

```
# Valuation by FFT
C_T = np.maximum(S - K, 0)
Q = np.zeros(M + 1, 'd')
Q[0] = q
Q[1] = 1 - q
l = np.sqrt(M + 1)
v1 = ifft(C_T) * l
v2 = (np.sqrt(M + 1) * fft(Q) / (l * (1 + r * dt))) ** M
C_0 = fft(v1 * v2) / l

# Result Output
print "Value of European call option is %8.3f" % np.real(C_0[0])
```

In this script, Python loops are entirely avoided—this is possible since for European options only the final payoffs are relevant (something one could also make use of for the previous implementations). The speed advantage of this algorithm is again considerable: it is 100 times faster than the vectorized algorithm from before and 1,000 times faster than the nested loop-based version (for 1,000 time steps).

A.2.3 Monte Carlo Approach

Finally, we apply Monte Carlo simulation (MCS) to value the same European call option in the Black-Scholes-Merton model $\mathcal{M}^{BSM}$. Here it is where pseudo-random numbers come into play. As with the FFT algorithm we only care about the final index level at T and simulate it by the use of pseudo-random numbers. We get the simple simulation algorithm shown as Algorithm 5.[7]

Although the algorithm seems to imply something like "looping over arrays", we can again avoid array loops completely on the Python interpreter level. The Python/NumPy implementation is really compact—only five lines of code for the core algorithm. With another five lines we can produce a histogram of the index levels at T as displayed in Figure A.3.

```
#
# Valuation of European Call Option
# via Monte Carlo Simulation
# A_pyt/g_MCS.py
#
import numpy as np
import matplotlib.pyplot as plt
from c_parameters import *

# Valuation via MCS
```

[7]Glasserman (2004) is a comprehensive reference on the Monte Carlo method applied to financial problems and models.

Algorithm 5: Monte Carlo Valuation Algorithm

---

1 Consider the date of maturity T and, for z_T being a standard normally distributed random variable, write

$$S_T = S_0 \cdot e^{\left(r - \frac{1}{2}\sigma^2\right) \cdot T + \sigma\sqrt{T}z_T}$$

for $i = 1, ..., I$ **do**

2 | Draw a standard normally distributed pseudo-random number $z_{T,i}$
3 | Simulate the index level value $S_{T,i}$ given equation (A.1) and $z_{T,i}$
4 | Determine the inner value of the call at T as $\max[S_{T,i} - K, 0]$

5 Sum up all inner values at T, take the average and discount back to $t = 0$ to arrive at the Monte Carlo estimator for the option value:

$$C_0(K, T) \approx e^{-rT} \cdot \frac{1}{I} \sum_I \max[S_T(i) - K, 0]$$

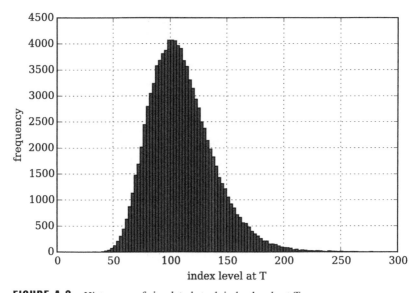

FIGURE A.3 Histogram of simulated stock index levels at T

```
I = 100000  # number of simulated values for S_T
rand = np.random.standard_normal(I)   # generate pseudo-random numbers
ST = S0 * np.exp((r - 0.5 * vola ** 2) * T + np.sqrt(T) * vola * rand)
     # simulate I values for S_T
pv = np.sum(np.maximum(ST - K, 0) * np.exp(-r * T)) / I  # MCS estimator


# Result Output
print "Value of European call option is %8.3f" % pv
```

```
# Graphical Output
plt.figure()
plt.hist(ST, 100)
plt.xlabel('index level at T')
plt.ylabel('frequency')
plt.grid(True)
```

The algorithm produces a quite accurate estimate for the European call option value although the implementation is rather simplistic (i.e. there are, for example, no variance reduction techniques involved):

```
1   In [10]: run g_MCS.py
2   Value of European call option is   15.649
3
4   In [11]:
```

A.3 SELECTED FINANCIAL TOPICS

A.3.1 Approximation

It is often the case in derivatives analytics that one has to approximate some function or object of interest to draw conclusions or apply the approximations within financial algorithms. Two important approximation techniques are regression and interpolation.[8]

The type of regression we consider is called ordinary least-squares regression (OLS). In its most simple form, monomials $x, x^2, x^3, \ldots$ are used to approximate a desired function $y = f(x)$ given a number N of observations $(y_1, x_1), (y_2, x_2), \ldots, (y_N, x_N)$. Say we want to approximate $f(x)$ with a polynomial of order 2, $g(x) = a_1 + a_2 \cdot x + a_3 \cdot x^2$ where the a_i are regression parameters. The task is then to solve the following minimization problem:

$$\min_{a_1, a_2, a_3} \sum_{n=1}^{N} \left(y_n - g(x_n; a_1, a_2, a_3) \right)$$

As an example, we want to approximate the cosine function over the interval $[0, \pi/2]$ given 20 observations. The code is straightforward since NumPy has built-in functions polyfit and polyval. From polyfit you get the minimizing regression parameters back, while you can use them with polyval to generate values based on these parameters. The result is shown in Figure A.4 for three different regression functions.

---

[8]Brandimarte (2006), sec. 3.3, introduces into these techniques.

```
#
# Ordinary Least Squares Regression
# A_pyt/h_REG.py
#
import numpy as np
import matplotlib.pyplot as plt

# Regression
x = np.linspace(0.0, np.pi / 2, 20)  # x values
y = np.cos(x)  # y values, i.e. those values to regress
g1 = np.polyfit(x, y, 0)  # OLS of degree 1
g2 = np.polyfit(x, y, 1)  # OLS of degree 2
g3 = np.polyfit(x, y, 2)  # OLS of degree 3

g1y = np.polyval(g1, x)  # calculate regressed values for x vector
g2y = np.polyval(g2, x)
g3y = np.polyval(g3, x)

# Graphical Output
plt.figure()  # initialize new figure
plt.plot(x, y, 'r', lw=3, label='cosine')  # plot original function values
plt.plot(x, g1y, 'mx', label='constant')  # plot regression function values
plt.plot(x, g2y, 'bo', label='linear')
plt.plot(x, g3y, 'g>', label='quadratic')
plt.legend(loc=0)
plt.grid(True)
```

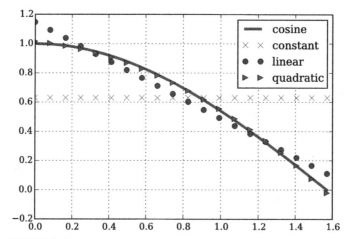

FIGURE A.4   Approximation of cosine function (line) by constant regression (crosses), linear regression (dots) and quadratic regression (triangles)

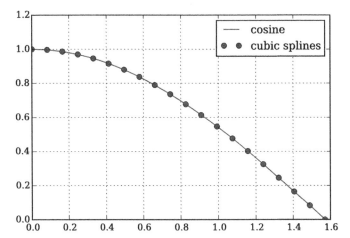

FIGURE A.5 Approximation of cosine function (line) by cubic splines interpolation (red dots)

The concept of interpolation is much more involved but nevertheless almost as straightforward in applications. The most common type of interpolation is with cubic splines for which you find functions in the sub-library scipy.interpolate. The example remains the same and the code is as compact as before while the result—see Figure A.5—seems perfect.

```
#
# Cubic Spline Interpolation
# A_pyt/i_SPLINE.py
#
import numpy as np
import scipy.interpolate as sci
import matplotlib.pyplot as plt

# Interpolation
x = np.linspace(0.0, np.pi / 2, 20)  # x values
y = np.cos(x)   # function values to interpolate
gp = sci.splrep(x, y, k=3)  # cubic spline interpolation
gy = sci.splev(x, gp, der=0)  # calculate interpolated values

# Graphical Output
plt.figure()
plt.plot(x, y, 'b', label='cosine')  # plot original function values
plt.plot(x, gy, 'ro', label='cubic splines')
  # plot interpolated function values
plt.legend(loc=0)
plt.grid(True)
```

Roughly speaking, cubic splines interpolation is (intelligent) regression between every two observation points with a polynomial of order 3. This is of course much more flexible than a single regression with a polynomial of, say, order 2. Two drawbacks in algorithmic terms are, however, that the observations have to be ordered in the x-dimension. Furthermore, cubic splines are of limited or no use for higher dimensional problems where OLS regression is applicable as easily as in the two-dimensional world.

A.3.2   Optimization

Strictly speaking, regression and interpolation are two special forms of optimization (some kind of minimization). However, optimization techniques are needed much more often in derivatives analytics. An important area is, for example, the calibration of model parameters to a given set of market-observed option prices or implied volatilities.

The two major approaches are *global* and *local* optimization. While the first looks for a global minimum or maximum of a function (which does not have to exist at all), the second looks for a local minimum or maximum. As an example, we take the sine function over the interval $[-\pi, 0]$ with a minimum function value of -1 at $-\pi/2$. Again, the library scipy delivers respective functions via the sub-library optimize. The code is as follows:

```
#
# Finding a Minimum of a Function
# A_pyt/j_OPT.py
#
import numpy as np
import scipy.optimize as sco

# Finding a Minimum


def y(x):
    ''' Function to Minimize. '''
    if x < -np.pi or x > 0:
        return 0.0
    return np.sin(x)

gmin = sco.brute(y, ((-np.pi, 0, 0.01), ), finish=None)  # global optimization
lmin = sco.fmin(y, -0.5)  # local optimization

# Result Output
print "Global Minimum is %8.6f" % gmin
print "Local Minimum is  %8.6f" % lmin
```

Both functions brute (global brute force algorithm) and fmin (local convex optimization algorithm) also work in multi-dimensional settings. In general, the solution of the local optimization is strongly dependent on the initialization; here the -0.5 did quite well in reaching $-\pi/2$ as the solution.

```
1    In [5]: run j_OPT.py
2    Optimization terminated successfully.
3             Current function value: -1.000000
4             Iterations: 18
5             Function evaluations: 36
6    Global Minimum is -1.571593
7    Local Minimum is  -1.570801
8
9    In [6]:
```

A.3.3 Numerical Integration

It is not always possible to analytically integrate a given function. Then numerical integration often comes into play. We want to check numerical integration where we can do it analytically as well

$$\int_0^1 e^x dx$$

The value of the integral is $e^1 - e^0 \approx 1.7182818284590451$. For numerical integration, again scipy helps out with the sub-library integrate which contains the function quad, implementing a numerical quadrature scheme:[9]

```python
#
# Numerically Integrate a Function
# A_pyt/k_INT.py
#
import numpy as np
from scipy.integrate import quad

# Numerical Integration


def f(x):
    ''' Function to Integrate. '''
    return np.exp(x)

int_value = quad(lambda u: f(u), 0, 1)[0]

# Output
print "Value of the integral is %10.9f" % int_value
```

---

[9]Brandimarte (2006), ch. 4, introduces into numerical integration.

The output of the numerical integration equals the analytical value (with rounding):

```
1   In [8]: run k_INT.py
2   Value of the integral is 1.718281828
3
4   In [9]:
```

A.4 ADVANCED PYTHON TOPICS

This section briefly illustrates some advanced Python topics, in particular object-oriented programming, basic input-output operations and reading data from Excel files.

A.4.1 Classes and Objects

So far, we have looked at modules and functions. The dominating coding paradigm of our time is, however, object-oriented programming. For example, the popularity of C++ for derivatives analytics stems to a great extent from the fact that it brings with it powerful object orientation.

On a rather basic level, almost anything is an object in Python. What we want to do now is to implement *new classes* of objects, i.e. we go one level higher. For example, we can define a new class for European call options. A class is characterized by its *attributes* which are stored in a function with name __init__ and so-called *methods*, like the valuation function of Black-Scholes-Merton as already implemented before. Here is a sample code for two classes:

```python
#
# Two Financial Option Classes
# A_pyt/1_CLASS.py
#
#
import math
import scipy.stats as scs

# Class Definitions


class Option:
    ''' Black-Scholes-Merton European call option class.

    Attributes
    ==========
    S0: float
        initial index level
    K: float
        strike price
    T: float
        time-to-maturity
```

```
    r: float
        constant short rate
    vola: float
        constant volatility factor
    '''

    def __init__(self, S0, K, T, r, vola):
        ''' Initialization of Object. '''
        self.S0 = float(S0)
        self.K = K
        self.T = T
        self.r = r
        self.vola = vola

    def d1(self):
        ''' Helper function. '''
        d1 = ((math.log(self.S0 / self.K) +
               (self.r + 0.5 * self.vola ** 2) * self.T)
             / (self.vola * math.sqrt(self.T)))
        return d1

    def value(self):
        ''' Method to value option. '''
        d1 = self.d1()
        d2 = d1 - self.vola * math.sqrt(self.T)
        call_value = (self.S0 * scs.norm.cdf(d1, 0.0, 1.0)
                      - self.K * math.exp(-self.r * self.T)
                      * scs.norm.cdf(d2, 0.0, 1.0))
        return call_value


class OptionVega(Option):
    ''' Black-Scholes-Merton class for Vega of European call option. '''

    def vega(self):
        ''' Method to calculate the Vega of the European call option. '''
        d1 = self.d1()
        vega = self.S0 * scs.norm.pdf(d1, 0.0, 1.0) * math.sqrt(self.T)
        return vega
```

The working becomes clear after executing the module and defining option objects by parametrizing the different classes:

```
1   In [12]: run 1_CLASS.py
2
3   In [13]: o1 = Option(105., 100., 1.0, 0.05, 0.25)
```

```
 4
 5   In [14]: o1.Value()
 6   Out[14]: 15.654719726823579
 7
 8   In [15]: o1.Vega()
 9   ---------------------------------------------------------------------
10   AttributeError                          Traceback (most recent call last)
11   ./python/A_pyt/<ipython-input-15-dbb35f94473d> in <module>()
12   ----> 1 o1.Vega()
13
14   AttributeError: Option instance has no attribute 'Vega'
15
16   In [16]: o2 = Option_Vega(105., 100., 1.0, 0.05, 0.25)
17
18   In [17]: o2.value()
19   Out[17]: 15.654719726823579
20
21   In [18]: o2.vega()
22   Out[18]: 36.588656569539303
23
24   In [19]:
```

The class Option contains a method called Value. The value of the option object o1 can be retrieved via invoking the method as in o1.Value(). However, the class Option has no method to calculate the vega[10] of the option. This, however, is what is included in the class OptionVega. This class is defined on the basis of the Option class via class OptionVega(Option) and inherits the attributes and methods of the other class. That is why we parametrize an object of this class in the same way and why we can calculate its value in the same way.

A.4.2 Basic Input-Output Operations

Saving and loading Python modules/scripts is really simple. However, the need to save and load Python objects also arises frequently. In this section, we want to illustrate a fundamental way of storing objects permanently (via pickling or serialization). The next sub-section illustrates how to store data in and retrieve data from spreadsheet files. This is an important functionality since Excel is still one of the most popular front-office tools in investment banks, hedge funds, etc.

Suppose we want to save our two option objects o1 and o2 to a file on disk. To this end, we can use the cPickle module. A respective session in IPython could look like the following:

---

[10]The vega of an option is the first derivative of the option value V with respect to the volatility σ, i.e. $\partial V / \partial \sigma$.

```
In [19]: o1 = Option(105., 100., 1.0, 0.05, 0.25)

In [20]: o2 = OptionVega(105., 100., 1.0, 0.05, 0.25)

In [21]: import cPickle as cp

In [22]: option = open('option_container', 'w')

In [23]: cp.dump(o1, option)

In [24]: cp.dump(o2, option)

In [25]: option.close()

In [26]: option
Out[26]: <closed file 'option_container', mode 'w' at 0x1fcd270>

In [27]: options = open('option_container', 'r')

In [28]: option1 = cp.load(options)

In [29]: option2 = cp.load(options)

In [30]: option1.value()
Out[30]: 15.654719726823579

In [31]: option2.vega()
Out[31]: 73.345040765170197

In [32]: options.close()

In [33]:
```

Notice that the objects are loaded in the sequence as stored ("first in, first out"). And you can never know (if you did not save the information as well) how many objects there are in the file. So it could be a good idea to store the two option objects not separately but as a list.

```
In [33]: options = open('option_container_2', 'w')

In [34]: cp.dump([option1, option2], options)

In [35]: options.close()

In [36]: optionstore = open('option_container_2', 'r')
```

```
 9   In [37]: olist = cp.load(optionstore)
10
11   In [38]: olist
12   Out[38]:
13   (<__main__.Option instance at 0x251b710>,
14    <__main__.OptionVega instance at 0x251b6c8>)
15
16   In [39]: len(olist)
17   Out[39]: 2
18
19   In [40]: olist[0]
20   Out[41]: <__main__.Option instance at 0x251b710>
21
22   In [42]: olist[0].value()
23   Out[43]: 15.654719726823579
24
25   In [44]: olist[1].vega()
26   Out[45]: 73.345040765170197
27
28   In [46]:
```

This seems to make life a bit more convenient.

A.4.3   Interacting with Spreadsheets

The topic of this sub-section is how to read and write data from and to Excel spreadsheets. To this end, a sample Excel workbook is needed. We produced one with quite a few DAX index quotes (source: http://finance.yahoo.com). The name of the file is DAX_data.xlsx and it contains data as displayed in Figure A.6.

The data analysis library pandas provides a number of convenient I/O tools. Among them is an Excel file reader which reads structured data contained in a spreadsheet into a pandas DataFrame object.[11] To access, print and plot the data contained in the Excel file, a script like this does the job:

```
#
# Reading Data from Excel Spreadsheet Files
# A_pyt/m_Excel_read.py
#
import pandas as pd
import matplotlib.pyplot as plt
```

---

[11] At the time of writing pandas is already a mighty data analysis package (cf. McKinney (2012)). This appendix can only give an initial impression of its capabilities. At the end of 2014, the PDF documentation of the library stood at more than 1,500 pages (for release 0.15.1). The subsequent section demonstrates how the library pandas can make life easier when it comes to handling financial time series and using them for valuation purposes.

```
# Open Excel Spreadsheet and Read Date
DAX = pd.read_excel('A_pyt/DAX_data.xlsx', 'sheet1',
                    index_col=0, parse_dates=True)

# Print 10 Most Current Daily Data Sets
print DAX.ix[-10:].to_string()

# Plot Close Levels for Whole Data Set
DAX['Close'].plot(label='DAX Index')
plt.legend(loc=0)
```

This module, once started, produces the following output:

```
In [10]: run m_Excel_read.py
                 Open      High       Low     Close       Volume   Adj Close
Date
2014-11-17   9162.27   9331.32   9161.60   9306.35     72034400     9306.35
2014-11-18   9323.75   9461.53   9323.52   9456.53     73982400     9456.53
2014-11-19   9462.05   9521.73   9439.16   9472.80     73153500     9472.80
2014-11-20   9460.40   9487.69   9382.23   9483.97     82097800     9483.97
2014-11-21   9521.24   9736.14   9508.17   9732.55    166634400     9732.55
2014-11-24   9722.31   9832.41   9711.77   9785.54     97612300     9785.54
```

FIGURE A.6 Sample spreadsheet in Excel format with DAX quotes (here shown with LibreOffice); source: finance.yahoo.com

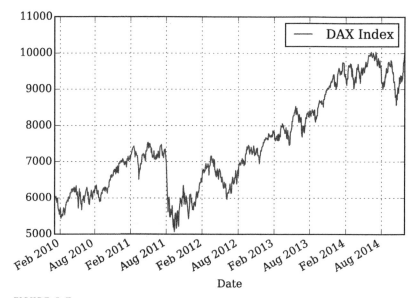

FIGURE A.7   Historic DAX index levels; source: http://finance.yahoo.com

```
10   2014-11-25   9790.03   9921.46   9787.26   9861.21   117773900   9861.21
11   2014-11-26   9894.60   9942.67   9868.35   9915.56    89124300   9915.56
12   2014-11-27   9934.78   9992.67   9920.86   9974.87    84700200   9974.87
13   2014-11-28   9990.70   9990.70   9902.40   9980.85    98906800   9980.85
14
15   In [11]:
```

The script also generates a plot as in Figure A.7.

A.5   RAPID FINANCIAL ENGINEERING

This section illustrates a whole valuation process implemented in Python and using again the powerful library pandas as the main tool. It shows how to address the following tasks that are typical for derivatives analytics in particular and financial engineering in general:

- data gathering (here: quotes for the German DAX index)
- data analysis (here: calculating daily log returns)
- generating graphics (here: plotting DAX quotes and log returns)
- implementing numerical methods (here: Monte Carlo simulation)
- data storage (here: DAX quotes with daily log returns)

The script exhibits a rather concise form—which justifies the term *rapid* financial engineering:

```python
#
# Retrieving Financial Data from the Web and
# Doing Data Analytics with pandas
# A_pyt/n_pandas.py
#
import math
import numpy as np
import pandas as pd
import pandas.io.data as web
import matplotlib.pyplot as plt


#
# 1. Data Gathering
#
DAX = web.DataReader('^GDAXI', data_source='yahoo',
                     start='1/1/2005', end='28/11/2014')
    # reads DAX data from Yahoo Finance


#
# 2. Data Analysis
#
DAX['Returns'] = np.log(DAX['Close'] / DAX['Close'].shift(1))
    # daily log returns


#
# 3. Generating Plots
#
plt.figure(figsize=(7, 5))
plt.subplot(211)
DAX['Adj Close'].plot()
plt.title('DAX Index')
plt.subplot(212)
DAX['Returns'].plot()
plt.title('log returns')
plt.tight_layout()


#
# 4. Numerical Methods
#
# Market Parameters
S0 = DAX['Close'][-1]  # start value of DAX for simulation
vol = np.std(DAX['Returns']) * math.sqrt(252)
  # historical, annualized volatility of DAX
r = 0.01  # constant risk-free short rate
```

```
# Option Parameters
K = 10000.  # strike price of the option to value
T = 1.0  # time-to-maturity of the option

# Simulation Parameters
M = 50  # number of time steps
dt = T / M  # length of time interval
I = 10000  # number of paths to simulate
np.random.seed(5000)  # fixed seed value

# Simulation
S = np.zeros((M + 1, I), dtype=np.float)  # array for simulated DAX levels
S[0] = S0  # initial values
for t in xrange(1, M + 1):
    ran = np.random.standard_normal(I)  # pseudo-random numbers
    S[t] = S[t - 1] * np.exp((r - vol ** 2 / 2) * dt
                             + vol * math.sqrt(dt) * ran)
        # difference equation to simulate DAX levels step-by-step
        # NumPy vectorization over all simulated paths

# Valuation
V0 = math.exp(-r * T) * np.sum(np.maximum(S[-1] - K, 0)) / I  # MCS estimator
print "MCS call value estimate is %8.3f" % V0

#
# 5. Data Storage
#
h5file = pd.HDFStore('DAX_data.h5')  # open HDF5 file as database
h5file['DAX'] = DAX  # write pandas.DataFrame DAX into HDFStore
h5file.close()  # close file
```

Here is some output from the script and from interacting with objects generated by it:

```
 1  In [24]: run n_pandas.py
 2  MCS call value estimate is  912.050
 3
 4  In [25]: DAX
 5  Out[25]:
 6  <class 'pandas.core.frame.DataFrame'>
 7  DatetimeIndex: 2535 entries, 2005-01-03 00:00:00 to 2014-11-28 00:00:00
 8  Data columns (total 7 columns):
 9  Open        2535 non-null float64
10  High        2535 non-null float64
11  Low         2535 non-null float64
12  Close       2535 non-null float64
13  Volume      2535 non-null int64
14  Adj Close   2535 non-null float64
```

```
15   Returns      2534 non-null float64
16   dtypes: float64(6), int64(1)
17   memory usage: 158.4 KB
18
19   In [26]: S0
20   Out[26]: 9980.8500000000004
21
22   In [27]: vol
23   Out[27]: 0.22005937913242066
24
25   In [28]: S
26   Out[28]:
27   array([[ 9980.85      ,    9980.85      ,    9980.85      , ...,
28            9980.85      ,    9980.85      ,    9980.85      ],
29          [ 10109.14261197,  10120.31053148,   9914.05151453, ...,
30            9623.88640669,  10528.55645662,  10060.46805893],
31          [ 9969.89401753,   9980.25807455,   9689.45433757, ...,
32            9459.14482363,   9892.4452775 ,  10298.72443737],
33          ...,
34          [ 8634.23391906,   8220.4710566 ,   7563.57734092, ...,
35            11602.42496642,  10136.19939927,  11625.19646252],
```

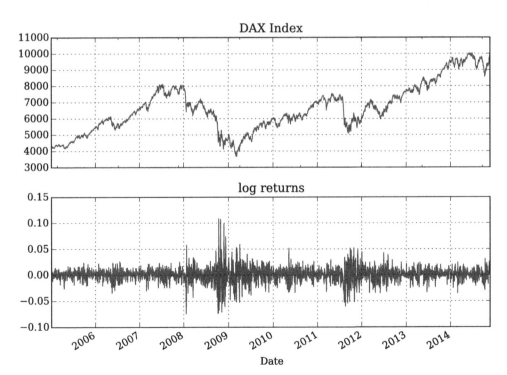

FIGURE A.8 DAX index quotes from 03. January 2005 to 28. November 2014 and daily log returns; source: http://finance.yahoo.com

```
36          [   8721.89783607,     8067.9006704 ,     7344.93794989,  ...,
37              11615.52504255,   10339.54117202,   10668.75438809],
38          [   8922.38372072,     8529.03134822,     7334.99586935,  ...,
39              11576.12919096,   10343.39920151,   10297.9093708 ]])
40
41   In [29]:
```

As one can see, the pandas DataFrame object DAX has stored 2, 535 different sets of daily quotes for the DAX index and 2, 534 daily log returns. The starting index level for the simulation is 9, 980.85 while the annualized volatility is calculated as 22.0%. Via simulation, the value for a European call option with strike $K = 10,000$ and time-to-maturity of $T = 1.0$ years is estimated as 913.334. Figure A.8 shows the graphical output of the script.

This concludes this appendix on the Python programming language for financial analytics.

Bibliography

Andersen, Leif (2008) Simple and Efficient Simulation of the Heston Stochastic Volatility Model, *Journal of Computational Finance*, 11(3), 1–42.

Andersen, Leif, Peter Jäckel and Christian Kahl (2010) Simulation of Square-Root Processes, in *Encyclopedia of Quantitative Finance*, Rama Cont (ed. in chief), John Wiley & Sons, Hoboken, New Jersey.

Andersen, Torben and Luca Benzoni (2009) Realized Volatility, in *Handbook of Financial Time Series*, Torben Andersen, Richard Davis, Jens-Peter Krieß, Thomas Mikosch (eds), Springer Verlag, Berlin, 555–575.

Bakshi, Gurdip, Charles Cao and Zhiwu Chen (1997) Empirical Performance of Alternative Option Pricing Models, *Journal of Finance*, 52(5), 2003–2049.

Bali, Turan and Liuren Wu (2006) A Comprehensive Analysis of the Short-Term Interest-Rate Dynamics, *Journal of Banking & Finance*, 30, 1269–1290.

Bates, David (1996) Jumps and Stochastic Volatility: Exchange Rates Processes Implicit in Deutsche Mark Options, *Review of Financial Studies*, 9(1), 69–107.

Baxter, Martin and Andrew Rennie (1996) *Financial Calculus—An Introduction to Derivative Pricing*, Cambridge University Press, Cambridge.

Bhattacharya, Rabi and Edward Waymire (2007) *A Basic Course in Probability Theory*, Springer Verlag, New York.

Bittman, James (2009) *Trading Options as a Professional*, McGraw-Hill, New York.

Björk, Tomas (2004) *Arbitrage Theory in Continuous Time*, 2nd ed., Oxford University Press, Oxford.

Björk, Tomas (2009) An Overview of Interest Rate Theory, in *Handbook of Financial Time Series*, Torben Andersen, Richard Davis, Jens-Peter Krieß, Thomas Mikosch (eds), Springer Verlag, Berlin, 615–651.

Black, Fischer and Myron Scholes (1973) The Pricing of Options and Corporate Liabilities, *Journal of Political Economy*, 81(3), 638–659.

Boyle, Phelim (1977) Options: A Monte Carlo Approach, *Journal of Financial Economics*, 4(4), 322–338.

Brandimarte, Paolo (2006) *Numerical Methods in Finance and Economics*, 2nd ed., John Wiley & Sons, Hoboken, New Jersey.

Brigo, Damiano and Fabio Mercurio (2001) On Deterministic-Shift Extensions of Short-Rate Models, *Working Paper*, Banca IMI, Milano, www.damianobrigo.it.

Brigo, Damiano and Fabio Mercurio (2006) *Interest Rate Models—Theory and Practice*, 2nd ed., Springer Verlag, Berlin.

Broadie, Mark and Özgür Kaya (2006) Exact Simulation of Stochastic Volatility and Other Affine Jump Diffusion Processes, *Operations Research*, 54(2), 217–231.

Carr, Peter and Dilip Madan (1999) Option Valuation using the Fast Fourier Transform, *Journal of Computational Finance*, 2(4), 61–73.

Černý, Aleš (2004) Introduction to Fast Fourier Transform in Finance, *Journal of Derivatives*, 12(1), 73–88.

Cetin, Umut, Robert Jarrow and Philip Protter (2004) Liquidity Risk and Arbitrage Pricing Theory, *Finance and Stochastics*, 8(3), 1–31.

Chaudhury, Mo (2014) Option Bid-Ask Spread and Liquidity, *Working Paper*, McGill University, Desautels Faculty of Management, www.ssrn.com.

Cheng, Peng and Olivier Scaillet (2007) Linear-Quadratic Jump-Diffusion Modeling, *Mathematical Finance*, 17(4), 575–598.

Cherubini, Umberto, Giovanni Della Lunga, Sabrina Mulinacci and Pietro Rossi (2009) *Fourier Transform Methods in Finance*, John Wiley & Sons, Chichester.

Christoffersen, Peter and Kris Jacobs (2004) The Importance of the Loss Function in Option Valuation, *Journal of Financial Economics*, 72, 291–318.

Cipra, Barry (2000) The Best of the 20th Century: Editors Name Top 10 Algorithms, *SIAM News*, 33(4), 1–2.

Clément, Emmanuelle, Damien Lamberton and Philip Protter (2002) An Analysis of a Least Squares Regression Algorithm for American Option Pricing, *Finance and Stochastics*, 17, 448–471.

Cont, Rama (2001) Empirical Properties of Asset Returns: Stylized Facts and Statistical Issues, *Quantitative Finance*, 1, 223–236.

Cont, Rama and Peter Tankov (2004a) *Financial Modelling With Jump Processes*, 2nd ed., CRC Press UK, London.

Cont, Rama and Peter Tankov (2004b) Non-Parametric Calibration of Jump-Diffusion Option Pricing Models, *Journal of Computational Finance*, 7(3), 1–49.

Cont, Rama, Peter Tankov and Ekaterina Voltchkova (2007) Hedging with Options in Models with Jumps, in *Stochastic Analysis and Applications—the Abel Symposium 2005*, Springer Verlag, Berlin.

Cooley, James and John Tukey (1965) An Algorithm for the Machine Calculation of Complex Fourier Series, *Mathematics of Computation*, 19(90), 297–301.

Cox, John, Jonathan Ingersoll and Stephen Ross (1985) A Theory of the Term Structure of Interest Rates, *Econometrica*, 53(2), 385–407.

Cox, John, Stephen Ross and Mark Rubinstein (1979) Option Pricing: A Simplified Approach, *Journal of Financial Economics*, 7(3), 229–263.

Crépey, Stéphane (2009) Tikhonov Regularization, in *Encyclopedia of Quantitative Finance*, Rama Cont (ed. in chief), John Wiley & Sons, Hoboken, 1807–1811.

Dai, Qiang and Kenneth Singleton (2000) Specification Analysis of Affine Term Structure Models, *Journal of Finance*, 55(5), 1943–1978.

Delbaen, Freddy and Walter Schachermayer (1994) A General Version of the Fundamental Theorem of Asset Pricing, *Mathematische Annalen*, 300, 463–520.

Delbaen, Freddy and Walter Schachermayer (1998) The Fundamental Theorem of Asset Pricing for Unbounded Stochastic Processes, *Mathematische Annalen*, 312, 215–250.

Delbaen, Freddy and Walter Schachermayer (2004) *The Mathematics of Arbitrage*, Springer Verlag, Berlin.

Detemple, Jerome (2006) *American-Style Derivatives—Valuation and Computation*, Chapman & Hall/CRC, Boca Raton.

Detlefsen, Kai (2005) Hedging Exotic Options in Stochastic Volatility and Jump Diffusion Models, *Master's Thesis*, Humboldt-University Berlin, Berlin.

de Weert, Frans (2008) *Exotic Options Trading*, John Wiley & Sons, Chichester.

Duffie, Darrell, Jun Pan and Kenneth Singleton (2000) Transform Analysis and Asset Pricing for Affine Jump-Diffusions, *Econometrica*, 68(6), 1343–1376.

Duffie, Darrell and Kenneth Singleton (2003) *Credit Risk—Pricing, Measurement and Management*, Princeton University Press, Princeton, New Jersey.

Elliot, Robert and Ekkehard Kopp (2005) *Mathematics of Financial Markets*, 2nd ed., Springer Verlag, New York.

Fengler, Matthias (2005) *Semi-Parametric Modeling of Implied Volatility*, Springer Verlag, Berlin.

Filipović, Damir (2009) *Term Structure Models—A Graduate Course*, Springer Verlag, Dordrecht.

Fletcher, Shayner and Christopher Gardener (2009) *Financial Modelling in Python*, John Wiley & Sons, Chichester.

Frey, Rüdiger (2000) Market Illiquidity as a Source of Model Risk in Dynamic Hedging, in *Model Risk: Concepts, Calibration and Pricing*, Rajna Gibson (ed.), Risk Publications, London, 125–136.

Fries, Christian (2008) Foresight Bias and Suboptimality Correction in Monte Carlo Pricing of Options with Early Exercise, *Mathematics in Industry*, 12, 645–649.

Galluccio, Stefano and Yann Le Cam (2008) Implied Calibration and Moments Asymptotics in Stochastic Volatility Jump Diffusion Models, *Working Paper*, BNP Paribas, London, www.ssrn.com.

Gatheral, Jim (2006) *The Volatility Surface—A Practitioner's Guide*, John Wiley & Sons, Hoboken, New Jersey.

Gilbert, Charles, K. Ravindran and Robert Reitano (2007) Results of the Survey on Variable Annuity Hedging Programs for Life Insurance Companies, *Report*, Society of Actuaries, www.soa.org.

Glasserman, Paul (2004) *Monte Carlo Methods in Financial Engineering*, Springer Verlag, New York.

Grzelak, Lech, Cornelis Oosterlee and Sacha van Weeren (2012) Extension of Stochastic Volatility Equity Models with Hull-White Interest Rate Process, *Quantitative Finance*, 12(1), 89–105.

Haastrecht, Alexander and Antoon Pelsser (2010) Efficient, Almost Exact Simulation of the Heston Stochastic Volatility Model, *International Journal of Theoretical and Applied Finance*, 13(1), 1–43.

Haenel, Valentin, Emmanuelle Gouillart and Gaël Varoquaux (2013) Python Scientific Lecture Notes, http://scipy-lectures.github.com.

Hansen, Lars and Eric Renault (2009) Pricing Kernels and Stochastic Discount Factors, in *Encyclopedia of Quantitative Finance*, Rama Cont (ed. in chief), John Wiley & Sons, Hoboken, 1418–1427.

Harrison, Michael and David Kreps (1979) Martingales and Arbitrage in Multiperiod Securities Markets, *Journal of Economic Theory*, 20, 381–408.

Harrison, Michael and Stanley Pliska (1981) Martingales and Stochastic Integrals in the Theory of Continuous Trading, *Stochastic Processes and their Applications*, 11, 215–260.

Haugh, Martin and Leonid Kogan (2004) Pricing American Options: A Duality Approach, *Operations Research*, 52(2), 258–270.

Heath, David, Robert Jarrow and Andrew Morton (1992) Bond Pricing and the Term Structure of Interest Rates: A New Methodology for Contingent Claims Valuation, *Econometrica*, 60(1), 77–105.

Heston, Steven (1993) A Closed-Form Solution for Options with Stochastic Volatility with Applications to Bond and Currency Options, *The Review of Financial Studies*, 6(2), 327–343.

Hilpisch, Yves (2001) *Dynamic Hedging, Positive Feedback, and General Equilibrium*, Dissertation Thesis, Saarland University, Saarbruecken, www.hilpisch.com.

Hilpisch, Yves (2014) *Python for Finance—Analyze Big Financial Data*, O'Reilly, Beijing.

Hull, John and Alan White (2013) LIBOR vs. OIS: The Derivatives Discounting Dilemma, *Journal of Investment Management*, 11(3), 14–27.

Jarrow, Robert (1999) In Honor of the Nobel Laureates Robert C. Merton and Myron S. Scholes: A Partial Differential Equation that Changed the World, *Journal of Economic Perspectives*, 13(4), 229–248.

Jarrow, Robert (2005) Liquidity Risk and Classical Option Pricing Theory, in *Mathematical Modeling of Market Liquidity Risk*, P. Neu and L. Matz (eds), John Wiley & Sons, Singapore.

Kahale, Nabil (2004) An Arbitrage-Free Interpolation of Volatilities, *Risk Magazine*, 17(May), 102–106.

Kahl, Christian (2007) *Modelling and Simulation of Stochastic Volatility in Finance*, Dissertation.com, Boca Raton.

Klössner, Stefan (2010) Grasping Economic Jumps by Sparse Sampling Using Intradaily Highs and Lows, *Working Paper*, Saarland University, Saarbruecken, http://econ.duke.edu/brossi/NBERNSF/Klossner.pdf.

Kohler, Michael (2009) A Review on Regression-based Monte Carlo Methods for Pricing American Options, *Working Paper*, Technical University of Darmstadt, Darmstadt, www.mathematik.tu-darmstadt.de.

Lamberton, Damien and Bernard Lapeyre (1996) *Introduction to Stochastic Calculus Applied to Finance*, Chapman & Hall, London.

Langtangen, Hans Petter (2009) *A Primer on Scientific Programming with Python*, Springer Verlag, Berlin.

Lee, Eileen (2010) Python takes a Bite, *WILMOTT Magazine*, March.

Lewis, Alan (2001) A Simple Option Formula for General Jump-Diffusion and Other Exponential Lévy Processes, *Working Paper*, OptionCity, www.optioncity.net.

Liberti, Leo (2008) Introduction to Global Optimization, *Working Paper*, École Polytechnique, Palaiseau, www.lix.polytechnique.fr.

London, Justin (2005) *Modeling Derivatives in C++*, John Wiley & Sons, Hoboken, New Jersey.

Longstaff, Francis and Eduardo Schwartz (2001) Valuing American Options by Simulation: A Simple Least Squares Approach, *Review of Financial Studies*, 14(1), 113–147.

Lord, Roger, Remmert Koekkoek and Dick van Dijk (2006) A Comparison of Biased Simulation Schemes for Stochastic Volatility Models, *Working Paper*, Erasmus University, Rotterdam, www.ssrn.com.

McKinney, Wes (2012) *Python for Data Analysis*, O'Reilly, Beijing.

Medvedev, Alexey and Olivier Scaillet (2010) Pricing American Options Under Stochastic Volatility and Stochastic Interest Rates, *Journal of Financial Economics*, 98, 145–159.

Merton, Robert (1973) Theory of Rational Option Pricing, *Bell Journal of Economics and Management Science*, 4, 141–183.

Merton, Robert (1976) Option Pricing when the Underlying Stock Returns are Discontinuous, *Journal of Financial Economics*, 3(3), 125–144.

Mikhailov, Sergei and Ulrich Nögel (2003) Heston's Stochastic Volatility Model—Implementation, Calibration and Some Extensions, *WILMOTT Magazine*, July, 74–79.

Moodley, Nimalin (2005) The Heston Model: A Practical Approach—With Matlab Code, *Bachelor's Thesis*, University of the Witwatersrand, Johannesburg, math.nyu.edu.

Nandi, Saikat and Daniel Waggoner (2000) Issues in Hedging Options Positions, *Economic Review*, 1st Qu., Federal Reserve Bank of Atlanta.

Pliska, Stanley (1997) *Introduction to Mathematical Finance*, Blackwell Publishers, Malden and Oxford.

Protter, Philip (2001) A Partial Introduction to Financial Asset Pricing Theory, *Stochastic Processes and their Applications*, 91, 169–203.

Protter, Philip (2005) *Stochastic Integration and Differenatial Equations*, 2nd ed., 3rd printing, Springer Verlag, Berlin.

Rebonato, Riccardo (2004) *Volatility and Correlation*, 2nd ed., John Wiley & Sons, Chichester.

Reinsberg, Rene (2006) *Pricing Options on the DAX—An Empirical Investigation*, Thesis, WHU–Otto Beisheim School of Management, Vallendar, www.ssrn.com.

Rudin, Walter (1970) *Real and Complex Analysis*, International Student Edition, McGraw-Hill, London.

Schmelzele, Martin (2010) Option Pricing Formulae using Fourier Transform: Theory and Application, *Working Paper*, www.pfadintegral.com.

Schoutens, Wim, Erwin Simons and Jurgen Tistaert (2004) A Perfect Calibration! Now What?, *WILLMOT Magazine*, March, 66–78.

Stentoft, Lars (2004) *Least Squares Monte-Carlo and GARCH Methods for American Options: Theory and Applications*, Dissertation Thesis, University of Aarhus, Denmark, www.samfundsvidenskab.au.dk.

Svoboda, Simona (2002) *An Investigation of Various Interest Rate Models and Their Calibration in the South African Market*, Dissertation Thesis, University of the Witwatersrand, Johannesburg, http://janroman.dhis.org.

Tankov, Peter and Ekaterina Voltchkova (2009) Jump-Diffusion Models: A Practitioner's Guide, *Banqué et Marchés*, 99, March–April.

Tsitsiklis, John and Benjamin Van Roy (2001) Regression Methods for Pricing Complex American-Style Options, *IEEE Transactions on Neural Networks*, 12, 694–730.

Wallner, Christian and Uwe Wystup (2004) Efficient Computation of Option Price Sensitivities for Options of American Style, *WILMOTT Magazine*, November, 2–11.

Wang, Yang and Russel Calfisch (2010) Pricing and Hedging American-Style Options: A Simple Simulation-based Approach, *Journal of Computational Finance*, 13(4), 95–125.

Williams, David (1991) *Probability with Martingales*, reprint 2001, Cambridge University Press, Cambridge.

Wilmott, Paul, Sam Howison and Jeff Dewynne (1995) *The Mathematics of Financial Derivatives*, Cambridge University Press, Cambridge.

Index

Index compiled by Terry Halliday

Printed and bound by CPI Group (UK) Ltd, Croydon, CR0 4YY

23/04/2025

14660950-0003